Abortion Bibliography

for 1985

Abortion Bibliography

for 1985

Compiled by
Polly T. Goode

The Whitston Publishing Company
Troy, New York
1988

TABLE OF CONTENTS

PREFACE

Abortion Bibliography for 1985 is the sixteenth annual list of books and articles surrounding the subject of abortion in the preceding year. It appears serially each fall as a contribution toward documenting in one place as comprehensively as possible the literature of one of our central social issues. It is an attempt at a comprehensive world bibliography.

Searches in compiling this material have covered the following sources:
Abstracts on Criminology & Penology
Abstracts on Police Science
Access
Air University Library Index to Military Periodicals
America: History and Life
American Humanities Index
American Reference Books Annual
Applied Science & Technology Index
Bibliographic Index
Biological Abstracts
Biological & Agricultural Index
British Humanities Index
Business Periodicals Index
C & P Abstracts
Canadian Education Index
Canadian Periodicals Index
Catholic Periodical & Literature Index
Communication Abstracts
College Student Personnel Abstracts
Criminal Justice Abstracts
Criminal Justice Periodical Index
Cumulative Book Index
Current Index to Journals in Education
Dissertation Abstracts International A. Humanities and
    Social Sciences
Dissertation Abstracts International: B. The Sciences and
    Engineering
Education Index
Environment Abstracts
Environment Index
Essay & General Literature Index
General Science Index
Hospital Literature Index

Hospital Literature Index
Human Resources Abstracts
Humanities Index
Index Medicus
Index to Jewish Periodicals
Index to Legal Periodicals
International Nursing Index
Media Review Digest
Music Index
Nursing and Allied Health Literature
PAIS
PAIS Foreign Language Index
Philosopher's Index
Popular Periodical Index
Psychological Abstracts
Readers Guide to Periodical Literature
Religion Index One: Periodicals (from: Index to Religious
PeriodicalLiterature)
Religious and Theological Abstracts
Sage Family Studies Abstracts
Sage Urban Studies Abstracts
Social Sciences Index
Social Work Research & Abstracts
Sociological Abstracts
Studies on Women's Abstracts
Women's Studies Abstracts.

The Bibliography is divided into two sections: a title section in alphabetical order; and a subject section. Thus, if the researcher does not wish to observe the subject heads of the compiler, he can use the title section exclusively. The subject heads have been issued from the nature of the material indexed rather than being imposed from Library of Congress subject heads or other standard lists.

The Subject Head Index includes page numbers.

Polly T. Goode
Troy, New York

LIST OF JOURNALS CITED

AFER: AFRICAN ECCLESIAL REVIEW
AJR: AMERICAN JOURNAL OF ROENTGENOLOGY
ANS: ADVANCES IN NURSING SCIENCE
ACTA ACADEMIAE MEDICINAE WUHAN
ACTA ANTHROPOGENETICA
ACTA CHIRURGICA ACADEMIAE SCIENTARUM HUNGARICAE
ACTA BIOMEDICA DE L'ATENEO PARMENSE
ACTA EUROPAEA FERTILITATIS
ACTA GASTROENTEROLOGICA LATINOAMERICANA
ACTA OBSTETRICIA ET GYNECOLOGICA SCANDINAVICA
ACTA PATHOLOGICA ET MICROBIOLOGICA SCANDINAVICA
ACTA PHARMACEUTICA HUNGARICA
ACTA PHYSIOLOGICA HUNGARICAE
ACTION NATIONALE
AD FORUM
ADOLESCENCE
ADVANCES IN HUMAN GENETICS
ADVERTISING AGE
AFRICAN JOURNAL OF MEDICINE AND MEDICAL SCIENCES
AHOT BE YISRAEL
AKUSHERSTVO I GINEKOLOGIIA
ALBERTA REPORT
ALCOHOL AND ALCOHOLISM
ALCOHOLISM: CLINICAL & EXPERIMENTAL RESEARCH
AMERICA
AMERICAN DEMOGRAPHICS
AMERICAN BAR ASSOCIATION JOURNAL
AMERICAN FAMILY PHYSICIAN
AMERICAN JOURNAL OF CLINICAL NUTRITION
AMERICAN JOURNAL OF EPIDEMIOLOGY
AMERICAN JOURNAL OF GASTROENTEROLOGY
AMERICAN JOURNAL OF HUMAN GENETICS
AMERICAN JOURNAL OF LAW AND MEDICINE
AMERICAN JOURNAL OF MEDICAL GENETICS
AMERICAN JOURNAL OF NURSING
AMERICAN JOURNAL OF OBSTETRICS AND GYNECOLOGY
AMERICAN JOURNAL OF OPTOMETRY AND PHYSIOLOGICAL OPTICS
AMERICAN JOURNAL OF PHYSIOLOGY
AMERICAN JOURNAL OF PSYCHOTHERAPY
AMERICAN JOURNAL OF PUBLIC HEALTH
AMERICAN JOURNAL OF REPRODUCTIVE IMMUNOLOGY & MICROBIOLOGY

AMERICAN JOURNAL OF THEOLOGY AND PHILOSOPHY
AMERICAN JOURNAL OF TRIAL ADVOCACY
AMERICAN JOURNAL OF VETERINARY RESEARCH
AMERICAN SPEECH
ANAESTHESIA AND INTENSIVE CARE
ANATOMISCHER ANZEIGER
ANDROLOGIA
ANESTHESIA AND ANALGESIA
ANNALES CHIRURGIAE ET GYNAECOLOGIAE
ANNALES DE GENETIQUE
ANNALES D'IMMUNOLOGIE
ANNALES DE MEDECINE INTERNE
ANNALES FRANCAISES D'ANESTHESIA ET DE REANIMATION
ANNALI DI OSTETRICIA GINECOLOGIA MEDICINA PERINATALE
ANNALS OF THE ACADEMY OF MEDICINE, SINGAPORE
ANNALS OF THE AMERICAN ACADEMY OF POLITICAL AND SOCIAL
    SCIENCE
ANNALS OF CLINICAL RESEARCH
ANNALS OF HUMAN BIOLOGY
ANNALS OF INTERNAL MEDICINE
ANNALS OF THE NEW YORK ACADEMY OF SCIENCES
ANNALS OF OPHTHALMOLOGY
ARCHIV DER PHARMAZIE
ARCHIVES OF ANDROLOGY
ARCHIVES OF GYNECOLOGY
ARCHIVES OF SEXUAL BEHAVIOR
ARCHIVOS DE BIOLOGIA Y MEDICINA EXPERIMENTALES
ARTHRITIS AND RHEUMATISM
ARZNEIMITTEL-FORSCHUNG
ASIA-OCEANIA JOURNAL OF OBSTETRICS AND GYNAECOLOGY
ASIAN PACIFIC JOURNAL OF ALLERGY AND IMMUNOLOGY
ASSIGNMENT CHILDREN
ATLANTIS
AUDIOLOGY
AUDUBON
AUSTRALIAN AND NEW ZEALAND JOURNAL OF OBSTETRICS AND
    GYNAECOLOGY
AUSTRALASIAN NURSES JOURNAL
AUSTRALIAN FAMILY PHYSICIAN
AUSTRALIAN JOURNAL OF SEX, MARRIAGE AND FAMILY
AUSTRALIAN VETERINARY JOURNAL
BC STUDIES
BALAI
BANGLADESH MEDICAL RESEARCH COUNCIL BULLETIN
BEHAVIORAL NEUROSCIENCE
BEIJING REVIEW
BIOLOGICAL RESEARCH IN PREGNANCY AND PERINATOLOGY
BIOLOGY OF REPRODUCTION
BIOMATERIALS
BIOMATERIALS, MEDICAL DEVICES AND ARTIFICIAL ORGANS
BIOMEDICAL PHARMACOTHERAPY
BIOSCIENCE

BIRTH DEFECTS
BODY POLITIC
BOLETIN DE LA OFICINA SANITARIA PANAMERICANA
BRATISLAVSKE LEKARSKE LISTY
BRIARPATCH
BRIGHAM YOUNG UNIVERSITY LAW REVIEW
BRISTOL MEDICO-CHIRURGICAL JOURNAL
BRITISH HEART JOURNAL
BRITISH JOURNAL OF ANAESTHESIOLOGY
BRITISH JOURNAL OF OBSTETRICS AND GYNAECOLOGY
BRITISH JOURNAL OF POLITICAL SCIENCE
BRITISH JOURNAL OF PSYCHIATRY
BRITISH MEDICAL JOURNAL
BROOKLYN JOURNAL OF INTERNATIONAL LAW
BUFFALO LAW REVIEW
BULLETIN OF CONCERNED ASIAN SCHOLARS
BULLETIN OF THE HONG KONG PSYCHOLOGICAL SOCIETY
BUSINESS INSURANCE
BUSINESS JAPAN
BUSINESS WEEK
CAHIERS D'ANESTHESIOLOGIE
CANADA AND THE WORLD
CANADIAN FORUM
CANADIAN JOURNAL OF PSYCHIATRY
CANADIAN JOURNAL OF PUBLIC HEALTH
CANADIAN MEDICAL ASSOCIATION JOURNAL
CANADIAN NURSE
CANADIAN OPERATING ROOM NURSES JOURNAL
CANADIAN REVIEW OF SOCIOLOGY AND ANTHROPOLOGY
CANCER DETECTION AND PREVENTION
CARCINOGENESIS
CASOPIS LEKARU CESKYCH
CATHOLIC DIGEST
CATHOLIC LAWYER
CELL AND TISSUE RESEARCH
CENTER JOURNAL
CENTRAL AFRICAN JOURNAL OF MEDICINE
CEPHALALGIA
CESKOSLOVENSKA GYNEKOLOGIE
CEYLON MEDICAL JOURNAL
CHALLENGE
CHARTIST
CHATELAINE
CHEMICAL AND ENGINEERING NEWS
CHEMICAL MARKETING REPORT
CHEMICAL WEEK
CHEST
CHILD ABUSE AND NEGLECT
CHILDREN TODAY
CHINA QUARTERLY
CHRISTIAN CENTURY
THE CHRISTIAN MINISTRY

CHRISTIAN SCHOLAR'S REVIEW
CHRISTIANITY AND CRISIS
CHRISTIANITY TODAY
CHUNG HSI I CHIEH HO TSA CHIH
CHUNG HUA FU CHAN KO TSA CHIH
CHUNG HUA I HSUEH TSA CHIH
CHUNG HUA HU LI TSA CHIH
CHURCH AND STATE
CIBA FOUNDATION SYMPOSIA
CLINICA E INVESTIGACION EN GINECOLOGIA Y OBSTETRICIA
CLINICAL AND EXPERIMENTAL IMMUNOLOGY
CLINICAL AND EXPERIMENTAL OBSTETRICS AND GYNECLOGY
CLINICAL CHEMISTRY
CLINICAL ELECTROENCEPHALOGRAPHY
CLINICAL GENETICS
CLINICAL OBSTETRICS AND GYNAECOLOGY
CLINICAL PHARMACY
CLINICAL REPRODUCTION AND FERTILITY
CLINICAL SOCIAL WORK JOURNAL
CLINICAL THERAPEUTICS
COMER EXTERIOR
COMMONWEAL
COMMUNIO
COMMUNIQU'ELLES
COMMUNITY HEALTH STUDIES
COMMUNITY MEDICINE
CONCEPTE
CONGRESSIONAL QUARTERLY WEEKLY REPORT
CONRAD GREBEL REVIEW
CONSERVATIVE DIGEST
CONSULTANT
CONSUMER REPORTS
CONSUMERS RESEARCH MAGAZINE
CONTEMPORARY REVIEW
CONTEMPORARY SOCIOLOGY
CONTRACEPTION
CONTRIBUTIONS TO NEPHROLOGY
CORRECTIONS DIGEST
COSMOPOLITAN
CRIME CONTROL DIGEST
CRIMINAL JUSTICE NEWSLETTER
CRIMINAL LAW REVIEW
CURRENT DIGEST OF THE SOVIET PRESS
CYTOGENETICS AND CELL GENETICS
DAI: DISSERTATION ABSTRACTS INTERNATIONAL:
    A. HUMANITIES AND SOCIAL SCIENCES
DAI: DISSERTATION ABSTRACTS INTERNATIONAL:
    B. SCIENCES AND ENGINEERING
DANISH MEDICAL BULLETIN
DEPAUL LAW REVIEW
DEMOGRAPHY
DEUTSCHE MEDIZINISCHE WOCHENSCHRIFT

GEOGRAPICAL MAGAZINE
GEOGRAPHY
GINECOLOGIA Y OBSTETRICIA DE MEXICO
GINEKOLOGIA POLSKA
GLAMOUR
GOOD HOUSEKEEPING
GOODWINS
GUARDIAN
GUILD NOTES
GYNAEKOLOGISCHE RUNDSCHAU
GYNAKOLOGE
GYNECOLOGIC AND OBSTETRIC INVESTIGATION
GYNECOLOGIC ONCOLOGY
HAREFUAH
HARPERS
HARVARD JOURNAL OF LAW AND PUBLIC POLICY
HARVARD JOURNAL OF LEGISLATION
HASTINGS CENTER REPORT
HEALTH
HEALTH BULLETIN
HEALTH EDUCATION
HEALTH EDUCATION QUARTERLY
HEALTH MANAGEMENT FORUM
HEALTH PAC BULLETIN
HEALTHRIGHT
HEALTHSHARING
HERIZONS
HOME MAGAZINE
HORIZONS
HOSPITAL AND COMMUNITY PSYCHIATRY
HOSPITAL PROGRESS
HUMAN EVENTS
HUMAN GENETICS
HUMAN LIFE REVIEW
HUMAN NUTRITION
HUMAN ORGANIZATION
HUMAN RELATIONS
HUMANIST
HYGIE
IMJ: ILLINOIS MEDICAL JOURNAL
IMPACT OF SCIENCE ON SOCIETY
IN THESE TIMES
INDIAN HEART JOURNAL
INDIAN JOURNAL OF EXPERIMENTAL BIOLOGY
INDIAN JOURNAL OF MEDICAL RESEARCH
INDIAN JOURNAL OF PUBLIC HEALTH
INDIANA LAW REVIEW
INDIANA MEDICINE
INFIRMIERE CANADIENNE
INFIRMIERE FRANCAISE
INTERCONTINENTAL PRESS
INTERNATIONAL AND COMPARATIVE LAW QUARTERLY

INTERNATIONAL ARCHIVES OF OCCUPATIONAL AND ENVIRONMENTAL
HEALTH
INTERNATIONAL JOURNAL OF CANCER
INTERNATIONAL JOURNAL OF EPIDEMIOLOGY
INTERNATIONAL JOURNAL OF FERTILITY
INTERNATIONAL JOURNAL OF GYNAECOLOGY AND OBSTETRICS
INTERNATIONAL JOURNAL OF NURSING STUDIES
INTERNATIONAL JOURNAL OF PSYCHOLOGY
INTENRATIONAL JOURNAL OF PSYCHOPHYSIOLOGY
INTERNATIONAL JOURNAL OF SOCIAL PSYCHIATRY
INTERNATIONAL JOURNAL OF WOMEN'S STUDIES
INTERNATIONAL NURSING REVIEW
INTERNATIONAL QUARTERLY OF COMMUNITY HEALTH AND EDUCATION
INTERNATIONAL VIEWPOINT
IOWA MEDICINE
ISIS
ISRAEL JOURNAL OF MEDICAL SCIENCES
ISSUES IN MENTAL HEALTH NURSING
JIKKEN DOBUTSU
JSSR: JOURNAL OF THE SCIENTIFIC STUDY OF RELIGION
JOURNAL DE GYNECOLOGIE, OBSTETRIQUE ET BIOLOGIE DE LA
REPRODUCTION
JOURNAL OF ADOLESCENT HEALTH CARE
JOURNAL OF AMERICAN COLLEGE HEALTH
JOURNAL OF THE AMERICAN MEDICAL WOMEN'S ASSOCIATION
JOURNAL OF THE AMERICAN OSTEOPATHIC ASSOCIATION
JOURNAL OF APPLIED BEHAVIOR ANALYSIS
JOURNAL OF APPLIED SOCIAL PSYCHOLOGY
JOURNAL OF BIOSOCIAL SCIENCE
JOURNAL OF CANADIAN STUDIES
JOURNAL OF CHRISTIAN NURSING
JOURNAL OF CHRONIC DISEASES
JOURNAL OF CLINICAL AND HOSPITAL PHARMACY
JOURNAL OF CLINICAL PATHOLOGY
JOURNAL OF CLINICAL PSYCHIATRY
JOURNAL OF CLINICAL PSYCHOLOGY
JOURNAL OF COMPARATIVE FAMILY STUDIES
JOURNAL OF COUNSELING AND DEVELOPMENT
JOURNAL OF COUNSELING PSYCHOLOGY
JOURNAL OF DEVELOPING AREAS
JOURNAL OF ECUMENICAL STUDIES
JOURNAL OF ENDOCRINOLOGY
JOURNAL OF EPIDEMIOLOGY AND COMMUNITY HEALTH
JOURNAL OF ETHNOPHARMACOLOGY
JOURNAL OF FAMILY ISSUES
JOURNAL OF FAMILY LAW
JOURNAL OF FAMILY WELFARE
JOURNAL OF FEMINIST STUDIES IN RELIGION
JOURNAL OF FORENSIC SCIENCES
JOURNAL OF GENETIC PSYCHOLOGY
JOURNAL OF HUMAN STRESS
JOURNAL OF IMMUNOLOGY

JOURNAL OF THE INDIAN MEDICAL ASSOCIATION
JOURNAL OF INTERDISCIPLINARY HISTORY
JOURNAL OF JEWISH COMMUNAL SERVICE
JOURNAL OF JUVENILE LAW
JOURNAL OF LEGAL MEDICINE
JOURNAL OF MARRIAGE AND THE FAMILY
JOURNAL OF THE MEDICAL ASSOCIATION OF THAILAND
JOURNAL OF MEDICAL ETHICS
JOURNAL OF MEDICAL GENETICS
JOURNAL OF THE MEDICAL SOCIETY OF NEW JERSEY
JOURNAL OF THE MOSCOW PATRIARCHATE
JOURNAL OF THE NATIONAL MEDICAL ASSOCIATION
JOURNAL OF NURSE-MIDWIFERY
JOURNAL OF NUTRITION EDUCATION
JOURNAL OF OCCUPATIONAL MEDICINE
JOURNAL OF PASTORAL COUNSELING
JOURNAL OF PERSONALITY AND SOCIAL PSYCHOLOGY
JOURNAL OF PSYCHOSOMATIC OBSTETRICS AND GYNECOLOGY
JOURNAL OF PSYCHOSOMATIC RESEARCH
JOURNAL OF REPRODUCTIVE AND INFANT PSYCHOLOGY
JOURNAL OF REPRODUCTIVE IMMUNOLOGY
JOURNAL OF REPRODUCTIVE MEDICINE
JOURNAL OF RESEARCH IN PERSONALITY
JOURNAL OF THE ROYAL COLLEGE OF GENERAL PRACTITIONERS
JOURNAL OF THE ROYAL SOCIETY OF HEALTH
JOURNAL OF THE ROYAL SOCIETY OF MEDICINE
JOURNAL OF SEX EDUCATION AND THERAPY
JOURNAL OF SEX RESEARCH
JOURNAL OF SOCIAL HISTORY
JOURNAL OF SOCIAL SERVICE RESEARCH
THE JOURNAL OF SOCIAL WELFARE LAW
JOURNAL OF SOCIAL WORK AND HUMAN SEXUALITY
JOURNAL OF SOUTHEAST ASIAN STUDIES
JOURNAL OF THE TENNESSEE MEDICAL ASSOCIATION
JOURNAL OF TROPICAL PEDIATRICS
JOURNAL OF UROLOGY
JOURNAL OF WOMEN AND RELIGION
JOURNEES ANNUELLES DE DIABETOLOGIE DE L'HOTEL-DIEU
JUDAISM
JUGOSLAVENSKA GINEKOLOGIJA I OPSTETRICIJA
JUSTICE QUARTERLY
KANGOGAKU ZASSHI
KLINISCHE WOCHENSCHRIFT
KRANKENPFLEGE JOURNAL
LABOUR/LE TRAVAIL
LAKARTIDNINGEN
LANCET
LESBIAN CONTRADICTION
LIFE SCIENCES
LINCOLN LAW REVIEW
MCN: AMERICAN JOURNAL OF MATERNAL-CHILD NURSING
MS MAGAZINE

MCCALLS
MACLEAN'S
MADEMOISELLE
MANAGEMENT SCIENCE
MATURITAS
MEDECINE TROPICALE
MEDICAL CARE
MEDICAL HISTORY
MEDICAL HYPOTHESES
MEDICAL JOURNAL OF AUSTRALIA
MEDICAL LETTER ON DRUGS AND THERAPEUTICS
MEDICINE AND LAW
MEDICINSKI PREGLED
MEDICO-LEGAL BULLETIN
MEDITSINSKAIA RADIOLOGIIA
MENTAL AND PHYSICAL DISABILITY LAW REPORTER
MICHIGAN MEDICINE
MICROSURGERY
MIDWIFE, HEALTH VISITOR AND COMMUNITY NURSE
MILITANT
MINERVA ANESTESIOLOGICA
MINERVA GINECOLOGIA
MONIST
MOTHER JONES
MOTHERING
MT. SINAI JOURNAL OF MEDICINE
MULTINATIONAL MONITOR
MUTATION RESEARCH
NATIONAL NOW TIMES
NATIONAL PRISON PROJECT JOURNAL
NATURWISSENSCHAFTEN
NATION
NATIONAL CATHOLIC REPORTER
NATIONAL REVIEW
NATURAL HISTORY
NATURE
NEBRASKA LAW REVIEW
NEDERLANDS TIJDSCHRIFT VOOR GENEESKUNDE
NEW AGE
NEW BLACKFRIARS
NEW DIRECTIONS FOR WOMEN
NEW ENGLAND JOURNAL OF MEDICINE
NEW HUMANIST
NEW LAW JOURNAL
NEW REPUBLIC
NEW SCIENTIST
NEW SOCIETY
NEW STATESMAN
NEW WOMEN'S TIMES
NEW YORK
NEW YORK LAW SCHOOL HUMAN RIGHTS ANNUAL
NEW YORK REVIEW OF BOOKS

NEW YORK STATE JOURNAL OF MEDICINE
NEW YORK TIMES MAGAZINE
NEW ZEALAND LAW JOURNAL
NEW ZEALAND MEDICAL JOURNAL
NEWSWEEK
NIPPON NAIKA GAKKAI ZASSHI
NIPPON SANKA FUJINKA GAKKAI ZASSHI
NORTH CAROLINA LAW REVIEW
NORTH DAKOTA QUARTERLY
NORTHWEST PASSAGE
NOT MAN APART
NURSE PRACTITIONER
NURSES DRUG ALERT
NURSING MIRROR AND MIDWIVE'S JOURNAL
NURSING STANDARD
NURSING TIMES
OBSERVER
OBSTETRICS AND GYNECOLOGY
OFF OUR BACKS
OHIO STATE MEDICAL JOURNAL
OKLAHOMA CITY UNIVERSITY LAW REVIEW
OKLAHOMA LAW REVIEW
ONCOLOGY NURSING FORUM
ORVOSI HETILAP
OVERTHROW
PACIFIC AFFAIRS
PADIATRIE UND PADOLOGIE
PAPUA NEW GUINEA MEDICAL JOURNAL
PARENTS MAGAZINE
PATHOLOGICA
PATHOLOGIE BIOLOGIE
PATHOLOGY ANNUAL
PATHOLOGY, RESEARCH AND PRACTICE
PATIENT CARE
PEDIATRIC NURSING
PEDIATRICS
PEOPLE WEEKLY
PEPPERDINE LAW REVIEW
PERCEPTION
PERSPECTIVES IN PEDIATRIC PATHOLOGY
PHARMAZIE
PHILADELPHIA MAGAZINE
PHILOSOPHICAL QUARTERLY
PHILOSOPHY
PHOENIX RISING
PHYSICIAN ASSISTANT
PLACENTA
PLANTA MEDICA
POLICE AND SECURITY BULLETIN
POLICY REVIEW
POPULATION
POPULATION AND DEVELOPMENT REVIEW

POPULATION AND ENVIRONMENT
POPULATION BULLETIN
POPULATION REPORTS
POPULATION RESEARCH AND POLICY REVIEW
POPULATION STUDIES
POPULI
POSTGRADUATE MEDICINE
PRACTITIONER
PRENATAL DIAGNOSIS
PREVENTION
PRO MUNDI VITA BULLETIN
PROBLEMY ENDOKRINOLOGII I GORMONOTERAPII
PROGRESS IN CLINICAL AND BIOLOGICAL RESEARCH
PROGRESSIVE
PROSTAGLANDINS
PROSTAGLANDINS LEUKOTRIENES AND MEDICINE
PROTECT YOURSELF
PSYCHOLOGICAL REPORTS
PSYCHOLOGIE MEDICALE
PSYCHOLOGY OF WOMEN QUARTERLY
PSYCHOLOGY TODAY
PUBLIC HEALTH
PUBLIC HEALTH REPORTS
PUBLIC HEALTH REVIEWS
PUBLIC OPINION
PUBLIC OPINION QUARTERLY
PUBLIC RELATIONS JOURNAL
PUBLIC WELFARE
QUARTERLY JOURNAL OF SPEECH
QUARTERLY REVIEWS ON DRUG METABOLISM AND DRUG INTERACTIONS
RADICAL AMERICAN
RADIOLOGIA DIAGNOSTICA
RECENTI PROGRESSI IN MEDICINA
REDBOOK
REFORMED JOURNAL
REFRACTORY GIRL
RELIGIOUS STUDIES REVIEW
RESEARCH IN NURSING AND HEALTH
RESOURCES FOR FEMINIST RESEARCH
RESPIRATION
REVIEW OF RELIGIOUS RESEARCH
REVISTA CHILENA DE OBSTETRICIA Y GINECOLOGIA
REVISTA DE ENFERMAGEN
REVISTA DE INVESTIGACION CLINICA
REVISTA DE SAUDE PUBLICA
REVISTA ESPANOLA DE INVESTIGACIONES SOCIOLOGICAS
REVUE D'EPIDEMIOLOGIE ET DE SANTE PUBLIQUE
REVUE DE L'INFIRMIERE
REVUE DE L'INSTITUT DE SOCIOLOGIE
REVUE FRANCAISE DE GYNECOLOGIE ET D'OBSTETRIQUE
REVUE MEDICALE DE LA SUISSE ROMANDE
RHODE ISLAND MEDICAL JOURNAL

RIGHTS AND BILL OF RIGHTS JOURNAL
RINSHO KETSUEKI
RUTGERS LAW REVIEW
RYUMACHI
ST. LOUIS UNIVERSITY LAW JOURNAL
SANTA CLARA LAW REVIEW
SASKATCHEWAN LAW REVIEW
SATURDAY EVENING POST
SCANDINAVIAN JOURNAL OF SOCIAL WORK
SCHWEIZERISCHE RUNDSCHAU FUR MEDIZIN PRAXIS
SCIENCE
SCIENCE DIMENSION
SCIENCE FOR PEOPLE
SCIENCE NEWS
SCIENCE, TECHNOLOGY AND HUMAN VALUES
SCOTTISH MEDICAL JOURNAL
SECURITY LETTER
SEVENTEEN
SEX ROLES
SEXUALLY TRANSMITTED DISEASES
SHMATE
SHENG LI KO HSUEH CHIN CHAN
SIECUS REPORT
SIMULATION AND GAMES
SOCIAL BIOLOGY
SOCIAL COMPASS
SECURITY SYSTEMS DIGEST
SOCIAL HISTORY
SOCIAL PSYCHIATRY
SOCIAL SCIENCE AND MEDICINE
SOCIAL SCIENCE QUARTERLY
SOCIAL SCIENCE RESEARCH
SOCIAL THEORY AND PRACTICE
SOCIAL WORK IN EDUCATION
SOCIAL WORK IN HEALTH CARE
SOCIALIST REVIEW
SOCIETY
SOCIOLOGICAL FOCUS
SOCIOLOGICAL PERSPECTIVES
SOCIOLOGICAL REVIEW MONOGRAPH
SOCIOLOGY AND SOCIAL RESEARCH
SOINS
SOINS CARDIOLOGIE
SOINS, GYNECOLOGIE, OBSTETRIQUE, PUERICULTURE, PEDIATRIE
SOINS. PATHOLOGIE TROPICALE
SOJOURNERS
SOUNDINGS
SOUTH AFRICAN MEDICAL JOURNAL
SOUTHERN EXPOSURE
SOUTHERN MEDICAL JOURNAL
SOVETSKAIA MEDITSINA
SPARE RIB

SPECIALTY LAW DIGEST: HEALTH CARE
SPORTS MEDICINE
STATE OF THE WORLD
STEROIDS
STUDIES IN FAMILY PLANNING
SUCCESSFUL FARMING
SUNDAY TIMES
SYGEPLEJERSKEN
T V GUIDE
TAIWAN I HSUEH HUI TSA CHIH
TEEN
TEMAS DE TRABOJO SOCIAL
TERATOLOGY
TEXAS OBSERVER
THEOLOGICAL STUDIES
THEOLOGY TODAY
THEORETICAL MEDICINE
THERAPIA HUNGARICA
THERAPIE
THIS WORLD
THROMBOSIS AND HAEMOSTASIS
THROMBOSIS RESEARCH
TIDSSKRIFT FOR DEN NORSKE LAEGEFORENING
TIJDSCHRIFT VOR ZIEKENVERPLEGING
TIME
TIMES (LONDON)
TIMES EDUCATIONAL SUPPLEMENT
TIMES HIGHER EDUCATIONAL SUPPLEMENT
TOHOKU JOURNAL OF EXPERIMENTAL MEDICINE
TOPICS IN EMERGENCY MEDICINE
TOPICS IN HEALTH RECORD MANAGEMENT
TRIAL
TROPICAL AND GEOGRAPHICAL MEDICINE
TUNISIE MEDICALE
UN MONTHLY CHRONICLE
US CATHOLIC
US NEW AND WORLD REPORT
USA TODAY
UTNE READER
UGESKRIFT FOR LAEGER
UNION MEDICALE DU CANADA
UNIVERSITY OF RICHMOND LAW REVIEW
UNIVERSITY OF TORONTO LAW JOURNAL
UPSALA JOURNAL OF MEDICAL SCIENCES
URBAN ANTHROPOLOGY
UROLOGY
VALPARAISO UNIVERSITY LAW REVIEW
VARDFACKET
VIATA MEDICALA
VIERTELJAHRSHEFTE FUR ZEITGESCHICHTE
VILLAGE VOICE
VOGUE

WHO BULLETIN
WHO CHRONICLE
WALL STREET JOURNAL
WEST INDIAN MEDICAL JOURNAL
WESTERN JOURNAL OF MEDICINE
WESTERN POLITICAL QUARTERLY
WIENER KLINISCHE WOCHENSCHRIFT
WILLAMETTE LAW REVIEW
WILSON QUARTERLY
WISCONSIN MEDICAL JOURNAL
WITNESS
WOMANEWS
WOMEN AND HEALTH
WOMEN AND POLITICS
WOMEN AND THERAPY
WOMEN'S PRESS
WOMEN'S REVIEW OF BOOKS
WOMEN'S RIGHTS LAW REPORTER
WOMEN'S ROLES
WORD AND WORLD
WORKING WOMAN
WORLD FUTURES
WORLD HEALTH STATISTICS QUARTERLY
WORLD PRESS REVIEW
ZEITSCHRIFT FUR AERZTLICHE FORTBILDUNG
ZEITSCHRIFT FUR GEBURTSCHILFE UND PERINATOLOGIE
ZEITSCHRIFT FUR HAUTKRANKHEITEN
ZEITSCHRIFT FUR KINDER-UND JUGENDPSYCHIATRIE
ZEITSCHRIFT FUR MISSIONSWISSENSCHAFT UND RELIGION-
    SWISSENSCHAFT
ZEITSCHRIFT FUR PSYCHOSOMATISCHE MEDIZIN UND PSYCHOANALYSE
ZENTRALBLATT FUR GYNAEKOLOGIE
YAO HSUEH HSUEH PAO

SUBJECT HEAD INDEX

BOOKS,
GOVERNMENT PUBLICATIONS,
AND MONOGRAPHS

Abdulah, Norma, and Jack Harewood. CONTRACEPTIVE USE AND FERTILITY IN THE COMMONWEALTH CARIBBEAN. International Statistics Institute, 1984.

Ahmed, Bashir-Ud-Din. DETERMINANTS OF FERTILITY IN BANGLADESH: DESIRED FAMILY SIZE, NATURAL FERTILITY, AND CONTRACEPTIVE USE. University of California, Berkeley, 1984. (Ph.D. dissertation)

Arce, F. and Gabriel C. Alvarez, editors. POPULATION CHANGE IN SOUTHEAST ASIA. Institute of Southeast Asian Studies, 1983.

Benderly, Beryl L. THINKING ABOUT ABORTION. New York: Dial Press, 1984.

Birdsall, Nancy, editor. THE EFFECTS OF FAMILY PLANNING PROGRAMS ON FERTILITY IN THE DEVELOPING WORLD. Washington, D.C.: International Bank for Reconstruction and Development, 1985.

Bongaarts, John and Susan Greenhalgh. AN ALTERNATIVE TO THE ONE-CHILD POLICY IN CHINA. New York: Population Council, 1985.

Callahan, Sidney and Daniel Callahan, editors. ABORTION: UNDERSTANDING DIFFERENCES. New York: Plenum Press, 1984.

Canada. Statistics Canada. Health Division. THERAPEUTIC ABORTIONS, 1982. Ottawa: The Division, 1984.

Cartoof, Virginia G. MASSACHUSETTS' PARENTAL CONSENT LAW: ORIGINS, IMPLEMENTATION AND IMPACT. Brandeis University, 1985. (Ph.D. dissertation)

Coleman, Samuel. FAMILY PLANNING IN JAPANESE SOCIETY; TRADITIONAL BIRTH CONTROL IN A MODERN URBAN CULTURE. Princeton: Princeton University Press, 1983.

Cook, Rebecca J. and Bernard M. Dickens. EMERGING ISSUES IN COMMONWEALTH ABORTION LAWS, 1982. Commonwealth Secretariat, 1983.

Fronhock, Fred M. ABORTION; A CASE STUDY IN LAW AND MORALS. Westport, CT: Greenwood Press, 1983.

Harper, Michael J. K. BIRTH CONTROL TECHNOLOGIES; PROSPECTS BY THE YEAR 2000. Austin: University of Texas Press, 1983.

Hernandez, Donald J. SUCCESS OR FAILURE? FAMILY PLANNING PROGRAMS IN THE THIRD WORLD. Westport, CT: Greenwood Press, 1984.

1

Herz, Barbara K. OFFICIAL DEVELOPMENT ASSISTANCE FOR POPULATION ACTIVITIES: A REVIEW. Washington, D.C.: International Bank for Reconstruction and Development, 1984.

International Conference on Population. FERTILITY AND FAMILY: PROCEEDINGS OF THE EXPERT GROUP ON FERTILITY AND FAMILY. New York: United Nations, 1984.

International Forum of African Women Leaders on Population and Development. UN FUND FOR POPULATION ACTIVITIES REPORT, 1984. New York: United Nations, 1984.

Kanyiri, Elisha M. THE SOCIOECONOMIC AND DEMOGRAPHIC FACTORS INFLUENCING CONTRACEPTIVE BEHAVIOR IN KENYA. Florida State University, 1984. (Ph.D. dissertation)

Kaufman, Joan. BILLION AND COUNTING; FAMILY PLANNING CAMPAIGNS AND POLICIES IN THE PEOPLE'S REPUBLIC OF CHINA. San Francisco: San Francisco Press, 1983.

Krason, Stephen M. ABORTION: POLITICS, MORALITY AND THE CONSTITUTION. Lanham, MD: University Press of America, 1984.

Legge, Jerome S., Jr. ABORTION POLICY: AN EVALUATION OF THE CONSEQUENCES FOR MATERNAL AND INFANT HEALTH. Albany: State University of New York Press, 1985.

Marin, Barbara V., et al. ATTITUDES AND PRACTICES OF LOW-INCOME HISPANIC CONTRACEPTIVES. Washington, D.C.: Spanish Speaking Mental Health Research Center Occasional Papers No. 13, 1981.

Neubauer, Erika. SCHWANGERSCHAFTSABBRUCH ALS SOZIALES UND PERSONALES PROBLEM; EINE EMPIRISCHE UNTERSUCHUNG ZUR SOZIOLOGIE DER FRAU. Weinheim, West Germany: Beltz, 1984.

POPULATION POLICY COMPENDIUM: AFGHANISTAN. New York: United Nations Department for International Economic and Social Affairs, 1983.

—: BRAZIL. New York: United Nations Department for International Economic and Social Affairs, 1983.

Potts, Malcolm, et al. TEXTBOOK OF CONTRACEPTIVE PRACTICE. New York: Cambridge University Press, 1983.

Reis, Hans. DAS LEBENSRECHT DES UNGEBORENEN KINDES ALS VERFASSUNGSPROBLEM. Tubingen, West Germany: Mohr, 1984.

Reiter, Johannes and Ursel Theile, editors. GENETIK UND MORAL: BEITRAGE ZU EINER ETHIK DES UNGEBORENEN. Mainz, West Germany: Matthias-Grunewald, 1985.

Reynolds, Brenda. HUMAN ABORTION; GUIDE FOR MEDICINE, SCIENCE AND RESEARCH WITH BIBLIOGRAPHY. Washington, D.C.: Abbe Publishing Association, 1984.

Sachdev, Paul, editor. PERSPECTIVES ON ABORTION. Metuchen, NJ: Scarecrow, 1985.

Sadik, Nafis, editor. POPULATION: THE UNFPA EXPERIENCE. New York: New York University Press, 1984.

Song, Jian, et al. POPULATION CONTROL IN CHINA: THEORY AND APPLICA-TIONS. New York: Praeger, 1985.

Splaver, Gail I. ABORTION SERVICES IN ENGLAND: FACTORS ASSOCIATED WITH SOCIAL WORKER ATTITUDES AND RECOMMENDATIONS. University of California, Berkeley, 1984. (Ph.D. dissertation)

SRI LANKA: CONTRACEPTIVE PREVALENCE SURVEY REPORT 1982. Westinghouse Health Systems Report, 1983.

Stettner, Allison G. and Anita P. Cowan. HEALTH ASPECTS OF FAMILY PLANNING; A GUIDE TO RESOURCES IN THE UNITED STATES. New York: Human Sciences Press, 1982.

STOPPING POPULATION GROWTH (STATE OF THE WORLD 1985). Washington, D.C.: Worldwatch Institute Report, 1985.

UNITED NATIONS FUND FOR POPULATION ACTIVITIES 1983 REPORT. New York: The Fund, 1983.

United Nations Fund for Population Activities. INVENTORY OF POPULATION PROJECTS IN DEVELOPING COUNTRIES AROUND THE WORLD, 1982/83: MULTILATERAL ASSISTANCE, BILATERAL ASSISTANCE, NON-GOVERNMENTAL ORGANIZATION ASSISTANCE. New York: The Fund, 1984.

—. —, 1983/84: MULTILATERAL ASSISTANCE, BILATERAL ASSISTANCE, NON-GOVERNMENTAL ORGANIZATION ASSISTANCE. New York: The Fund, 1985.

United States. Congress. Joint Economic Committee. Subcommittee on Interna-tional Trade, Finance, and Security Economics. POPULATION GROWTH AND DEVELELOPMENT IN THE WORLD ECONOMY: HEARING, MARCH 20, 1984. Washington: GPO, 1984.

United States. Congress. Senate. Committee on the Judiciary. Subcommittee on the Constitution. CONSTITUTIONAL AMENDMENTS RELATING TO ABORTION; HEARINGS BEFORE THE SUBCOMMITTEE ON THE CONSTITU-TION OF THE COMMITTEE ON THE JUDICIARY. Washington: GPO, 1983.

United States. House Committee on Post Office and Civil Service. Subcommittee on Census and Population. U.S. POLICY ON POPULATION ASSISTANCE: HEARING, JULY 25, 1984. Washington: GPO, 1984.

3

A-bombs and abortions, by C. R. Wood. FUNDAMENTALIST JOURNAL 3(7):66, July-August 1984.

AFFPA medical task force guidelines. Medical Task Force of the Australian Federation of Family Planning Associations. MEDICAL JOURNAL OF AUSTRALIA 143(4):162-163, August 19, 1985.

AID tightens antiabortion measures, by C. Holden. SCIENCE 227:1318-1319, March 15, 1985.

AID turns down IPPF, by C. Holden. SCIENCE 227:37, January 4, 1985.

AIDS. Condoms and gay abandon [letter], by C. J. Mitchell. MEDICAL JOURNAL OF AUSTRALIA 142(11):617, May 27, 1985.

Aborted sibling factor: a case study, by A. H. Weiner, et al. CLINICAL SOCIAL WORK JOURNAL 12(3):209-215, 1984.

Abortion. CANADIAN MEDICAL ASSOCIATION JOURNAL 133(4):318A-318B, August 15, 1985.

Abortion [letter], by N. E. MacLean. NEW ZEALAND MEDICAL JOURNAL 98(771): 22, January 23, 1985.

Abortion amendments mar Civil Rights Bill. OFF OUR BACKS 15(7):13, July 1985.

Abortion and the Catholic Church. HUMANIST 8(1):28, Spring 1985.

Abortion and the Christian feminist: a dilemma?, by C. Smith. NEW BLACKFRIARS 66:62-67, February 1985.

Abortion and the Christian feminist: profilers of survival, by S. Dowell. NEW BLACK-FRIARS 66:67-72, February 1985.

Abortion and the conscience of the nation, by R. Reagan. FUNDAMENTALIST JOURNAL 3(1):19-25, January 1984.

Abortion and elections/Bishops try to do in dems, by E. Bader. GUARDIAN 37(1):91, October 3, 1984.

Abortion and the ethics manual [letter], by C. D. Gibson, Jr. ANNALS OF INTERNAL MEDICINE 102(1):133-134, January 1985.

Abortion and the Holocaust, by R. M. Brown. CHRISTIAN CENTURY 101:1004-1005, October 31, 1984.

Abortion and infanticide. Is there a difference?, by D. Cannon. POLICY REVIEW 32:12-17, 1985.

Abortion and medical discipline [letter]. NEW ZEALAND MEDICAL JOURNAL 98(778): 348, May 8, 1985.

Abortion and medical discipline [letter]. NEW ZEALAND MEDICAL JOURNAL 98(780):451-452, June 12, 1985.

Abortion and medical discipline [letter], by F. R. Duncanson. NEW ZEALAND MEDICAL JOURNAL 98(776):251, April 10, 1985.

Abortion and medical discipline [letter], by K. B. Fitzsimons, et al. NEW ZEALAND MEDICAL JOURNAL 98(781):507-508, June 26, 1985.

Abortion and moral consensus: beyond Solomon's choice, by M. Kolbenschlag. CHRISTIAN CENTURY 102:179-183, February 20, 1985.

Abortion and the right, by J. Hardisty. SHMATE 11:36, Summer 1985.

Abortion and the state. OFF OUR BACKS 15(4):4, April 1985.

Abortion and sterilization in the United States: demographic dynamics, by P. J. Sweeney. UNION MEDICALE DU CANADA 113(7):587-593, July 1984.

Abortion and subsequent pregnancy, by C. F. Bradley. CANADIAN JOURNAL OF PSYCHIATRY 29(6):494-498, October 1984.

Abortion and theology [views of K. Luker], by M. E. Marty. CHRISTIAN CENTURY 101:1018-1020, October 31, 1984.

An abortion anniversary, by W. Shapiro. NEWSWEEK 105:22, February 4, 1985.

Abortion as a stigma: in the eyes of the beholder, by G. Weidner, et al. JOURNAL OF RESEARCH IN PERSONALITY 18:359-371, September 1984.

Abortion as "violence against women", by R. Petchesky. RADICAL AMERICAN 18(2):64, 1984.

Abortion battle in America, by M. Potts. NEW SOCIETY 71:204-206, February 7, 1985.

Abortion bias: how network coverage has tilted to the prolifers: even anti-abortion forces acknowledge that the nightly news is paying more attention to their side of the explosive issue, by Joanmarie Kalter. TV GUIDE 33:6, November 9, 1985.

Abortion Bill "unconstitutional." BRIARPATCH 14(5):9, June 1985.

Abortion bills and smokescreens, by T. L. Langford. TEXAS OBSERVER 77(3):12-14, February 22, 1985.

Abortion: a christian response, by S. J. Grenz. CONRAD GREBEL REVIEW 2(1): 21-30, 1984.

Abortion: a civilized exchange, by E. Van Den Haag, et al. NATIONAL REVIEW 37:37-39, September 6, 1985.

Abortion clinic bombings and the Reagan administration, by L. Woehrle. OFF OUR BACKS 15:2, January 1985.

Abortion clinic bombings present new American crime and security problems.
POLICE AND SECURITY BULLETIN 16(9):1, January 1985.

Abortion clinic closed; clinic closed because of abuse against women. OFF OUR
BACKS 15:3, January 1985.

Abortion clinic sues protesters [news]. CHRISTIANITY TODAY 29(14):69, October 4,
1985.

Abortion clinic violence: How far will it go?, by L. Speare. WOMEN'S PRESS 14(5):1,
November 1984.

Abortion clinic: what goes on, by S. K. Reed. PEOPLE WEEKLY 24:103-106,
August 26, 1985.

Abortion clinics intensify security to avert bombings. SECURITY SYSTEMS DIGEST
16(2):7, January 21, 1985.

Abortion clinics lose coverage after attacks, by S. Taravella. BUSINESS INSURANCE
19:3+, January 21, 1985.

Abortion clinics: terror, but not terrorism. ECONOMIST 294:18-19, January 5, 1985.

Abortion clinics under fire. GUILD NOTES 9(1):1, Winter 1985.

Abortion conflict: what it does to one doctor, by D. Clendinan. NEW YORK TIMES
MAGAZINE August 11, 1985, p. 18-22+.

Abortion, contraception, infanticide, by P. E. Devine. PHILOSOPHY 58:513-520,
October 1983.

Abortion controversy slows radical 'civil rights' bill: but foes still face uphill battle.
HUMAN EVENTS 45:1+, August 10, 1985.

Abortion controversy: a study in law and politics, by A. M. Pearson, et al. HARVARD
JOURNAL OF LAW AND PUBLIC POLICY Spring 1985, p. 427-464.

Abortion cuts in California?, by T. Woody. IN THESE TIMES 8(37):4, October 3,
1984.

Abortion debate. CHRISTIAN CENTURY 101:1032, November 7, 1984.

Abortion denied—outcome of mothers and babies [letter], by C. Del Campo. CANA-
DIAN MEDICAL ASSOCIATION JOURNAL 131(6):546+, September 15, 1984.

Abortion dialogue, by J. A. Brix. CHRISTIAN CENTURY 102:21-24, January 2-9,
1985.

Abortion dilemma, by A. Finlayson. WORLD PRESS REVIEW 32:56, January 1985.

Abortion: the devisive issue [editorial], by A. Yankauer. AMERICAN JOURNAL OF
PUBLIC HEALTH 75(7):714-715, July 1985.

Abortion: the enduring debate. ECONOMIST 292:26+, September 22, 1984.

Abortion experience among obstetric patients at Korle-Bu Hospital, Accra, Ghana, by
P. Lamptey, et al. JOURNAL OF BIOSOCIAL SCIENCE 17(2):195-203, April
1985.

7

Abortion fight gets set for a new round, by T. Gest. U S NEWS AND WORLD RE-
PORT 98:69, January 28, 1985.

Abortion following prenatal diagnosis of genetic defects, by W. Weise. ZENTRAL-
BLATT FUR GYNAEKOLOGIE 107(14):855-862, 1985.

Abortion following recent myocardial infarct, by B. Köhler. ZENTRALBLATT FUR
GYNAEHOLOGIE 107(8):508-511, 1985.

Abortion in Canada: a new phase in the conflict, by T. Sinclair-Faulkner. CHRIS-
TIAN CENTURY 102:923-926, October 16, 1985.

Abortion in early pregnancy [letter], by I. R. Walker. MEDICAL JOURNAL OF
AUSTRALIA 142(8):489, April 15, 1985.

Abortion in Great Britain: one Act, two laws, by K. M. Norrie. THE CRIMINAL LAW
REVIEW August 1985, p. 475-488.

Abortion in Greece, by S. Ginger. CONTEMPORARY REVIEW 243:253-255,
November 1983.

Abortion in Thailand and Sweden: health services and short-term consequences, by
T. N. Singnomklao. CIBA FOUNDATION SYMPOSIUM 115:54-66, 1985.

Abortion-inducing effect of prostaglandin F2-alpha in the mid-trimester of pregnancy,
by A. Pajor, et al. ACTA CHIRURGICA ACADEMIAE SCIENTARUM
HUNGARICAE 25(4):229-238, 1984.

Abortion induction in the 2d pregnancy trimester. Endocervical PGE2 gel administration, intramuscular sulprostone administration and combined treatment, by W.
Schmidt, et al. GEBURTSHILFE UND FRAUENHEILKUNDE 45(4):261-264, April
1985.

Abortion is not convenient [letters]. VILLAGE VOICE 29:8-9, October 16, 1984.

Abortion is not a crime/Spanish women fight, by E. Lamas. INTERNATIONAL VIEW-
POINT 76:28, May 20, 1985.

Abortion is not murder, by G. Scialabba. VILLAGE VOICE 29:8, October 16, 1984.

Abortion issue is not so simple, by T. C. Fox. NATIONAL CATHOLIC REPORTER
20:12, October 19, 1984.

Abortion: the issue is women's rights, by P. Grogan. MILITANT 48(44):11, November
30, 1984.

Abortion: an issue to grieve?, by S. S. Joy. JOURNAL OF COUNSELING AND
DEVELOPMENT 63:375-376, February 1985.

Abortion issues reach into hospital ORs. AMERICAN JOURNAL OF NURSING
84:1535, December 1984.

Abortion lottery: it's where you live that counts, by A. Neustatter. SUNDAY TIMES
November 10, 1985, p. 36.

Abortion: medical progress and social implications. CIBA FOUNDATION SYMPOSIA
115:1-285, 1985.

Abortion—moral and religious aspects. NATIONAL CATHOLIC REPORTER 21(1):
53, February 15, 1985.

Abortion: new arguments on an old issue [news]. CHRISTIANITY TODAY 29(18):56-57, December 13, 1985.

Abortion: no going back. GUARDIAN 37(17):18, January 30, 1985.

Abortion: opinion roundup. charts. PUBLIC OPINION 8:25-28, April-May 1985.

Abortion or premature delivery?, by R. Perkins. MEDICAL JOURNAL OF AUSTRALIA 142(5):313-314, March 4, 1985.

Abortion outcome as a function of sex-role identification, by R. C. Alter. PSYCHOLOGY OF WOMEN QUARTERLY 8:211-233, Spring 1984.

Abortion pill goes on trial, by N. Docherty. NEW SCIENTIST 106:5, June 20, 1985.

Abortion policy and the argument from uncertainty, by R. S. Pfeiffer. SOCIAL THEORY AND PRACTICE 11(3):371-386, 1985.

Abortion policy in Canada as a women's issue, by S. McDaniel. ATLANTIS 10(2):74, Spring 1985.

Abortion, a psychological argument, by J. D. Hunt. EMOTIONAL FIRST AID: A JOURNAL OF CRISIS INTERVENTION 1(4):34-42, Winter 1984.

Abortion question [forced abortions for population control. ECONOMIST 294:44, March 2, 1985.

Abortion re-examined, by E. Monk. HEALTHSHARING 6(1):20, Winter 1984.

Abortion, right and wrong, by R. S. Smith. MICHIGAN MEDICINE 84(6):350+, June 1985.

Abortion, right and wrong, by R. R. Smith. NEWSWEEK 105:16, March 25, 1985.

Abortion rights: some setbacks but more gains. GUARDIAN 37(10):9, December 5, 1984.

Abortion service of Ste-Therese in danger, by P. Duchesne. COMMUNIQU 'ELLES 11(3):6, May 1985.

Abortion services in Slovenia, by L. Andolsek. CIBA FOUNDATION SYMPOSIA 115:21-25, 1985.

Abortion, the state and freedom, by N. Hunter. OFF OUR BACKS 14(10):15, November 1984.

Abortion statistics 1983. HEALTH BULLETIN 42(5):272-273, September 1984.

Abortion: stories from North and South. HEALTHSHARING 6(1):21, Winter 1984.

Abortion terrorism: the toll rises. MS MAGAZINE 13:19, March 1985.

Abortion: trying to hold on to what we have, by P. Krebs, et al. OFF OUR BACKS 15:1-2, February 1985.

Abortion: understanding differences, by S. Callahan, et al. FAMILY PLANNING PERSPECTIVES16(5):219-221, September-October 1984.

Abortion using health insurance, by O. Gritschneder. GEBURTSHILFE UND FRAUENHEILKUNDE 44(9):604-607, September 1984.

Abortion. A viable proposition?, by R. Shapiro. NURSING TIMES 81(32):17-18, August 7-13, 1985.

Abortion: why don't we all get smart [editorial]. CHRISTIANITY AND CRISIS 45:123-125, April 15, 1985.

Abortion wins another round, by H. Quinn. MACLEAN'S 97:46, November 19, 1984.

Abortion's other victims. Women discuss post-abortion trauma, by M. Gallagher. POLICY REVIEW 32:20-22, 1985.

Abortions rights actions planned, by D. Wang. INTERCONTINENTAL PRESS 23(17): 544, September 9, 1985.

Absence of correlation between oral contraceptive usage and cardiovascular mortality, by R. A. Wiseman. INTERNATIONAL JOURNAL OF FERTILITY 29(4):198-208, 1984.

Absence of histopathology in somatic tissues of rats made infertile with gossypol, by S. J. Engler, et al. ARCHIVES OF ANDROLOGY 13(1):93-100.

About TOP risks and about mammography, by E. Trimmer. MIDWIFE, HEALTH VISITOR AND COMMUNITY NURSE 20(9):322, September 1984.

Acceptance of effective contraceptive methods after induced abortion, by A. Bulut. STUDIES IN FAMILY PLANNING 15:281-284, November-December 1984.

Accuracy of spontaneous abortion recall, by A. J. Wilcox, et al. AMERICAN JOURNAL OF EPIDEMIOLOGY 120(5):727-733, November 1984.

Achieving expected parities: a reanalysis of Freedman et al's data, by D. M. Sloane, et al. DEMOGRAPHY 21(3):413-422, August 1984.

Acne and oral contraceptives, by H. L. van der Meeren, et al. NEDERLANDS TIJD-SCHRIFT VOOR GENEESKUNDE 128(28):1333-1337, July 14, 1984.

Action program on anesthesia gases: pregnant employees should have the right to change positions, by J. Björdal. VARDFACKET 8(13-14):8-9, August 16, 1984.

Actions refocus nation's abortion debate/women's, by L. Lederer. NATIONAL NOW TIMES 18(1):1, January 1985.

Activists urge fightback against bombers, by A. Finger. GUARDIAN 37(16):3, January 23, 1985.

Acupuncture for the induction of cervical dilatation in preparation for first-trimester abortion and its influence on HCG, by Y. K. Ying, et al. JOURNAL OF REPRO-DUCTIVE MEDICINE 30(7):530-534, July 1985.

Acute placentitis and spontaneous abortion caused by chlamydia psittaci of sheep origin: a histological and ultrastructural study, by S. Y. Wong, et al. JOURNAL OF CLINICAL PATHOLOGY 38(6):707-711, June 1985.

Acute renal insufficiency in pregnancy. A case of the uremic-hemolytic syndrome in the post-partum period, by S. Federico, et al. MINERVA GINECOLOGIA 36(7-8): 395-398, July-August 1984.

Additional studies on pregnancy termination and inhibition of the monkey corpus l luteum with 5-oxa-17-phenyl-18,19,20-trinor-PGF1 apha methyl ester and structurally related prostaglandins, by J. W. Wilks, et al. PROSTAGLANDINS 28(3):323-332, September 1984.

Administrative, counseling and medical practices in National Abortion Federation facilities, by U. Landy, et al. FAMILY PLANNING PERSPECTIVES 14(5):257-262, September-October 1982.

Adolescent and voluntary interruption of pregnancy in the hospital milieu, by C. Mazière, et al. SOINS, GYNECOLOGIE, OBSTETRIQUE, PUERICULTURE, PEDIATRIE 45:37-44, February 1985.

Adolescent contraception: factors to consider before you prescribe, by L. B. Tyrer, et al. CONSULTANT 25(10):75-79+, July 1985.

Adolescent contraceptive use and pregnancy: the role of the male partner, by P. E. Abrons. DAI: SCIENCES AND ENGINEERING 45(12), June 1985.

Adolescent Family Life Act and the promotion of religious doctrine, by P. Donovan. FAMILY PLANNING PERSPECTIVES16(5):222-228, September-October 1984.

Adolescent mothers and fetal loss, what is learned from experience, by P. B. Smith, et al. PSYCHOLOGICAL REPORTS 55:775-778, December 1984.

Adolescent pregnancy and sex roles, by C. J. Ireson. SEX ROLES 11:189-201, August 1984.

Adolescent pregnancy: contributing factors, consequences, treatment and plausible solutions, by C. Black, et al. ADOLESCENCE 20:281-290, Summer 1985.

Adolescents' communication styles and learning about birth control, by R. DePietro, et al. ADOLESCENCE 19:827-837, Winter 1984.

Adolescents' values, sexuality, and contraception in a rural New York county, by N. McCormick, et al. ADOLESCENCE 20:385-395, Summer 1985.

Adverse effect of an overdistended bladder on first-trimester sonography, by M. E. Baker, et al. AJR 145(3):597-599, September 1985.

Adverse effects of contraceptive sponges. NURSES DRUG ALERT 9(2):9, February 1985.

Aetna's defense costs capped under Dalkon Shield agreement, by S. Tarnoff. BUSINESS INSURANCE 18:1+, November 26, 1984.

Affecting fatherhood: a research team at the University of Western Ontario may have found a low-risk reversible male contraceptive, by S. Bars. SCIENCE DIMENSION 17(2):14-19, 1985.

Affirmation of life: a nurse wrestles with questions of abortion and justice [photos], by L. Rozzell. SOJOURNERS 14(6):34-37, June 1985.

After contraception: dispelling rumors about later childbearing. POPULATION REPORTS 12(5):697-731, September-October 1984.

After a lawyer turns whistle-blower, the company that made the Dalkon Shield warns women of its dangers, by J. S. Podesta. PEOPLE WEEKLY 23:61+, January 14, 1985.

Against the might of the moral right, by J. Mellor. SPARE RIB 152:11, March 1985.

Age of consent and the sexual dilemma, by A. Langslow. AUSTRALASIAN NURSES JOURNAL 14(8):50-51, March 1985.

Age variation in use of a contraceptive service by adolescents, by S. G. Philliber, et al. PUBLIC HEALTH REPORTS 100:34-40, January-February 1985.

Aged gametes, adverse pregnancy outcomes and natural family planning. An epidemiologic review, by R. H. Gray. CONTRACEPTION 30(4):297-309, October 1984.

Aid and abortion: leave it to Malthus. ECONOMIST 291:27, June 30, 1984.

Alleged miscarriages of Catherine of Aragon and Anne Boleyn, by J. Dewhurst. MEDICAL HISTORY 28(1):49-56, January 1984.

Allosensitization in tumor therapy and prophylaxis, and in female contraception—a prospect for clinical use, by A. Bukovskv, et al. MEDICAL HYPOTHESES 16(3):241-251, March 1985.

Alteration of convulsive threshold and conditioned avoidance response in mice fed diets containing contraceptive steroids, by H. C. Yen-Koo, et al. DRUG AND CHEMICAL TOXICOLOGY 7(6):541-549, 1984.

Alternative approach to initiating oral contraceptives. AMERICAN FAMILY PHYSICIAN 31:137, March 1985.

Amenorrhoea traumatica following therapeutic abortion: an approach to management, by W. K. Tang. ASIA-OCEANIA JOURNAL OF OBSTETRICS AND GYNAECOLOGY 10(4):479-483, December 1984.

American Association of Gynecologic Laparoscopists' 1982 membership survey, by J. M Phillips, et al. JOURNAL OF REPRODUCTIVE MEDICINE 29(8):592-594, August 1984.

American Catholic family: signs of cohesion and polarization, by W. V. D'Antonio. JOURNAL OF MARRIAGE AND THE FAMILY 47(2):395-405, May 1985.

American Life Lobby strives to outlaw taxes for abortion [news], by A. D. Blanchard. FUNDAMENTALIST JOURNAL 4(5):60, May 1985.

American nuns face Vatican ultimatum, by J. M. Wall. CHRISTIAN CENTURY 102:67-68, January 23, 1985.

American physicians and birth control, 1936-1947, by J. M. Ray, et al. JOURNAL OF SOCIAL HISTORY 18:399-411, Spring 1985.

American scholar on abortion in China, by S. W. Mosher. CATHOLIC DIGEST November 1985, p. 111+.

America's abortion dilemma [special section]. NEWSWEEK 105:20-29, January 14, 1985.

America's battle over abortion, by M. Potts. NEW SOCIETY 71(1154):204-206, 1985.

Anaesthesia for suction termination of pregnancy, by S. L. West, et al. ANAESTHESIA 40(7):669-672, July 1985.

Analysis of Borowski v. The Attorney -General of Canada and The Minister of Finance of Canada, by T. Campbell. SASKATCHEWAN LAW REVIEW 49:359-367, 1984-1985.

Analysis of outcome predictors of migraine towards chronicity, by A. Baldrati, et al. CEPHALALGIA 5(Suppl. 2):195-199, May 1985.

And at the end of the day who is holding the baby?, by J. South. NEW STATES-MAN November 15, 1985, p. 10-12.

Anemia in the etiology of threatened late abortion and premature labor, by T. Mardesíc. CESKOSLOVENSKA GYNEKOLOGIE 50(5):356-359, June 1985.

Anesthesia for termination of pregnancy: midazolam compared with methohexital, by R. Verma, et al. ANESTHESIA AND ANALGESIA 64(8):792-794, August 1985.

Angels who wear not a halo but a coil, by J. Tweedie. GUARDIAN 19:11, July 1985.

Annulment of a medical treatment contract in violation of the abortion prohibition of Paragraph 218 StGB, by G. H. Schlund. GEBURTSHILFE UND FRAUENHEIL-KUNDE 44(8):537-538, August 1984.

Antecedents and prevention of unwanted pregnancy, by M. Gerrard, et al. ISSUES IN MENTAL HEALTH NURSING 5(1/4):85-101, 1983.

Anti-abortion efforts fail in 5 out of 6 states. NATIONAL NOW TIMES 17(6):5, November 1984.

Antiabortion violence. FAMILY PLANNING PERSPECTIVES 17(1):4, January-February 1985.

Antiabortion violence on the rise, by L. C. Wohl. MS MAGAZINE 13:135-136+, October 1984.

Antifertility activity and general pharmacological properties of ORF 13811: a synthetic analog of zoapatanol, by D. W. Hahn, et al. 30(1):39-53, July1984.

Antifertility effect of citrus hystrix DC, by P. Piyachaturawat, et al. JOURNAL OF ETHNOPHARMACOLOGY 13(1):105-110, March 1985.

Antiprogesterones are coming: menses induction, abortion, and labour?, by D. L. Healy, et al. BRITISH MEDICAL JOURNAL 290(6468):580-581, February 23, 1985.

Appalling implications of Morgentaler's unjust acquittal, by T. Byfield. ALBERTA REPORT 11:60, November 26, 1984.

Appeal of certainty. ECONOMIST 298:18, December 22, 1984.

Archbishop, governor, and veep, by M. Novak. NATIONAL REVIEW 36:45, September 21, 1984.

Are there adverse effects of periconceptual spermicide use?, by J. L. Mills, et al. FERTILITY AND STERILITY 43(3):442-446, 1985.

Are there any absolute medical contraindications to the progestogen only oral contraceptive?, by J. Guillebaud. BRITISH MEDICAL JOURNAL 289(6451):1079, October 20, 1984.

Are we failing our teenagers? Value of a family planning service for teenagers within the sexually transmitted disease clinic, by J. M. Tobin, et al. BRITISH MEDICAL JOURNAL 290(6465):376-378, February 2, 1985.

Array of anti-abortion amendments planned, by N. Cohodas. CONGRESSIONAL QUARTERLY WEEKLY REPORT 43:2201-2202, November 2, 1985.

Article III, § 2/14th amendment, § 5 congressional responses to Roe [Roe v. Wade, 93 S. Ct. 705] from Lincoln's Dred Scott [Dred Scott, v. Sanford 60 U. S. 393] viewpoint, by G. S. Swan. LINCOLN LAW REVIEW 16:63-89, 1985.

Artificial termination of pregnancy in patients with uterine myoma, by L. N. Vasil-evskaia, et al. AKUSHERSTVO I GINEKOLOGIIA (2):47-50, February 1985.

As the abortion issue reaches a political flashpoint, two Catholic experts clash in debate, by D. Grogan. PEOPLE WEEKLY 22:93+, October 22, 1984.

Ask a lawyer: do I need my husband's consent to have an abortion?, by L. S. Dranoff. CHATELAINE 58:20+, April 1985.

Aspects of the choice of contraceptives after legal abortion in relation to psycho-logical masculinity: femininity and psychosocial functions, by L. Jacobsson, et al. JOURNAL OF PSYCHOSOMATIC OBSTETRICS AND GYNAECOLOGY 3(1):53-58, May 1984.

Association between diaphragm use and urinary tract infection, by S. D. Fihn, et al. JAMA 254:240-245, July 12, 1985.

An association with birth control pills. Moyamoya, by W. Sequeira, et al. IMJ 166(6): 434-436, December 1984.

Association between unfavorable outcomes in successive pregnancies, by H. C. Miller, et al. AMERICAN JOURNAL OF OBSTETRICS AND GYNECOLOGY 153(1):20-24, September 1, 1985.

At last, good news about the pill, by J. Langone. DISCOVER 6:8, February 1985.

Attack on teen abortion, by E. Bader. GUARDIAN 37(23):1, March 13, 1985.

Attacks of anti-abortionists, by C. Walter. WOMANEWS 6(2):1, February 1985.

Attempted suicide in response to refusal of elective abortion, by L. Gabinet. OHIO STATE MEDICAL JOURNAL 80(11):801-803, November 1984.

Attitude towards abortion among teenagers in Bendel State of Nigeria, by O. G. Oshodin. JOURNAL OF THE ROYAL SOCIETY OF HEALTH 105(1):22-24, February 1985.

Attitudes of sterilized women to contraceptive sterilization, by P. E. Børdahl. SCAN-DINAVIAN JOURNAL OF SOCIAL MEDICINE 12(4):191-194, 1984.

Attitudes toward marriage and childbearing of individuals at risk for Huntington's disease, by M. Schoenfeld, et al. SOCIAL WORK IN HEALTH CARE 9(4):73-81, Summer 1984.

Attributions, expectations, and coping with abortion, by B. Major, et al. JOURNAL OF PERSONALITY AND SOCIAL PSYCHOLOGY 48(3):585-599, March 1985.

Avoidance of anger, by K. J. Lindgren, et al. MCN 10(5):320-323, September-October 1985.

Baby Doe and Ginny: a reason for treating "the least of these", by D. Brown. EVAN-
GELICAL JOURNAL 3(1):13-20, 1985.

Baby killers and fetus fetishists, by P. Addelson. WOMEN'S REVIEW OF BOOKS
2(2):14, November 1984.

Baby's first breath not always welcomed [live birth abortions; news]. FUNDAMENTAL-
IST JOURNAL 2(1):58-59, January 1983.

Back on the bandwagon: the effect of opinion polls on public opinion, by C. Marsh.
BRITISH JOURNAL OF POLITICAL SCIENCE 15:51-74, January 1985.

Backing down on abortion regulation: Saskatchewan's Tories pass a pro-life hot
potato to the courts, by L. Cohen. ALBERTA REPORT 12:49, July 8, 1985.

Baclofen as an analgesic in operations for uterine dilation, aspiration and curettage,
by O. Corli, et al. MINERVA ANESTESIOLOGICA 50(7-8):401-405, July-August
1984.

Bacteriology, clinical course, and histoplacental, myometrial and hysterographic findings in the infected ovum between 10 and 26 weeks, by A. Ovalle, et al.
REVISTA CHILENA DE OBSTETRICIA Y GINECOLOGIA 48(6):449-462, 1983.

La baisse de la fécondité depuis 1965: moins d enfants désirés et moins de
grossesses non désirées. Tables and charts, by H. Leridon. POPULATION
40(3):507-525, 1985.

Balanced rearrangement of chromosomes 2, 5, and 13 in a family with duplication 5q
and fetal loss, by M. I. Evans, et al. AMERICAN JOURNAL OF MEDICAL
GENETICS 19(4):783-790, December 1984.

Bangladesh: involuntary sterilization. NATION 239(22):705, December 29, 1984.

Bankruptcy of contraception?, by F. P. Wibaut. NEDERLANDS TIJDSCHRIFT VOOR
GENEESKUNDE 128(50):2349-2353, December 15, 1984.

Bankruptcy 'shield' against Dalkon claims. NEW SCIENTIST 107:21, August 29,
1985.

Barrier contraception, by A. Mills. CLINICAL OBSTETRICS AND GYNECOLOGY
11(3):641-660, December 1984.

Barrier methods of contraception, by R. L. Skrine. PRACTITIONER 229(1403):441-
446, May 1985.

Barriers to effective family planning in Nepal, by S. R. Schuler, et al. STUDIES IN
FAMILY PLANNING 16:260-270, September-October 1985.

Barring the way to gonococci . . . synergistic effect between spermicides and barrier
contraceptives. EMERGENCY MEDICINE 16(20):92, November 30, 1984.

Basic considerations in the choice of contraceptive methods for male and female, by
J. Hammerstein. GYNAKOLOGE 17(3):156-174, September 1984.

Becoming voluntarily childless: an exploratory study in a Scottish city, by E. Campbell.
SOCIAL BIOLOGY 30(3):307-317, Fall 1983.

Belfast/on the abortion trial. CHARTIST 104:6, May 1985.

Belgium/Women's right to choose on trial. INTERNATIONAL VIEWPOINT 83:26, September 30, 1985.

Beliefs, attitudes, intentions and contraceptive behavior of college students, by D. McLittle. DAI: HUMANITIES AND SOCIAL SCIENCES 45(7), January 1985.

Benefits of oral contraceptives, by A. A. Kubba. JOURNAL OF THE ROYAL SOCIETY OF HEALTH 105(2):73-74, April 1985.

Benign breast disease, oral contraceptive use, and the risk of breast cancer [letter], by C. La Vecchia. JOURNAL OF CHRONIC DISEASES 37(11):869-870, 1984.

Between pro-life and pro-choice, by V. A. Sackett. PUBLIC OPINION 8:53-55, April-May 1985.

Beyond "choice," by S. Clancy. LESBIAN CONTRADICTION 11:16, Summer 1985.

"Beyond family planning" in Indonesia. POPULI 2(3):20, 1984.

Beyond the pill?. . . vaginal contraceptive sponge, by P. Holmes. NURSING TIMES 81(7):19, 13-19, February 1985.

Bible, abortion, and common sense, by N. L. Geisler. FUNDAMENTALIST JOURNAL 4(5):24-27, May 1985.

Big payout [A. H. Robins' liability for Dalkon Shield]. TIME 125:86, April 15, 1985.

Billings method of family planning: an assessment. STUDIES IN FAMILY PLANNING 15:253-266, November-December 1984.

Bioethics seminar 10. The roots and overview of family planning, by T. Kimura. KANGOGAKU ZASSHI 48(11):1301-1304, November 1984.

Biological paternity, social maternity: on abortion and infanticide as unrecognised indicators of the cultural character of maternity. THE SOCIOLOGICAL REVIEW MONOGRAPH 28:232-240, June 1979.

Bipolar coagulation in surgical laparoscopy, by I. Les, et al. CESKOSLOVENSKA GYNEKOLOGIE 50(4):289-290, May 1985.

Bipolar tubal cautery failures [letter]. FERTILITY AND STERILITY 43(6):943-947, June 1985.

Birth control after 35. PREVENTION 37:57-61, August 1985.

Birth control: the appeal of certainty. ECONOMIST 293:18, December 22, 1984.

Birth control clinic controversy [teen-age pregnancy; Chicago's DuSable High School; editorial], by J. M. Wall. CHRISTIAN CENTURY 102:907-908, October 16, 1985.

Birth control clinics in high schools brew controversy nationwide [Chicago's DuSable High School]. JET 69:10-11, October 14, 1985.

Birth control considerations during chemotherapy, by C. C. Tarpy. ONCOLOGY NURSING FORUM 12(2):75-78, March-April 1985.

Birth control: facts you should know [teenagers], by S. S. Soria. TEEN 29:6+, February 1985.

Birth control in school [DuSable High School, Chicago]. CHRISTIANITY TODAY 29(16):58, November 8, 1985.

Birth control movement in England and the United States: the first 100 years, by T. Perse. JOURNAL OF THE AMERICAN MEDICAL WOMEN'S ASSOCIATION 40(4):119-122, July-August 1985.

Birth control use means more clinic visits. JET 67:37, January 28, 1985.

Birth control: surprising news!, by M. H. J. Farrell. GOOD HOUSEKEEPING 200:315, May 1985.

Birth control update, by A. B. Eagan. MCCALLS 112:18+, February 1985.

Birth control update, by K. McCoy. SEVENTEEN 44:75-76+, September 1985.

Birth control use by teenagers: 1 and 2 years postabortion, by M. Abrams. JOURNAL OF ADOLESCENT HEALTH CARE 6(3):196-200, 1985.

Birth planning and fertility transition [People's Republic of China: conference paper]. ANNALS OF THE AMERICAN ACADEMY OF POLITICAL AND SOCIAL SCIENCE 476:128-141, November 1984.

Bitter pill [pro life opposition to birth control], by A. E. Schwartz. NEW REPUBLIC 192:10-12, February 18, 1985.

Bitter silent scream, by M. McDonald. MACLEANS 98:58, February 25, 1985.

Black fertility patterns—Cape Town and Ciskei, by M. Roberts, et al. SOUTH AFRI-CAN MEDICAL JOURNAL 66(13):481-484, September 29, 1984.

Blood hormone levels in threatened abortion, by M. V. Fedorova, et al. AKUSHER-STVO I GINEKOLOGIIA 12:31-33, December 1984.

Blood loss and nausea during legal abortion, by J. Carcey, et al. ANNALES FRANCAISES D'ANESTHESIA ET DE REANIMATION 4(3):271-273, 1985.

Bloodletting continues [abortion; perspective], by L. Mooneyham. FUNDA-MENTALIST JOURNAL 2(9):12-13, October 1983.

Bold stand on birth control [views of John Paul II], by R. N. Ostling. TIME 124:66, December 3, 1984.

Bombing feminism, by R. P. Petchesky. NATION 240:101, February 2, 1985.

Bombings: abortion clinic attacks not called terrorism, but may bring FBI action. SECURITY LETTER 15(1):2, January 2, 1985.

Book maps out reproductive battle, by A. Dermansky. NEW DIRECTIONS FOR WOMEN November1984, p. 5.

Book withdrawn [Brave new people by D. G. Jones withdrawn by Inter-Varsity Press]. CHRISTIAN CENTURY 101:920, October 10, 1984.

Born again: how an abortion crusader became a right-to-lifer, by J. Klein. NEW YORK 18:40-45, January 7, 1985.

Breaking up with the pill: is it hard to do?, by E. Goldbaum. MADEMOISELLE 91:52+, February 1985.

Breast cancer and oral contraceptives: critique of the proposition that high potency progestogen products confer excess risk, by F. M. Sturtevant. BIOMEDICAL PHARMACOTHERAPY 38(8):371-379, 1984.

Breast-feeding, birth spacing and pregnancy care: prevalence and outcome, by R. P. Bernard, et al. JOURNAL OF TROPICAL PEDIATRICS 30(5):279-286, October 1984.

Breastfeeding—the leading contraceptive in the world, by S. Bergström. LAKART-IDNINGEN 82(6):398-403, February 6, 1985.

Breastfeeding and contraception: why the inverse association?, by S. Millman. STUDIES IN FAMILY PLANNING 16(2):61-75, March-April 1985.

Breastfeeding, contraception, and birth intervals in developing countries, by D. P. Smith. STUDIES IN FAMILY PLANNING 16(3):154-163, May-June 1985.

Breath of life and unwanted pregnancy, by J. B. Ashbrook. THE CHRISTIAN MINISTRY 16(4):15-17, July 1985.

CNA position on family planning. CANADIAN NURSE 80:8, December 1984.

Cabbages and condoms: packaging and channels of distribution, by M. Potts. CLINICAL OBSTETRICS AND GYNAECOLOGY 11(3):799-809, December 1984.

Calculating risk ratios for spontaneous abortions: the problem of induced abortions, by J. Olsen. INTERNATIONAL JOURNAL OF EPIDEMIOLOGY 13(3):347-350, September 1984.

California referendum on abortion?, by E. Baaer. GUARDIAN 37(43):2, September 4, 1985.

Can anesthesia be employed for male or female sterilization with impunity?, by O. Zaffiri. MINERVA ANESTESIOLOGICA 51(1-2):57-59, January-February 1985.

Can Congress settle the abortion issue?, by M. C. Segers. HASTINGS CENTER REPORT 12(3), June 20-28.

Canada/abortion-rights doctors targeted Socialist voice. INTERCONTINENTAL PRESS 23(1):30, January 21, 1985.

Canadian birth control movement on trial, 1936-1937, by D. Dodd. SOCIAL HISTORY 16(32):411-428, 1983.

Candy wrappers, beer bottles and abortions, J. Lankford. CATHOLIC DIGEST 11:13, March 1985.

Capital punishment: helplessness and power, by R. M. Cooper. ENCOUNTER 46:163-175, Spring 1985.

Cardinal Bernardin and the need for Catholic social teaching. CENTER JOURNAL 1:9-28, Winter 1984.

Cardiomonitoring in the evaluation of fetal condition in threatened abortion in the second and third trimesters, by I. D. Khokhlova. AKUSHERSTVO I GINE-KOLOGIIA 10:35-38, October 1984.

Cardiovascular disease mortality in Denmark before and after the introduction of oral contraceptives, by E. H. Larsen, et al. UGESKRIFT FOR LAEGER 146(36):2677-2680, September 3, 1984.

Carrie Buck's daughter [forced eugenic sterilization], by S. J. Gould. NATURAL HIS-
TORY 93:14-18, July 1984.

Case against Depo-Provera. MULTINATIONAL MONITOR 6:3-22, February-March
1985.

Case-control study of galactorrhea and its relationship to the use of oral contraceptives, by S. J. Taler, et al. OBSTETRICS AND GYNECOLOGY 65(5):665-668,
May 1985.

Case for birth control before 1850: Nantucket reexamined, by B.J. Logue.
JOURNAL OF INTERDISCIPLINARY HISTORY 15:371-391, Winter 1985.

Case for untidiness, by A. Hertzberg. COMMONWEAL 111:655-656, November 30,
1984.

Case of Evans' syndrome: thrombocytopenia improved by artificial abortion, by T.
Ohtsuki, et al. RINSHO KETSUEKI 25(11):1814-1818, November 1984.

Case of materno-foetal histocompatibility—implications for leucocyte transfusion
treatment for recurrent aborters, by D. C. Kilpatrick. SCOTTISH MEDICAL
JOURNAL 29(2):110-112, April 1984.

Case of the Peacenik Provacateur, by P. Maass. NATION 240(24):751, June 22,
1985.

Case study. A. H. Robins and the Dalkon Shield, by C. Policano. PUBLIC RELA-
TIONS JOURNAL 41:16-19+, March 1985.

Catalogue of killing: a pro-choice film fuels the abortion debate, by O. Roberts, et al.
ALBERTA REPORT 11:48-49, October 29, 1984.

Catholic father of the pill, by D. Nyhan. NATIONAL CATHOLIC REPORTER 21:7,
December 28, 1984.

Catholic physician, the contraception issue and the three questions of ethics, by
J. A. O'Donohoe. JOURNAL OF PASTORAL COUNSELING 18:34-46,
Spring-Summer 1983.

Catholic politicians and abortion, by J. F. Donceel. AMERICA 152:81-83, February 2,
1985.

Catholic theologian at an abortion clinic, by D. C. Maguire. MS MAGAZINE 13:129-
132, December 1984.

Catholics and abortion: authority vs. dissent, by R. R. Ruether. CHRISTIAN
CENTURY 102:859-862, October 2, 1985.

Caught in the abortion backlash, by V. Safran. PROGRESSIVE 49:16, May 1985.

Cell mediated immune response in spontaneous abortion and toxaemia of pregnancy, by J. Naithani, et al. INDIAN JOURNAL OF MEDICAL RESEARCH
81:149-156, February 1985.

Census-derived estimates of fertility by duration since first marriage in the Republic of
Korea. DEMOGRAPHY 21:537-558, November 1984.

Cervical cap as a contraceptive alternative, by M. A. Johnson. NURSE PRACTI-
TIONER 10(1):37+, January 1985.

Cervical cerclage following prior delivery [letter], by J. H. Harger. AMERICAN JOURNAL OF OBSTETRICS AND GYNECOLOGY 151(8):1141-1142, April 15, 1985.

Cervical dilatation for early abortion (new approach), by M. B. Purwar, et al. ASIA-OCEANIA JOURNAL OF OBSTETRICS AND GYNAECOLOGY 10(3):275-279, September 1984.

Cervical dysplasia: association with sexual behavior, smoking, and oral contraceptive use?, by E. A. Clarke, et al. AMERICAN JOURNAL OF OBSTETRICS AND GYNECOLOGY 151(5):612-616, March 1985.

Cervical occlusion due to adhesions following therapeutic abortion: an uncommon sequel to vacuum curettage, by I. S. Fraser. AUSTRALIAN AND NEW ZEALAND JOURNAL OF OBSTETRICS AND GYNAECOLOGY 24(4):292-293, November 1984.

Cervix-dilative effect of PGF2 alpha after intracervical and extraovular administration, by A. Pajor, et al. GINEKOLOGIA POLSKA 55(6):421-425, June 1984.

Cervix priming in induced abortion in the 1st trimester using intracervical administration of sulprostone gel, by W. Rath, et al. GEBURTSHILFE UND FRAUENHEILKUNDE 45(1):51-56, January 1985.

Cervix ripening and labor induction in therapeutic abortion in the middle and late 2d trimester using intracervical and extra-amniotic prostaglandin gel administration, by W. Rath, et al. WIENER KLINISCHE WOCHENSCHRIFT 97(11):486-493, May 24, 1985.

Change of mind following failed abortion doesn't relieve the physician of liability. FORTSCHRITTE DER MEDIZIN 103(9):70-71, March 7, 1985.

Changes in the age at marriage and its effects on fertility: a study of slum dwellers in Greater Bombay, by P. K. Bhargava. JOURNAL OF FAMILY WELFARE 31:32-36, September 1984.

Changing pattern of contraception in Lahore, Pakistan: 1963-1980, by F. Yusuf, et al. JOURNAL OF BIOSOCIAL SCIENCE 17(3):317-325, July 1985.

Characteristics and bioefficacy of monoclonal antigonadotropin releasing hormone antibody, by S. K. Gupta, et al. AMERICAN JOURNAL OF REPRODUCTIVE IMMUNOLOGY AND MICROBIOLOGY 7(3):104-108, March 1985.

Characteristics of abortion patients in the United States, 1979 and 1980, by S. K. Henshaw, et al. FAMILY PLANNING PERSPECTIVES 15(1):5-8+, January-February 1983.

Characteristics of family planning acceptors at a primary health care project in Lagos, Nigeria, by A. A. Olukoya. PUBLIC HEALTH 99(1):37-44, January 1985.

Characteristics of patients attending Harare Hospital with incomplete abortion, by C. Crowther, et al. CENTRAL AFRICAN JOURNAL OF MEDICINE 31(4):67-70, April 1985.

Characteristics of the treatment of pregnant women with septic abortion and pyelonephritis complicated by acute renal failure, by V. L. Cherniakov, et al. AKUSHERSTVO I GINEKOLOGIIA 5:52-53, May 1985.

Chemical fertility control and wildlife management, by J. F. Kirkpatrick, et al. BIOSCIENCE 35:485-491, September 1985.

Chemistry and abortion, by R. Block. MACLEANS 98:58, May 27, 1985.

Chewing more than he's bitten off, by A. Cockburn. NATION 241:39, July 20-27, 1985.

Child in the womb is a human being, by L. Nogrady. PERCEPTION 8:19-22, March-April 1985.

Child sacrifice to the modern Molech, by M.D. Bray. FUNDAMENTALIST JOURNAL 3(1):15-17, January 1984.

Childlessness and marital stability in remarriages, by J. D. Griffith, et al. JOURNAL OF MARRIAGE AND THE FAMILY 46:577-585, August 1984.

Childlessness: a panel study of expressed intentions and reported fertility, by L. G. Pol. SOCIAL BIOLOGY 30:318-327, August 1983.

China: the abortion question. THE ECONOMIST 294:44, March 2, 1985.

China pushes efforts to reduce population growth. CHEMICAL AND ENGINEERING NEWS 63:50-51, January 14, 1985.

China's fertility transition: the one-child campaign, by E. Platte. PACIFIC AFFAIRS 57:646-671, Winter 1984-1985.

China's population policy, by G. Iver. OFF OUR BACKS 15(3):15, March 1985.

China's population policy: 'fewer but better' children. UN MONTHLY CHRONICLE 21:xiv, June 1984.

Chinese express views on Mosher to Stanford, by M. Sun. SCIENCE 226:28-29, October 5, 1984.

Choice. MS 13:97, March 1985.

Choice of contraception for the diabetic woman, by N. Athea, et al. JOURNEES ANNUELLES DE DIABETOLOGIE DE L'HOTEL-DIEU 253:61, 1983.

Choice vs. life. PEOPLE WEEKLY 24:70-72+, August 5, 1985.

Chorion biopsy, cytogenetic diagnosis, and selective termination in a twin pregnancy at risk of haemophilia, by M. T. Mulcahy, et al. LANCET 2(8407):866-867, October 13, 1984.

Christmas and abortion [sermon; Luke 2:12; Matthew 2:16], by J. Killinger. THE CHRISTIAN MINISTRY 16(6):26-27, November 1985.

Chromosomal abnormalities in the Kaiser-Permanente Birth Defects Study, with special reference to contraceptive use around the time of conception, by S. Harlap, et al. TERATOLOGY 31(3):381-387, June 1985.

Chromosome abnormalities in 118 couples with recurrent spontaneous abortions, by A. Tóth, et al. GYNECOLOGIC AND OBSTETRIC INVESTIGATION 18(2):72-77, 1984.

Chromosome analysis in couples with recurrent abortions, by K. Soh, et al. TOHOKU JOURNAL OF EXPERIMENTAL MEDICINE 144(2):151-163, October 1984.

Chromosome analysis of female baboons following treatment with STS 557 and levonorgestrel, by J. Strecke, et al. ZENTRALBLATT FUR GYNAEKOLOGIE 107(5):304-307, 1985.

Chromosome anomalies in spontaneously aborted fetuses and a study of mutagenesis in a human population, by J. Dejmek, et al. BRATISLAVSKE LEKARSKE LISTY 83(6):637-645, June 1985.

Chromosome studies of 500 couples with two or more abortions, by E. S. Sachs, et al. OBSTETRICS AND GYNECOLOGY 65(3):375-378, March 1985.

Chromosome study in repeated abortions, by K. Larsen, et al. UGESKRIFT FOR LAEGER 147(4):285-287, January 21, 1985.

Church and Cuomo [Catholic Church]. COMMONWEAL 111:517-518, October 5, 1984.

Churches' response to abortion [official positions of 16 US churches], by R. J. Enquist. WORD AND WORLD 5,414:425, Fall 1985.

Circulating immune complexes and ribonuclease and 5'-nucleotidase activity in the blood of women with threatened abortion treated with acupuncture-reflexo-therapy, by L. I. Ksendzov, et al. AKUSHERSTVO I GINEKOLOGIIA 12:36-37, December 1984.

Civil war, by J. Hoffman, et al. VILLAGE VOICE 30:14, February 12, 1985.

Claims for malpractice and complications following female sterilization 1975-1979, by E. Ryde-Blomqvist. LAKARTIDNINGEN 81(42):3810-3812, October 17, 1984.

Claims for malpractice and complications following legal abortions 1975-1979, by E. Ryde-Blomqvist. LAKARTIDNINGEN 81(42):3808-3810, October 17, 1984.

Classic methods of contraception, by G. A. Hauser. GYNAKOLOGE 17(3):194-199, September 1984.

Classification and mechanisms of spontaneous abortion, by D. I. Rushton. PERSPECTIVES IN PEDIATRIC PATHOLOGY 8(3):269-287, Fall 1984.

Clastogenicity of a male contraceptive, gossypol, in mammalian cell cultures with and without the metabolic activation by S9 mix, by J. C. Liang, et al. ENVIRONMENTAL RESEARCH 36:138-143, February 1985.

Clinic bombings: government policy incarnate, by S. Poggi. GAY COMMUNITY 12(27):3, January 26, 1985.

Clinical and pathological comparison of young adult women with hepatocellular carcinoma with and without exposure to oral contraceptives, by R. A. Hromas, et al. AMERICAN JOURNAL OF GASTROENTEROLOGY 80(6):479-485, June 1985.

Clinical chemistry in women treated with six levonorgestrel covered rods or with a copper IUD, by S. Díaz, et al. CONTRACEPTION 31(4):321-330, April 1985.

Clinical evaluation of Rigevidon used for contraception, by L. Marianowski, et al. GINEKOLOGIA POLSKA 55(8):631-635, August 1984.

Clinical forum. 1. Postabortion counseling, by S. Anthony, et al. NURSING MIRROR 156(4):31-37, January 26, 1983.

Clinical, immunologic, and genetic definitions of primary and secondary recurrent spontaneous abortions, by J. A. McIntyre, et al. FERTILITY AND STERILIZATION 42(6):849-855, December 1984.

Clinical trial of gossypol as a male contraceptive: a randomized controlled study, by G. Z. Liu. CHUNG HUA I HSUEH TSA CHIH 65(2):107-109, February 1985.

Clustering of abortion scale scores, by R. Lane, Jr. JSSR 24:403-406, December 1985.

Coevcion in a soft state: the family planning program of India, by M. Vicziany. PACIFIC AFFAIRS 55:373-402, Fall 1982.

—. PACIFIC AFFAIRS 55:557-592, Winter 1982.

Collagen sponge as vaginal contraceptive barrier: critical summary of seven years of research, by M. Chvapil, et al. AMERICAN JOURNAL OF OBSTETRICS AND GYNECOLOGY 151(3):325-329, February 1, 1985.

College students' attitudes toward shared responsibility in decisions about abortion: implications for counseling, by I. J. Ryan, et al. JOURNAL OF AMERICAN COLLEGE HEALTH 31:231-235, June 1983.

Colorado voters amend the state's constitution to outlaw public funding of abortions. CHRISTIANITY TODAY 29:46-47, January 18, 1985.

Combined contraceptives in experimental liver damage, by A. Kulcsár, et al. ACTA PHARMACEUTICA HUNGARICA 54(6):272-279, November 1984.

Combined hormonal oral contraceptive. Comparative study of 4 schemes, by R. L. Reynoso, et al. GINECOLOGIA Y OBSTETRICIA DE MEXICO 52(329):221-223, September 1984.

Comments on two Hungarian television educational series, by A. Pázsy. PROGRESS IN CLINICAL AND BIOLOGICAL RESEARCH 163C:351-354, 1985.

Commons debates the Warnock Report, by N. Fowler. NURSING STANDARD 376:8, December 6, 1984.

Communicating contraception. POPULI 2(2):31, 1984.

Communication and contraceptive practices in adolescent couples, by Polit-O'Hara. ADOLESCENCE 20:33-43, September 1985.

Communist Party and woman question 1922-1929, by J. Sangster. LABOUR/LE TRAVAIL 15:25, Spring 1985.

Chromosome aberrations in 334 individuals with various types of abortion (including 144 couples), by J. M. Cantú, et al. REVISTA DE INVESTIGACION CLINICA 37(2):131-134, April-June 1985.

Community reaction to the establishment of an abortion clinic in Duluth, Minnesota, by C. M. MacLeod. NORTH DAKOTA QUARTERLY 52(1):34-47, 1984.

Comparative analysis of methods of the immunotherapy or spontaneous abortions, by V. I. Govallo, et al. AKUSHERSTVO I GINEKOLOGIIA 3:41-43, March 1985.

Comparative clinical trial of the contraceptive sponge and Neo Sampoon tablets, by E. Borko, et al. OBSTETRICS AND GYNECOLOGY 65(4):511-515, April 1985.

Comparative evaluation of contraceptive efficacy of norethisterone oenanthate (200 mg) injectable contraceptive given every two or three monthly. Indian Council of Medical Research Task Force on hormonal contraception, by S. K. Banerjee, et al. CONTRACEPTION 30(6):561-574, December 1984.

Comparative métabolic effects of oral contraceptive preparations containing different progestagens. Effects of desogestrel + ethinylestradiol on the haemostatic balance, by I. Rákoczi, et al. ARZNEIMITTEL-FORSCHUNG 35(3):630-633, 1985.

Comparative risks and costs of male and female sterilization, by G. L. Smith, et al. AMERICAN JOURNAL OF PUBLIC HEALTH 75:370-374, April 1985.

Comparative safety of second-trimester abortion methods, by D. A. Grimes, et al. CIBA FOUNDATION SYMPOSIA 115:83-101, 1985.

Comparative study of applications for abortions for the years 1979 and 1980, by E. G. Pérez. TEMAS DE TRABOJO SOCIAL 4(1):67-82, January-June 1982.

Comparative study of recidivists and contraceptors along the dimensions of lows of control and impulsivity, by G. D. Gibb. INTERNATIONAL JOURNAL OF PSY-CHOLOGY 19(6):581-591, December 1984.

Comparative study of topical anesthesia for laparoscopic sterilization with the use of the tubal ring, by S. Koetsawang, et al. AMERICAN JOURNAL OF OBSTETRICS AND GYNECOLOGY 150(8):931-933, December 15, 1984.

Comparative trial of the Today contraceptive sponge and diaphragm, by D. A. Edel-man, et al. AMERICAN JOURNAL OF OBSTETRICS AND GYNECOLOGY 150(7):869-876, December 1, 1984.

Comparing contraceptives, by J. Willis. FDA CONSUMER 19:28-35, May 1985.

Comparison of high-dose estrogens versus low-dose ethinylestradiol and norgestrel combination in postcoital interception: a study in 493 women, by M. R. Van Santen, et al. FERTILITY AND STERILIZATION 43(2):206-213, February 1985.

Comparison of interval and postabortal/puerperal laparoscopic sterilization with the tubal ring procedure, by L. Heisterberg, et al. ACTA OBSTETRICIA ET GYNECOLOGICA SCANDINAVICA 64(3):223-225, 1985.

Comparison of the methods for terminating pregnancy, by V. M. Sadauskas, et al. AKUSHERSTVO I GINEKOLOGIIA 3:37-39, March 1985.

Comparison of plasma cholesterol, triglycerides and high density lipoprotein choles-terol levels in women using contraceptive pills and a control group, by D. Yeshurun, et al. GYNECOLOGIC AND OBSTETRIC INVESTIGATION 18(4):169-173, 1984.

Comparison of prostaglandin E2 pessaries and laminaria tents for ripening the cervix before termination of pregnancy, by S. R. Killick, et al. BRITISH JOURNAL OF OBSTETRICS AND GYNAECOLOGY 92(5):518-521, 1985.

Comparison of the psychosocial situation of 125 abortion patients before and after the abortion, by P. Goebel. ZEITSCHRIFT FUR PSYCHOSOMATISCHE MEDIZIN UND PSYCHOANALYSE 30(3):270-281, 1984.

Comparison of three social-psychological models of attitude and behavioral plan: prediction of contraceptive behavior, by M. D. Pagel, et al. JOURNAL OF PERSONALITY AND SOCIAL PSYCHOLOGY 47:517-533, September 1984.

Comparison of a 2-phase preparation (Oviol 22) with a low-dose 1-phase preparation, by M. Dik, et al. GEBURTSHILFE UND FRAUENHEILKUNDE 44(12):808-812, December 1984.

Complex translocation in habitual abortion, by A. Smith, et al. HUMAN GENETICS 70(3):287, 1985.

Complications and short-term consequences of tubal sterilization. A personal three- and twelve-month follow-up investigation, by P. E. Børdahl, et al. ACTA OBSTETRICIA ET GYNECOLOGICA SCANDINAVICA 63(6):481-486, 1984.

Complications in pregnancy, by R. K. Smith, et al. TOPICS IN EMERGENCY MEDICINE 7(2):9-18, July 1985.

Compulsory birth control and fertility measures in India: a simulation approach, by S. S. Halli. SIMULATION AND GAMES 14(4):429-444, December 1983.

Compulsory pregnancy: it's still 1984. FRYING PAN December 1984, p. 16.

Computerized histories facilitate patient care in a termination of pregnancy clinic: the use of a small computer to obtain and reproduce patient information, by R. J. Lilford, et al. BRITISH JOURNAL OF OBSTETRICS AND GYNAECOLOGY 92(4):333-340, April 1985.

Concentration-dependent mechanisms of ovulation inhibition by the progestin ST-1435, by P. L. Lähteenmäki, et al. FERTILITY AND STERILIZATION 44(1):20-24, July 1985.

Conception-waits in fertile women after stopping oral contraceptives, by S. Harlap, et al. INTERNATIONAL JOURNAL OF FERTILITY 29(2):73-80, 1984.

Condom a day keeps the doctor away, by J. McBeth. FAR EASTERN ECONOMIC REVIEW 126:49-50, October 11, 1984.

Condom spots stun Spanish, by M. Specht. ADVERTISING AGE 55:3+, October 4, 1984.

Conference de Mexico: l'avortement en vedette, by P. Allen. ACTION NATIONALE 74:185, October 1984.

Confronting the teenage pregnancy issue: social marketing as an interdisciplinary approach, by W. Marsiglio. HUMAN RELATIONS 38(10):983-1000, 1985.

Congenital afibrinogenemia and recurrent early abortion: a case report, by S. Evron, et al. EUROPEAN JOURNAL OF OBSTETRICS, GYNECOLOGY AND REPRODUCTIVE BIOLOGY 19(5):307, May 1985.

Congress facing a bitter battle on population control abroad; tighter abortion controls?, by J. Felton. CONGRESSIONAL QUARTERLY WEEKLY REPORT 42:2142-2146, September 1, 1984.

Conscientious objection, by J. S. O'Neill. NEW ZEALAND LAW JOURNAL 272-274+, August 1984.

Consequences of abortion legislation. Special issue: women changing therapy: new assessments, values and strategies in feminist therapy, by M. Braude. WOMEN AND THERAPY 2(2-3):81-90, Summer-Fall, 1983.

Considerations in relation to severe toxicoseptic abortion, by M. Buhaciuc, et al. VIATA MEDICALA 32(8):171-172, August 1984.

Consistency for the sake of life [abortion and nuclear weapons], by P. Narciso. SOJOURNERS 14(8):12, August-September 1985.

Constitutional law: the minor's right to consent to abortion: how far is Oklahoma from Akron. OKLAHOMA LAW REVIEW 37:780-809, Winter 1984.

Constitutionality of a city ordinance regulating the performance of abortion. US Supreme Court. Decision Nos. 81746, 811172, June 15, 1983. MEDICINE AND LAW 4(1):85-90, 1985.

Contact lens wear problems: implications of penicillin allergy, diabetic relatives, and use of birth control pills, by D. P. Harrison. AMERICAN JOURNAL OF OPTOMETRY AND PHYSIOLOGICAL OPTICS 61(11):674-678, November 1984.

Contemporary American abortion controversy: stages in the argument by C. C. Railsback. QUARTERLY JOURNAL OF SPEECH 70(4):410-424, 1984.

Continuation and effectiveness of contraceptive practice: a cross-sectional approach, by J. E. Laing. STUDIES IN FAMILY PLANNING 16(3):138-153, May-June 1985.

Contraception and abortion of mentally handicapped female adolescents under German law, by A. Eser. MEDICINE AND LAW 4(6):499-513, 1985.

Contraception and fertility in the Netherlands, by E. Ketting. FAMILY PLANNING PERSPECTIVES 15(1):19-25, January-February 1983.

Contraception and religiousness in a general practice population in Israel, by A. Sandiuk, et al. FAMILY PRACTICE 1(1):37-41, March 1984.

Contraception and the use of care systems, by M. H. Bouvier-Colle, et al. JOURNAL DE GYNECOLOGIE, OBSTETRIQUE ET BIOLOGIE DE LA REPRODUCTION 14(2):155-162, 1985.

Contraception and voluntary pregnancy interruption in public hospital establishments. Circular DGS/2A No. 12-82 of 12 October 1982, by J. Latrille. SOINS, GYNECOLOGIE, OBSTETRIQUE, PUERICULTURE, PEDIATRIE (27-28):61-64, August-September 1983.

Contraception consultation. Choice of contraception method, by J. C. Guillat. SOINS, GYNECOLOGIE, OBSTETRIQUE, PUERICULTURE, PEDIATRIE (14-15):29-31, July-August 1982.

Contraception: dilemmas for the relatively infertile, by S. Craig, et al. HEALTH-RIGHT 4:13-16, February 1985.

—, by M. Flynn. HEALTHRIGHT 4:25-26, May 1985.

Contraception for the adolescent, by R. B. Shearin, et al. POSTGRADUATE MEDICINE 78(3):209-211+, September 1, 1985.

Contraception for teenagers. SOCIETY 23:35-52, November-December 1985.

Contraception in adolescents, by G. Freund. FORTSCHRITTE DER MEDIZIN 103(22):610-612, June 13, 1985.

Contraception: introduction, by J. C. Guillat. SOINS, GYNECOLOGIE, OBSTETRIQUE, PUERICULTURE, PEDIATRIE, July-August 1982.

Contraception—the morning after. FAMILY PLANNING PERSPECTIVES 16:266-270, November-December 1984.

Contraception the 'morning after.' A too little used opportunity, by C. Schumann. FORTSCHRITTE DER MEDIZIN 102(33):807-810, September 6, 1984.

Contraception research lagging [news], by C. Holden. SCIENCE 229(4718):1066, September 13, 1985.

Contraception update. CLINICAL OBSTETRICS AND GYNAECOLOGY 11(3):549-819, December 1984.

Contraception with long-acting subdermal implants. A five-year clinical trial with Silastic covered rod implants containing levonorgestrel. The International Committee for Contraception Research (ICCR) of the Population Council, by D. N. Robertson, et al. CONTRACEPTION 31(4):351-359, April 1985.

Contraception with progesterone pellets during lactation, by O. Peralta, et al. REVISTA CHILENA DE OBSTETRICIA Y GINECOLOGIA 49(5):337-345, 1984.

Contraception with subdermal ST-1435 capsules: side-effects, endocrine profiles and liver function related to different lengths of capsules, by H. Kurunmäki, et al. CONTRACEPTION 31(3):305-318, March 1985.

Contraceptive advice for the postpartum period, by I. Couvreur, et al. SOINS, GYNE-COLOGIE, OBSTETRIQUE, PUERICULTURE, PEDIATRIE 35:39-41, April 1984.

Contraceptive attitudes and practice in women choosing sterilization, by K. D. Bledin, et al. JOURNAL OF THE ROYAL COLLEGE OF GENERAL PRACTITIONERS 34(268):595-599, November 1984.

Contraceptive behavior in college-age males related to Fishbein model, B. M. Ewald, et al. ANS 7(3):63-69, April 1985.

Contraceptive behavior in 1877 dispensary users. Which to use? What were the motives for their suspension?, by R. Maggi, et al. ANNALI DI OSTETRICIA GINECOLOGIA MEDICINA PERINATALE 105(1):5-13, January-February 1984.

Contraceptive compatibility, S. Bryant-Johnson. ESSENCE 16:20+, September 1985.

Contraceptive continuation rates in Papua, New Guinea, by P. K. Townsend. PAPUA NEW GUINEA MEDICAL JOURNAL 26(2):114-121, June 1983.

Contraceptive controversy [in British media; Law Lords decision; news]. CHRISTIAN CENTURY 102:994, November 6, 1985.

Contraceptive decision-making in urban, black female adolescents: its relationship to cognitive development, by B. Sachs. INTERNATIONAL JOURNAL OF NURSING STUDIES 22(2):117-126, 1985.

Contraceptive dilemma [Dalkon Shield IUD recall and counterfeit Ovulen-21 pills], by P. Ohlendorf. MACLEANS 97:74+, November 26, 1984.

Contraceptive efficacy and hormonal profile of ferujoi: a new coumarin from Ferula jaeschkeana, by M. M. Singh, et al. PLANTA MEDICA 3:268-270, June 1985.

Contraceptive futurology or 1984 in 1984, by E. Diczfalusy. CONTRACEPTION 31(1):1-10, January 1985.

Contraceptive habits in women born in 1936. Results of a health survey at the ages of 40 and 45, by K. Garde, et al. UGESKRIFT FOR LAEGER 147(4):314-318, January 21, 1985.

Contraceptive implant [Norplant], by M. Clark. NEWSWEEK 105:70, March 11, 1985.

Contraceptive knowledge and use of birth control as a function of sex guilt, by C. IBerger, et al. INTERNATIONAL JOURNAL OF WOMEN'S STUDIES 8:72-79, January-February 1985.

Contraceptive knowledge of 14 to 17-year-old students of a suburban district, by I. Mehlan, et al. ZEITSCHRIFT FUR AERZTLICHE FORTBILDUNG 79(5):205-207, 1985.

Contraceptive method switching among American female adolescents, 1979, by M. B. Hirsch, et al. JOURNAL OF ADOLESCENT HEALTH CARE 6(1):1-7, January 1985.

Contraceptive practice among American women, 1973-1982, by C. A. Bachrach. FAMILY PLANNING PERSPECTIVES 16:253-259, November-December 1984.

Contraceptive practices and reproductive patterns in sickle cell disease, by J. H. Samuels-Reid, et al. JOURNAL OF THE NATIONAL MEDICAL ASSOCIATION 76(9):879-883, September 1984.

Contraceptive practices of women attending the Sexually Transmitted Disease Clinic in Nashville, Tennessee, by R. W. Quinn, et al. SEXUALLY TRANSMITTED DISEASES 12(3):99-102, July-September 1985.

Contraceptive prevalence: the influence of organized family planning programs, by R. J. Lapham, et al. STUDIES IN FAMILY PLANNING 16(3):117-137, May-June 1985.

Contraceptive product advertising, by A. Kastor. SIECUS REPORT 13:6-7, July 1985.

Contraceptive risktaking among never-married youth, by S. Krishnamoorthy, et al. AUSTRALIAN JOURNAL OF SEX, MARRIAGE AND FAMILY 4(3):151-157, August 1983.

Contraceptive risk-taking behavior among young women: an investigation of psycho-social variables, by M. A. Gutman. DAI: SCIENCES AND ENGINEERING 46(6),. December 1986.

Contraceptive role of breastfeeding, by J. P. Habicht, et al. POPULATION STUDIES 39:213-232, July 1985.

Contraceptive sponge patient insert warns of TSS. FDA DRUG BULLETIN 14(2):18-19, August 1984.

Contraceptive trends [editorial], by K. Wellings, et al. BRITISH MEDICAL JOURNAL 289(6450):939-940, October 13, 1984.

Contraceptive update, by H. Pengelley. PROTECT YOURSELF August 1985, p. 50-57.

Contraceptive usage during lactation: analysis of 1973 and 1976 national survey of family growth: age and race, by M. Labbok, et al. AMERICAN JOURNAL OF PUBLIC HEALTH 75:75-77, January 1985.

Contraceptive use among Mormons, 1965-1975, by B. Heaton, et al. DIALOGUE 16(3):106-109, 1983.

Contraceptive use and efficacy in a genetically counseled population, by D. C. Wertz, et al. SOCIAL BIOLOGY 30:328-334, August 1983.

Contraceptive use and fertility in Guatemala. Tables, by R. S. Monteith, et al. 16:279-288, September-October 1985.

Contraceptive use before tubal sterilization, by G. S. Grubb, et al. JOURNAL OF REPRODUCTIVE MEDICINE 30(4):345-350, April 1985.

Contraceptive use during lactation in developing countries, by A. R. Pebley, et al. STUDIES IN FAMILY PLANNING 16(1):40-51, January-February 1985.

Contraceptive use in Georgia: estimation by telephone survey, by A. M. Spitz, et al. SOUTHERN MEDICAL JOURNAL 78(3):323-328, March 1985.

Contraceptive use, pregnancy and fertility patterns among single American women in their 20s, by K. Tanfer, et al. FAMILY PLANNING PERSPECTIVES 17(1):10-19, January-February 1985.

Contraceptives for the relatively infertile, by G. T. Kovacs. HEALTHRIGHT 4:17-19, February 1985.

Contragestion by antiprogestin: a new approach to human fertility control, by E. E. Baulieu. CIBA FOUNDATION SYMPOSIA 115:192-210, 1985.

Control definition in case-control studies of ectopic pregnancy, by N. S. Weiss, et al. AMERICAN JOURNAL OF PUBLIC HEALTH 75:67-68, January 1985.

Controlled comparison of the Pomeroy resection technique and laparoscopic electro-coagulation of the tubes, by P. E. Børdahl, et al. ANNALES CHIRURGIAE ET GYNAECOLOGIAE 73(5):288-292, 1984.

Controlled study of 16,16-dimethyl-trans-delta 2 prostaglandin E1 methyl ester vagi-nal pessaries prior to suction termination of first trimester pregnancies, by P. R. Fisher, et al. BRITISH JOURNAL OF OBSTETRICS AND GYNAECOLOGY 91(11):1141-1144, November 1984.

Controlled trial of treatment of recurrent spontaneous abortion by immunisation with paternal cells, by J. F. Mowbray, et al. LANCET 1(8435):941-943, April 27, 1985.

Controversial abortion drug finally approved for use [Preglandin]. BUSINESS JAPAN 29:35, October 1984.

Coping with abortion, by L. Cohen, et al. JOURNAL OF HUMAN STRESS 10(3): 140-145, Fall 1984.

Corporate bottom line. HEALTHSHARING 5(4):4, Fall 1984.

Corpus luteum function assessed by serial serum progesterone measurements after laparoscopic endotherm sterilization, by R. Kirschner, et al. ACTA EUROPAEA FERTILITATIS 16(3):169-173, May-June 1985.

Corpus luteum insufficiency, the primary cause of habitual abortion: its successful therapy, by G. Siklósi, et al. ORVOSI HETILAP 125(42):2549-2553, October 14, 1984.

Correlation of moral development with use of birth control and pregnancy among teenage girls, by J. Jurs. PSYCHOLOGICAL REPORTS 55:1009-1010, December 1984.

Cosmo's update on contraception, by A. Ferrar. COSMOPOLITAN 197:240-243, October 1984.

Costs and benefits of Title XX and Title XIX family planning services in Texas, by D. Malitz. EVALUATION REVIEW 8:519-536, August 1984.

Course of pregnancy following spontaneous abortion, by B. Rud, et al. ACTA OBSTETRICIA ET GYNECOLOGICA SCANDINAVICA 64(3):277-278, 1985.

Court of Appeals rules DHSS notice on family planning contrary to law, by D. Brahams. LANCET 1(8419):59-61, January 5, 1985.

Court to reconsider abortion issue. CONGRESSIONAL QUARTERLY WEEKLY REPORT 43:1002, May 25, 1985.

Crack in the Catholic Monolith, by B. Maschinot. IN THESE TIMES 9(1):7, November 7, 1984.

Crimes against the unborn: protecting and respecting the potentiality of human life [through criminal law; United States], by J. A. Parness. HARVARD JOURNAL OF LEGISLATION 22:97-172, Winter 1985.

Crimes—feticide—statutes—vagueness. THE FAMILY LAW REPORTER: COURT OPINIONS December 11, 1984, p. 1074.

Critical analysis of 75 therapeutic abortions, by N. J. Leschot, et al. EARLY HUMAN DEVELOPMENT 10(3-4):287-293, January 1985.

Critical look at current regulation of interruption of pregnancy as it is called according to section 218 et seq. of the Criminal Code (FRG), by E. Backhaus. CONCEPTE 4:95-112, 1984.

Cross-country study of commercial contraceptive sales programs: factors that lead to success, by M. S. Boone, et al. STUDIES IN FAMILY PLANNING 16(1):30-39, January-February 1985.

Crucial new direction for international family planning, by F. P. Hosken. HUMANIST 44:5-8+, January-February 1984.

Cruelty to animals [letter], by C. E. Horner. AUSTRALIAN VETERINARY JOURNAL 61(12):414-415, December 1984.

Cry with the mother, by M. S. Shea. THEOLOGY TODAY 41:325-326, October 1984.

Cuomo and the lay voice, by A. McCarthy. COMMONWEAL 111:550-551, October 19, 1984.

Current antiabortion propaganda, by S. L. Polchanova. FEL'DSHER I AKUSHERKA 49(8):43-48, August 1984.

Current aspects of abortion assistance, by P. E. Treffers. NEDERLANDS TIJD-SCHRIFT VOOR GENEESKUNDE 128(31):1476-1478, August 4, 1984.

Current status of intrauterine devices, by D. R. Mishell, Jr. NEW ENGLAND JOURNAL OF MEDICINE 312:984-985, April 11, 1985.

Current trends in antifertility vaccine research, by D. C. Covey, et al. WESTERN JOURNAL OF MEDICINE 142(2):197-202, February 1985.

Cytogenetic findings in 311 couples with infertility and reproductive disorders, by B. Raczkiewicz, et al. ACTA ANTHROPOGENETICA 7(4):355-366, 1983.

Cytogenetics of aborters and abortuses: a review, by P. J. Noor, et al. SINGAPORE MEDICAL JOURNAL 25(5):306-312, October 1984.

Cytogenetics of pregnancy wastage, by A. Boué, et al. ADVANCES IN HUMAN GENETICS 14:1-57, 1985.

Cytologic identification of trophoblastic epithelium in products of first-trimester abortion, by E. S. Jacobson, et al. OBSTETRICS AND GYNECOLOGY 66(1):124-126, July 1985.

D. A. pickets abortion clinic, by Barbara Fischkin. [Denis Dillon pickets clinic in Nassau County, New York, run by Bill Baird]. MS 14:19, December 1985.

Dalkon Shield is finally recalled. CONSUMER REPORTS 50:447, August 1985.

Dalkon Shield IUD health risk hushed, by G. Evans. SPARE RIB 156:10, July 1985.

Dalkon Shield/a very serious business, by P. Duchesne. COMMUNIO 11(4):6, July 1985.

Daughters of the sexual revolution, by J. Sadgrove. GUARDIAN November 12, 1985, p. 10.

Day of the yam, by A. Rosser. NURSING TIMES 81(18):47, May 1-7, 1985.

Days of our Dalkon [A. H. Robins Co., manufacturer of the Dalkon Shield, reported a deficit because of a special fund set up to deal with lawsuits by injured women], by A. Fugh-Berman. OFF OUR BACKS 15:6, May 1985.

Dear friends of pro-choice, by E. Mcauster. NATIONAL CATHOLIC REPORTER 21:14-15, November 16, 1984.

Death before birth. [Grief after therapeutic abortion], by E. Dunn. SUNDAY TIMES December 8, 1985, p. 38.

Death is also life, by F. Belliard. REVUE DE L'INFIRMIERE 35(2):9-13, January 1985.

Deaths from spontaneous abortion in the United States, by S. M. Berman, et al. JAMA 253(21):3119-3123, June 7, 1985.

Debate continues: recent works on abortion, by J. O'Connor. RELIGIOUS STUD-IES REVIEW 11:105-114, April 1985.

Debate rages over pro-abortion book. FUNDAMENTALIST JOURNAL 3(9):64, October 1984.

Debating abortion again [H. Morgentaler's clinic in Toronto], by S. MacKay. MAC-LEANS 97:40, December 24, 1984.

Decidual morphology and F prostaglandin in amniotic fluid in stretch-induced abortion, by Y. Manabe, et al. OBSTETRICS AND GYNECOLOGY 64(5):661-665, November 1984.

Decision to undergo tubal ligation, by J. G. Fontaine. UNION MEDICALE DU CANADA 113(7):604-606, July 1984.

Deep vein thrombosis and the oestrogen content in oral contraceptives. An epidemiological analysis, by A. Kierkegaard. CONTRACEPTION 31(1):29-41, January 1985.

Defending against assaults on abortion rights, by E. Bader. GUARDIAN 37(3):9, October 17, 1984.

Demise of the trimester standard? City of Akron v. Akron Center for Reproductive Health, Inc. [103 S. Ct. 2481]. JOURNAL OF FAMILY LAW 23:267-286, February 1984.

Democrats versus Catholic church, by J. Judis. IN THESE TIMES 8(37):7, October 3, 1984.

Demographic transition in a Punjab village. POPULATION AND DEVELOPMENT REVIEW 10(4):661, December 1984.

Demography comes of age [World Bank's World Development Report]. ECONOMIST 292:76-77, July 14, 1984.

Dependence, reliance and abortion, by M. Strasser. PHILOSOPHICAL QUARTERLY 35:73-82, January 1985.

Depo-Provera: blessing or curse?, by U. Vaid. THE NATIONAL PRISON PROJECT JOURNAL 4:1+, Summer 1985.

Depot medroxyprogesterone acetate: clinical and metabolic effects (lipids, glucose, hemostasis), by Y. Hyjazi, et al. JOURNAL DE GYNECOLOGIE, OBSTETRIQUE ET BIOLOGIE DE LA REPRODUCTION 14(1):93-103, 1985.

Depression and self-blame [women who use contraception and become pregnant anyway], by C. Turkington. PSYCHOLOGY TODAY 18:18, December 1984.

Destiny and liberty. Notes on the interruption of pregnancy in Western Societies, by A. Ines. REVISTA ESPANOLA DE INVESTGAGIONES SOCIOLOGICAS 21: 135-150, January-March 1983.

Determinants of birth-interval length in the Philippines, Malaysia and Indonesia: a hazard model. DEMOGRAPHY 22(2):145, May 1985.

Determinants of contraceptive use in Nepal, by J. M. Tuladhar. JOURNAL OF BIOSOCIAL SCIENCE 17(2):185-193, April 1985.

Determinants of opposition to abortion. An analysis of the hard and soft scales, by M. H. Benin. SOCIOLOGICAL PERSPECTIVES 28(2):199-216, 1985.

Determination of certain physical and chemical characteristics of the activating serum factor from preparturient women and women with habitual abortions, by J. Lukanov, et al. EXPERIENTIA 41(1):68-70, January 15, 1985.

Development of a low-dose monthly injectable contraceptive system: I. Choice of compounds, dose and administration route, by J. Garza-Flores, et al. CONTRACEPTION 30(4):371-379, October 1984.

Development of a scale to measure attitude toward the condom as a method of birth control, by I. S. Brown. JOURNAL OF SEX RESEARCH 20:255-263, August 1984.

Development of a simplified laparoscopic sterilization technique, by S. D. Khandwala. JOURNAL OF REPRODUCTIVE MEDICINE 29(8):586-588, August 1984.

Diabetes and spontaneous abortion [letter], by H. Kalter. AMERICAN JOURNAL OF OBSTETRICS AND GYNECOLOGY 152(5):603-604, July 1, 1985.

Diagnosis of extrauterine pregnancy in mini-abortions, by M. Dejmek, et al. CESKOS-LOVENSKA GYNEKOLOGIE 49(7):484-487, August 1984.

Diagnostic efficacy of 'routine' thoracic radiography preparatory to abortion, by M. Hanisch. RADIOLOGIA DIAGNOSTICA 26(2):233-238, 1985.

Diaphragm: an accomplice in recurrent UTI [letter], by G. E. Leach. UROLOGY 24(5): 524, November 1984.

Diazepam and ketamine for voluntary interruptions of pregnancy, by G. Bovyn. CAHIERS D'ANESTHESIOLOGIE 30(8):1019-1025, December 1982.

Did Searle closes its eyes to a health hazard? [Copper 7 IUD], by W. B. Glaberson. BUSINESS WEEK October 14, 1985, p. 120-122.

Dilatation of the cervix by oral PGE2 before first-trimester termination of pregnancy, by C. Somell, et al. ACTA OBSTETRICIA ET GYNECOLOGICA SCANDINAVICA 63(7):625-628, 1984.

Discoveries and dissimulations: the impact of abortion deaths on maternal mortality in British Columbia, by A. McLaren, et al. BC STUDIES 64:3-26, 1984-1985.

Dissent and reaction [controversy over abortion advertisement signed by Catholic religious]. AMERICA 152:37, January 19, 1985.

Diversity claimed [survey of Catholic theologians and scholars]. CHRISTIAN CEN-TURY 102:240, March 6, 1985.

Doctor and the underage girl [contraception; from our British correspondent, by K. Slack. CHRISTIAN CENTURY 102:174-176, February 20, 1985.

Doctor cleared in abortion trial, by T. Pugh. GUARDIAN 37(8):12, November 12, 1984.

Doctor couple arrested for phony abortions in N.Y. [M. Samuel and J. Cameau-Samuel]. JET 68:38, April 1, 1985.

Doctor's dilemma [H. Morgentaler's clinics], by R. Block. MACLEANS 97:52, December 17, 1984.

Doctors ordered to consult parents before prescribing. College regrets appeal ban on contraception for girls under 16. NURSING STANDARD 379:2, January 10, 1985.

Does diethylstilbestrol also affect the ovaries of the fetus?, by T. K. Eskes, et al. NEDERLANDS TIJDSCHRIFT VOOR GENEESKUNDE 128(34):1601-1603, August 25, 1984.

Does a man give a damn—about birth control?, by P. Nelson. MADEMOISELLE 91:100, June 1985.

Does ultrasound examination render biochemical tests obsolete in the prediction of early pregnancy failure?, by J. G. Westergaard, et al. BRITISH JOURNAL OF OBSTETRICS AND GYNAECOLOGY 92(1):77-83, January 1985.

Dorval's erotic zone, by P. Duchesne. COMMUNIQU'ELLES 11(3):7, May 1985.

Double-blind placebo-controlled trial of baclofen, alone and in combination, in patients undergoing voluntary abortion, by O. Corli, et al. CLINICAL THERAPEUTICS 6(6):800-807, 1984.

Double standard [bombings, Planned Parenthood offices, abortion clinics; editorial], by B. C. Harris. WITNESS 68(2):16, February 1985.

Down syndrome live births and prior spontaneous abortions of unknown karyotype, by E. B. Hook. PROGRESS IN CLINICAL AND BIOLOGICAL RESEARCH 163C:21-24, 1985.

Drawing lines: the abortion perplex and the presuppositions of applied ethics, by A. Weston. MONIST 67:589-604, October 1984.

E.R.A. and abortion: really separate issues?, by D. Johnson, et al. AMERICA 150: 432-437, June 9, 1984.

Early and late abortion methods, by D. A. van Lith, et al. CLINICAL OBSTETRICS AND GYNAECOLOGY 11(3):585-601, December 1984.

Early biopsy of chorionic villi. Personal experience and review of the literature, by A. Treisser, et al. REVUE FRANCAISE DE GYNECOLOGIE ET D'OBSTETRIQUE 80(6):397-412, May 1985.

Early complications of legal abortions, Canada, 1975-1979, by S. Wadhera, et al. WORLD HEALTH STATISTICS QUARTERLY 37(1):84-97, 1984.

Early embryonic loss: report of the study group, by A. F. Zakharov. PROGRESS IN CLINICAL AND BIOLOGICAL RESEARCH 163C:3-7, 1985.

Early spontaneous abortion, by J. L. Parmentier. SOINS, GYNECOLOGIE, OBSTETRIQUE, PUERICULTURE, PEDIATRIE 24:5-7, May 1983.

Early symptoms and discontinuation among users of oral contraceptives in Sri Lanka. STUDIES IN FAMILY PLANNING 15(6):285, November-December 1984.

Early total operative occlusion of the cervix in anamnestic abortion and premature labor risk, E. Saling. GYNAKOLOGE 17(4):225-229, December 1984.

Echographic and anatomo-pathologic aspects of a blighted ovum. Clinical and prognostic importance, by F. Borruto, et al. MINERVA GINECOLOGIA 36(7-8):413-417, July-August 1984.

Echographic diagnosis of gestational age and law 194, by F. Chiavazza, et al. ACTA BIOMEDICA DE L'ATENEO PARMENSE 56(2):63-67, 1985.

Economic and demographic interrelationships in sub-Saharan Africa, by E. Boserup. POPULATION AND DEVELOPMENT REVIEW 11:383-397, September 1985.

Economic and other determinants of annual change in U. S. fertility: 1917-1976. SOCIAL SCIENCE RESEARCH 13(3):250-267, September 1984.

Ectopic pregnancies following female sterilization. A matched case-control analysis, by I. C. Chi, et al. ACTA OBSTETRICIA ET GYNECOLOGICA SCANDINAVICA 63(6):517-521, 1984.

Ectopic pregnancy and spontaneous abortions following in-vitro fertilization and embryo transfer, by S. Lindenberg, et al. ACTA OBSTETRICIA ET GYNECOLOGICA SCANDINAVICA 64(1):31-34, 1985.

Ectopic pregnancy in a distal tubal remnant, by B. G. Molloy, et al. INTERNATIONAL JOURNAL OF GYNAECOLOGY AND OBSTETRICS 23(2):135-136, April 1985.

Ectopic pregnancy in relation to previous induced abortion, by J. R. Daling. JAMA 253(7):1005-1008, 1985.

Edinburgh diary [General Assembly, Church of Scotland, annual meeting], by K. Slack. CHRISTIAN CENTURY 102:636-637, July 3-10, 1985.

Educating for marriage and responsible parenthood in the field of health care, by J. Dunovsky. CASOPIS LEKARU CESKYCH 124(10):289-292, March 8, 1985.

Education. Gaining and giving insight, by K. Hills. NURSING MIRROR AND MID-WIVE'S JOURNAL 160(6):28-29, February 6, 1985.

Education and the timing of motherhood: disentangling causation, by R. R. Rindfuss. JOURNAL OF MARRIAGE AND THE FAMILY 46:981-984, November 1984.

Education related to birth control. BEIJING REVIEW 28:27-28, August 19, 1985.

Educational transition in rural South India. POPULATION AND DEVELOPMENT REVIEW 11(1):29, March 1985.

Eerdmans takes over publication of controversial InterVarsity book [Brave new people, by D. G. Jones]. CHRISTIANITY TODAY 28:53, December 14, 1984.

Effect of anionic polymeric hydrogels on spermatozoa motility, by H. Singh, et al. BIOMATERIALS 5(5):307-309, September 1984.

Effect of aspirin containing silastic implants placed adjacent to epididymis on fertility of rats, by W. D. Ratnasooriya, et al. INDIAN JOURNAL OF EXPERIMENTAL BIOLOGY 22(2):75-77, February 1984.

Effect of birth spacing on childhood mortality in Pakistan, by J. G. Cleland, et al. POPULATION STUDIES 38:401-418, November 1984.

Effect of chemical intravaginal contraceptives and Betadine on Ureaplasma urealyticum, by A. J. Amortegui, et al. CONTRACEPTION 30(2):135-141, August 1984.

Effect of continuous local microdose norethisterone enanthate on the epididymis of adult rat, by U. K. Srivastava. ANDROLOGIA 15(4):333-338, July-August 1983.

Effect of contraceptive knowledge source upon knowledge accuracy and contraceptive behavior, by A. J. Pope, et al. HEALTH EDUCATION 16:41-44, June-July 1985.

Effect of gossypol on macromolecular synthesis in rat testis. An in vitro study, by P. Kainz, et al. CONTRACEPTION 31(2):151-158, February 1985.

Effect of induced abortion on the state of the cervix uteri in nulliparae, by V. O. Vekhnovskii. AKUSHERSTVO I GINEKOLOGIIA 12:42-43, December 1984.

Effect of legal abortion on teenage fertility in Trieste, Italy, by G. Benussi, et al. FAMILY PLANNING PERSPECTIVES 17(1):23-24, January-February 1985.

Effect of marital dissolution on contraceptive protection, by L. Bumpass, et al. FAMILY PLANNING PERSPECTIVES 16:271-284, November-December 1984.

Effect of a new contraceptive ring releasing 20 micrograms levonorgestrel daily on blood lipid levels and glucose tolerance, by M. G. Elder, et al. CONTRACEPTION 30(1):55-60, July 1984.

Effect of a once-a-month oral contraceptive on serum prolactin levels, by M. C. Jia, et al. CHUNG HUA FU CHAN KO TSA CHIH 20(2):113-116, March 1985.

Effect of oral contraceptive drug on cardiovascular system, liver and kidneys, by C. Chaudhuri, et al. INDIAN HEART JOURNAL 37(2):96-100, March-April 1985.

Effect of oral contraceptive formulation and field-workers: a cautionary tale, by P. C. Miller, et al. INTERNATIONAL JOURNAL OF GYNAECOLOGY AND OBSTETRICS 23(1):13-20, February 1985.

Effect of oral contraceptives and some psychological factors on the menstrual experience, by C. M. Harding, et al. JOURNAL OF BIOSOCIAL SCIENCE 17(3):291-304, July 1985.

Effect of oral contraceptives in malaria infections in rhesus monkey, by W. E. Collins, et al. WHO BULLETIN 62(4):627-637, 1984.

Effect of oral medroxyprogesterone acetate and methyltestosterone on sexual functioning in a male contraceptive trial, by K. Doody, et al. CONTRACEPTION 31(1):65-70, January 1985.

Effect of postcoital oestradiol treatment upon transport, growth, differentiation and viability of preimplantation mouse embryos, by L. S. Roblero, et al. ARCHIVOS DE BIOLOGIA Y MEDICINA EXPERIMENTALES 16(1):55-59, August 1983.

Effect of 7 alpha- and 7 beta-methyl-10 beta, 17 beta-diacetoxy-delta 4-estren-3-one on terminating early pregnancy, by Y. H. Chu, et al. YAO HSUEH HSUEH PAO 19(3):173-177, March 1984.

Effect of a single midcycle administration of 0.5 or 2.0 mg dienogest (17 alpha-cyanomethyl-17beta-hydroxy-estra-4,9-dien-3-one) on pituitary and ovarian function—investigation for the use as a postcoital contraceptive, by G. Köhler, et al. EXPERIMENTAL AND CLINICAL ENDOCRINOLOGY 84(3):299-304, December 1984.

Effect of a topical contraceptive on endocervical culture for Neisseria gonorrhoeae, by C. H. Livengood, et al. AMERICAN JOURNAL OF OBSTETRICS AND GYNECOLOGY 150(3):319-320, October 1, 1984.

Effect of tubal ligation on the incidence of epithelial cancer of the ovary, by M. Koch, et al. CANCER DETECTION AND PREVENTION 7(4):241-245, 1984.

Effectiveness of Bricanyl (terbutaline) treatment in the prevention and management of threatened abortion and premature delivery, respectively, within the frames of out-patients' services, by B. Toth, et al. THERAPIA HUNGARICA 30(2):88-92, 1982.

Effectiveness of family planning clinics in serving adolescents, by E. E.Kisker. FAMILY PLANNING PERSPECTIVES 16:212-218, September-October 1984.

Effectiveness of injectable contraceptives in Mexican women, by J. Garza-Flores, et al. BOLETIN DE LA OFICINA SANITARIA PAN AMERICANA 98(2):181-186, February 1985.

Effects of abortion on a marriage, by J. Mattinson. CIBA FOUNDATION SYMPOSIA 115:165-177, 1985.

Effects of birth rank, maternal age, birth interval, and sibship size on infant and child mortality: evidence from 18th and 19th century reproductive histories, by J. Knodel, et al. AMERICAN JOURNAL OF PUBLIC HEALTH 74:1098-1106, October 1984.

Effects of a combination of cigarette smoking and oral contraception on coagulation and fibrinolysis in human females, by J. Harenberg, et al. KLINISCHE WOCHEN-SCHRIFT 63(5):221-224, March 1, 1985.

Effects of common environmental exposures on spontaneous abortion of defined karyotype, by D. Warburton. PROGRESS IN CLINICAL AND BIOLOGICAL RESEARCH 163C:31-36, 1985.

Effects of elevated female sex steroids on ethanol and acetaldehyde metabolism in humans, by C. M. Jeavons, et al. ALCOHOLISM: CLINICAL AND EXPERI-MENTAL RESEARCH 8(4):352-358, July-August 1984.

Effects of female sterilization: one year follow-up in a prospective controlled study of psychological and psychiatric outcome, by J. E. Cooper, et al. JOURNAL OF PSYCHOSOMATIC RESEARCH 29(1):13-22, 1985.

Effects of information on patient stereotyping, by B. M. DeVellis, et al. RESEARCH IN NURSING AND HEALTH 7(3):237-244, September 1984.

Effects of miscarriage on a man, by D. D. Cumings. EMOTIONAL FIRST AID: A JOURNAL OF CRISIS INTERVENTION 1(4):47-50, Winter 1984.

Effects of oral contraceptives and obesity on protein C antigen, by T. W. Meade, et al. THROMBOSIS AND HAEMOSTASIS 53(2):198-199, April 22, 1985.

Effects of oral contraceptives on vitamins B6, B12, C, and folacin, by K. S. Veninga. JOURNAL OF NURSE-MIDWIFERY 29(6):386-390, November-December 1984.

Effects of the ovarian and contraceptive cycles on absolute thresholds, auditory fatigue and recovery from temporary threshold shifts at 4 and 6 kHz, by J.-C. Petiot, et al. AUDIOLOGY 23(6):581-598, November-December 1984.

Effects of paced coital stimulation on estrus duration in intact cycling rats and ovariec-tomized and ovariectomized-adrenal-octomized hormone-primed rats, by M. S. Erskine. BEHAVIORAL NEUROSCIENCE 99(1):151-161, February 1985.

Effects of social setting and family planning programs on recent fertility declines in developing countries: a reassessment, by S. E. Tolnay, et al. SOCIOLOGY AND SOCIAL RESEARCH 69(1):72-89, October 1984.

Effects of sterilization on menstruation, by J. Foulkes, et al. SOUTHERN MEDICAL JOURNAL 78(5):544-547, May 1985.

Effects of three techniques of tubal occlusion on ovarian hormones and menstrua-tion, by P. Virutamasen, et al. JOURNAL OF THE MEDICAL ASSOCIATION OF THAILAND 67(4):201-210, April 1984.

Effects of US decision to withdraw aid for worldwide family planning programmes. LANCET 1(8420):97, January 12, 1985.

Effects on menstruation of elective tubal sterilization: a prospective controlled study, by K. D. Bledin, et al. JOURNAL OF BIOSOCIAL SCIENCE 17:19-30, January 1985.

Efficacy of allylestrenol in the prevention of habitual abortion, by R. Grio, et al. MINERVA GINECOLOGIA 37(4):171-172, April 1985.

Efficacy of using thymalin in different types of peritonitis in obstetrical practice, by B. I. Kuznik, et al. AKUSHERSTVO I GINEKOLOGIIA 9:50-52, September 1984.

Elective sterilization: no guarantees, by J. K. Avery. JOURNAL OF THE TENNESSEE MEDICAL ASSOCIATION 77(9):540-541, September 1984.

Electroconvulsive therapy [letter], by S. Barza. CANADIAN JOURNAL OF PSYCHIATRY 30(4):310, June 1985.

Electroimpulse test as a method for the diagnosis of threatened abortion and to evaluate the effectiveness of treatment, by V. I. Orlov. AKUSHERSTVO I GINEKOLOGIIA 12:33-35, December 1984.

Elevating ambulatory record systems: a case study, by L. Brooks. TOPICS IN HEALTH RECORD MANAGEMENT 5(3):47-50, March 1985.

Embryos from spontaneous abortions with chromosomal aberrations, by J. Kleinebrecht, et al. ANATOMISCHER ANZEIGER 157(1):3-33, 1984.

Empirical investigation of the determinants of congressional voting on federal financing of abortions and the ERA, by J. M. Netter. JOURNAL OF LEGAL STUDIES 14:245-257, January 1985.

End this TV taboo: Sets' run birth control ads during "Dallas" and "Dynasty," by J. Kalter. TV GUIDE 33:30, November 23, 1985.

Endocrine abortions, by J. L. Parmentier. SOINS, GYNECOLOGIE, OBSTETRIQUE, PUERICULTURE, PEDIATRIE 24:15-16, May 1983.

Endocrine function of the reproductive system after early abortion by vacuum-aspiration, by T. M. Likhacheva. AKUSHERSTVO I GINEKOLOGIIA 2:37-39, February 1985.

Epidemiologic analysis of fetal death in utero in Singapore, by K. C. Tan, et al. INTERNATIONAL JOURNAL OF GYNAECOLOGY AND OBSTETRICS 22(3): 181-188, June 1984.

Equal-opportunity banning, by N. Hentoff. VILLAGE VOICE 29:8, October 30, 1984.

Experience with adolescents seeking an abortion, by M. Berger. ZEITSCHRIFT FÜR KINDER-UND JUGENDPSYCHIATRIE12(3):250-265, 1984.

An error in the calculation of the percentage of conceptions with an unbalanced chromosome rearrangement that survive birth, by W. L. Russell. MUTATION RESEARCH 142(4):217, April 1985.

Estrogen and progesterone receptors in the decidual tissue of women administered prostaglandins and experiencing spontaneous abortion, by M. K. Asribekova, et al. PROBLEMY ENDOKRINOLOGII I GORMONOTERAPII 31(2):26-29, March-April 1985.

Estrogen-progestoyen agents and megaloblastic anemia, by D. Mottier, et al. JOURNAL DE GYNECOLOGIE, OBSTETRIQUE ET BIOLOGIE DE LA REPRODUCTION 13(6):707-710, 1984.

Estrogen treatment for victims of rape [letter]. NEW ENGLAND JOURNAL OF MEDI-CINE 312(15):988-989, April 11, 1985.

Estroprogestational minipills: breast diseases and functional cysts of the ovary. Apropos of 87 cases, by M. Vincens, et al. THERAPIE 40(3):177-180, May-June 1985.

Ethical dilemma of late pregnancy termination in cases of gross fetal malformations, by J. R. Leiberman, et al. ISRAEL JOURNAL OF MEDICAL SCIENCES 20(11): 1051-1055, November 1984.

Ethical implications of alternatives to induced abortion and corrective surgery [letter], by P. Cholnoky. ORVOSI HETILAP 126(2):118, January 13, 1985.

Ethical issues in reproductive medicine: a Mormon perspective [photo], by L. E. Bush. DIALOGUE 18:40-66, Summer 1985.

Ethics in caring, by T. Keighley. NURSING STANDARDS 365:8, September 20, 1984.

Ethnic differences in contraceptive use in Sri Lanka, by K. R. Murty, et al. STUDIES IN FAMILY PLANNING 15:222-232, September-October 1984.

Ethnicity, locus of control for family planning, and pregnancy counselor credibility, by D. R. Atkinson, et al. JOURNAL OF COUNSELING PSYCHOLOGY 32:417-421, July 1985.

Etymology of condom, by Z. P. Thundy. AMERICAN SPEECH 60:177-179, Summer 1985.

Evaluation of intra-amniotic administration of 120 gm of urea with 5 mg of prostaglan-din F2 alpha for midtrimester termination of pregnancy between 20 and 24 weeks' gestation, by R. V. Haning, Jr., et al. AMERICAN JOURNAL OF OBSTETRICS AND GYNECOLOGY 151(1):92-96, January 1, 1985.

Evidence of immunosuppressor factor in the serum of women taking oral contracep-tives, by J. Bousquet, et al. GYNECOLOGIC AND OBSTETRIC INVESTIGATION 18(4):178-182, 1984.

Evolution and reversibility of damage to rabbit fallopian tubes after five sterilization methods, by N. Garcea, et al. MICROSURGERY 6(1):20-25, 1985.

Evolution of the minor complications due to the use of copper intrauterine device, by A. Albert, et al. CLINICA E INVESTIGACION EN GINECOLOGIA Y OBSTETRICIA 10(1):16-22, 1983.

Exogenous hormone use and fibrocystic breast disease by histopathologic compon-ent, by G. S. Berkowitz, et al. INTERNATIONAL JOURNAL OF CANCER 34(4): 443-449, October 15, 1984.

Exotic reaction to tubal ligation, by S. Lockwood. AUSTRALIAN FAMILY PHYSICIAN 13(6): 446-447, June 1984.

Experience from a local authority clinic for advice on contraception. A consecutive study of 1000 women attending a clinic for advice on contraception in the Munici-pality of Fredriksberg, by E. Schroeder, et al. AGESKRIFT FOR LAEGER 146(26):1953-1957, June 25,1984.

Experience with laparoscopic interval sterilization with fallopian tube rings, by A. F. Haenel, et al. FORTSCHRITTE DER MEDIZIN 103(5):87-90, February 7, 1985.

Experience with levonorgestrel in postcoital contraception, by E. Canzler, et al. ZENTRALBLATT FÜR GYNAEKOLOGIE 106(17):1182-1191, 1984.

Experimental study of pathological and normal early pregnancy with the E rosette test, by R. R. Strache, et al. ZENTRALBLATT FÜR GYNAEKOLOGIE 107(4): 201-207, 1985.

Exploratory study of life-change events, social support and pregnancy decisions in adolescents, by M. L. Carlson, et al. ADOLESCENCE 19:765-780, Winter 1984.

Explosions over abortion [terrorist bombings of clinics], by E. Magnuson. TIME 125:16-17, January 14, 1985.

Extermination of Jews in self-defense? The legends around T. N. Kaufman, by W. Benz. VIERTELJAHRSHEFTE FUR ZEITGESCHICHTE 29(4):615-630, 1981.

"F factor": the New Testament in some white, feminist, Christian theological construction, by J. C. Lambert. JOURNAL OF FEMINIST STUDIES IN RELIGION 1(2):93-113, Fall 1985.

FBI director was right not to usurp ATF in bombings, by R. J. O'Connell. CRIME CONTROL DIGEST 19(7):1-2, February 18, 1985.

Facing the facts. TIMES EDUCATIONAL SUPPLEMENT 3596:35, May 31, 1985.

Factors associated with adolescent use of family planning clinics, by J. A. Shea, et al. AMERICAN JOURNAL OF PUBLIC HEALTH 74(11):1227-1230, November 1984.

Factors associated with married women's selection of tubal sterilization and vasectomy, by R. N. Shain, et al. FERTILITY AND STERILITY 43(2):234-244, February 1985.

Factors in adolescent contraceptive use . . . knowledge, self-esteem and religiosity, by K. G. Kellinger. NURSE PRACTITIONER 10(9):55+, September 1985.

Factors influencing the success of microsurgical tuboplasty for sterilization reversal, by P. J. Paterson. CLINICAL REPRODUCTION AND FERTILITY 3(1):57-64, March 1985.

Factors predicting pregnancy resolution decision satisfaction of unmarried adolescents, by M.Eisen, et al. JOURNAL OF GENETIC PSYCHOLOGY 145(2): 231-239, December 1984.

Factors related to delay for legal abortions performed at a gestational age of 20 weeks or more, by C. Joseph . JOURNAL OF BIOSOCIAL SCIENCE 17(3):327-337, July 1985.

Failed tubal ligation: bringing a wrongful birth case to trial, by G. I. Strausberg. TRIAL 21(5):30-33, May 1985.

Family issues and the right, by V. Hardisty. SHMATE 11:33, Summer 1985.

Family issues and the right, by S. Sturgis. OFF OUR BACKS 15(8):17, August 1985.

Family planning and culture, by B. Qureshi. JOURNAL OF THE ROYAL SOCIETY OF HEALTH 105(1):11-14, February 1985.

Family planning and female sterilization in the United States, by T. M. Shapiro, et al. SOCIAL SCIENCE AND MEDICINE 17(23):1847-1855, 1983.

Family planning and sexual counseling . . . the nurse's role, by J. Glover. NURSING MIRROR AND MIDWIVE'S JOURNAL 160(3):28-29, January 16, 1985.

Family planning clinic services in the United States, 1983, by A. Torres, et al. FAMILY PLANNING PERSPECTIVES 17(1):30-35, January -February 1985.

Family planning experience. POPULI 2(1):36, 1984.

Family planning for deer, by T. Levenson. DISCOVER 5:34-35+, December 1984.

Family planning: general practice and clinic services, by S. Rowlands. JOURNAL OF THE ROYAL COLLEGE OF GENERAL PRACTITIONERS 35(273):199-200, April 1985.

Family planning: the global challenge, by J. A. Loraine. PRACTITIONER 229(1403): 407-412, May 1985.

Family planning in Japanese society, by N. Engel. BULLETIN OF CONCERNED ASIAN SCHOLARS 17(2):71, April 1985.

Family planning in rural and semirural areas, by M. R. Santamaría Valladolid. REVISTA DE ENFERMAGEN 7(74):63-66, October 1984.

Family planning in the service of human development, by H. Mahler. WHO CHRONICLE 38(6):239-242, 1984.

Family planning in Singapore, by C. Ng. ASIA-OCEANIA JOURNAL OF OBSTETRICS AND GYNAECOLOGY 10(4):559-563, December 1984.

Family planning in USSR found wanting. CURRENT DIGEST OF THE SOVIET PRESS 37:10-12+, October 23, 1985.

Family planning performance at a major hospital in Sri Lanka, by S. Tennakoon. CEYLON MEDICAL JOURNAL 28(4):233-238, December 1983.

Family planning programme in India: the non governmental sector, by A. B. Wadia. JOURNAL OF FAMILY WELFARE 30:11-46, June 1984.

Family planning services in the commonwealth Caribbean [editorial], by L. Matadial. WEST INDIAN MEDICAL JOURNAL 34(1):1-2, March 1985.

Family planning: U. S. policy changing?, by J. Raloff. SCIENCE NEWS 128:55, July 27, 1985.

Fatal in utero salicylism, by T. A. Rejent, et al. JOURNAL OF FORENSIC SCIENCES 30(3):942-944, July 1985.

Favorable response to Metrulen in Von Willebrand's disease (type III), by J. Moreb, et al. HAREFUAH 107(10):283-285, November 15, 1984.

Federal law enforcement role at issue in abortion bombings. CRIMINAL JUSTICE NEWSLETTER 16(3):7-8, February 1, 1985.

Female infanticide and amniocentesis, by R. Jeffery, et al. SOCIAL SCIENCE AND MEDICINE 19(11):1207-1212, 1984.

Female sterilization: free choice and oppression, by C. Barroso. REVISTA DE SAUDE PUBLICA 18(2):170-180, April 1984.

Female sterilization monitored by laparoscopy. Evaluation of 2 electrosurgical occlusive technics, by L. C. Uribe Ramirez, et al. GINECOLOGIA Y OBSTETRICIA DE MEXICO 52(322):33-40, February 1984.

Female sterilization—safe and irreversible?, by O. Lalos, et al. LAKARTIDNINGEN 81(38):3358-3360, September 19, 1984.

Feminism in Japan, by A. Henry. OFF OUR BACKS 14(10):12, November 1984.

Feminist morality; excerpt from *Not an easy choice: a feminist re-examines abortion*, by K. McDonnell. CANADIAN FORUM 64:18-20, November 1984.

Fertility control in the bitch by active immunization with porcine zonae pellucidae: use of different adjuvants and patterns of estradiol and progesterone levels in estrous cycles, by C. A. Mahi-Brown, et al. BIOLOGY OF REPRODUCTION 32(4):761-772, May 1985.

Fertility effects of isolated spouse separations in relation to their timing, by R. G. Potter, et al. SOCIAL BIOLOGY 30:279-289, August 1983.

Fertility of couples following cessation of contraception, by N. Spira, et al. JOURNAL OF BIOSOCIAL SCIENCE 17(3):281-290, July 1985.

Fertility survey of different birth cohort women in Beijing city, S. X. Wang. CHUNG HUA FU CHAN KO TSA CHIH 20(1):30-33, January 1985.

Fetal malformations following progesterone therapy during pregnancy: a preliminary report, by J. A. Rock, et al. FERTILITY AND STERILITY 44(1):17-19, July 1985.

Fetal research and the problem of consent, by C. Perry. WORLD FUTURES 20(1-2):55-67, 1984.

Fever during pregnancy and spontaneous abortion, by J. Kline, et al. AMERICAN JOURNAL OF EPIDEMIOLOGY 121(6):832-842, June 1985.

Fewer under-16s seek pill advice [Gellick ruling in Great Britain], by J. Last. TIMES EDUCATIONAL SUPPLEMENT 3599:16, June 12, 1985.

Fibrinopeptide A plasma levels during low-estrogen oral contraceptive treatment, by G. B. Melis, et al. CONTRACEPTION 30(6):575-583, December 1984.

15(S)-15-methyl-prostaglandin F2 alpha used for induction of delivery in the case of intra-uterine fetal death, by M. Osler, et al. ACTA OBSTETRICIA ET GYNECOLOGICA SCANDINAVICA 64(2):131-132, 1985.

Fight for abortion rights, by S. Arnott. GAY COMMUNITY 12(28):1, February 2, 1985.

Film program in health and family planning in rural Zaire, by M. Carael, et al. HUMAN ORGANIZATION 43:341-348, Winter 1984.

Filshie clip for female sterilization [letter], by D. Casey. CONTRACEPTION 31(4):441-442, April 1985.

First aid in pastoral care: pastoral care in marriage, by J. Thompson. EXPOSITORY TIMES 96:324-329, August 1985.

First campaigns for birth control clinics in British Columbia, by A. McLaren. JOURNAL OF CANADIAN STUDIES 19(3):50-64, 1984.

Flames of fanaticism: abortion clinic bombings are only the latest actions in America's little-known history of violence in the name of God, by A. J. Menendez. CHURCH AND STATE 38:4-7, February 1985.

Flipchart nutrition reference for family planning, by J. Van Gurp. JOURNAL OF NUTRITION EDUCATION 17:18B, March 1985.

Florida: more abortion bombings. NEWSWEEK 105:17, January 7, 1985.

Focus on life issues [editorial]. NATIONAL CATHOLIC REPORTER 21:16, January 25, 1985.

Foetal protection against abortion: is it immunosuppression or immunostimulation?, by T. G. Wegmann. ANNALES D'IMMUNOLOGIE 135D(3):309-312, November-December 1984.

Foetuses, famous violinists, and the right to continued aid, by M. Davis. PHILO-SOPHICAL QUARTERLY 33:259-278, July 1983 and 35:73-82, January 1985.

Follow-up study of children born to women denied abortion, by Z. Matejcek, et al. CIBA FOUNDATION SYMPOSIA 115:136-149, 1985.

Foreign aid birth control campaigns: the disability connection—in whose interest?, by Anne Gajerski-Cauley. RESOURCES FOR FEMINIST RESEARCH 14:14-18, March 1985.

Foreign travel alert for women on the pill. GLAMOUR 83:51, June 1985.

Formulation and noncontraceptive uses of the new, low-dose oral contraceptive, by F. R. Batzer. JOURNAL OF REPRODUCTIVE MEDICINE 29(7 Suppl):503-512, July 1984.

Formulation of a potential antipregnancy vaccine based on the beta-subunit of human chorionic gonadotropin (beta-hCG). I. Alternative macromolecular carriers, by Y. Y. Tsong, et al. JOURNAL OF REPRODUCTIVE IMMUNOLOGY 7(2):139-149, February 1985.

—II. Use of compounds of the muramyl dipeptide (MDP) family as adjuvants, by H. A. Nash, et al. JOURNAL OF REPRODUCTIVE IMMUNOLOGY 7(2):151-162, February 1985.

—III. Evaluation of various vehicles and adjuvants, by C. C. Chang, et al. JOURNAL OF REPRODUCTIVE IMMUNOLOGY 7(2):163-169, February 1985.

Foundation power [critical views of American foundation funding in the areas of population control and abortion, by M. Meehan. HUMAN LIFE REVIEW 10:42-60, Fall 1984.

Four-year follow-up of insertion of quinacrine hydrochloride pellets as a means of nonsurgical female sterilization, by R. Bhatt, et al. FERTILITY AND STERILIZA-TION 44(3):303-306, September 1985.

Fragile sites and chromosome breakpoints in constitutional rearrangements II. Spontaneous abortions, stillbirths and newborns, by F. Hecht, et al. CLINICAL GENETICS 26(3):174-177, September 1984.

Freestanding abortion clinics: services, structure, fees, by S. K. Henshaw. FAMILY PLANNING PERSPECTIVES 14(5):248-250+, September-October 1982.

From biotechnology to bioethics: the shock of the future, by E. Boné. PRO MUNDI VITA BULLETIN 101:1-42, 1985.

From the viewpoint of the hospital physician. 7 years after the reform of paragraph 218, by A. Kayser. KRANKENPFLEGE JOURNAL 22(11):28-32, November 1, 1984.

Functional state of the pituitary-ovaries system in women with a history of habitual abortion, by T. K. Baituraeva, et al. PROBLEMY ENDOKRINOLOGII I GORMONOTERAPII 30(6):25-27, November-December 1984.

Further reflections on changes in fertility expectations and preferences, by A. D. Thornton, et al. DEMOGRAPHY 21(3):423-429, August 1984.

Gains and losses for women, by M. Simms. NEW HUMANIST 100:18-21, Spring 1985.

Gallbladder disease related to use of oral contraceptives and nausea in pregnancy, by A.Järnfelt-Samsioe, et al. SOUTHERN MEDICAL JOURNAL 78(9):1040-1043, September 1985.

Gallup poll shows Americans are mistaken about contraceptives. AMERICAN FAMILY PHYSICIAN 31:18, April 1985.

Gender slap, by J. Lukomnik. HEALTH PAC BULLETIN 15(4):11, July 1984.

General yeast infection in Bangladeshi women using contraceptives, by K. M. Rahman, et al. BANGLADESH MEDICAL RESEARCH COUNCIL BULLETIN 10(2):65-70, December 1984.

Generation of one-child families? FUTURIST 19:49-50, June 1985.

Generational differences in fertility among Mexican Americans: implications for assessing the effects of immigration, by F. D. Bean, et al. SOCIAL SCIENCE QUARTERLY 65:573-582, June 1984.

Genesis of contemporary Italian feminism, by J. Barkan. RADICAL AMERICAN 18(5):31, 1984.

Genetic amniocentesis: impact of placental position upon the risk of pregnancy loss, by J. P. Crane, et al. AMERICAN JOURNAL OF OBSTETRICS AND GYNE-COLOGY 150(7):813-816, December 1984.

Genetic diseases; problems of prenatal testing, by T. Beardsley. NATURE 314:211, March 21, 1985.

Genetic medicine in the perspective of Orthodox halakhah, by R. M. Green. JUDAISM 34:261-277, Summer 1985.

Genetics and a woman's rights [letter], by A. B. Masters. CANADIAN MEDICAL ASSOCIATION JOURNAL 131(12):1433, December 15, 1984.

Genital infections in women undergoing therapeutic abortion, by D. Avonts, et al. EUROPEAN JOURNAL OF OBSTETRICS, GYNECOLOGY AND REPRO-DUCTIVE BIOLOGY 20(1):53-59, July 1985.

Geraldine Ferraro's abortion dilemma: hypothetical dialogue with the candidate, by D. D'Souza. HUMAN EVENTS 44:23, November 3, 1984.

Germ cell survival, differentiation, and epididymal transit kinetics in mouse testis subjected to high in vivo levels of testosterone enanthate, by R. B. Goldberg. CELL AND TISSUE RESEARCH 237(2):337-342, 1984.

German euthanasia program [letter], by J. E. McArthur. NEW ZEALAND MEDICAL JOURNAL 98(784):656, August 14, 1985.

Getting rid of old habits, by M. Lauer. MOTHER JONES 10(2):10, February 1985.

Global politics in Mexico City, by D. Wulf, et al. FAMILY PLANNING PERSPECTIVES 16(5):228-232, September-October 1984.

Global prospects NOT MAN APART 15(3):12, March 1985.

Glucose-6-phosphate dehydrogenase in couples with habitual abortion, by J. Guizar Vázquez, et al. GINECOLOGIA Y OBSTETRICIA DE MEXICO 50(308):325-328, December 1982.

Go forth and multiply—like rabbits?[Latin America], by A. Hiller. HUMANIST 44:15-19, November-December 1984.

Go thou and do likewise [face the facts], by C. Thomas. FUNDAMENTALIST JOURNAL 3(1):26, January 1984.

Gonadal steroids in athletic women contraception, complications and performance, by J. C. Prior, et al. SPORTS MEDICINE 2(4):287-295, July-August 1985.

Good news about the pill, by N. Mallovy. HOME MAGAZINE 20:48E-48H, May 1985.

Good news about vasectomies, by E. Michaels. CHATELAINE 58:18, February 1985.

Gossypol in female fertility control: ovum implantation and early pregnancy inhibited in rats, by Y. C. Lin, et al. LIFE SCIENCES 37(1):39-47, July 8, 1985.

Government steps up attacks on abortion rights, by J. Baker. INTERNATIONAL VIEWPOINT 81:4, July 29, 1985.

Governmental abortion policies and the right to privacy: the rights of the individual and the rights of the unborn. BROOKLYN JOURNAL OF INTERNATIONAL LAW 11:103-126, Winter 1985.

Governor and the bishops [M. Cuomo at Notre Dame]. NEW REPUBLIC 191:7-9, October 8, 1984.

Gradualist response to Robert Wennberg, by W. Hasker. CHRISTIAN SCHOLAR'S REVIEW 14(4,362)):369, 1985.

Grand multiparity: benefits of a referral program for hospital delivery and postpartum tubal ligation, by P. Barss, et al. PAPUA NEW GUINEA MEDICAL JOURNAL 28(1):35-39, March 1985.

Grappling with the population programme, by A. Maranan. BALAI 11:22, 1985.

Great Britain fighting for a woman's right/choos. INTERNATIONAL VIEWPOINT 73:26, April 8,1985.

Groping for God's kind face again, by J. G. Swank. CHRISTIANITY TODAY 29:68, June 14, 1985.

Group discussion on contraceptive issues, by B. A. Rienzo. HEALTH EDUCATION 16:52-53, August-September 1985.

Groups protest: abortion is not an erotic act. COMMUNIQU'ELLES 10(6):6, November 1984.

Guide to contraceptive choices for women with disabilities. RESOURCES FOR FEMINIST RESEARCH 14:106-108, March 1985.

Guidelines for overcoming design problems in family planning operations research, by A. A. Fisher, et al. STUDIES IN FAMILY PLANNING 16(2):100-105, March-April 1985.

Guilty of trying to self-abort, by E. Rader. GUARDIAN 37(13):2, December 26, 1984.

Gyn game: FDA and contraceptive sponge, by D. St. Clair. HEALTH PAC BULLETIN 15(5):13, September 1984.

Gynaecology of middle-aged women—menstrual and reproductive histories, by A. Hagstad, et al. MATURITAS 7(2):99-113, July 1985.

HHS discriminates religiously, by C. Schiff. WOMANEWS 6(3):5, March 1985.

HLA compatibility and human reproduction, by P. F. Bolis, et al. CLINICAL AND EXPERIMENTAL OBSTETRICS AND GYNECOLOGY 12(1-2):9-12, 1985.

HLA sharing and spontaneous abortion in humans, by M. L. Thomas, et al. AMERICAN JOURNAL OF OBSTETRICS AND GYNECOLOGY 151(8):1053-1058, April 15, 1985.

HLA typing in couples with repetitive abortion, by P. F. Bolis, et al. BIOLOGICAL RESEARCH IN PREGNANCY AND PERINATOLOGY 5(3):135-137, 1984.

Habitual abortion, by E. Maroni. SCHWEIZERISCHE RUNDSCHAU FUR MEDZIN PRAXIS 74(15):371-377, April 9, 1985.

Habitual abortion of chromosomal etiology, by S. S. Bessudnova, et al. AKUSHERSTVO I GINEKOLOGIIA (12):8-10, December 1984.

Hardest question, by K. L. Woodward. NEWSWEEK 105:29, January 14, 1985.

Health belief model and the contraceptive behavior of college women: implications for health education, by N. R. Hester, et al. JOURNAL OF AMERICAN COLLEGE HEALTH 33:245-252, June 1985.

Health belief model approach to adolescents' fertility control: some pilot program findings, by M. Eisen, et al. HEALTH EDUCATION QUARTERLY 12(2):185-210, Summer 1985.

Health education and beyond: a Soviet women's group experience, by M. Coughlin, et al. JOURNAL OF JEWISH COMMUNAL SERVICE 60(1):65-69, 1983.

Health insurance study: no increased risk for fetal abnormalities in women working with video display terminals, by A. Ericson, et al. LAKARTIDNINGEN 82(23):2180-2184, June 5, 1985.

Helping hand for back-alley abortionists, by R. MacKay. GUARDIAN 37(30):15, May 1, 1985.

Hentoff, are you listening, by K. Pollitt. MOTHER JONES 10(2):60, February 1985.

Hepatic adenoma and oral contraception: apropos of a hemorrhagic complication, by J. Maurice, et al. REVUE MEDICALE DE LA SUISSE ROMANDE 105(3):211-217, March 1985.

Hepatitis and diaphragm fitting, by L. A. Lettau, et al. JAMA 254(6):752, August 9, 1985.

Hepatobiliary complications of female hormonal contraception, by F. Darnis. SOINS (437):3-7, September 1984.

High-and low-tech control, by L. R. Brown. NATURAL HISTORY 94:77, April 1985.

High court hears horrors of illegal abortion, by E. Bader. GUARDIAN 37(46):3, September 25, 1985.

High court to re-examine state abortion regulations, by E. Witt. CONGRESSIONAL QUARTERLY WEEKLY REPORT 43:2153-2155, October 26, 1985.

High failure rate of a plactic tubal (Bleier) clip, by R. Adelman. OBSTETRICS AND GYNECOLOGY 64(5):721-724, November 1984.

High resolution cytogenetic evaluation of couples with recurring fetal wastage, by T. L. Yang-Feng, et al. HUMAN GENETICS 69(3):246-249, 1985.

Histology of the placenta in spontaneous abortion, by V. Bianco, et al. ANNALI DI OSTETRICIA GINECOLOGIA MEDICINA PERINATALE 105(4):219-224, July-August 1984.

Holding the center against "right" rhetoric, by J. M. Wall. CHRISTIAN CENTURY 102:203-204, February 27, 1985.

Holocaust, Nazism and abortion [euphemisms], by W. Brennan. FUNDAMENTALIST JOURNAL 2(1):30-33, January 1983.

Holy war, by P. Donovan. FAMILY PLANNING PERSPECTIVES 17(1):5-9, January-February 1985.

Holy war in Pensacola, by P. Carlson. PEOPLE WEEKLY 23:20-25, January 21, 1985.

Horizons unclear for herizons, by P. Duchesne. COMMUNIQU'ELLES 11(4):4, July 1985.

Hormonal contraception and IUDs in adolescents, by M. Mall-Haefeli. FORT-SCHRITTE DER MEDIZIN 102(33):823-824, September 6, 1984.

Hormonal contraceptive methods, by J. McEwan. PRACTITIONER 229(1403):415-423, May 1985.

Hormonal factors and melanoma in women, by A. Green, et al. MEDICAL JOURNAL OF AUSTRALIA 142(8):446-448, April 15, 1985.

Hormone levels in amniotic fluid and maternal serum in women who undergo spontaneous abortion after second trimester amniocentesis, by K. Bremme, et al. GYNECOLOGIC AND OBSTETRIC INVESTIGATION 18(2):78-82, 1984.

Hormone load tests in the first half of pregnancy—a diagnostic and therapeutic approach, by I. Gerhard, et al. BIOLOGICAL RESEARCH IN PREGNANCY AND PERINATOLOGY 5(4):157-173, 1984.

Hormones in the etiology and prevention of breast and endometrial cancer, by R. D. Gambrell, Jr. SOUTHERN MEDICAL JOURNAL 77(12):1509-1515, December 1984.

Hospitalization for miscarriage and delivery outcome among Swedish nurses working in operating rooms 1973-1978, by H. A. Ericson, et al. ANESTHESIA AND ANALGESIA 64(10):981-988, October 1985.

House panel rejects birth control notification. CONGRESSIONAL QUARTERLY WEEKLY REPORT 43:943, May 18, 1985.

House prohibits use of DC funds for abortion, by L. Sorrel. OFF OUR BACKS 15(8): 10, August 1985.

Household fertility decisions in West Africa: a comparison of male and female survey results, by F. L. Mott, et al. STUDIES IN FAMILY PLANNING 16(2):88-99, March-April 1985.

How IUDs cause infertility, by I. Anderson. NEW SCIENTIST 106:6, April 18, 1985.

How the number of living sons influences contraceptive use in Menoufia Governorate, Egypt, by S. Gadalla, et al. STUDIES IN FAMILY PLANNING 16(3):164-169, May-June 1985.

How patients view mandatory waiting periods for abortion, by M. Lupfer, et al. FAMILY PLANNING PERSPECTIVES 13(2):75-79, 1981.

How reliable is female sterilization? 211 pregnancies after 35,599 operations, by V. Odlind, et al. LAKARTIDNINGEN 81(38):3357-3358, September 19, 1984.

How risky is the pill? ECONOMIST 295:16, April 6, 1985.

How Robins will go on paying for the Dalkon Shield, by C. S. Eklund, et al. BUSINESS WEEK April 15, 1985, p. 50.

How to go off the pill. MCCALLS 112:79-80, November 1984.

Human sterilization emerging technologies and reemerging social issues. SCIENCE, TECHNOLOGY AND HUMAN VALUES 9(3):8, Summer 1984.

Husband or wife? A multivariate analysis of decision making for voluntary sterilization, by M. D. Clark, et al. JOURNAL OF FAMILY ISSUES 3(3):341-360, 1982.

Hydatidiform mole with a coexistent fetus, by H. A. Sande, et al. ACTA OBSTETRICIA ET GYNECOLOGICA SCANDINAVICA 64(4):353-355, 1985.

Hypergonadotropic amenorrhea following laparoscopic tubal sterilization, by A. W. Kowatsch, et al. WIENER KLINISCHE WOCHENSCHRIFT 97(11):504-505, May 24, 1985.

Hyperprolactinemia and contraception: a prospective study, by A. A. Luciano, et al. OBSTETRICS AND GYNECOLOGY 65(4):506-510, April 1985.

Hypocrisy of abortion, by A. J. Longo. CANADIAN MEDICAL ASSOCIATION JOURNAL 133(1):13-14, July 1, 1985.

Hypothalamic-pituitary function in women after abortion or premature labor, by H. Morishita, et al. NIPPON SANKA FUJINKA GAKKAI ZASSHI 36(10):1807-1812, October 1984.

I had an abortion; I kept my baby, by M. A. Kellogg. SEVENTEEN 43:144-145+, October 1984.

IUD, by P. Duchesne. COMMUNIQU'ELLES 11(4):5, July 1985.

IUD alert [Dalkon Shield], by C. SerVaas. SATURDAY EVENING POST 257:108-109, January-February 1985.

IUD-infertility link, by J. Silberner. SCIENCE NEWS 127:229, April 13, 1985.

IUDs and infertility. AMERICAN FAMILY PHYSICIAN 31:244+, June 1985.

—. MCCALLS 112:57, August 1985.

IVF versus nature [letter], by R. Winston, et al. LANCET 1(8423):284, February 2, 1985.

Identification of fetal bloodstains by enzyme-linked immunosorbent assay for human a-fetoprotein, by Y. Katsumata. JOURNAL OF FORENSIC SCIENCES 30(4): 1210-1215, October 1985.

Ideology and politics at Mexico City: the United States at the 1984 International Conference on population. POPULATION AND DEVELOPMENT REVIEW 11(1):1, March 1985.

Ideology of the general interest and legislative issues concerning abortion, by B. M. Pereira. REVUE DE L'INSTITUT DE SOCIOLOGIE 1-2:239-256, 1984.

Idolized pill: a pill to be gilded . . . or resistance to oral contraception, by M. Debout. PSYCHOLOGIE MEDICALE 14(8):1173-1179, June 1982.

IgM gammopathy and the lupus anticoagulant syndrome in habitual aborters, by N. Gleicher, et al. JAMA 253(22):3278-3281, June 14, 1985.

Illegally induced abortion observation at Ramathibodi Hospital, by S. Pongthai, et al. JOURNAL OF THE MEDICAL ASSOCIATION OF THAILAND 67(Suppl. 2):50-53, October 1984.

Illicit abortion, a public health problem in Kinshasa (Zaire), by K. Tshibangu, et al. JOURNAL DE GYNECOLOGIE, OBSTETRIQUE ET BIOLOGIE DE LA REPRO-DUCTION 13(7):759-763, 1984.

Illinois abortion statute for incompetent persons struck down. MENTAL AND PHYSI-CAL DISABILITY LAW REPORTER 8(5):450, September-October 1984.

Immediate postabortal contraception with Norplant: levonorgestrel, gonadotropin, estradiol, and progesterone levels over two postabortal months and return of fertility after removal of Norplant capsules, by H. Kurunmäki, et al. CONTRA-CEPTION 30(5):431-442, November 1984.

Immunisation can prevent miscarriage. NEW SCIENTIST 106:20, May 9, 1985.

Immunogenetic studies of spontaneous abortion in mice. Preimmunization of females with allogeneic cells, by N. Kiger, et al. JOURNAL OF IMMUNOLOGY 134(5):2966-2970, May 1985.

Immunogenicity and the vascular risk of oral contraceptives, by C. Plowright, et al. BRITISH HEART JOURNAL 53(5):556-561, May 1985.

Immunogenicity of synthetic sex hormones and thrombogenesis, by V. Beaumont, et al. PATHOLOGIE BIOLOGIE 33(4):245-249, April 1985.

Immunology of abortion, by J. F. Mowbray, et al. CLINICAL AND EXPERIMENTAL IMMUNOLOGY 60(1):1-7, April 1985.

Impact of development and population policies on fertility in India, by A. K. Jain. STUDIES IN FAMILY PLANNING 16:181-198, July-August 1985.

Impact of family planning programs on fertility, by J. D. Sherris, et al. POPULATION REPORTS (29):1733-1771, January-February 1985.

Impact of family planning service in rural Yangoru, by P. Roscoe. PAPUA NEW GUINEA MEDICAL JOURNAL 27(1):16-19, March 1984.

Impact of the Hyde amendment on Congress, by S. Tolchin. WOMEN AND POLITICS 5(1):1, Spring 1985.

Impact of PKU on the reproductive patterns in collaborative study families, by J. K. Burns, et al. AMERICAN JOURNAL OF MEDICAL GENETICS 19(3):515-524, November 1984.

Impacts of behavioral intentions, social support, and accessibility on contraception: a cross-cultural study, by S. Kar, et al. POPULATION AND ENVIRONMENT 7(1): 17-31, Spring 1984.

Impairment of caffeine clearance by chronic use of low-dose oestrogen-containing oral contraceptives, by D. R. Abernethy, et al. EUROPEAN JOURNAL OF CLINI-CAL PHARMACOLOGY 28(4):425-428, 1985.

Implementation of abortion policy in Canada as a women's issue, by S. A. McDaniel. ATLANTIS 10:74-91, Spring 1985.

Importance of the ketamine-flunitrazepam combination in elective abortion, by R. Cordebar. CAHIERS D'ANESTHESIOLOGIE 32(Suppl. 8):59-63, December 1984.

Importance of replicating a failure to replicate: order effects on abortion items, by G. F. Bishop, et al. PUBLIC OPINION QUARTERLY 49(1):105-114, 1985.

Impossible choice [abortion vs. defective child], by M. V. Hunt. MCCALLS 112:44+, July 1985.

In the bombsight: abortion clinics. U S NEWS AND WORLD REPORT 98:8, January 14, 1985.

In defense of women's right to abortion, by P. Grogan. MILITANT 48(45):5, December 7, 1984.

In praise of Laminaria . . . seaweed to dilate the cervix. EMERGENCY MEDICINE 17(5):153+, March 15, 1985.

In Turner's syndrome womanhood is important and not chromosomes, by E. M. Sarroe. SYGEPLEJERSKEN 84(31):14-15, August 1, 1984.

In vitro amplification of toxic shock syndrome toxin-1 by intravaginal devices, by P. M. Tierno, Jr., et al. CONTRACEPTION 31(2):185-194, February 1985.

In vitro and in vivo evaluation of latex condoms using a two-phase nonoxynol 9 system, by N. Rodgers-Neame, et al. FERTILITY AND STERILITY 43(6):931-936, June 1985.

In vitro growth and chromosome constitution of placental cells. I. Spontaneous and elective abortions, by P. A. Hunt, et al. CYTOGENETICS AND CELL GENETICS 39(1):1-6, 1985.

Incidence of chromosome anomalies in 123 married couples with reproductive loss, by M. Lukácová, et al. BRATISLAVSKE LEKARSKE LISTY 83(6):658-669, June 1985.

Incidence of gestational trophoblastic disease in induced abortion, by S. Tangtrakul, et al. JOURNAL OF THE MEDICAL ASSOCIATION OF THAILAND 67(Suppl. 2:54-55, October 1984.

Incidence, significance and remission of tubal spasm during attempted hysteroscopic tubal sterilization, by J. M. Cooper, et al. JOURNAL OF REPRODUCTIVE MEDICINE 30(1):39-42, January 1985.

Incomplete abortion, by A. P. Kiriushchenkov. FEL'DSHER I AKUSHERKA 49(7):46-50, July 1984.

Increased frequency of lymphocytic mitotic non-disjunction in recurrent spontaneous aborters, by R. C. Juberg, et al. JOURNAL OF MEDICAL GENETICS 22(1):32-35, February 1985.

Increased UDP-glucuronyltransferase in putative preneoplastic foci of human liver after long-term use of oral contraceptives, by G. Fischer, et al. NATURWISSENSCHAFTEN 72(5):277-278, May 1985.

Increasing appointment keeping by reducing the call-appointment interval, by J. Benjamin-Bauman, et al. JOURNAL OF APPLIED BEHAVIOR ANALYSIS 17:295-301, Fall 1984.

Indications for prevalence and implications of hysterectomy: a discussion, by K. Wijma, et al. JOURNAL OF PSYCHOSOMATIC OBSTETRICS AND GYNECOLOGY 3(2):69-77, August 1984.

Indrani and Nirmaladevi speak out. OFF OUR BACKS 14(10):4, November 1984.

Induced abortion by the suction method. An analysis of complication rates, by B. I. Nesheim. ACTA OBSTETRICIA ET GYNECOLOGICA SCANDINAVICA 63(7): 591-595, 1984.

Induced abortion operations and their early sequelae. Joint study of the Royal College of General Practitioners and the Royal College of Obstetricians and Gynaecologists. JOURNAL OF THE ROYAL COLLEGE OF GENERAL PRACTITIONERS 35(273):175-180, April 1985.

Infant K's case. MACLEANS 98:21, May 13, 1985.

Inflationary note from India: the going rate for sterilization, by C. Levine. HASTINGS CENTER REPORT 15:3, April 1985.

Influence of cigarette smoke and treatment with contraceptive hormones on the fibrinolytic activity in the rat, by A. Kjaeldgaard, et al. THROMBOSIS RESEARCH 36(6):571-578, December 15, 1984.

Influence of client-provider relationships on teenage women's subsequent use of contraception, by C. A. Nathanson, et al. AMERICAN JOURNAL OF PUBLIC HEALTH 75(1):33-38, January 1985.

Influence of parents, church, and peers on the sexual attitudes and behaviors of college students, by L. R. Daugherty, et al. ARCHIVES OF SEXUAL BEHAVIOR 13(4):351-359, August 1984.

Influence of sexual level of knowledge in contraceptive devices and venereal diseases on pelvic infections, by M. Shiloach. AHOT BE YISRAEL 39(124):9-12, June 1984.

Inhibiting effect of artificial cryptorchidism on spermatogenesis, by R. Mieusset, et al. FERTILITY AND STERILITY 43(4):589-594, April 1985.

Inhibition by gossypol of testosterone production by mouse Leydig cells in vitro, by A. Donaldson, et al. CONTRACEPTION 31(2):165-171, February 1985.

Inhibition of luteal phase progesterone levels in the rhesus monkey by epostane, by B. W. Snyder, et al. CONTRACEPTION 31(5):479-486, May 1985.

Inhibition of 3 beta-hydroxysteroid dehydrogenase (3 beta-HSD) activity in first- and second-trimester human pregnancy and the luteal phase using Epostane, by N. S. Pattison. FERTILITY AND STERILITY 42(6):875-881, December 1984.

Initiating contraceptive use: how do young women decide, by J. E. White. PEDIATRIC NURSING 10(5):347-352, September-October 1984.

Injectable contraception, by M. G. Elder. CLINICAL OBSTETRICS AND GYNAECOLOGY 11(3):723-741, December 1984.

Injectable contraception using depot progestagens, by V. V. Murillo, et al. GINECOLOGIA Y OBSTETRICIA DE MEXICO 51(315):191-197, July 1983.

Institutional abuse tubal sterilization in a population at risk of ill-treating their children, by Y. Englert, et al. CHILD ABUSE AND NEGLECT 9(1):31-35, 1985.

Institutional factors affecting teenagers' choice and reasons for delay in attending a family planning clinic, by L. S. Jabin, et al. FAMILY PLANNING PERSPECTIVES 15(1):25-29, January-February 1983.

Instructions for starting the use of oral contraceptives [letter], by N. B. Loudon, et al. NEW ENGLAND JOURNAL OF MEDICINE 311(25):1634-1635, December 20, 1984.

Integrated family planning services: a Nigerian experience, by O. Ayangade. EAST AFRICAN MEDICAL JOURNAL 61(5):412-419, May 1984.

Interaction between sex hormone binding globulin and levonorgestrel released for vaginal rings in women, by S. Z. Cekan, et al. CONTRACEPTION 31(4):431-439, April 1985.

Interactions between beta-mimetics and indices of feto-placental function, by M. Forcucci-Zulli, et al. MINERVA GINECOLOGIA 37(3):89-92, March 1985.

Interception II: postcoital low-dose estrogens and norgestrel combination in 633 women, by M. R. Van Santen, et al. CONTRACEPTION 31(3):275-293, March 1985.

International dilemma, by A. Finlayson. MACLEANS 97:54, November 19, 1984.

International feminists target sterilization programs. OVERTHROW 6(4):7, December 1984.

Interruption of pregnancy by private physicians. Opinion of the Baden-Würtemberg Superior Court of 1-30-1985, by H. J. Rieger. DEUTSCHE MEDIZINISCHE WOCHENSCHRIFT 110(13):519-521, March 29, 1985.

Interval tubal sterilization in obese women—an assessment of risks, by I. C. Chi, et al. AMERICAN JOURNAL OF OBSTETRICS AND GYNECOLOGY 152(3):292-297, June 1, 1985.

InterVarsity Press bows to pressure, withdraws abortion book, by D. G. Jones. FUNDAMENTALIST JOURNAL 3(10):64, November 1984.

Intervention analysis of the effects of legalized abortion upon U. S. fertility [impact of the 1973 decision of the United States Supreme Court invalidating statutes that restrict access to abortion], by T. D. Hogan. POPULATION RESEARCH AND POLICY REVIEW 3:201-218, October 1984.

Interview with Dr. Henry Morgentaler. CANADIAN MEDICAL ASSOCIATION JOURNAL 133(5):490-495, September 1, 1985.

Interview with a pro-choice activist. INTERNATIONAL VIEWPOINT 71:26, March 11, 1985.

Intestinal absorption of ST-1435 in rats, by P. L. Lähteenmäki. CONTRACEPTION 30(2):143-151, August 1984.

Intracervical administration of prostaglandin E2 prior to vacuum aspiration. A prospective double-blind randomized study, by T. Iversen, et al. INTERNATIONAL JOURNAL OF GYNAECOLOGY AND OBSTETRICS 23(2):95-99, April 1985.

Intramuscular administration of Prostin for abortion in the second trimester, by F. Curic, et al. JUGOSLAVENSKA GINEKOLOGIJA I OPSTETRICIJA 24(3-4):68-70, May-August 1984.

Intraperitoneal bleeding from ectopic decidua following hormonal contraception. Case report, by L. C. Tang, et al. BRITISH JOURNAL OF OBSTETRICS AND GYNAECOLOGY 92(1):102-103, January 1985.

Intrauterine and ectopic pregnancies after a tubal ligation with documented tubal occlusion, by A. G. Shapiro. SOUTHERN MEDICAL JOURNAL 78(8):1014-1015, August 1985.

Intrauterine bone contraceptive device: an accident of nature, by Y. F. Dajani, et al. FERTILITY AND STERILITY 43(1):149-150, January 1985.

Intra-uterine contraceptive devices, by J. Elias. PRACTITIONER 229(1403):431-436, May 1985.

Intrauterine device insertion following induced abortion, by L. Querido, et al. CONTRACEPTION 31(6):603-610, 1985.

Intrauterine devices and long-term risks, by E. Michaels. CHATELAINE 58:18, February 1985.

Intrauterine hematoma: a prognostic enigma in threatened abortion, by F. R. Raymond, et al. JOURNAL OF THE AMERICAN OSTEOPATHIC ASSOCIATION 85(1):65-70, January 1985.

Intrauterine synechiae complicated with threatened abortion and preterm labor. Combined therapy with terbutaline and magnesium sulfate, by T. Kawarabayashi, et al. ASIA-OCEANIA JOURNAL OF OBSTETRICS AND GYNAECOLOGY 10(4): 449-455, December 1984.

Invasive cervical cancer and combined oral contraceptives [letter], by J. A. Fortney, et al. BRITISH MEDICAL JOURNAL 290(6481):1587, May 25, 1985.

Investigations on Dierrenbachia amoena Gentil. I: Endocrine effects and contraceptive activity, by R. Costa de Pasquale, et al. JOURNAL OF ETHNOPHARMACOLOGY 12(3):293-303, December 1984.

Ireland sex and violence in the Dail. ECONOMIST 294:40+, February 23, 1985.

Irish bastards, by S. G.r Davies. SPECTATOR 254:11, February 2, 1985.

Iron stores in users of oral contraceptive agent, by E. P. Frassinelli-Gunderson, et al. AMERICAN JOURNAL OF CLINICAL NUTRITION 41:703-712, April 1985.

Is the boycott against the Upjohn Company working. CHRISTIANITY TODAY 29(15): 45-46, October 18, 1985.

Is Depo Provera still being incautiously used?, by P. Cohen. NEW STATESMAN 108:6, October 19, 1984.

Is Rome anti-Catholic?, by P. Steinfels. COMMONWEAL 112:4-5, January 11, 1985.

Islam and birth planning: an interview with the Grand Mufti of Egypt. POPULI 2(2):40, 1984.

Islamic populations: limited demographic transition, by J. I. Clarke. GEOGRAPHY 70:118-128, April 1985.

Italy: abortion and nationalized health care, by M. Mori. HASTINGS CENTER REPORT 14:22-23, December 1984.

Japanese miscarriages blamed on computer terminals. NEW SCIENTIST 106:7, May 23, 1985.

Jerry Falwell meets the sisters of Justice [Columbus, Ohio, radical feminist group protests Falwell's ideas, especially the opposition to abortion rights], by B. Khan. OFF OUR BACKS 16:15, February 1986.

Journal from an obscure place: thoughts on abortion from an unborn child, by J. Miles. JOURNAL OF CHRISTIAN NURSING 1(3):8-12, Fall 1984.

Judge biased against Robins, court says, by S. Tarnott. BUSINESS INSURANCE 18:2+, November 12, 1984.

Judging risks versus benefits of oral contraceptives [editorial], by J. K. Jones, et al. CLINICAL PHARMACY 3(5):521-522, September-October 1984.

Judgment without justice: abortion on demand 10 years later, by J.Falwell. FUNDAMENTALIST JOURNAL 2(1):8-35, January 1983.

Judicial decision making and biological fact: Roe v. Wade and the unresolved question of fetal viability, by R. H. Blank. WESTERN POLITICAL QUARTERLY 37: 584-602, December 1984.

Jury discards abortion law; AG ponder appeal, by L. Waldorf. BODY POLITIC (109):9, December 1984.

Just the facts [networks reject a TV spot]. TIME 126:57, August 19, 1985.

Justice asks Supreme Court to overturn Roe/Wade, by M. Anderson. NATIONAL NOW TIMES 18(5):1, August 1985.

Justice asks court to reverse Roe v. Wade (which declared abortion on demand to be a constitutional right). HUMAN EVENTS 45:5, July 27, 1985.

Justice asks Supreme Court to overturn Roe/Wade, by M. Anderson. NATIONAL NOW TIMES 18(5):1, August 1985.

Justice Department wants Roe reversal; NOW protests, by L. Sorrel. OFF OUR BACKS 15(8):10, August 1985.

Justice O'Connor, the constitution, and the trimester approach to abortion: a liberty on a collision course with itself, by R. F. Duncan. CATHOLIC LAWYER 29:275-285, Summer 1984.

Karyotype in couples with spontaneous abortion, by F. Bernardi, et al. MINERVA GINECOLOGIA 36(7-8):391-394, July-August 1984.

Know thyself—adolescents self-asessment of compliance behavior, by I. F. Litt. PEDIATRICS 75(4):693-696, April 1985.

Knowledge, attitude and practice of family planning in Hausa women, by N. Rehan. SOCIAL SCIENCE AND MEDICINE 18(10):839-844, 1984.

Labor force participation and fertility: a social analysis of their antecedents and simultaneity, by M. Van Loo. HUMAN RELATIONS 37:941-968, November 1984.

Lack of tubal occlusion by intrauterine quinacrine and tetracycline in the primate, by L. J. Zaneveld, et al. CONTRACEPTION 30(2):161-167, August 1984.

Lactation promoting contraception, by K. Biering-Sørensen, et al. UGESKRIFT FOR LAEGER 147(14):1213, April 1, 1985.

Laparoscopic findings and contraceptive use in women with signs and symptoms suggestive of acute salpingitis, by P. Wølner-Hanssen, et al. OBSTETRICS AND GYNECOLOGY 66(2):233-238, August 1985.

Laparoscopic salpingoclasia. Comparative study of 3 methods, by J. Vázquez Méndez, et al. GINECOLOGIA Y OBSTETRICIA DE MEXICO 53(335):75-78, March 1985.

Laparoscopic sterilization in a free-standing clinic: a report of 1,092 cases, by S. Y. Lee, et al. CONTRACEPTION 30(6):545-553, December 1984.

Laparoscopic sterilization of the bitch and queen by uterine horn occlusion, by D. E. Wildt, et al. AMERICAN JOURNAL OF VETERINARY RESEARCH 46(4):864-869, April 1985.

Laparoscopic tubal sterilization. Endothermy coagulation and cross-clipping, by O. Storeide, et al. TIDSSKRIFT FOR DEN NORSKE LAEGEFORENING 104(23): 1544-1545, August 20, 1984.

Laparoscopy in the puerperium, by A. Molina Sosa, et al. GINECOLOGIA Y OBSTET-
RICIA DE MEXICO 51(319):301-306, November 1983.

Late abortions and the crime of child destruction: a reply [and] a rejoinder, by V.
Tunkel, et al. CRIMINAL LAW REVIEW March 1985, p. 133-142.

Late complications of medical termination of pregnancy: a study in the civil hospital,
Surat, by C. Somasundaram, et al. JOURNAL OF FAMILY WELFARE 30:76-84,
June 1984.

Late infertile days in early postpartum cycles, by L. I. Hatherley. CLINICAL REPRO-
DUCTION AND FERTILITY 3(1):73-80, March 1985.

Late is too late. ECONOMIST August 17, 1985, p. 25.

Latest views on pill prescribing, by C. R. Kay. JOURNAL OF THE ROYAL COLLEGE
OF GENERAL PRACTITIONERS 34(268):611-614, November 1984.

Law pregnancy interruption and the consequences for the nurse burdened by conscience, by H. Hulsebosch. TIJDSCHRIFT VOR ZIEKENVERPLEGING 37(24):
754-757, November 27, 1984.

Laws and policies affecting fertility: a decade of change. POPULATION REPORTS
12(6):105, November 1984.

Learning the facts of life [legal contraception], by T. Clifton. NEWSWEEK 105:48,
March 11, 1985.

Learning the "real" facts of life [interview with J. Irving]. GLAMOUR 83:118+, July
1985.

Legacy of life, by T. Elkins. CHRISTIANITY TODAY 29(1):18-25, January 18, 1985.

Legal abortion in England and Wales, by D. B. Paintin. CIBA FOUNDATION SYM-
POSIA 115:4-20, 1985.

Legal abortion in Italy: 1980-1981, by S. L. Tosi, et al. FAMILY PLANNING PER-
SPECTIVES 17:19-23, January-February 1985.

Legal abortion: limits and contributions to human life, by R. J. Cook. CIBA FOUN-
DATION SYMPOSIA 115:211-227, 1985.

Legal aspects of medical genetics in Wisconsin, by E. W. Clayton. WISCONSIN
MEDICAL JOURNAL 84(3):28-32, March 1985.

Legal issues in sterilization using tubal coagulation, by G. H. Schlund. GEBURT-
SHILFE UND FRAUENHEILKUNDE 44(10):692-693, October 1984.

Legalized abortion: the Singapore experience. STUDIES IN FAMILY PLANNING
16(3):170, May-June 1985.

Legislation on contraception and abortion for adolescents, by R. Roemer. STUD-
IES IN FAMILY PLANNING 16:241-251, September-October 1985.

Liberty and family rights, by R. Stott. CANADIAN FORUM 64:20-21+, November
1984.

Life or death split in America, by C. Thomas. TIMES February 13, 1985, p. 11.

Liittle changes in 14 years in attitudes on abortion. JET 69:5, September 16, 1985.

Little give-and-take in abortion debate, by J. Walsh. IN THESE TIMES 9(10):3, January 30, 1985.

Long-term effects of Depo-Provera on carbohydrate and lipid metabolism, by D. F. Liew, et al. CONTRACEPTION 31(1):51-64, January 1985.

Long-term experience with Norplant contraceptive implants in Finland, by P. Holma. CONTRACEPTION 31(3):231-241, March 1985.

Long-term follow-up of children breast-fed by mothers receiving depot-medroxy-progesterone acetate, by J. Jimenez, et al. CONTRACEPTION 30(6):523-533, December 1984.

Long-term regret among 216 sterilized women. A six-year follow-up investigation, by P. E. Børdahl. SCANDINAVIAN JOURNAL OF SOCIAL WORK 13(1):41-47, 1985.

Long-term risk of menstrual disturbances after tubal sterilization, by F. DeStefano, et al. AMERICAN JOURNAL OF OBSTETRICS AND GYNECOLOGY 152(7 Pt 1): 835-841, August 1, 1985.

Long-term toxicity of a hydrogelic occlusive device in the isthmus of the human oviduct. A light microscopic study, by J. Brundin, et al. ACTA PATHOLOGICA ET MICROBIOLOGICA SCANDINAVICA 93(3):121-126, May 1985.

Long view of elder activists, by A. Braden. SOUTHERN EXPOSURE 13(2):34, March 1985.

Looking past abortion rhetoric, by J. A. Brix. CHRISTIAN CENTURY 101:986-988, October 24, 1984.

Low-dose prostaglandin E2 analogue for cervical dilatation prior to pregnancy termination, by M. Borten, et al. AMERICAN JOURNAL OF OBSTETRICS AND GYNECOLOGY 150(5 Pt 1):561-565, November 1, 1984.

Low risk reversible [male] contraceptive tested. CANADIAN NURSE 81:15, September 1985.

Luteinizing hormone releasing hormone analogues for contraception, by S. J. Nillius. CLINICAL OBSTETRICS AND GYNECOLOGY 11(3):551-572, December 1984.

Magazine versus physicians: the influence of information source on intentions to use oral contraceptives, by D. F. Halpern, et al. WOMEN AND HEALTH 10(1):9-23, Spring 1985.

Maguires' ire [discussion of January 11, 1985 article, Is Rome anti-Catholic?], by P. Steinfels. COMMONWEAL 112:130+, March 8, 1985.

Mainline churches reassess prochoice stand on abortion [Protestant denominations]. CHRISTIANITY TODAY 28:72, December 14, 1984.

Make sure your diaphragm is still protecting you. GLAMOUR 83:80, April 1985.

Making the decision for female sterilization, by A. Alvarado Durán, et al. GINECOLOGIA Y OBSTETRICIA DE MEXICO 51(313):131-136, May 1983.

Making distinctions [discussion of February 8, 1985 article, Understanding Mario Cuomo], by J. Tagg. NATIONAL REVIEW 37:36+, April 5, 1985.

Making news: Asian women in the west, by U. Butalia. ISIS 1984, p. 114.

Making of the pill, by C. Djerassi. SCIENCE 5:127-129, November 1984.

Malaysian integrated population program performance: its relation to organizational and integration factors [family planning with health], by C. O. Fong. MANAGEMENT SCIENCE 31:50-65, January 1985.

Male attitudes towards family planning in Khartoum, Sudan, by M. A. Mustafa, et al. JOURNAL OF BIOSOCIAL SCIENCE16(4):437-449, October 1984.

Male contraception. Gonadal and adrenal functions in men treated with medroxy-progesterone, by M. Roger, et al. PATHOLOGIE BIOLOGIE 32(8):895-898, October 1984.

Male contraception—a review, by D. Donaldson. JOURNAL OF THE ROYAL SOCIETY OF HEALTH 105(3):91-98, June 1985.

Male ideology of privacy! A feminist perspective on the right of abortion, by C. MacKinnon. RADICAL AMERICAN 17(4):23-35, 1983.

Malformations and chromosome anomalies in spontaneously aborted fetuses with single umbilical artery, by J. Byrne, et al. AMERICAN JOURNAL OF OBSTETRICS AND GYNECOLOGY 151(3):340-342, February 1, 1985.

Managing patients on oral contraceptives, by M. Block, et al. AMERICAN FAMILY PHYSICIAN 32(2):154-168, August 1985.

Mandatory parental involvement in contraceptive services for minors, by K. H. Gould. SOCIAL WORK IN EDUCATION 7(1):7-12, 1984.

Margaret Sanger and the International Planned Parenthood Federation, by M. Golden. AFER 27:109-114, April 1985.

Mario and Gerry had it coming. (their lambasting from American bishops over abortion), by P. J. Buchanan. HUMAN EVENTS 44:5, August 23, 1984.

Mario slips through [views of M. Cuomo], by D. R. Carlin, Jr. COMMONWEAL 112: 392-393, July 12, 1985.

Marriage in the Greek Orthodox Church, by D. J. Constantelos. JOURNAL OF ECUMENICAL STUDIES 22:21-27, Winter 1985.

Marriage in Roman Catholicism, by D. L. Carmody. JOURNAL OF ECUMENICAL STUDIES 22:28-40, Winter 1985.

Marvelon—an OC with a new progestagen. DRUG AND THERAPEUTICS BULLETIN 22(18):69-70, September 1984.

Mass media and population problem in Egypt [3 articles]. POPULATION STUDIES 11:41-60, April-June 1984.

Maternal age-specific rates of numerical chromosome abnormalities with special reference to trisomy, by T. Hassold, et al. HUMAN GENETICS 70(1):11-17, 1985.

Maternal antipaternal immunity in couples predisposed to repeated pregnancy losses, by P. R. McConnachie, et al. AMERICAN JOURNAL OF REPRODUCTIVE IMMUNOLOGY 5(4):145-150, June 1984.

Maternal employment and the chromosomal characteristics of spontaneously aborted conceptions, by J. Silverman, et al. JOURNAL OF OCCUPATIONAL MEDICINE 27(6):427-438, June 1985.

Maternal lactation as a method of contraception? 1. The epidemiology of maternal lactation in a suburban region of Tunis, by S. Khadraoui, et al. TUNISIE MEDICALE 61(6):431-437, November-December 1983.

—2. The epidemiology of postpartum amenorrhea, by H. Chaabouni, et al. TUNISIE MEDICALE 62(1):83-90, January-February 1984.

—3. Comparison of maternal lactation with current methods of contraception, by A. Fourati, et al. TUNISIE MEDICALE 62(2):137-141, March-April 1984.

Maternal reproductive loss and cleft lip with or without cleft palate in human embryos, by K. Shiota. AMERICAN JOURNAL OF MEDICAL GENETICS 19(1):121-129, September 1984.

Meaning of the abortion conflict, by Carole Joffe. CONTEMPORARY SOCIOLOGY 14(1):26-29, January 1985.

Meaning of Morgentaler [acquittal in Toronto abortion clinic trial; special section]. MACLEANS 97:44-50+, November 19, 1984.

Meaning of motherhood [review article], by B. Townsend. AMERICAN DEMO-GRAPHICS 7:8+, January 1985.

Meanings of the notion "desire for a child": some considerations based on an empir-ical study of 400 patients applying for legal abortion, by A. T. Teichmann. JOUR-NAL OF PSYCHOSOMATIC OBSTETRICS AND GYNAECOLOGY 3(3-4):215-222, December 1984.

Measuring accessibility to family planning services in rural Thailand, by N. Chayovan, et al. STUDIES IN FAMILY PLANNING 15:201-211, September-October 1984.

Measuring early pregnancy loss: laboratory and field methods, by A. J. Wilcox, et al. FERTILITY AND STERILITY 44(3):366-374, September 1985.

Measuring the effect of sex preference on fertility: the case of Korea. DEMO-GRAPHY 22(2):280, May 1985.

Medicaid and abortion, by R. A. McCormick. THEOLOGICAL STUDIES 45(4):715-721, 1984.

Medical clinical responsibility in control studies in pregnancy and curettage of the uterus long after fetal death, by G. H. Schlund. GEBURTSHILFE UND FRAUEN-HEILKUNDE 44(12):827-828, December 1984.

Medical criminals: physicians and white-collar offenses, by P. D. Jesilow, et al. JUSTICE QUARTERLY 2(2):149-165, June 1985.

Medical progress and the social implications of abortion: summing-up, by M. Potts. CIBA FOUNDATION SYMPOSIA 115:263-268, 1985.

Medical Termination of Pregnancy Act1983 (Barbados), by P. K. Menon. INTER-NATIONAL AND COMPARATIVE LAW QUARTERLY 34:630-636, July 1985.

Medroxyprogesterone acetate does not perturb the profile of steroid metabolites in urine during pregnancy, by J. L. Yovich, et al. JOURNAL OF ENDOCRINOLOGY 104(3):453-459, March 1985.

Men and abortion. FUTURIST 19:60-62, April 1985.

Men with ties to church arrested for abortion clinic bombings. CHRISTIANITY TODAY 29:34-35, March 1, 1985.

Menses induction in rhesus monkeys using a controlled-release vaginal delivery system containing (15S) 15-methyl prostaglandin F2 alpha methyl ester, by C. H. Spilman, et al. FERTILITY AND STERILITY 42(4):638-643, October 1984.

Menstrual cycle from a bio-behavioral approach: a comparison of oral contraceptive and non-contraceptive users, by K. F. Garrett, et al. INTERNATIONAL JOURNAL OF PSYCHOPHYSIOLOGY 1(2):209-214, February 1984.

Menstrual induction: surgery versus prostaglandins, by D. T. Baird, et al. CIBA FOUNDATION SYMPOSIA 115:178-191, 1985.

Menstrual pattern changes following minilap/Pomeroy, minilap/ring and laparoscopy /ring sterilization: a review of 5982 cases, by P. P. Bhiwandiwala, et al. INTERNATIONAL JOURNAL OF GYNAECOLOGY AND OBSTETRICS 22(3):251-256, June 1984.

Menstrual patterns after female sterilization: variables predicting change, by L. P. Cole, et al. STUDIES IN FAMILY PLANNING 15:242, September-October 1984.

Menstrual regulation by (15S)-15 methyl prostaglandin F2 alpha by intramuscular route, by P. R. Bhattacharaya, et al. ASIA-OCEANIA JOURNAL OF OBSTETRICS AND GYNAECOLOGY 10(4):435-437, December 1984.

Mental health and female sterilization: a follow-up. Report of a WHO Collaborative prospective study. JOURNAL OF BIOSOCIAL SCIENCE 17(1):1-18, January 1985.

Mesenteric vein thrombosis associated with oral contraceptive administration during pregnancy, by M. Friedman, et al. ANNALES CHIRURGIAE ET GYNACOLOGIAE 73(5):296-298, 1984.

Mesenteric venous thrombosis and oral contraceptive use, by V. Naraynsingh, et al. TROPICAL AND GEOGRAPHICAL MEDICINE 37(2):192-193, June 1985.

Metabolic and vascular consequences of hormonal contraception in non-diabetics, by A. Basdevant, et al. JOURNEES ANNUELLES DE DIABETOLOGIE DE L'HOTEL -DIEU 1983, p. 223-237.

Metabolism of 14-C-arachidonic acid in platelets and antiaggregatory potency of prostacyclin in women taking oral contraceptives, by K. Jaschonek, et al. PROSTAGLANDINS LEUKOTRIENES AND MEDICINE 15(2):275-276, August 1984.

Metronidazole prophylaxis in elective first trimester abortion, by L. Heisterberg, et al. OBSTETRICS AND GYNECOLOGY 65(3):371-374, March 1985.

Microbial flora in septic abortion, by R. M. Nava y Sánchez, et al. GINECOLOGIA Y OBSTETRICIA DE MEXICO 51(317):229-235, September 1983.

Microbiological and histological findings in the fallopian tubes of women using various contraceptive methods, by J. A. Collins, et al. CONTRACEPTION 30(5):457-466, November 1984.

Mid-trimester pregnancy termination in teenage women, by J. Misra, et al. JOURNAL OF THE INDIAN MEDICAL ASSOCIATION 83(1):9-10, January 1985.

Mid-trimester pregnancy termination with ethacridine lactate, by S. Shukla, et al. JOURNAL OF THE INDIAN MEDICAL ASSOCIATION 82(12):432-434, December 1984.

Midtrimester termination of pregnancy using intravaginal gemeprost (16,16 dimethyl-trans delta 2 PGE1 methyl ester, cervagem), by G. V. Nair, et al. SINGAPORE MEDICAL JOURNAL 1985.

Mid-trimester therapeutic abortion by vaginal suppository of 16, 16-dimethyl-trans-delta 2-prostaglandin E1, by K. Kato, et al. ASIA OCEANIA JOURNAL OF OBSTETRICS AND GYNAECOLOGY 11(2):163-167, June 1985.

Migraine drug could be a new contraceptive, by L. Veltman. NEW SCIENTIST 105: 22, March 7, 1985.

Mini pills, IUDs and abortion, by J. F. Kippley. JOURNAL OF CHRISTIAN NURSING 2(1):32, Winter 1985.

Minilaparotomy and laparoscopy: safe, effective, and widely used, by L. Liskin, et al. POPULATION REPORTS (9):C125-167, May 1985.

Minors' right of privacy: access to abortions without parental notification. JOURNAL OF JUVENILE LAW 9:101-105, 1985.

(-)-gossypol: an active male antifertility agent, by S. A. Matlin, et al. CONTRACEPTION 31(2):141-149, February 1985.

Miscarriage: a loss that must be acknowledged. EMOTIONAL FIRST AID: A JOURNAL OF CRISIS INTERVENTION 1(4):43-46, Winter 1984.

'Missed pill' conception: fact of fiction?, by B. G. Molloy, et al. BRITISH MEDICAL JOURNAL 290(6480):1474-1475, May 18, 1985.

'Missed pill' conception: fact or fiction? [letter]. BRITISH MEDICAL JOURNAL 291(6488):136-137, July 13, 1985.

'Missed pill' conception: fact or fiction? [letter], by P. Bye. BRITISH MEDICAL JOURNAL 290(6485):1905, June 22, 1985.

Missed pill conception: fact or fiction? [letter], by S. R. Killick, et al. BRITISH MEDICAL JOURNAL 291(6493):487, August 17, 1985.

Model of fertility control in a Puerto Rican Community, by S. L. Schensul, et al. URBAN ANTHROPOLOGY 11(1):81-99, Spring 1982.

Moderate drinking during pregnancy and foetal outcome, by I. G. Barrison, et al. ALCOHOL AND ALCOHOLISM 19(2):167-172, 1984.

Moral norms: an update, by R. A. McCormick. THEOLOGICAL STUDIES 46:50-64, March 1985.

Moral significance of spontaneous abortion, by T. F. Murphy. JOURNAL OF MEDICAL ETHICS 11(2):79-83, June 1985.

Morality struggle: anti-abortionists gain as the furor spreads and uneasiness grows; they exploit progress made in treatment of fetuses; President's support helps, by E. Hume. WALL STREET JOURNAL 205:1+, April 15, 1985.

Morbidity and mortality from second-trimester abortions, by D. A. Grimes, et al. JOURNAL OF REPRODUCTIVE MEDICINE 30(7):505-514, July 1985.

Morbidity in tubal occlusion by laparoscopy, by F. Castro Carvajal, et al. GINECOL-OGIA Y OBSTETRICIA DE MEXICO 52(321):19-22, January 1984.

Morbidity risk among young adolescents undergoing elective abortion, by R. T. Burkman, et al. CONTRACEPTION 30(2):99-105, August 1984.

More about natural family planning [letter], by L. A. Bennett. AUSTRALIAN FAMILY PHYSICIAN 13(6):396-397, June 1984.

More pick sterilization, but not many black men do. JET 68:39, August 5, 1985.

Morgentaler and abortion, by F. Orr. ALBERTA REPORT 12:34-38, January 28, 1985.

Morgentaler's escalating crusade, by S. McKay. MACLEANS 98:12, August 19, 1985.

Morgentaler's march: acquittal brings his Alberta abortions closer, by A. Elash, et al. ALBERTA REPORT 11:34, November 26, 1984.

Mortality caused by cardiovascular diseases in Denmark before and after the introduction of the pill (letter), by O. Lidegaard. UGESKRIFT FOR LAEGER 147(1):39-40, December 31, 1984.

Mortality due to abortion at Kenyatta National Hospital, 1974-1983, by S. Wanjala, et al. CIBA FOUNDATION SYMPOSIA 115:41-53, 1985.

Mosher affair, by P. V. Ness. WILSON QUARTERLY 8(1):160-172, 1984.

Mother Church and daughter Geraldine. (Geraldine Ferraro and her difficulties with the Church over her stand on abortion). HUMAN EVENTS 44:4+, August 11, 1984.

Motivation for parenthood: a factor analytic study of attitudes towards having children, by J. Stephen Bell, et al. JOURNAL OF COMPARATIVE FAMILY STUDIES 16(1):111-119, Spring 1985.

Mrs. Gillick and the Wisbech Area Health Authority, by J. Griffiths. BRISTOL MEDICO-CHIRURGICAL JOURNAL 100(374):37, April 1985.

Mucus and moonlight: low-tech birth control. UTNE READER 10:17, June 1985.

Multilevel model of family planning availability and contraceptive use in rural Thailand, by B. Entwisle, et al. DEMOGRAPHY 21:559-574, November 1984.

Multiple interventions: a lesson on utility and weakness—Dominican Republic, by J. A. Ballweg. PUBLIC HEALTH REVIEWS 12(3-4):240-245, 1984.

Multivariate analysis of family planning knowledge differentials in rural Ghana. JOURNAL OF FAMILY WELFARE 30:47-60, June 1984.

Muslims battle over birth control, by D. MacKenzie. NEW SCIENTIST 107:21, July 18, 1985.

My baby or my life: how could I choose?. . . hyperemesis gravidarum, by V. Kennedy. JOURNAL OF CHRISTIAN NURSING 1(3):4-6, Fall 1984.

Mycoplasma, ureaplasma and spontaneous abortion. AMERICAN FAMILY PHYSICIAN 27:256, April 1983.

Myth of the month. HEALTH 17:82, February 1985.

NARAL Speakout, by P. De La Fuente. NEW DIRECTIONS FOR WOMEN 14(3):1, May 1985.

NOW challenges hierarchy, by Rogers, et al. NATIONAL NOW TIMES 18(4):1, June 1985.

NOW holds over 30 weekend vigils in abortion clinic, by M. Anderson. NATIONAL NOW TIMES 18(1):3, January 1985.

Nairobi conference [includes outside the Nairobi conference, inside Nairobi, trip to Kibwezi, family planning, International Council of African Women report, find markets (workshop)], by A. Henry. OFF OUR BACKS 15:1-9, November 1985.

Naproxen sodium for pain relief in first-trimester abortion, by K. Suprapto, et al. AMERICAN JOURNAL OF OBSTETRICS AND GYNECOLOGY 150(8):1000-1001, December 15, 1984.

Nation since "Blood Monday."(political aspects of the abortion issue), by P. B. Gemma, Jr. CONSERVATIVE DIGEST 11:16, February 1985.

Natural family planning [discussion of May 1985 article, comparing contraceptives], by J. Willis. FDA CONSUMER 19:2, September 1985.

Natural family planning (NFP) (letter), by G. Luh-Hardegg. GEBURTSHILFE UND FRAUENHEILKUNDE 44(12):829-830, December 1984.

Natural family planning in Mauritas, Indian Ocean: utilization patterns and continuance predictors, by G. L. Conner, et al. JOURNAL OF SOCIAL SERVICE RESEARCH 8(1):29-48, 1984.

National Family Welfare Programme in India, by C. S. Dawn. JOURNAL OF THE INDIAN MEDICAL ASSOCIATION 82(5):177-180, May 1984.

Natural methods of family planning, by A. M. Flynn. CLINICAL OBSTETRICS AND GYNECOLOGY 11(3):661-678, December 1984.

Necessity defense aids protestors, by M. Byrne. IN THESE TIMES 9(27):16, June 12, 1985.

Need for routine sonography prior to late abortion, by F. A. Chervenak, et al. NEW YORK STATE JOURNAL OF MEDICINE 85(1):4-5, January 1985.

Negative effect of the IUCD on the occurrence of heteroploidy—correlated abnormalities in spontaneous abortions: an update, by L. H. Honoré. CONTRACEPTION 31(3):253-260, March 1985.

Neither incompetent nor indifferent, by D. N. O'Steen. COMMENTARY 111:179-182, March 23, 1984.

Nets pressed to run contraceptive ads, by M. Christopher. ADVERTISING AGE 55:66+, October 8, 1984.

Never again/abortion 1954, by S. Matulis. FEMINIST CONNECTION January 1985, p. 1.

New aid in fighting AIDS? [spermicide nonoxynol-9]. NEWSWEEK 105:85, February 18, 1985.

New applications for the assay of placental proteins, by A. Klopper, et al. PLACENTA 6(2):173-184, March-April 1985.

New attacks on abortion clinics, by M. Koppel. INTERCONTINENTAL PRESS 23(3): 87, February 18, 1985.

New birth control implant safer than taking pill [Norplant]. JET 68:29, March 25, 1985.

New civil war, by M. Potts. WORLD PRESS REVIEW 32:44, April 1985.

New class of non-hormonal contragestational agents: pharmacodynamic-pharmacokinetic relationships, by A. Assandri, et al. QUARTERLY REVIEWS ON DRUG METABOLISM AND DRUG INTERACTIONS 4(2-3):237-261, 1982.

New contraceptive tries again, by D. A. Fuller. AD FORUM 6:11+, January 1985.

New HWC guidelines for oral contraceptive users, manufacturers and health professionals, by P. LaCroix. CANADIAN NURSE 81:13, October 1985.

New heat over an old issue, by R. T. Zintl. TIME 125:17, February 4, 1985.

New Jersey constitutional law: Medicaid funding for abortion after Right to Choose v. Byrne. RUTGERS LAW REVIEW 36:665-702, Spring 1984.

New look at progestogens, by K. Fotherby. CLINICAL OBSTETRICS AND GYNAE-COLOGY 11(3):701-722, December 1984.

New method for estimation of illegal abortions, by O. Nørgaard. DANISH MEDICAL BULLETIN 32(1):76-78, March 1985.

New pill: should you take it?, by A. Boroff Eagan. MS MAGAZINE 14:35-36+, October 1985.

New prostaglandin E1 analog in late interruption of pregnancy, in utero deaths and very premature ruptures of the membranes. Apropos of 117 cases, by R. Henrion, et al. JOURNAL DE GYNECOLOGIE, OBSTETRIQUE ET BIOLOGIE DE LA REPRODUCTION 13(8):939-946, 1984.

New technology confab, by J. Stein. NEW DIRECTIONS FOR WOMEN 14(2):7, March 1985.

New technology leaves spayed heifers with ovary tissue [ovarian autograft technique]. SUCCESSFUL FARMING 83:B1, August 1985.

New twist in the abortion funding controversy: Planned Parenthood v. Arizona. DEPAUL LAW REVIEW 33:835-355, Summer 1984.

New woman, the new family and the rationalization of sexuality; the sex reform movement in Germany 1928 to 1933, by A. Grossmann. DAI:THE HUMANITIES AND SOCIAL SCIENCES 45(7), January 1985.

NY Diocese blocks abortion clinic. OFF OUR BACKS 15(3):16, March 1985.

New York's controversial Archbishop, by A. L. Goldman. NEW YORK TIMES MAGA-ZINE October 14, 1984, p. 38+.

Nightmare of Kiko Martinez, by D. Martinez. GUILD NOTES 9(2):4, Spring 1985.

1983 abortion decisions: clarification of the permissible limits of abortion regulation. UNIVERSITY OF RICHMOND LAW REVIEW Fall 1983, p. 137-159.

1983 abortion decisions: Virginia distinguished. MEDICO-LEGAL BULLETIN 32(4): 1-7, July-August 1983.

No aid for abortion. ECONOMIST 294:32, February 16, 1985.

No link is found between 'pill' and breast cancer. JET 68:39, June 24, 1985.

No monolithic view [discussion of September 7, 1984 article, Religion and politics: clearing the air]. COMMONWEAL 111:548+, October 19, 1984.

No more griseofulvin for pill users: another clinically important interaction?, by L. Offerhaus. NEDERLANDS TIJDSCHRIFT VOOR GENEESKUNDE 128(33):1579-1580, August 18, 1984.

No one is realistic about family planning, by Y. A. Eraj. INTERNATIONAL NURSING REVIEW 31(6):179, November-December 1984.

Nobel laureate speaks in defense of unborn life, by Mother Teresa. CHRISTIANITY TODAY 29:62-63, September 6, 1985.

Noncompliance among oral contraceptive acceptors in rural Bangladesh, by B. Seaton. STUDIES IN FAMILY PLANNING 16(1):52-59, January-February 1985.

Non-hormonal methods of contraception in diabetic women. Reliability, risks, precautions, surveillance, by D. Buchsenschutz. JOURNEES ANNUELLES DE DIABETOLOGIE DE L'HOTEL-DIEU 1983, p. 239-252.

Nonimmunologically induced habitual abortion, by E. Maroni. GYNAEKOLOGISCHE RUNDSCHAU 24(Suppl. 1):1-8, 1984.

Not quite the baby I expected . . ., by J. Chase. GOOD HOUSEKEEPING 199:68+, October 1984.

Not Reagan's way. ECONOMIST 292:30+, August 11, 1984.

Notes from the fringe, by M. H. Brown. HARPERS 270:20, June 1985.

Notes on moral theology, by R. A. McCormick. THEOLOGICAL STUDIES 46(1):50-114, 1985.

Nova Scotia responds to Morgentaler. HEALTHSHARING 6(3):7, Summer 1985.

Now what?, by J. Walsh. IN THESE TIMES 9(21):2, April 24, 1985.

Nuptiality, fertility and family planning practices in rural Bangladesh: a case study, by S. B. Bhuyan, et al. JOURNAL OF FAMILY WELFARE 31:62-75, September 1984.

Nurse confident of acquittal, by T. Pugh. BRIARPATCH 14(2):2, March 1985.

Nurses attitude to therapeutic abortion, by C. Webb. NURSING TIMES 81(1):44-47, January 2-8, 1985.

Nutrition and the pill, by L. B. Tyrer. JOURNAL OF REPRODUCTIVE MEDICINE 29(Suppl. 7):547-550, July 1984.

Observation on plasma fibrinogen level in cases of incomplete abortions, by R. B. Thakur. JOURNAL OF THE INDIAN MEDICAL ASSOCIATION 82(10):353-354, October 1984.

Obstacles to successful fertility control in Nigeria, by E. O. Udjo. SOCIAL SCIENCE AND MEDICINE 19(11):1167-1171, 1984.

Obstetric-gynecologic day hospital: analgesia for voluntary interruption of pregnancy, by D. Laveneziana, et al. ANNALI DI OSTETRICIA GINECOLOGIA MEDICINA PERINATALE 106(1):48-51, January-February 1985.

Oestrogen deficiency after tubal ligation, by J. Cattanach. LANCET 1(8433):847-849, April 13, 1985.

Offer they can't refuse, by C. Thomas. CONSERVATIVE DIGEST 11:24, August-September 1985.

On the barricades for abortion rights, by J. Sutherland. FREE SOCIETY 9(1):32, Fall 1984.

On brain death, organ transplantation, artificial abortion, euthanasia and embryo transport, by K. Takagi. NIPPON NAIKA GAKKAI ZASSHI 73(8):1111-1127, August 1984.

On the immunogenicity of the beta subunit of ovine luteinizing hormone (oLH beta) and equine chorionic gonadotropin (eCG) in the chimpanzee (Pan troglodytes): effect of antiserum on monkey cycle and early pregnancy, by N. R. Moudgal, et al. AMERICAN JOURNAL OF REPRODUCTIVE IMMUNOLOGY AND MICRO-BIOLOGY 8(4):120-124, August 1985.

On the origin and histological structure of adenocarcinoma of the endocervix in women under 50 years of age, by G. Dallenbach-Hellweg. PATHOLOGY, RESEARCH, AND PRACTICE 179(1):38-50, September 1984.

On pills, IUDs and condoms, by S. Evangelista. BALAI 11:21, 1985.

On risks, costs of sterilization [letter], by D. A. Grimes, et al. AMERICAN JOURNAL OF PUBLIC HEALTH 75(10):1230, October 1985.

One-child population policy, modernization, and the extended Chinese family, by C. Xiangming. JOURNAL OF MARRIAGE AND THE FAMILY 47:193-202, February 1985.

One son is no sons [India], by S. A. Freed, et al. NATURAL HISTORY 94:10+, January 1985.

Oops! There goes your right to choose, by H. Levine. GUARDIAN 37(41):7, August 7, 1985.

Open all hours . . . birth control clinic, by J. Seymour. NURSNG MIRROR AND MID-WIVES JOURNAL 161(16):22-24, October 16, 1985.

Opinions and opinion changes of white South Africans concerning abortion, by J. D. Venter. HUMANITAS 7(2):131-141, 1981.

Oral contraception and cancer of the female reproductive system, by K. L. Woods. JOURNAL OF CLINICAL AND HOSPITAL PHARMACY 10(2):123-135, June 1985.

Oral contraception asnd coagulation, by M. Notelovitz. CLINICAL OBSTETRICS AND GYNAECOLOGY 28(1):73-83, March 1985.

Oral contraception and metabolism, by A. Harlay. INFIRMIERE FRANCAISE (257):19-21, July 1984.

Oral contraception and serious psychiatric illness: absence of an association, by M. P. Vessey, et al. BRITISH JOURNAL OF PSYCHIATRY 146:45-49, January 1985.

Oral contraception, coital frequency, and the time required to conceive, by C. F. Westoff, et al. SOCIAL BIOLOGY 29:157-167, Spring-Summer, 1982.

Oral contraception for the adolescent, by L. B. Tyrer. JOURNAL OF REPRODUC-TIVE MEDICINE 29(Suppl. 7):551-559, July 1984.

Oral contraception in Bangladesh, by S. Bhatia, et al. STUDIES IN FAMILY PLAN-NING 15:233-241, September-October 1984.

Oral contraception—starting, stopping or changing. DRUG THERAPY BULLETIN 23(10):37-39, May 20, 1985.

Oral contraceptive failure. AMERICAN JOURNAL OF NURSING 85:694, June 1985.

Oral contraceptive failure . . . drugs taken concurrently can reduce its effectiveness. NURSES DRUG ALERT 9(6):42-43, June 1985.

Oral contraceptive PPI: its effect on patient knowledge, feelings, and behavior, by C. D. Sands, et al. DRUG INTELLIGENCE AND CLINICAL PHARMACY 18(9):730-735, September 1984.

Oral contraceptive pill and benign intracranial hypertension [letter], by N. D. Soysa. NEW ZEALAND MEDICAL JOURNAL 98(784):656, August 14, 1985.

Oral contraceptive use and breast cancer in young women in Sweden [letter], by H. Olsson, et al. LANCET 1(8431):748-749, March 30, 1985.

Oral contraceptive use: prospective follow-up of women with suspected glucose intolerance, by T. J. Duffy, et al. CONTRACEPTION 30(3):197-208, September 1984.

Oral contraceptives, by R. P. Shearman. AUSTRALIAN FAMILY PHYSICIAN 13(9): 685-691, September 1984.

Oral contraceptives and breast cancer: the current controversy, by M. C. Pike, et al. JOURNAL OF THE ROYAL SOCIETY OF HEALTH 105(1):5-10, February 1985.

Oral contraceptives and cardiovascular disease: a critique of the epidemiologic stud-ies, by J. P. Realini, et al. AMERICAN JOURNAL OF OBSTETRICS AND GYNE-COLOGY 152(6 Pt 2):729-798, July 15, 1985.

Oral contraceptives and cervical cancer, by J. M. Piper. GYNECOLOGIC ONCOLOGY 22(1):1-14, September 1985.

Oral contraceptives and the cobalamin (vitamin B12) metabolism, by K. Hjelt, et al. ACTA OBSTETRICIA ET GYNECOLOGICA SCANDINAVICA 64(1):59-63, 1985.

Oral contraceptives and neoplasia, by P. G. Stubblefield. JOURNAL OF REPRO-DUCTIVE MEDICINE 29(Suppl. 7):524-529, July 1984.

Oral contraceptives and nonfatal vascular disease, by J. B. Porter, et al. OBSTET-RICS AND GYNECOLOGY 66(1):1-4, July 1985.

Oral contraceptives and pituitary response to GnRH: comparative study of progestin-related effects, by A. Römmler, et al. CONTRACEPTION 31(3):295-303, March 1985.

Oral contraceptives and reproductive mortality [letter], by W. M. Gerhold. NEW ENGLAND JOURNAL OF MEDICINE 311(24):1583, December 13, 1984.

Oral contraceptives and surgery: reduced antithrombin and antifactor Xa levels without postoperative venous thrombosis in low-risk patients, by A. S. Gallus, et al. THROMBOSIS RESEARCH 35(5):513-526, September 1, 1984.

Oral contraceptives and venous thrombosis [letter], by C. Hougie. WESTERN JOURNAL OF MEDICINE 141(5):688-689, November 1984.

Oral contraceptives, Chlamydia trachomatis infection, and pelvic inflammatory disease. A word of caution about protection, by A. E. Washington, et al. JAMA 253(15):2246-2250, April 19, 1985.

Oral contraceptives come of age . . . decrease the susceptibility to many diseases. CANADIAN OPERATING ROOM NURSES JOURNAL 3(3):44, May-June 1985.

Oral contraceptives containing chlormadinone acetate and cancer incidence at selected sites in the German Democratic Republic—a correlation analysis, by P. Nischan, et al. INTERNATIONAL JOURNAL OF CANCER 34(5):671-674, November 15, 1984.

Oral contraceptives. The current risk-benefit ratio, by E. B. Connell. JOURNAL OF REPRODUCTIVE MEDICINE 29(Suppl. 7):513-523, July 1984.

Oral contraceptives in the 1980s, by S. R. Miliken. PHYSICIAN ASSISTANT 9(5):29-30+, May 1985.

Oral contraceptives in 1984, by E. K. Chapler. IOWA MEDICINE 74(10):439-440, October 1984.

Oral contraceptives, lipids and cardiovascular disease, by K. Fotherby. CONTRA-CEPTION 31(4):367-394, April 1985.

Oral contraceptives market benefits from new products. CHEMICAL MARKETING REPORT 227:20-21, March 25, 1985.

Oral contraceptives, 1985: a synopsis, by D. Woods. CANADIAN MEDICAL ASSO-CIATION JOURNAL 133(5):463-465, September 1, 1985.

Order and disorder in anti-abortion rhetoric: a logological view, by R. A. Lake. QUAR-TERLY JOURNAL OF SPEECH 70:425-443, November 1984.

Organization of multi-level medical services for women with abortions and for premature infants, by M. F. V'iaskova, et al. AKUSHERSTVO I GINEKOLOGIIA (5):60-61, May 1985.

Out of the courts and into the streets. CANADA AND THE WORLD 50:11-12, April 1985.

Outcome of pregnancy after threatened abortion, by J. B. Hertz, et al. ACTA OBSTETRICIA ET GYNECOLOGICA SCANDINAVICA 64(2):151-156, 1985.

Outcome of pregnancy following induced abortion. Report from the joint study of the Royal College of General Practitioners and the Royal College of Obstetricians and Gynaecologists, by P. I. Frank, et al. BRITISH JOURNAL OF OBSTETRICS AND GYNAECOLOGY 92(4):308-316, April 1985.

Outflanking the abortionists: pro-life street tactics come to Alberta to head off Morgentaler, by M. McKinley. ALBERTA REPORT 12:34, December 31, 1984.

Outpatient interval female sterilization at the University College Hospital, Ibadan, Nigeria, by E. O. Otolorin, et al. AFRICAN JOURNAL OF MEDICINE AND MEDICAL SCIENCES 14(1-2):3-9, March-June 1985.

Ovabloc. Five years of experience, by T. P. Reed. JOURNAL OF REPRODUCTIVE MEDICINE 29(8):601-602, August 1984.

Ovarian function following ligation of the fallopian tubes, by X. D. Sun. CHUNG HUA FU CHAN KO TSA CHIH 19(3):166-167, July 1984.

Ovarian function in monkeys after bilateral salpingectomy, by J. R. Zhao, et al. INTERNATIONAL JOURNAL OF FERTILITY 29(2):118-121, 1984.

Overpopulation problem as it affects the United States: a step toward a societal response [Catholic Church position], by S. D. Mumford. HUMANIST 45:14-17+, July-August 1985.

Ovulation inhibitors and tumors, by G. Freund, et al. DEUTSCHE MEDIZINISCHE WOCHENSCHRIFT 110(35):1346-1350, August 30, 1985.

Oxford-Family Planning Association contraceptive study, by M. P. Vessey, et al. CLINICAL OBSTETRICS AND GYNAECOLOGY 11(3):743-757, December 1984.

Oxytocin-induced water intoxication. A case report, by F. J. Muller, et al. SOUTH AFRICAN MEDICAL JOURNAL 68(5):340-341, August 1985.

PID associated with fertility regulating agents. Task Force on intrauterine devices, special programme of research, development and research training in human reproduction, World Health Organization. CONTRACEPTION 30(1):1-21, July 1984.

Panel says Depo-Provera not proved safe, by M. Sun. SCIENCE 226:950-951, November 23, 1984.

Paracentric inversion: a study of 2 new cases, by N. Morichon-Delvallez, et al. REVUE FRANCAISE DE GYNECOLOGIE ET D'OBSTETRIQUE 80(5):275-277, April 1985.

Parental consent—does doctor know best after all? The Gillick case, by D. Brahams. NEW LAW JOURNAL 135:8-10, January 4, 1985.

Parental HLA compatibility, fetal wastage and neural tube defects: evidence for a T/t-like locus in humans, by B. Schacter, et al. AMERICAN JOURNAL OF HUMAN GENETICS 36(5):1082-1091, September 1984.

Parental response to mid-trimester therapeutic abortion following amniocentesis, by O. W. Jones, et al. PRENATAL DIAGNOSIS 4(4):249-256, July-August 1984.

Parents right to decide [letter], by H. C. Moss. INDIANA MEDICINE 77(1):28, January 1984.

Paternal mosaic 45, X/46, XYq+ and recurrent spontaneous abortions without monosomy X [letter], by V. Izakovic, et al. CLINICAL GENETICS 27(3):285-286, March 1985.

Paternal Robertsonian translocation t(13q; 14q) and maternal reciprocal translocation t(7p; 13q) in a couple with repeated fetal loss, by P. R. Scarbrough, et al. JOURNAL OF MEDICAL GENETICS 21(6):463-464, December 1984.

69

Pathologic early pregnancy. Evaluation of new pregnancy tests, by J. A. Steier, et al. TIDSSKRIFT FOR DEN NORSKE LAEGEFORENING 105(7):496-498, March 10, 1985.

Pathos and promise of Christian ethics: a study of the abortion debate, by W. Werpehowski. HORIZONS 12:284-310, Fall 1985.

Patient understanding of oral contraceptive side effects, by N. Goldfield, et al. WESTERN JOURNAL OF MEDICINE 142(3):417-418, March 1985.

Pattern and attitude of Nigerian women in Benin City towards female sterilization, by A. F. Omu, et al. ASIA OCEANIA JOURNAL OF OBSTETRICS AND GYNAECOLOGY 11(1):17-21, March 1985.

Patterns of contraceptive method of use by California family planning clinic clients, 1976-84, by B. M. Aved. AMERICAN JOURNAL OF PUBLIC HEALTH 75(10): 1210-1212, October 1985.

Paving the way for parenthood . . . family planning nurse, by G. Rands. NURSING TIMES 81(4):46-47, January 23-29, 1985.

Paying high price for the pill [damages awarded in P. Buchan's suit against Ortho Pharmaceutical Canada], by R. Block. MACLEANS 97:52, April 30, 1984.

Pediatric drug information, by R. G. Fischer. PEDIATRIC NURSING 11(5):384, September-October 1985.

Peers, parents, and partners. Determining the needs of the support person in an abortion clinic, by P. B. Beeman. JOURNAL OF OBSTETRICS, GYNECOLOGY AND NEONATAL NURSING 14(1):54-58, January-February 1985.

Pelvic inflammatory disease: pill risk, by D. D. Bennett. SCIENCE NEWS 127:263, April 27, 1985.

Pensacola, D C bombers found guilty, by M. Anderson. NATIONAL NOW TIMES 18(4):3, June 1985.

People like us [pro-lifers]. NATIONAL REVIEW 37:18, February 22, 1985.

Perforation of angular pregnancy during elective pregnancy termination. A case report, by Y. Rahmani, et al. JOURNAL OF REPRODUCTIVE MEDICINE 30(4): 366-367, April 1985.

Peroperative penicillins, bacteremia, and pelvic inflammatory disease in association with induced first-trimester abortion, by L. Heisterberg, et al. DANISH MEDICAL BULLETIN 32(1):73-75, March 1985.

Persistence of high fertility in Kenya, by I. Sindiga. SOCIAL SCIENCE AND MEDICINE 20(1):71-84, 1985.

Personal experience with tubal sterilizations performed by the posterior uterine vault approach, by J. Adamec, et al. CESKOSLOVENSKA GYNEKOLOGIE 50(1):44-47, February 1985.

Personhood, covenant, and abortion, by M. R. Maguire. AMERICAN JOURNAL OF THEOLOGY AND PHILOSOPHY 6(1):28-46, 1985.

Pharmacokinetic and pharmacodynamic investigations with monthly injectable contraceptive preparations, by A. R. Aedo, et al. CONTRACEPTION 31(5):453-469, May 1985.

Pharmacokenetic observations on ST-1435 administered subcutaneously and intra-vaginally, by P. L. Lähteenmäki, et al. CONTRACEPTION 30(4):381-389, October 1984.

Pharmacological basis of therapeutics: gossypol, an oral male contraceptive?, by S. M. Penningroth. JOURNAL OF THE MEDICAL SOCIETY OF NEW JERSEY 81(8):663-665, August 1984.

Photosensitized decomposition of contraceptive steroids: a possible explanation for the observed (photo) allergy of the oral contraceptive pill, by A. Sedee, et al. ARCHIV DER PHARMAZIE 318(2):111-119, February 1985.

Physician's counseling in conflict about pregnancy. Dilemma and chance, by W. Schuth, et al. DEUTSCHE MEDIZINISCHE WOCHENSCHRIFT 110(30):1175-1178, July 26, 1985.

Physiological basis of birth control, by W. X. Li, et al. SHENG LI KO HSUEH CHIN CHAN 15(1):87-92, January 1984.

Picture costs ten thousand words, by D. O. Stewart. AMERICAN BAR ASSOCIATION JOURNAL 71:62-66, January 1985.

Pill and the liver, by L. Schiff. ACTA GASTROENTEROLOGICA LATINOAMERICANA 13(2):188-191, 1983.

Pill and thrombosis, by I. Thranov, et al. UGESKRIFT FOR LAEGER 146(36):2709-2711, September 3, 1984.

Pill for men, by G. Levoy. NEW AGE February 1985, p. 19.

Pill formulations and their effect on lipid and carbohydrate metabolism, by P. G. Brooks. JOURNAL OF REPRODUCTIVE MEDICINE 29(Suppl. 7):539-546, July 1984.

Pill that 'might defuse the abortion issue' [morning after pills], by R. Rhein, Jr., et al. BUSINESS WEEK April 1, 1985, p. 85+.

Pill/25 years of uncertainty, by P. Duchesne. COMMUNIQU'ELLES 11(4):6, July 1985.

Pill's armed competitor. DISCOVER 6:7, May 1985.

Pill's eclipse [survey on forms of birth control]. TIME 124:79, December 17, 1984.

Pitfalls of linking cancer to the pill, by S. Connor. NEW SCIENTIST 105:3, April 4, 1985.

Pituitary microadenoma. Subsequent pregnancies (clinical cases), by C. Wainstein. REVISTA CHILENA DE OBSTETRICIA Y GINECOLOGIA 46(1):20-24, 1981.

Placenta percreta associated with a second-trimester pregnancy termination, by M. D. Hornstein, et al. AMERICAN JOURNAL OF OBSTETRICS AND GYNECOLOGY 150(8):1002-1003, December 15, 1984.

Placing of antifertility drugs in food supplies: one answer to our global population crisis?, by S. Lesse. AMERICAN JOURNAL OF PSYCHOTHERAPY 39(2):155-158, April 1985.

Planned Parenthood [Planned Parenthood Ass'n v. Dep't of Human Resources, 687 p.2d 785 (Or.)] aborts state funding limits. WILLIAMETTE LAW REVIEW 21:405-410, Spring 1985.

Planned Parenthood seeks support via newspaper ads. EDITOR AND PUBLISHER-THE FOURTH ESTATE 117:30, October 13, 1984.

Planning programs for pregnant teenagers, by M. R. Burt, et al. PUBLIC WELFARE 43(2):28-36, Spring 1985.

Plasma pyridoxal phosphate in women taking oral contraceptives for at least five years, by A. Hamfelt, et al. UPSALA JOURNAL OF MEDICAL SCIENCES 89(3):285-286, 1984.

Plasmapheresis for the treatment of repeated early pregnancy wastage associated with anti-P, by J. A. Rock, et al. OBSTETRICS AND GYNECOLOGY 66(Suppl. 3):57S-60S, September 1985.

Plastic (Bleier) clip high failure rate [letter], by L. Hammond. OBSTETRICS AND GYNECOLOGY 66(2):297-298, August 1985.

Polemic on abortion in the U.S.: lessons from an experience, by A. de Miguel. REVISTA ESPANOLA DE INVESTIGACIONES SOCIOLOGICAS 21:151-179, January-March 1983.

Police raid abortion clinic, by J. Walkington. INTERCONTINENTAL PRESS 23(13):393, July 1985.

Politics and abortion, by J. I. Rosoff. CIBA FOUNDATION SYMPOSIA 115:244-262, 1985.

Politics, morality, and the Catholic Church, by G. a. Kelly. USA TODAY 113:68-73, March 1985.

Politics of abortion, by N. Hentoff. VILLAGE VOICE 29:8, October 2, 1984.

Politics of motherhood, by M. O. Steinfels. CHRISTIANITY AND CRISIS 44:342-343, October 1, 1984.

Politics of population control, by L. Sundberg. HERIZONS 2(7):9, November 1984.

Politics of procreation. SCIENCE FOR PEOPLE (57):15, 1985.

Popular contraception. AMERICAN FAMILY PHYSICIAN 31:290, April 1985.

Population and politics. HEALTHSHARING (1):16, Winter 1984.

Population and U. S. policy [U.N. conference on population]. NATIONAL REVIEW 36:13-14, September 7, 1984.

Population control: no-women decide, by A. Henry. OFF OUR BACKS 14(9):2, October 1984.

Population control vs. freedom in China, by V. Bullough, et al. FREE INQUIRY 4:12-15, Winter 1983-84.

Population dynamics and policy in the People's Republic of China [compared with Japan, Korea, and Taiwan; conference paper], by L.-J. Cho. ANNALS OF THE AMERICAN ACADEMY OF POLITICAL AND SOCIAL SCIENCE 476:111-127, November 1984.

Population in the Asian scene questions, by R. Toledo. BALAI (11):2, 1985.

Population policies and proposals: when big brother becomes big daddy [family planning and other population policies as functions of the state and as individual human rights], by Laura E. Farrell. BROOKLYN JOURNAL OF INTERNATIONAL LAW 10:83-114, Winter 1984.

Population policy analysis and development planning, by O. G. Simmons. JOURNAL OF DEVELOPING AREAS 18:433-448, July 1984.

Population policy and trends in China, 1978-83, by J. Banister. CHINA QUARTERLY December 1984, p. 717-741.

Population policy: country experience [Mexico, Indonesia, and India], by M. Ainsworth. FINANCE AND DEVELOPMENT 21:18-20, September 1984.

Population policy in Egypt: a case in public policy analysis [family planning policies adopted since 1962], by A. S. Hassan. POPULATION STUDIES 11:19-25, April-June 1984.

Population update [Reagan administration stand on cutting aid to governments that sanction abortion]. HUMANIST 45:43, May-June 1985.

Possible antidepressant effect of oral contraceptives: case report, by P. Roy-Byrne, et al. JOURNAL OF CLINICAL PSYCHIATRY 45(8):350-352, August 1984.

Possible hepatitis from diaphragm fitting [letter], by L. C. Wislicki. JAMA 252(23): 3251, December 21, 1984.

Possible potentiation of suicide risk in patients with EEG dysrhythmias taking oral contraceptives: a speculative empirical note, by F. A. Struve. CLINICAL ELECTROENCEPHALOGRAPHY 16(2):88-90, April 1985.

Postabortal pelvic infection associated with Chlamydia trachomatis and the influence of humoral immunity, by S. Osser, et al. AMERICAN JOURNAL OF OBSTETRICS AND GYNECOLOGY 150(6):699-703, November 15, 1984.

Post-abortion and post-partum psychiatric hospitalization, by H. P. David. CIBA FOUNDATION SYMPOSIA 115:150-164, 1985.

Post-cesarean section insertion of intrauterine devices, by I. C. Chi, et al. AMERICAN JOURNAL OF PUBLIC HEALTH 74:1281-1282, November 1984.

Post-coital birth control family planning. OFF OUR BACKS 15(2):7, February 1985.

Post-coital contraception, by P. D. Bromwich. PRACTITIONER 229(1403):427-429, May 1985.

Postcoital contraception, by P. Draca, et al. MEDICINSKI PREGLED 38(3-4):205-206, 1985.

Post-coital contraception, by A. A. Kubba. JOURNAL OF THE ROYAL SOCIETY OF HEALTH 104(6):212-213, December 1984.

Postcoital contraception, by A. A. Yuzpe. CLINICAL OBSTETRICS AND GYNAECOLOGY 11(3):787-797, December 1984.

Post-coital contraception using a combination of d-norgestrel and ethinyloestradiol, by Chi Nguyen Duy, et al. JOURNAL DE GYNECLOGIE, OBSTETRIQUE ET BIOLOGIE DE LA REPRODUCTION 14(4):523-526, 1985.

Post-coital contraception with estrogens. Mechanism of action, results and sequelae in a caseload of 123 cases, by F. Monasterolo. MINERVA GINECOLOGIA 36(7-8):451-454, July-August 1984.

Postcoital contraception with steroid hormones, by G. Köhler, et al. ZENTRALBLATT FUR GYNAEKOLOGIE 106(17):1173-1181, 1984.

Postcoital contraception (without prostaglandins), by R. Wyss. GYNAKOLOGE 17(3): 200-203, September 1984.

Postcoital intervention [letter], by G. Kovacs, et al. MEDICAL JOURNAL OF AUS-TRALIA 142(7):424-425, April 1, 1985.

Postcoital pill, by E. Weisberg. HEALTHRIGHT 4:17-19, August 1985.

Post conception failures in reproduction: infectious diseases and immunitary pro-blems, by G. Scarselli, et al. ACTA EUROPAEA FERTILITATIS 15(5):363-367, September-October 1984.

Postconception menses induction using prostaglandin vaginal suppositories, by H. W. Foster, Jr., et al. OBSTETRICS AND GYNECOLOGY 65(5):682-685, May 1985.

Postconceptional induction of menses with double prostaglandin F2 alpha impact, by M. Borten, et al. 150(8):1006-1007, December 15, 1984.

Postpartum sterilization and the private practitioner, by V. P. DeVilliers. SOUTH AFRI-CAN MEDICAL JOURNAL 67(4):132-133, January 26, 1985.

Post-tubal-ligation syndrome, by J. A. Vázquez. GINECOLOGIA Y OBSTETRICIA DE MEXICO 51(317):237-240, September 1983.

Post-tubal sterilization syndrome—a misnomer, by M. C. Rulin, et al. AMERICAN JOURNAL OF OBSTETRICS AND GYNECOLOGY 151(1):13-19, January 1 1985.

Potential impact of changes in fertility on infant, child and maternal mortality, by J. Trussell, et al. STUDIES IN FAMILY PLANNING 15:267-280, November-December 1984.

Potential use of postcoital contraception to prevent unwanted pregnancy, by T. A. Johnston, et al. BRITISH MEDICAL JOURNAL 290(6474):1040-1041, April 6, 1985.

Powell plays tricks with his bill, by S. Ardill. SPARE RIB (155):132, June 1985.

Prayer for the woman who has miscarried, by G. Nefyodov. JOURNAL OF THE MOSCOW PATRIARCHATE 8:77-78, 1983.

Precautionary tales . . . , by C. Doyle. OBSERVER January 20, 1985, p. 24-29.

Predicting contraceptive behavior among university men: the role of emotions and behavioral intentions, by W. A. Fisher. JOURNAL OF APPLIED SOCIAL PSYCHOLOGY 14:104-123, March-April 1984.

Predictors of repeat pregnancies among low-income adolescents, by M. Gispert, et al. HOSPITAL AND COMMUNITY PSYCHIATRY 35:719-723, July 1984.

Pregnancy and systemic sclerosis [letter], by M. Giordano, et al. ARTHRITIS AND RHEUMATISM 28(2):237-238, February 1985.

Pregnancy following repeated abortions in uterine abnormalities, by J. Schmid. GYNAEKOLOGISCHE RUNDSCHAU 24(3):140-144, 1984.

Pregnancy impairment in mice by antibodies to subcellular placenta fractions, by J. Morenz, et al. INTERNATIONAL JOURNAL OF FERTILITY 29(2):91-97, 1984.

Pregnancy in Fanconi's anemia, by H. Zakut, et al. HAREFUAH 107(9):238-239, November 1, 1984.

Pregnancy loss in mothers of multiple births and in mothers of singletons only, by G. Wyshak. ANNALS OF HUMAN BIOLOGY 12(1):85-89, January-February 1985.

Pregnancy outcome in the Seveso area after ICDD contamination, by G. M. Fara, et al. PROGRESS IN CLINICAL AND BIOLOGICAL RESEARCH 163B:279-285, 1985.

Pregnancy prevention by intravaginal delivery of a progesterone antagonist: RU486 tampon for menstrual induction and absorption, by G. D. Hodgen. FERTILITY AND STERILITY 44(2):263-267, August 1985.

Pregnancy protection index: a framework for the Systematic Study of Pregnancy Protection. JOURNAL OF SEX RESEARCH 20(3):14, August 1984.

Pregnancy terminating effect and toxicity of an active constituent of Aristolochia mollissima Hance, aristolochic acid A, by W. H. Wang, et al. YAO HSUEH HSUEH PAO 19(6):405-409, June 1984.

Pregnancy termination for genetic indications: the impact on families, by R. M. Furlong, et al. SOCIAL WORK IN HEALTH CARE 10(1):17-34, Fall 1984.

Pregnancy termination in Switzerland. Development 1979-1981, by P. A. Gloor, et al. SCHWEIZERISCHE RUNDSCHAU FUR MEDIZIN PRAXIS 74(17):434-438, April 23, 1985.

Pregnancy termination: not for family planning. The legal difference between sterilization and pregnancy termination is decisive, by H. Krautkrämer. FORTSCHRITTE DER MEDIZIN 102(36):78, September 27, 1984.

Pregnancy wastage and prenatal diagnosis, by B. Grünfeld, et al. TIDSSKRIFT FOR DEN NORSKE LAEGEFORENING 105(15):1079-1081, May 30, 1085.

Pregnant women's attitudes toward the abortion of defective fetuses, by R. C. Faden, et al. POPULATION AND ENVIRONMENT 6(4):197-209, 1983.

Premarital contraceptive use: a discriminant analysis approach, by A. R. Sack, et al. ARCHIVES OF SEXUAL BEHAVIOR 14(2):165-182, April 1985.

Premath of hysterectomy, by R. Kasrawi, et al. JOURNAL OF PSYCHOSOMATIC OBSTETRICS AND GYNECOLOGY 3(3-4):233-236, December 1984.

Prenatal genetic diagnosis [letter], by R. A. Jones. MEDICAL JOURNAL OF AUSTRALIA 143(3):127, August 5, 1985.

Prenatal selection and fetal development disturbances occurring in carriers of G6PD deficiency, by D. Toncheva, et al. HUMAN GENETICS 69(1):88, 1985.

Preoperative cervical priming by intracervical application of a new sulprostone gel, by W. Rath, et al. CONTRACEPTION 31(3):207-216, March 1985.

Presbyterian Church (USA) decides to give higher priority to evangelism, by R. L. Frame. CHRISTIANITY TODAY 29(10):36+, July 12, 1985.

Presbyterians in Indianapolis [197th general assembly of Presbyterian Church (USA), June 1985; editorial], by D. J. Brouwer. REFORMED JOURNAL 35(7):3-4, July 1985.

Prescribing contraceptives for under-age-girls—the doctor's legal position, by D. Brahams. PRACTITIONER 229(1403):461-463, May 1985.

Prescribing oral contraceptives in 1985, by L. H. Labson. PATIENT CARE 19(6):16-18+, March 30, 1985.

Prevalence and trends in oral contraceptive use in premenopausal females ages 12-54 years, United States, 1971-1980, by R. Russell-Briefel, et al. AMERICAN JOURNAL OF PUBLIC HEALTH 75(10):1173-1176, October 1985.

Preventing febrile complications of suction curettage abortion, by T. K. Park, et al. AMERICAN JOURNAL OF OBSTETRICS AND GYNECOLOGY 152(3):252-255, June 1, 1985.

Prevention of post-abortion complications, by A. A. Radionchenko, et al. SOVETS-KAIA MEDITSINA (11):108-110, 1984.

Prevention of pregnancy and abortion in adolescence, by L. Ruusuvaara. DUODE-CIM 101(2):156-158, 1985.

Prevention of recurrent spontaneous abortions by leukocyte transfusions, by C. G. Taylor, et al. JOURNAL OF THE ROYAL SOCIETY OF MEDICINE 78(8):623-627, August 1985.

Preventive use of heparin in women with septic abortion and pyelonephritis in pregnancy, by H. Zrubek, et al. GINEKOLOGIA POLSKA 55(11):855-858, November 1984.

Previous child with trisomy 21 and abortion rate, by S. Aymé, et al. PROGRESS IN CLINICAL AND BIOLOGICAL RESEARCH 163C:15-19, 1985.

Previous experience of induced abortion as a risk factor for fetal death and preterm delivery, by T. K. Park, et al. INTERNATIONAL JOURNAL OF GYNAECOLOGY AND OBSTETRICS 22(3):195-202, June 1984.

Price of unemployment, by M. Olesen. BRIARPATCH 14(5):14, June 1985.

Primary tubal infertility in relation to the use of an intrauterine device [also tubal infertility and the intrauterine device by Daniel W. Cramer, pp. 941-947, and current status of intrauterine devices by Daniel R. Mishell (editorial), pp. 984-985], by J. R. Daling, et al. NEW ENGLAND JOURNAL OF MEDICINE 312:937-941, April 11, 1985.

Privacy: control over stimulus input, stimulus output, and self-regarding conduct, by P. Siegel. BUFFALO LAW REVIEW 33(1):35-84, 1984.

Pro-abortion media shaken by "Silent Scream" (new film shows horrors of abortion), by W. F. Willoughby. HUMAN EVENTS 45:18+, March 23, 1985.

Pro-abortionist infiltrates sex education course (abortion clinic employee gives talk in public school sex ed course), by P. Schlafly. HUMAN EVENTS 45:20, May 18, 1985.

Pro-abortionists to battle "Silent Scream" (angry over anti-abortion film). HUMAN EVENTS 45:4+, March 9, 1985.

Pro-choice and "Silent No More", by M. Bowen. GUARDIAN 37(35):2, June 5, 1985.

Pro-choice and still catholic, by E. Bader. GUARDIAN 37(5):6, October 31, 1984.

Pro-choice movement: new directions, reexaminations, by K. Dubinsky, et al. PERCEPTION 8:16-18, March-April 1985.

Pro-choice pioneer recalls the bad old days, by A. Camen. GUARDIAN 37(46):3, September 25, 1985.

Pro-choice protest of a pro-choice protest [editorial], by L. M. Delloff. CHRISTIAN CENTURY 102:1084-1085, November 27, 1985.

Pro-choice vs. pro-life is a moral dilemma, says Daniel Callahan: we carry both traditions within us [interview], by G. Breu. PEOPLE WEEKLY 24:89-91+, August 12, 1985.

Professional satisfaction and client outcomes: a comparative organizational analysis, by C. S. Weisman, et al. MEDICAL CARE 23(10):1179-1192, October 1985.

Profile of contraceptive clients in Katsina, northern Nigeria, by H. P. Naghma-E-Rehan, et al. JOURNAL OF BIOSOCIAL SCIENCE 16:427-436, October 1984.

Prognostic significance of various hormonal parameters in pregnancies complicated by threatened abortion, by S. Marsico, et al. MINERVA GINECOLOGIA 36(7-8): 381-389, July-August 1984.

Prognostic value of ultrasonic scanning and serum estradiol in threatened abortion, by S. J. Sederberg-Olsen, et al. UGESKRIFT FOR LAEGER 146(25):1853-1855, June 18, 1984.

Progress in oral contraception. Advantages of a levonorgestrel-containing 3-stage preparation over low-dose levonorgestrel and desogestrel containing monophasic combination preparations, by U. Lachnit-Fixson. FORTSCHRITTE DER MEDIZIN 102(33):825-830, September 6, 1984.

Prohibition analogy as a dry try to make free abortion palatable, by T. Blackburn. NATIONAL CATHOLIC REPORTER 21:14-15, November 2, 1984.

Prolife activists escalate the war against abortion, by R. Frame. CHRISTIANITY TODAY 28:40-42, November 9, 1984.

Pro-life delegates protest party's platform: "Shutout of party." HUMAN EVENTS 44(28):4+, July 28, 1984.

Pro life equals violence, by I. Lloyd. SPARE RIB (152):11, March 1985.

Pro-life gains: a U of A study shows less support for abortions, by J. Davidson, et al. ALBERTA REPORT 12:39, March 18, 1985.

Pro-life in word or deed?, by E. I. Goulding. JOURNAL OF CHRISTIAN NURSING 1(1):32, Spring 1984.

Prolife vs. prochoice. CHRISTIAN CENTURY 102:410, April 24, 1985.

Pro-lifers sense impending victory: new court majority eyed. HUMAN EVENTS 45:5+, February 2, 1985.

Pro-lifers winning on many key issues. HUMAN EVENTS 45:6, August 31, 1985.

Promoting abortion, by M. Golden. AFER 27:245-249, August 1985.

Promoting the sponge: learning from experience. PUBLIC RELATIONS JOURNAL 41:20-21, March 1985.

Propaganda war over abortion, by A. Spake. MS MAGAZINE 14:88-92+, July 1985.

Prophylactic antibiotics for currettage abortion, by D. A. Grimes, et al. AMERICAN JOURNAL OF OBSTETRICS AND GYNECOLOGY 150(6):689-694, November 15, 1984.

Prophylactic antibodies unjustified for unselected abortion patients [letter], by J. A. McGregor. AMERICAN JOURNAL OF OBSTETRICS AND GYNECOLOGY 152(6 Pt 1):722-725, July 15, 1985.

Prophylaxis with lymecycline in induced first-trimester abortion: a clinical, controlled trial assessing the role of Chlamydia trachomatis and Mycoplasma hominis, by L. Heisterberg, et al. SEXUALLY TRANSMITTED DISEASES 12(2):72-75, April-June 1985.

Pro-puppies, pro-parrots, but not pro-people, by C. Thomas. FUNDAMENTALIST JOURNAL 2(10):34, November 1983.

Prospective study of Chlamydia trachomatis in first trimester abortion, by H. Shioøtz, et al. ANNALS OF CLINICAL RESEARCH 17(2):60-63, 1985.

Prostaglandins mediate postoperative pain in Falope ring sterilization, by B. L. Brodie, et al. AMERICAN JOURNAL OF OBSTETRICS AND GYNECOLOGY 151(2):175-177, January 15, 1985.

Protection of potential human life in Illinois: policy and law at odds, by J. A. Parness. NORTHERN ILLINOIS UNIVERSITY LAW REVIEW 5:1-30, Winter 1984.

Protestants push pro-life: Evangelicals now fight on their own terms, by T. Fennell. ALBERTA REPORT 12:46, May 13, 1985.

Protesting abortion [Morgentaler clinic, Toronto]. MACLEANS 98:17, August 12, 1985.

Proteus septicemias. Apropos of 4 cases, by P. Leniaud, et al. MEDECINE TROPICALE 44(2):137-142, April-June 1984.

Provision of abortion services in the United States, by D. A. Grimes. CIBA FOUNDATION SYMPOSIA 115:26-40, 1985.

Proximate determinants of fertility: sub-national variations. POPULATION STUDIES 39(1):113, March 1985.

Prudence, politics and the abortion issue [Catholic position], by D. A. Degnan. AMERICA 152:121-124, February 16, 1985.

Psychological and social disorders of Turkish women during an unaccepted pregnancy in a foreign country, by H. Berzewski. INTERNATIONAL JOURNAL OF SOCIAL PSYCHIATRY 30(4):275-282, Winter 1984.

Psychological aspects of voluntary interruption of pregnancy, by C. Mouniq, et al. PSYCHOLOGIE MEDICALE 14(8):1181-1185, June 1982.

Psychological considerations in the wish for refertilization, by H. Herrmann, et al. GEBURTSHILFE UND FRAUENHEILKUNDE 45(3):170-175, March 1985.

Psychological contributions to understanding gynaecological problems, by M. Tsoi. BULLETIN OF THE HONG KONG PSYCHOLOGICAL SOCIETY 14:9-16, January 1985.

Psychological effects of hysterectomy in premenopausal women, by S. Kav-Venaki, et al. JOURNAL OF PSYCHOSOMATIC OBSTETRICS AND GYNECOLOGY 2(2):76-80, June 1983.

Psychological factors related to adjustment after tubal ligation, by M. M. Tsoi, et al. JOURNAL OF REPRODUCTIVE AND INFANT PSYCHOLOGY 2(1):1-6, April 1984.

Psychological factors that predict reaction to abortion, by D. T. Moseley, et al. JOURNAL OF CLINICAL PSYCHOLOGY 37(2):276-279, 1981.

Psychological functioning after non-cancer hysterectomy: a review of methods and results, by K. Wijma. JOURNAL OF PSYCHOSOMATIC OBSTETRICS AND GYNAECOLOGY 3(3-4):133-154, December 1984.

Psychological problems following hysterectomy, by L. Millet, et al. PSYCHOLOGIE MEDICALE 14(8):1239-1244, June 1982.

Psychopathological effects of voluntary termination of pregnancy on the father called up for military service, by J.-C. DuBouis-Bonnefond, et al. PSYCHOLOGIE MEDICALE 14(8):1187-1189, June 1982.

Psychosexual problems, by P. Tunnadine. PRACTITIONER 229(1403):453-455+, May 1985.

Psychosocial and psychosexual aspects of contraception, by M. Guay. INFIRMIERE CANADIENNE 27(1):23-26, January 1985.

Psychosomatic complications of contraception, by P. Cepicky, et al. CESKO-SLOVENSKA GYNEKOLOGIE 49(10):758-759, December 1984.

Public and the pill: is the pill making a comeback?, by J. D. Forrest. AMERICAN JOURNAL OF PUBLIC HEALTH 75(10):1131-1132, October 1985.

Public board of inquiry advises that Depo-Provera not be approved for use as contraceptive in U. S. FAMILY PLANNING PERSPECTIVES 17(1):38-39, January-February 1985.

Public findings of contraceptive, sterilization and abortion services, 1983 [United States], by R. B. Gold, et al. FAMILY PLANNING PERSPECTIVES 17:25-30, January-February 1985.

Public misinformed about safety of the pill. GALLUP REPORT March 1985, p. 27-29.

Public opinion and the legalization of abortion; with French summary, by T. F. Hartnagel, et al. CANADIAN REVIEW OF SOCIOLOGY AND ANTHROPOLOGY 22:411-430, August 1985.

Public opinion on and potential demand for vasectomy in semi-rural Guatemala, by R. Santiso, et al. JOURNAL OF PUBLIC HEALTH 75:73-75, January 1985.

Public policy: contract, abortion, and the CIA, by P.H. Brietzke. VALPARAISO UNIVERSITY LAW REVIEW 18:741-940, Summer 1984.

Public policy on human reproduction and the historian, by J. Reed. JOURNAL OF SOCIAL HISTORY 18:383-398, Spring 1985.

Publishers disagree over controversial ad, by A. Radolf. EDITOR AND PUBLISHER-THE FOURTH ESTATE 118:15, March 30, 1985.

Pulling the plug on sterilization [fallopian tube plug allows reversible sterilization; work of C. Irving Meeker and Wilfred Roth], by J. Silberner. SCIENCE NEWS 127:166, March 16, 1985.

Putting off children. AMERICAN DEMOGRAPHICS 6(9):30, September 1984.

Quinacrine nonsurgical female sterilization: a reassessment of safety and efficacy, by E. Kessel, et al. FERTILITY AND STERILITY 44(3):293-298, September 1985.

RNs take to court in abortion cases. AMERICAN JOURNAL OF NURSING 85:830, July 1985.

Radioimmunological study of the gonadotropic function of the pituitary in women during reestablishment of the menstrual cycle, by V. I. Chemodanov, et al. MEDIT-SINSKAIA RADIOLOGIIA 30(3):62-64, March 1985.

Raising a child of rape[woman sues Dr. J. Novoa because morning-after pill Estrace proves ineffective], by P. Carlson. PEOPLE WEEKLY 23:30-35, March 25, 1985.

Rajiv steps in where Sanjay failed, by R. Ford. TIMES August 29, 1985, p. 10.

Ranitidine prophylaxis before anaesthesia in early pregnancy, by B. L. Duffy, et al. ANAESTHESIA AND INTENSIVE CARE 13(1):29-32, February 1985.

A rare case in gynecologic practice, by K. Durveniashki. AKUSHERSTVO I GINE-KOLOGIIA 23(4):364-365, 1984.

Rational basis? Strict scrutiny? Intermediate scrutiny? Judicial review in the abortion cases. OKLAHOMA CITY UNIVERSITY LAW REVIEW Summer 1984, 317-353.

Reagan fiddles as the clinic burns, E. Bader. RIGHTS AND BILL OF RIGHTS JOUR-NAL 31(2):5, July 1985.

Reagan's international war against abortion, by L. Gersing. IN THESE TIMES 9(36):5, September 25, 1985.

Reagan's world agenda for women, by L. Woods. INTERNATIONAL VIEWPOINT (71):25, March 11, 1985.

Real and false risks of contraceptive information, by M. D. Béran. GYNAEKOLO-GISCHE RUNDSCHAU 24(Suppl. 1):49-53, 1984.

Real and false risks of hormonal contraceptives, by J. Belaïsch. GYNAEKOLO-GISCHE RUNDSCHAU 24(Suppl. 1):12-19, 1984.

Real and false risks of injectable hormonal contraception, by C. Revaz. GYNAKOLO-GISCHE RUNDSCHAU 24(Suppl. 1):20-25, 1984.

Real and false risks of local contraception: spermicides and the diaphragm, by M. M. Zufferey. JOURNAL DE GYNECOLOGIE, OBSTETRIQUE ET BIOLOGIE DE LA REPRODUCTION 14(3):359-363, 1985.

Real and false risks of local contraception: spermicides, diaphragm, by M. M. Zufferey. GYNAEKOLOGISCHE RUNDSCHAU 24(Suppl. 1):26-28, 1984.

Real and false risks of male contraception, by J. Belaïsch. GYNAEKOLOGISCHE RUNDSCHAU 24(Suppl. 1):43-48, 1984.

Recant or else [American nuns, diversity of opinion on morality of abortion; news]. CHRISTIAN CENTURY 102:9, January 2-9, 1985.

Recantation or dismissal [nuns asking for dialogue on Catholic antiabortion stand: news]. CHRISTIAN CENTURY 102:793, September 11-18, 1985.

Recent cases: children, by M. A. Jones. THE JOURNAL OF SOCIAL WELFARE LAW May 1985, p. 157-162.

Recent cases: constitutional law. JOURNAL OF FAMILY LAW 23(3):462-464, 1984-85.

Reciprocal balanced translocation of the long arm of chromosome 8 to the short arm of chromosome 7 in a woman with two spontaneous abortions, by H. Hatzisse-vastou-Loukidou, et al. HUMAN GENETICS 70(4):379, 1985.

Reciprocal influences of family and religion in a changing world, by A. Thornton. JOURNAL OF MARRIAGE AND THE FAMILY 47(2):381-394, May 1985.

Recovery for rearing healthy child ruled out in District of Columbia. THE FAMILY LAW REPORTER: COURT OPINIONS 10(39):1532-1533, August 7, 1984.

Recurrent abortions and circulating anticoagulant. Relation to lupic disease: 6 cases, by A. Mathieu, et al. ANNALES DE MÉDECINE INTERNE 135(7):502-506, 1984.

Recurrent abortions, thromboses, and a circulating anticoagulant, by K. Eswaran, et al. AMERICAN JOURNAL OF OBSTETRICS AND GYNECOLOGY 151(6):751-752, March 15, 1985.

Recurrent spontaneous abortion, by M. J. Bennett. HEALTHRIGHT 4:8-13, May 1985.

Recurrent spontaneous abortions associated with lupus anticoagulant in patients with collagen-vascular diseases, by Y. Ichikawa, et al. RYUMACHI 25(2):87-94, April 1985.

Recurrent thrombotic thrombocytopenic purpura in early pregnancy: effect of uterine evacuation, by E. A. Natelson, et al. OBSTETRICS AND GYNECOLOGY 66(Suppl. 3):54S-56S, September 1985.

Reduced risk of pelvic inflammatory disease with injectable contraceptives [letter], by R. H. Gray. LANCET 1(8436):1046, May 4, 1985.

Reducing noncompliance to follow-up appointment keeping at a family practice center, by J. M. Rice, et al. JOURNAL OF APPLIED BEHAVIOR ANALYSIS 17:303-311, Fall 1984.

Reexamining the oral contraceptive issues, by R. Orne, et al. JOURNAL OF OBSTETRICS, GYNECOLOGY AND NEONATAL NURSING 14(1):30-36, January-February 1985.

Referrals vetoed [shelter operated by J. Vaughan, Los Angeles; news]. CHRISTIAN CENTURY 102:177, February 20, 1985.

Reflections on a new generation of oral contraceptives, by U. Gaspard. JOURNAL DE GYNECOLOGIE, OBSTETRIQUE ET BIOLOGIE DE LA REPRODUCTION 14(1): 85-92, 1985.

Regenerative nodular hyperplasia, hepatocellular carcinoma and oral contraceptives (letter), by J. F. Bretagne, et al. GASTROENTEROLOGIE CLINIQUE ET BIOLOGIQUE 8(10):768-679, October 1984.

Regret after decision to have a tubal sterilization, by G. S. Grubb, et al. FERTILITY AND STERILITY 44(2):248-253, August 1985.

Regulation of fertility by means of vaginal rings medicated with estradiol and levonorgestrel, by S. Diaz, et al. REVISTA CHILENA DE OBSTETRICIA Y GINECOLOGIA 47(4):266-273, 1982.

Regulation of male fertility: an immunological approach, by A. Tjokronegoro. ASIAN PACIFIC JOURNAL OF ALLERGY AND IMMUNOLOGY 1(2):161-167, December 1983.

Regulation of births in Africa, by J. C. Cazenave, et al. SOINS, PATHOLOGIE TROPICALE (46):3-6, March-April 1984.

Rejoinder. [Discussion of late abortions and the crime of child destruction: a reply], by V. Tunkel. CRIMINAL LAW REVIEW March 1985, p. 133-140.

Relation between postpartum bleeding and abortion, by A. L. Zhou. CHUNG HUA HU LI TSA CHIH 20(1):13-15, February 1985.

Relation between Trichomonas vaginalis and contraceptive measures, by H. A. el-Boulaqi, et al. JOURNAL OF THE EGYPTIAN SOCIETY OF PARASITOLOGY 14(2):495-499, December 1984.

Relationship between contraceptive method and vaginal flora, by B. A. Peddie, et al. AUSTRALIAN AND NEW ZEALAND JOURNAL OF OBSTETRICS AND GYNAECOLOGY 24(3):217-218, August 1984.

Relationship of estrogen and progesterone to breast disease, by P. G. Brooks. JOURNAL OF REPRODUCTIVE MEDICINE 29(Suppl. 7):530-538, July 1984.

Relationship of maternal age and trisomy among trisomic spontaneous abortions, by T. Hassold, et al. AMERICAN JOURNAL OF HUMAN GENETICS 36(6):1349-1356, November 1984.

Relationship of the menstrual cycle and thyroid hormones to whole-body protein turnover in women, by D. R. Garrel, et al. HUMAN NUTRITION 39C:29-37, January 1985.

Relative body weight as a factor in the decision to abort, by T. H. Thelen, et al. PSYCHOLOGICAL REPORTS 52:763-775, June 1983.

Relative oxytocic properties of fenprostalene compared with cloprostenol, prostaglandin F2 alpha, and oxytocin in the ovarietomized ewe, by R. Garcia-Villar, et al. AMERICAN JOURNAL OF VETERINARY RESEARCH 46(4):841-844, April 1985.

Religion and gender: a comparison of Canadian and American student attitudes, by M. B. Brinkerhoff, et al. JOURNAL OF MARRIAGE AND THE FAMILY 47(2):415-429, May 1985.

Religion and opposition to abortion reconsidered, by A. Lewis Rhodes. REVIEW OF RELIGIOUS RESEARCH 27(2):158-168, December 1985.

Religion, values and attitudes toward abortion, by R. J. Harris, et al. JOURNAL OF THE SCIENTIFIC STUDY OF RELIGION 24:137-154, June 1985.

Religious affiliation and the fertility of married couples, by W. D. Mosher, et al. JOURNAL OF MARRIAGE AND THE FAMILY 46:671-677, August 1984.

Religious belief and public morality, by M. Cuomo. NEW YORK REVIEW OF BOOKS 31:32-37, October 25, 1984.

Religious correlates of male sexual behavior and contraceptive use, by M. Young. HEALTH EDUCATION 16:20-25, August-September 1985.

Religious identity and attitudes toward contraceptives among university students in Nigeria, by I. Owie. SOCIAL BIOLOGY 30:101-105, Spring 1983.

Religious influences and congressional voting on abortion, by R. A. Dentler. JOURNAL FOR THE SCIENTIFIC STUDY OF RELIGION 16(2):145-164, 1984.

Remove that shield, by A. Henry. OFF OUR BACKS 14(11):12, December 1984.

Renewed abortion fight, by G. Moir. MACLEANS 98:54, April 8, 1985.

Renewed fight over abotion [trial of H. Morgentaler in Toronto], by S. McKay. MACLEANS 97:48, November 5, 1984.

Renin-angiotensin mechanisms in oral contraceptive hypertension in conscious rats, by W. L. Fowler, Jr., et al. AMERICAN JOURNAL OF PHYSIOLOGY 248(5 Pt 2): H695-699, May 1985.

Repeated first-trimester pregnancy loss: evaluation and management, by P. G. McDonough. AMERICAN JOURNAL OF OBSTETRICS AND GYNECOLOGY 153(1):1-6, September 1, 1985.

Repeated pregnancy loss due to alpha-thalassemia—report of 3 cases, by C. K. Kuo, et al. TAIWAN I HSUEH HUI TSA CHIH 83(7):724-729, July 1984.

Repeated spontaneous abortion, by F. Charvet, et al. REVUE FRANCAISE DE GYNECOLOGIE ET D'OBSTETRIQUE 80(7):555-558, July 1985.

Reports and surveys for the Center for Sociological Investigation on Abortion: 1979-1983. REVISTA ESPAÑOLA DE INVESTIGACIONES SOCIOLOGICAS 21:255-302, January-March 1983.

Rep. Henry J. Hyde challenges Cuomo on church-state issue. HUMAN EVENTS 44:8+, October 6, 1984.

Rep. Jack Kemp (R.NY) presses anti-abortion measure. HUMAN EVENTS 45:5+, November 30, 1985.

Reproduction and exposure to lead, by M. Saric. ANNALS OF THE ACADEMY OF MEDICINE, SINGAPORE 13(Suppl. 2):383-388, April 1984.

Reproduction and immune factors in women. Pregnancy, habitual abortion and HLA histocompatibility, by R. C. Martin-du-Pan, et al. JOURNAL DE GYNECOLOGIE, OBSTETRIQUE ET BIOLOGIE DE LA REPRODUCTION 14(3):291-293, 1985.

Reproduction law and medical consent, by B. M. Dickens. UNIVERSITY OF TORONTO LAW JOURNAL 35:255-286, Summer 1985.

Reproduction law—part one, by B. M. Dickens. HEALTH MANAGEMENT FORUM 6(2):22-34, Summer 1985.

Reproductive loss in man: total and chromosomally determined, by A. F. Zakharov. PROGRESS IN CLINICAL AND BIOLOGICAL RESEARCH 163C:9-14, 1985.

Reproductive patterns and the risk of gestational trophoblastic disease, by F. Parazzini, et al. AMERICAN JOURNAL OF OBSTETRICS AND GYNECOLOGY 152(7 Pt 1):866-870, August 1, 1985.

Reproductive rights in North Carolina, by S. Poggi. GAY COMMUNITY 13(5):2, August 10, 1985.

Requests for late termination of pregnancy: Tower Hamlets, 1983, by W. Savage. BRITISH MEDICAL JOURNAL 290(6468):621-623, February 23, 1985.

Requirement that doctor notify husband of abortion struck down. THE FAMILY LAW REPORTER: COURT OPINIONS 10(48):1659-1660, October 9, 1984.

Residential care as an alternative to abortion. HOSPITAL PROGRESS 60(1):41-44, 1979.

Resorption of prostaglandin E2 following various methods of local administration for ripening of the cervix and end the induction of labor, by R. Reichel, et al. WIENER KLINISCHE WOCHENSCHRIFT 97(11):500-503, May 24, 1985.

Response of patients and doctors to the 1983 'pill scare', by L. D. Ritchie, et al. JOURNAL OF THE ROYAL COLLEGE OF GENERAL PRACTITIONERS 34(268):600-602, November 1984.

Results obtained in patients with cerclage, by O. Valderrama. REVISTA CHILENA DE OBSTETRICIA Y GINECOLOGIA 49(4):251-255, 1984.

Retinal manifestations of thrombotic thrombocytopenic purpura (TTP) following use of contraceptive treatment, by M. Snir, et al. ANNALS OF OPHTHALMOLOGY 17(2):109-112, February 1985.

Retreat on Depo-provera, by P. Prakash. ECONOMIC AND POLITICAL WEEKLY 19:2072-2073, December 8, 1984.

Rev. Stone and his ghoulish tactics, by R. Sharpe. MS MAGAZINE 14:20, August 1985.

Reversibility of female sterilization, by A. M. Siegler, et al. FERTILITY AND STERILIZATION 43(4):499-510, April 1985.

Reversing Roe vs Wade, by P. C. Cunningham. CHRISTIANITY TODAY 29:20-22, September 20, 1985.

Revival of the male pill, by E. Fogg. NEW SCIENTIST 104:25, December 20-27, 1984.

Rhode Island abortion statute is struck down by Federal Court. THE FAMILY LAW REPORTER 11(9):1108-1109, January 8, 1985.

Right of privacy—mandatory hospitalization for all second trimester abortions invalidated as not being reasonably related to maternal health—City of Akron v. Akron Center for Reproductive Health, Inc., 103 S. Ct. 2481. SANTA CLARA LAW REVIEW 24:789-801, Summer 1984.

Right-to-life' bombers strike again, by J. Callum. GUARDIAN 37(4):9, October 24, 1984.

Right-to-life convention, by Adriane J. Fugh-Berman. OFF OUR BACKS 15:7, August-September 1985.

Right to life of the unborn—an assessment of the eighth amendment to the Irish constitution. BRIGHAM YOUNG UNIVERSITY LAW REVIEW 1984, p. 371-402.

Right to life or right to lie?, by B. Abas. PROGRESSIVE 49:24-25, June 1985.

Right-to-life porn, by J. Morley. NEW REPUBLIC 192:8-10, March 25, 1985.

"Right-to-life" scores new victory at AID, by C. Holden. SCIENCE 229:1065-1067, September 13, 1985.

Right of privacy and minors' confidential access to contraceptives, by S. Ebers. NEW YORK LAW SCHOOL HUMAN RIGHTS ANNUAL 2:131-149, Fall 1984.

Rights threatened [on amendments proposed by Jesse Helms, Orrin Hatch and Jack Kemp to legislation funding Title X placing severe limitations on the use of private and federal funds for family planning], by P. Sheldrick. NEW DIRECTIONS FOR WOMEN 15:1+, January-February 1986.

Risk of current methods in contraception, by M. M. Zufferey. REVUE MEDICALE DE LA SUISSE ROMANDE 105(2):147-150, February 1985.

Risk of premarital first pregnancy among metropolitan-area teenagers: 1976 and 1979, by M. A. Koenig, et al. FAMILY PLANNING PERSPECTIVES 14(5):239-241+, September-October 1982.

Risk of serious complications from induced abortion: do personal characteristics make a difference?, by J. W. Buehler, et al. AMERICAN JOURNAL OF OBSTETRICS AND GYNECOLOGY 153(1):14-20, September 1, 1985.

Risk of spontaneous abortion after early prenatal diagnosis performed by chorion biopsy, by B. Gustavii. LAKARTIDNINGEN 82(21):1959-1960, May 22, 1985.

Risk of spontaneous abortion in ultrasonically normal pregnancies [letter], by R. D. Wilson, et al. LANCET 2(8408):920-921, October 20, 1984.

Risks from Dalkon Shield, by J. Willis. FDA CONSUMER 19:35, May 1985.

Risks of new contraception methods, by M. M. Zufferey. GYNAEKOLOGISCHE RUNDSCHAU 24(Suppl. 1):40-42, 1984.

Risky business: why you gamble with birth control [excerpt from Swept away], by C. Cassell. MADEMOISELLE 90:194-195+, October 1984.

Robins' costly reserve fund [for lawsuits brought by users of its Dalkon Shield intra-uterine birth-control device]. DUNS BUSINESS MONTHLY 125:22, May 1985.

Robins nuns for shelter [files for bankruptcy to cope with Dalkon Shield disaster], by C. P. Alexander. TIME 126:32-33, September 2, 1985.

Robins sees continuing Dalkon problem. CHEMICAL MARKETING REPORT 227:9+, June 3, 1985.

Robins sets fund for Dalkon Shield claims. CHEMICAL AND ENGINEERING NEWS 63:8, April 8, 1985.

Roe v. Wade: a retrospective look at a judicial oxymoron, by J. J. Coleman, III. ST. LOUIS UNIVERSITY LAW JOURNAL 29:7-44, December 1984.

Role of advertising in birth control use and sexual decision making, by J. McKillip, et al. JOURNAL OF SEX EDUCATION AND THERAPY 10:44-48, Fall-Winter 1984.

Role of Brucella abortus in spontaneous abortion among the black population, by T. J. Fernihough, et al. SOUTH AFRICAN MEDICAL JOURNAL 68(6):379-380, September 14, 1985.

Role of maternal and child health clinics in education and prevention: a case study from Papua New Guinea, by J. Reid. SOCIAL SCIENCE AND MEDICINE 19(3): 291-303, 1984.

Role of prostaglandins in human fertility, by M. P. Embrey. RECENTI PROGRESSI IN MEDICINA 76(1):34-47, January 1985.

Role of tobacco and oral contraception in myocardial infarction in the female. Description of a case, by A. Leone, et al. PATHOLOGICA 76(1044):493-498, July-August 1984.

Root and branch of Roe v. Wade, by J. T. Noonan, Jr. NEBRASKA LAW REVIEW 63:668-679, 1984.

Royal College of General Practitioners' oral contraception study: some recent observations, by C. R. Kay. CLINICAL OBSTETRICS AND GYNAECOLOGY 11(3):759-786, December 1984.

Royal College of Nursing. Retrograde step. NURSING STANDARD (383):4, February 7, 1985.

Rubella susceptibility among prenatal and family planning clinic populations, by S. F. Dorfman, et al. MT. SINAI JOURNAL OF MEDICINE 52(4):248-252, April 1985.

Rules for liberals [Catholics opposed to abortion], by D. R. Carlin, Jr. COMMON-WEAL 111:486-487, September 21, 1984.

Rural poverty breeds fertility, by A. Vajpayee. NATURE 316:773, August 29, 1985.

Russell rominates: his stand on birth control shocks some pro-lifers, by A. Singer. ALBERTA REPORT 12:28, July 1, 1985.

Safe sterilization, by F. Diamond. HEALTHSHARING 6(1):6, Winter 1984.

Safety of abortion and tubal sterilization performed separately versus concurrently, by H. H. Akhter, et al. AMERICAN JOURNAL OF OBSTETRICS AND GYNE-COLOGY 152(6 Pt 1):619-623, July 15, 1985.

Safety of the contraceptive pill—a 24 year trial [letter], by Y. R. Dugas. SOUTH AFRI-CAN MEDICAL JOURNAL 68(1):9-10, July 6, 1985.

Safety of termination of pregnancy: NHS versus private [letter], by P. Diggory. LAN-CET 2(8409):989, October 27, 1984.

Salpingitis after laparoscopic sterilization, by J. Blaakaer, et al. UGESKRIFT FOR LAEGER 146(44):3373, October 29, 1984.

Sample size needed to assess risk of abortion after chorionic villus sampling [letter], by W. Holzgreve, et al. LANCET 1(8422):223, January 26, 1985.

Sandra Day O'Connor and the justification of abortion, by P. H. Werhane. THEORET-ICAL MEDICINE 5(3):360-363, October 1984.

Save-a-baby: a viable alternative. FUNDAMENTALIST JOURNAL 2(1):24-25, January 1983.

School-based health clinics: a new approach to preventing adolescent pregnancy?, by J. Dryfoos. FAMILY PLANNING PERSPECTIVES 17:70-75, March-April 1985.

Screening for biological activity of different plant parts of Tabernaemontana dichotoma, known as divi kaduru in Sri Lanka, by P. Perera, et al. JOURNAL OF ETHNOPHARMACOLOGY 11(2):233-241, July 1984.

"Seamless garment": life in its beginnings, by L. S. Cahill. THEOLOGICAL STUDIES 46:64-80, March 1985.

Search for a tubal ligation, by L. Haught. FEMINIST CONNECTION 5(3):30, December 1984.

2d papal visit to Kenya and the 43rd International Eucharist Congress [news]. AFER 27:196+, August 1985.

Second-trimester abortion: a difficult, unresolved problem, by P. Audra, et al. REVUE FRANCAISE DE GYNECOLOGIE ET D'OBSTETRIQUE 79(4):285-288, April 1984.

Second trimester abortions discontinued, by T. Puch. BRIARPATCH 14(1):7, February 1985.

Second-trimester abortions in the United States [1972-1981], by D. A. Grimes. FAMILY PLANNING PERSPECTIVES 16:260-266, November-December 1984.

Second-trimester abortions induced by dinoprost, by J. P. Feldman, et al. REVUE FRANCAISE DE GYNECOLOGIE ET D'OBSTETRIQUE 80(2):93-96, February 1985.

Secondary infertility following induced abortion. STUDIES IN FAMILY PLANNING 15:291-295, November-December 1984.

Seeking better contraceptives. POPULI 2(2):24, 1984.

Segregation and fertility analysis in an autosomal reciprocal translocation, t(1;8)(q41; q23.1), by A. E. Vauhkonen, et al. AMERICAN JOURNAL OF HUMAN GENETICS 37(3):533-542, May 1985.

Selective abortion—thoughts from several countries, by A. Henry. OFF OUR BACKS 14(10):13, November 1984.

Selective survival of only the healthy fetus following prenatal diagnosis of thalassaemia major in binovular twin gestation, by A. Antsaklis, et al. PRENATAL DIAGNOSIS 4(4):289-296, July-August 1984.

Senate kills proposal to prevent federal funding of abortions for women inmates. CORRECTIONS DIGEST 16:23, November 6, 1985.

Sentencing—castration of rapists—cruel and unusual punishment. THE CRIMINAL LAW REPORTER: COURT DECISIONS 36(24):2463, March 20, 1985.

Separate stitches tubal sterilization, a modified Pomeroy's technic: an analysis of the procedure, complications and failure rate, by P. Rimdusit. JOURNAL OF THE MEDICAL ASSOCIATION OF THAILAND 67(11):602-607, November 1984.

Septic shock as a complication of criminal abortion, by A. P. Kiriushchenkov. FEL'DSHER I AKUSHERKA 49(9):48-52, September 1984.

Sequelae and support after termination of pregnancy for fetal malformation, by J. Lloyd, et al. BRITISH MEDICAL JOURNAL 290(6472):907-909, March 23, 1985.

Sequelae of induced abortion, by P. Frank. CIBA FOUNDATION SYMPOSIA 115:67-82, 1985.

Sequelae of therapeutic abortion [letter], by S. D. Clarke. MEDICAL JOURNAL OF AUSTRALIA 142(7):425, April 1, 1985.

Sequelae of tubal ligation, by C. F. Alvarez. GINECOLOGIA Y OBSTETRICIA DE MEXICO 53(334):35-37, February 1985.

Sequelae of tubal ligation: an anlysis of 75 consecutive hysterectomies, by R. J. Stock. SOUTHERN MEDICAL JOURNAL 77(10):1255-1260, October 1984.

Serum copper concentration significantly less in abnormal pregnancies, by P. K. Buamah, et al. CLINICAL CHEMISTRY 30(10):1676-1677, October 1984.

Serum lipid and lipoprotein changes induced by new oral contraceptives containing ethinylestradiol plus levonorgestrel or desogestrel, by U. J. Gaspard, et al. CONTRACEPTION 31(4):395-408, April 1985.

Serum progesterone levels in early imminent abortion, by A. Balogh, et al. ACTA PHYSIOLOGICA HUNGARICA 65(3):275-279, 1985.

75 years of abortion-law landmarks, by M. Janigan. MACLEANS 97:50, November 19, 1984.

Sex and the single cat, by S. L. Gerstenfeld. PARENTS MAGAZINE 60:166, June 1985.

Sex and the under-age girl, by M. McFadyean. NEW SOCIETY 72:386-388, June 14, 1985.

Sex ratio associated with natural family planning [letter], by A. Perez, et al. FERTILITY AND STERILITY 43(1):152-153, January 1985.

Sex supplies: Calgary's free condom shop starts charging, by T. Fennell. ALBERTA REPORT 11:41, November 5, 1984.

Sexual reformation and counterreformation in law and medicine, by J. Money. MEDICINE AND LAW 4(5):479-488, 1985.

Shaming 'Dr. Death': pro-lifers picket abortionists' homes, by A. Elash. ALBERTA REPORT 12:45-46, July 29, 1985.

Shared dreams/disability/reproductive rights. RADICAL AMERICAN 18(4):51, 1984.

Shielding dalkon. OFF OUR BACKS 14(9):7, October 1984.

Short-course antibiotic prophylaxis in first-trimester abortion, by J. DiOrio. RHODE ISLAND MEDICAL JOURNAL 67(11):499-500, November 1984.

Short term effect of medroxyprogesterone acetate on the rat intestinal digestive and absorptive functions, by R. Singh, et al. INDIAN JOURNAL OF MEDICAL RESEARCH 81:186-192, February 1985.

Short-term effects of teenage parenting programs on knowledge and attitudes, by M. W. Roosa. ADOLESCENCE 19(75):659-666, Fall 1984.

Shot fired into Blackman home believed to be accidental. CRIMINAL JUSTICE NEWSLETTER 16(6):8, March 15, 1985.

Shrill! Abrasive! Acerbic! Inflammatory!, by A. Gaylor. FEMINIST CONNECTION January 1985, p. 5.

Shutting the door on dissent [American nuns threatened with expulsion for disagreeing with the Vatican's stand], by J. Castro. TIME 125:83, January 7, 1985.

Significance of human leukocyte antigen profiles in human infertility, recurrent abortion, and pregnancy disorders, by A. C. Menge, et al. FERTILITY AND STERILITY 43(5):693-695, May 1985.

Silent no more [pro-choice advocates], by J. V. Lamar, Jr. TIME 125:32, May 27, 1985.

Silent scream [antiabortion film], by C. Wallis. TIME 125:62, March 25, 1985.

Silent scream airs at White House, by J. McManus, et al. NATIONAL CATHOLIC REPORTER 21:5, February 22, 1985.

Silent scream, population, parochiaid, by E. Doerr. HUMANIST 45:41-42, July-August 1985.

Silent scream: seeking an audience. NEWSWEEK 105:37, February 25, 1985.

"Silent scream" a study in deception. HERIZONS 3(6):11, September 1985.

Simplified chromosome preparations from chorionic villi obtained by choriocentesis or derived from induced abortions, by D. Pitmon, et al. ANNALES DE GENETIQUE 27(4):254-256, 1984.

Sister Margaret Traxler and the Vatican 24—standing up to the Pope on choice and the church, by C. Kleiman. MS MAGAZINE 13:124, April 1985.

Six small capsule implants may change the way the world conceives of birth control [Norplant system gradually releases levonorgestrel]. PEOPLE WEEKLY 23:137, March 18, 1985.

16-Phenoxy-prostaglandin-E2 for inducing abortion in intact and complicated pregnancy, by W. Lichtenegger. GEBURTSHILFE UND FRAUENHEILKUNDE 44(11):752-757, November 1984.

$615 million reserve set for Dalkon Shield claims, by M. Fletcher. BUSINESS INSURANCE 19:3+, April 8, 1985.

Slaughter of the innocents, by F. A. Schaeffer, et al. FUNDAMENTALIST JOURNAL 2(1):21-22, January 1983.

Social and gynaecological background of 218 sterilized women, by P. E. Børdahl. SCANDINAVIAN JOURNAL OF SOCIAL MEDICINE 12(4):183-190, 1984.

Social and gynecological long-term consequences of tubal sterilization. A personal six-year follow-up investigation, by P. E. Børdahl. ACTA OBSTETRICIA ET GYNECOLOGICA SCANDINAVICA 63(6):487-495, 1984.

Social and psychological perspectives on voluntary sterilization: a review, by S. G. Philliber, et al. STUDIES IN FAMILY PLANNING 16(1):1-29, January-February 1985.

Social class distribution of surgical patients: an assessment of Oxford Record Linkage Study data, by K. Hunt, et al. COMMUNITY MEDICINE 6(4):291-298, November 1984.

Social class, religion and contraceptive failure in a sample of pregnant women in Brisbane, by J. M. Najman, et al. COMMUNITY HEALTH STUDIES 8(3):323-331, 1984.

Social communication, organization and community development: family planning in Thailand, by L. J. Duhl. ASSIGNMENT CHILDREN 65(68):117-136, 1984.

Social discipline in Singapore: an alternative for the resolution of social problems, by S. R. Quah. JOURNAL OF SOUTHEAST ASIAN STUDIES 14:266-289, September 1983.

Socialist-feminism and reproductive rights. SOCIALIST REVIEW (78): 110, November 1984.

Socioeconomic and demographic characteristics of induced abortion cases, by T. K. Chatterjee. INTERNATIONAL JOURNAL OF GYNAECOLOGY AND OBSTETRICS 23(2):149-152, April 1985.

Socio-economic and demographic factors and their influence on family planning behavior among non-adopters, by M. M. Reddy. JOURNAL OF FAMILY WELFARE 30:92, June 1984.

Socio-economic change in Korea, by T. Hongsoon Han. ZEITSCHRIFT FUR MISSIONSWISSENSCHAFT UND RELIGIONSWISSENSCHAFT 69:140-149, April 1985.

Socio-economic correlates of fertility and contraceptive practices amongst target couples of a rural community, by M. Bhattacharya, et al. INDIAN JOURNAL OF PUBLIC HEALTH 28(3):139-146, July--September 1984.

Socioeconomic status and fertility in rural Bangladesh, by K. Shaikh, et al. JOURNAL OF BIOSOCIAL SCIENCE 17:81-90, January 1985.

Some aspects of late abortion for congenital abnormality, by S. L. Barron. CIBA FOUNDATION SYMPOSIA 115:102-121, 1985.

Some aspects of sexual knowledge and sexual behavior of local women. Results of a survey. 1. General sexual knowledge and attitude to abortion, pregnancy and contraception, by V. Atputharajah. SINGAPORE MEDICAL JOURNAL 25(3):135-140, June 1984.

— 5. Sexual intercourse, by V. Atputharajah. SINGAPORE MEDICAL JOURNAL 26(2):155-160, April 1985.

Some prochoice advocates acknowledge prolife impact of film depicting an abortion [The silent scream], by S. Anderson. CHRISTIANITY TODAY 29:46-47, April 5, 1985.

Some thoughts on autonomy and equality in relation to Roe v. Wade, by R. B. Ginsburg. NORTH CAROLINA LAW REVIEW 63:375-386, January 1985.

Spain and abortion [news]. CHRISTIAN CENTURY 102:490, May 15, 1985.

Spermicidal contraceptives and poor reproductive outcomes: —the epidemiologic evidence against an association, by M. B. Bracken. AMERICAN JOURNAL OF OBSTETRICS AND GYNECOLOGY 151(5):552-556, March 1, 1985.

Spermicides and birth defects: no clear link, by M. Engel. GLAMOUR 83:160, August 1985.

Spermicides and congenital malformations: no relation. NURSES DRUG ALERT 9(6): 47, June 1985.

—: AMERICAN JOURNAL OF NURSING 85:699, June 1985.

Spermicides and pregnancy. AMERICAN FAMILY PHYSICIAN 31:248, June 1985.

Spermicides and teratgenesis. Family Planning Association of NSW. Medical advisory board. HEALTHRIGHT 4:31, May 1985.

Spermicides given green light [study by James L. Mills and Joe L. Simpson], by J. Silberner. SCIENCE NEWS 127:326, May 25, 1985.

Split verdict. What Americans think about abortion. POLICY REVIEW 32(18-19), 1985.

Sponge is selling again, by T. Carson. BUSINESS WEEK June 17, 1985, p. 65+.

Spontaneous abortion among insulin-dependent diabetic women, by M. Miodovnik, et al. AMERICAN JOURNAL OF OBSTETRICS AND GYNECOLOGY 150(4):372-376, October 15, 1984.

Spontaneous abortions among female industrial workers, by I. Figá-Talamanca. INTERNATIONAL ARCHIVES OF OCCUPATIONAL AND ENVIRONMENTAL HEALTH 54(2):163-171, 1984.

Spontaneous abortions and malformations in the offspring of nurses exposed to anaesthetic gases, cytostatic drugs, and other potential hazards in hospitals, based on registered information of outcome, by K. Hemminki, et al. JOURNAL OF EPIDEMIOLOGY AND COMMUNITY HEALTH 39(2):141-147, June 1985.

Spontaneous abortions and newborn infants with malformations, by A. Cvejic. MEDICINSKI PREGLED 37(9-10):401-407, 1984.

Spontaneous abortions and stillbirths in relation to prenatal examinations in Denmark. Report from the Cytogenetic Central Register, by U. Friedrich, et al. UGESKRIFT FOR LAEGER 146(25):1848-1849, June 18, 1984.

Spontaneous fetal loss rate in early pregnancy [letter], by D. H. Gilmore, et al. LANCET 1(8420):107, January 12, 1985.

'Squeal rule' and a minor's right to privacy, by P. A. Olah. SPECIALTY LAW DIGEST: HEALTH CARE 7(4):5-37, June 1985.

Squeal rule: statutory resolution and constitutional implications—burdening the minor's right of privacy. DUKE LAW JOURNAL December 1984, p. 1325-1357.

Stalemate on abortion [H. Morgentaler's clinics], by H. Quinn. MACLEANS 97:66, November 26, 1984.

State legislatures versus the Supreme Court: abortion legislation in the 1980's, by B. J. George, Jr. PEPPERDINE LAW REVIEW 12:427-513, January 1985.

Statistical comparison of Pearl rates, by J. E. Higgins, et al. AMERICAN JOURNAL OF OBSTETRICS AND GYNECOLOGY 151(5):656-659, March 1, 1985.

Statutes and ordinances—abortion. THE CRIMINAL LAW REPORTER: COURT DECISIONS 37(12):2226, June 19, 1985.

Statutes and ordinances—feticide—vagueness. THE CRIMINAL LAW REPORTER: COURT DECISIONS 36(9):2163, November 28, 1984.

Sterile debate. NEW SCIENTIST 104:2, November 29, 1984.

Sterilization, by J. R. Newton. CLINICAL OBSTETRICS AND GYNAECOLOGY 11(3): 603-640, December 1984.

Sterilisation. PRACTITIONER 229(1403):449-451, May 1985.

Sterilization: all the dif between forced and free, by E. Bader. GUARDIAN 37(20):5, February 20, 1985.

Sterilization among American Indian and Chicano Mothers, by K. I. Hunter, et al. INTERNATIONAL QUARTERLY OF COMMUNITY HEALTH AND EDUCATION 4(4):343-352, 1983-84.

Sterilization by composite rubber clip [letter], by P. W. Ashton. AUSTRALIAN AND NEW ZEALAND JOURNAL OF OBSTETRICS AND GYNAECOLOGY 25(1):78, February 1985.

Sterilization failures and their causes, by R. M. Soderstrom. AMERICAN JOURNAL OF OBSTETRICS AND GYNECOLOGY 152(4):395-403, June 15, 1985.

Sterilization failures with bipolar tubal cautery, by J. W. Ayers, et al. FERTILITY AND STERILITY 42(4):526-530, October 1984.

Sterilization in the northeast of Brazil, by B. Janowitz, et al. SOCIAL SCIENCE AND MEDICINE 20(3):215-221, 1985.

Sterilization: an informed decision?, by C. Toomey. TIMES August 9, 1985, p. 9.

Sterilization: making the choice, by P. A. Hillard. PARENTS MAGAZINE 60:124+, March 1985.

Sterilization methods in China [letter], by V. L. Bullough, et al. AMERICAN JOURNAL OF PUBLIC HEALTH 75(6):689, June 1985.

Sterilization of the mentally retarded, by A. Rousso. MEDICINE AND LAW 3(4):353-362, 1984.

Sterilization of women, by H. A. Hirsch. GYNAKOLOGE 17(3):210-215, September 1984.

Sterilization via minilaparotomy using a Chinese retractor, by K. Leikanger. TIDS-SKRIFT FOR DEN NORSKE LAEGEFORENING 104(27):1916-1917, September 30, 1984.

Sterilizations in a community hospital, by O. Storeide, et al. TIDSSKRIFT FOR DEN NORSKE LAEGEFORENING 104(23):1534-1535, August 20, 1984.

Sterilizing statistics [survey by National Center for Health Statistics]. CONSUMERS RESEARCH MAGAZINE 68:38, March 1985.

Steroid chemistry: history and recent developments, by P. Crabbé. IMPACT OF SCIENCE ON SOCIETY 136:389-396, 1984.

Stimulation of uterine contraction in fetal death, by B. L. Gurtovoi, et al. AKUSHERS-TVO I GINEKOLOGIIA (10):65-67, October 1984.

Stopping population growth, by L. R. Brown. STATE OF THE WORLD 1985, p. 200-221.

Strange definition of terrorism, by P. Simpson. WORKING WOMAN 10:44, April 1985.

Strengthening government health and family planning programs: findings from an Action Research Project in rural Bangladesh, by R. Simmons, et al. STUDIES IN FAMILY PLANNING 15:212-221, September-October 1984.

Structural approach to the evaluation of the quality of contraception services, by J. Ananijevic-Pandey, et al. JUGOSLAVENSKA GINEKOLOGIJA I OPSTETRICIJA 24(5-6):91-95, September-December 1984.

Structure of pregnancy intervals by planning status, by N. B. Ryder. POPULATION STUDIES 39:193-211, July 1985.

Structuro-functional activity of lymphocyte chromatin in abortion, by M. G. Kubatova, et al. AKUSHERSTVO I GINEKOLOGIIA (5):39-41, May 1985.

Studies in antifertility agents—Part XLI: Secosteroids—X syntheses of various stereoisomers of (+/-) 2,6 beta—diethyl-7 alpha -ethynyl-3-(p-hydroxyphenyl)-trans-bicyclo[4.30]nonan beta-ol, by A. G. Thingran, et al. STEROIDS 42(6):627-634, December 1983.

Studies in spiro heterocycles. Part 4(1): investigation of the reactions of fluorinated 3-aroylmethylene-indol-2-ones with hydrazine and phenylhydrazine and synthesis of spiro [indole-3,3'-pyrazol]-2-ones, by K. C. Joshi, et al. PHARMAZIE 40(1): 21-22, January 1985.

Study of the intravaginal insert (IVI): acceptability, side effects, and post-coital spermicidal activity, by M. Ahmad, et al. ACTA EUROPAEA FERTILITATIS 15(5):369-376, September-October 1984.

Study of local fibrinolysis in abortion, by M. Ikeuchi. NIPPON SANKA FUJINKA GAKKAI ZASSHI 37(7):1215-1223, July 1985.

Study of occupational exposure to antineoplastic drugs and fetal loss in nurses, by S. G. Selevan, et al. NEW ENGLAND JOURNAL OF MEDICINE 313(19):1173-1178, November 7, 1985.

Studies on fertility control—the formation and antifertility effect of polyvinyl-pyrrolidone-gossypol complex, by Z. W. Gu, et al. BIOMATERIALS, MEDICAL DEVICES AND ARTIFICIAL ORGANS 12(1-2):1-14, 1984.

Studies on implantation traces in rats. I. Size, observation period and staining, by T. Yamada, et al. JIKKEN DOBUTSU 34(1):17-22, January 1985.

Study on ovarian function following tubal ligation, by X. D. Sun, et al. ACTA ACADE-MIAE MEDICINAE WUHAN 5(2):119-120, 1985.

Subclinical autoimmune disease and unexplained abortion, by S. Cowchock, et al. AMERICAN JOURNAL OF OBSTETRICS AND GYNECOLOGY 150(4):367-371, October 15, 1984.

Subcutaneous implantation of gestagens. A new alternative for safe contraception, by V. Odlind, et al. LAKARTIDNINGEN 81(39):3494-3496, September 26, 1984.

Subdermal contraceptive implants [letter], by H. J. Orford. SOUTH AFRICAN MEDICAL JOURNAL 67(3):80, January 19, 1985.

Successful induction of abortion in intrauterine fetal death and operated pulmonary embolism, by H. Kölbl, et al. ZEITSCHRIFT FUR GEBURTSCHILFE UND PERINATOLOGIE 188(6):285-286, November-December 1984.

Summary report of the results of a sociological investigation of abortion by means of group discussion, by R. Ramos. REVISTA ESPANOLA DE INVESTIGACIONES SOCIOLOGICAS 21:243-254, January-March 1983.

Support for prenatal decision following an abnormal amniocentesis: structure, dynamics, and outreach, by P. A. Park. BIRTH DEFECTS 20(6):91-95, 1984.

Support from significant others and loneliness following induced abortion, by J. M. Robbins, et al. SOCIAL PSYCHIATRY 20(2):92-99, 1985.

Supreme Court and abortion. THE HASTINGS CENTER REPORT 10(6):14-19, December 1980.

Supreme Court will review state abortion laws, by E. Kennelly. NATIONAL NOW TIMES 18(4):3, June 1985.

Surgery and the pill [editorial], by J. Guillebaud. BRITISH MEDICAL JOURNAL 291(6494):498-499, August 24, 1985.

Surgical management of habitual abortion caused by uterus bicornis (metroplasty), by Z. Papp, et al. ORVOSI HETILAP 126(7):389-392+, February 17, 1985.

Surgical pathologist examines the placenta, by C. H. Sander. PATHOLOGY ANNUAL 20(Pt 2):235-288, 1985.

Survey of attitudes concerning contraception and the resolution of teenage pregnancy, by C. Rinck, et al. ADOLESCENCE 18(72):923-929, Winter 1983.

Survey reveals childbirth attitudes. BEIJING REVIEW 28:30, June 17, 1985.

Swedish solutions, by J. Trost. SOCIETY 23:44-48, November-December 1985.

Symposium on the philosophy of Alan Donagan. I. Taking a human life. II. Moral absolutism and abortion: Alan Donagan on the hysterectomy and craniotomy cases. III. Comments on Dan Brock and Terrence Donagan, by D. W. Brock, et al. ETHICS 95(4):851-886, 1985.

Symptothermal method of natural family planning, by K. Hamilton. PHYSICIAN ASSISTANT 8(11):143-144+, November 1984.

Syndrome of thrombosis, abortion, and neurological disease, by G. R. Hughes, et al. CONTRIBUTIONS TO NEPHROLOGY 43:9-11, 1984.

Synthetic gestagens and endocervical adenocarcinoma [letter], by G. Dallenbach-Hellweg. INTERNATIONAL JOURNAL OF GYNECOLOGY AND PATHOLOGY 3(2):241, 1984.

Systematic karyotyping of couples in early spontaneous abortion: a reliable examination in the prevention of chromosome anomalies, by A. Salesses. PROGRESS IN CLINICAL AND BIOLOGICAL RESEARCH 163C:25-29, 1985.

T- and B-lymphocyte dynamics in patients following septic abortion, by M. A. Repina, et al. AKUSHERSTVO I GINEKOLOGIIA (3):43-45, March 1985.

TV, sex and prevention, by K. Foltz. NEWSWEEK 106:72, September 9, 1985.

Tactics of the United States right-to-life movement [letter], by J. C. Willke. LANCET 1(8426):453, February 23, 1985.

Take out Dalkon Shield. FDA CONSUMER 19:37, February 1985.

Taking precautions, by R. Shapiro. NURSING TIMES 81(9):20-21, February -March 1985.

Taking Roe to the limits: treating viable feticide as murder. INDIANA LAW REVIEW 17:1119-1142, Winter 1984.

Taste of victory [Planned Parenthood organization; Face the Facts], by C. Thomas. FUNDAMENTALIST JOURNAL 4(3):57, March 1985.

Taxation—child support—abortion. THE FAMILY LAW REPORTER: COURT OPINIONS 11(40):1515, August 20, 1985.

Teaching about abortion as a public issue. WOMEN'S ROLES 10:885-902, June 1984.

Teaching laparoscopic sterilization, by C. L. Cook, et al. JOURNAL OF REPRODUCTIVE MEDICINE 29(9):693-696, September 1984.

Teenage confidence and consent. BRITISH MEDICAL JOURNAL 290(6462):144-145, January 12, 1985.

Teens just want to have fun?, by K. Mitchell. PEDIATRIC NURSING 11(4):256+, July-August 1985.

Tell it to the Marines [letter], by P. Gerber. MEDICAL JOURNAL OF AUSTRALIA 142(9):530-531, April 29, 1985.

Temporal changes in chromosome abnormality rate in human spontaneous abortions: evidence for an association between sex-chromosome monosomy and trisomy 16, by T. Hassold, et al. CYTOGENETICS AND CELL GENETICS 38(3):200-205, 1984.

Teratological evaluation of a novel antiabortifacient, dibenzyloxyindanpropionic acid. I. Dysmorphological and histopathological studies, by F. R. del Vecchio, et al. GENERAL PHARMACOLOGY 15(6):461-469, 1984.

—. II. Postnatal morphological and behavioral development, by F. R. Del Vecchio, et al. DRUG AND CHEMICAL TOXICOLOGY 7(4):357-381, 1984.

Termination of anencephalic pregnancies, by M. Lancet, et al. HAREFUAH 105(8): 211-212, October 16, 1983.

Termination of pregnancy by a slow release device containing 16, 16-dimethyl-trans-delta 2 PGE1 methyl ester, by M. Bygdeman, et al. ASIA OCEANIA JOURNAL OF OBSTETRICS AND GYNAECOLOGY 10(3):359-365, September 1984.

Termination of pregnancy or its prevention?, by L. Hirnle. GINEKOLOGIA POLSKA 55(9):701-703, September 1984.

Terror hits the clinics, [Army of God's violent attacks on legalized abortion, by A. Brummer. GUARDIAN January 2, 1985, p. 13.

Terrorsim for the glory of God, by B. Quinn. NORTHWEST PASSAGE 25(6):5, February 1985.

Terrorism or not? GUILD NOTES 9(1):6, Winter 1985.

Terrorist attacks intensify. NATIONAL NOW TIMES 17(6):5, November 1984.

Terrorist attacks on abortion clinics, by I. Canright. SOUTHERN EXPOSURE 12(6): 111, November 1984.

Testimony on constitutional amendments to negate *Roe v. Wade* given before the Subcommittee on the Constitution of the Senate Judiciary Committee, March 7, 1983. WOMEN'S RIGHTS LAW REPORTER 8:179-183, Summer 1985.

Theory of marital fertility transition, by R. D. Retherford. POPULATION STUDIES 39: 249-268, July 1985.

Therapeutic abortion following midtrimester amniocentesis [letter], by N. J. Leschot, et al. PRENATAL DIAGNOSIS 5(3):243-244, May-June 1985.

Therapeutic abortions following rubella infection in pregnancy: the potential impact on the incidence of congenital rubella syndrome, by M. K. Serdula, et al. AMERICAN JOURNAL OF PUBLIC HEALTH 74:1249-1251, November 1984.

Therapeutic use of prostaglandins, by J. Hruda, et al. CASOPIS LEKARU CESKYCH 123(50):1527-1530, December 14, 1984.

This old lady, by E. Rogers. SOUTHERN EXPOSURE 13(2):2, March 1985.

This we believe about life and its value: Nurses Christian Fellowship 1980 position statement. JOURNAL OF CHRISTIAN NURSING 1(3):7, Fall 1984.

Threshold hypothesis. Evidence from less developed Latin American countries, 1950 to 1980. DEMOGRAPHY 21(4):459, November 1984.

Tidewater NOW uncover abortion scam, by M. Franke. OFF OUR BACKS 14(9):10, October 1984.

Time for new thinking about teenage pregnancy . . . young women may want and need more direct personal guidance about contraception, by J. G. Dryfoos. AMERICAN JOURNAL OF PUBLIC HEALTH 75(1):13-14, January 1985.

Time to catch up with public opinion, by G. Rogerson. BODY POLITIC (113):6, April 1985.

To the backstreet by the backdoor, by J. South. NEW STATESMAN November 22, 1985, p. 14-15.

To have and have not [children], by A. Hinde. TIMES HIGHER EDUCATIONAL SUPPLEMENT 666:13, August 9, 1985.

To have or have not. (Is sterilization the contraceptiivefor you?), by E. Michaud. PHILADELPHIA MAGAZINE 76:121+, March 1985.

To have or not to have a pregnancy, by L. Klein. OBSTETRICS AND GYNECOLOGY 65(1):1-4, January 1985.

Tomorrow's contraception, by C. C. Standley, et al. REVUE DE'L'INFIRMIERE 35(4): 16-19, February 1985.

Too young to live, by E. Procter. NURSING MIRROR 160(20):31, May 15, 1985.

Tooley's immodest proposal, by C. H. Sommers. HASTINGS CENTER REPORT 15:39-42, June 1985.

Torision of the fallopian tube sterilization by electrocoagulation via a laparoscope, by B. Ottesen, et al. EUROPEAN JOURNAL OF OBSTETRICS, GYNECOLOGY AND REPRODUCTIVE BIOLOGY 19(5):297-300, May 1985.

Torts—medical malpractice—wrongful birth. THE FAMILY LAW REPORTER: COURT OPINIONS 11(32):1397, June 18, 1985.

Toxic shock syndrome associated with the use of the vaginal contraceptive sponge [letter], by R. C. Dart, et al. JAMA 253(13):1877, April 5, 1985.

Tragedy of abortion [letter], by L. Huapaya. CANADIAN MEDICAL ASSOCIATION JOURNAL 132(2):93+, January 15, 1985.

Transcervical intra-amniotic induction with PgF2 alpha in missed abortion and labor in the 3d trimester of pregnancy with dead fetus. II, by E. Rizzuto, et al. MENERVA GINECOLOGIA 37(4):137-139, April 1985.

Transferrin and HLA: spontaneous abortion, neural tube defects, and natural selection, by L. R. Weitkamp, et al. NEW ENGLAND JOURNAL OF MEDICINE 313(15): 925-932, October 10, 1985.

Transient reduction in serum HDL-cholesterol following medroxyprogesterone acetate and testosterone cypionate administration to healthy men, by K. E. Friedl, et al. CONTRACEPTION 31(4):409-420, April 1985.

Treatment and minors: issues not involving lifesaving treatment, by P. A. King. JOURNAL OF FAMILY LAW 23(2):241-265, 1984-85.

Treatment for habitual aborters . . . LE-anticoagulant can be suppressed with corticotropin, prednisone or azathioprine. NURSES DRUG ALERT 8(4):28-29, April 1984.

Treatment of mitral cardiomyopathies 3. Gynecologic-obstetric prevention and treatment, by J. Droniou. SOINS CARDIOLOGIE (24):17-18, February 1985.

Treatment of recurrent spontaneous abortions by immunisation with paternal leucocytes [letter], by M. F. Reznikoff-Etievant, et al. LANCET 1(8442):1398, June 5, 1985.

Treatment of threatened abortion with traditional Chinese medicine—a clinical analysis of 62 cases, by H. Y. Huang. CHUNG HSI I CHIEH HO TSA CHIH 5(4):214-216, April 1985.

Treatment of women habitually aborting, by N. T. Gudakova, et al. AKUSHERSTVO I GINEKOLOGIIA (12):38-39, December 1984.

Trends in legalized abortion in South Australia 1970-81, by F. Yusuf, et al. JOURNAL OF BIOSOCIAL SCIENCE 17(2):215-221, April 1985.

Trends in Moslem fertility and the application of the demographic transition model, by M. H. Nagi. SOCIAL BIOLOGY 30:245-262, August 1983.

Tri-Norinyl and Ortho-Novum 7/7/7—two triphasic oral contraceptives. MEDICAL LETTER ON DRUGS AND THERAPEUTICS 26(672):93-94, October 12, 1984.

Trials target abortion clinics, by I. Dequeecker. INTERCONTINENTAL PRESS 23(17): 543, July 8, 1985.

Triphasil—a new triphasic oral contraceptive. MEDICAL LETTER ON DRUGS AND THERAPEUTICS 27(688):48, May 24, 1985.

Triplet pregnancy with second trimester abortion and delivery of twins at 35 weeks' gestation, by M. T. Banchi. OBSTETRICS AND GYNECOLOGY 64(5):728-730, November 1984.

Trojan horse goes to court: Bolger v. Youngs Drug Products Corp., by M. Mason. AMERICAN JOURNAL OF LAW AND MEDICINE 10(2):203-227, Summer 1984.

Truth about The silent scream, by A. Spake. MS MAGAZINE 14:92, July 1985.

Truth behind a moving piece of propaganda. [Controversial] US-made anti-abortion video], by A. Kent. GUARDIAN January 9, 1985, p. 8.

Tubal infertility and the intrauterine device, by D. W. Cramer, et al. NEW ENGLAND JOURNAL OF MEDICINE 312:941-947, April 11, 1985.

Tubal infertility in relation to prior induced abortion, by J. R. Daling, et al. FERTILITY AND STERILITY 43(3):389-394, March 1985.

Tubal litigation by minilaparotomy, by C. Grudsky, et al. REVISTA CHILENA DE OBSTETRICIA Y GINECOLOGIA 46(4):198-205, 1981.

Tubal ligation by a vaginal approach, by S. A. Guzman, et al. GINECOLOGIA Y OBSTETRICIA DE MEXICO 52(327):171-174, July 1984.

Tubal ligation in Milne Bay Province, Papua New Guinea, by P. Barss, et al. PAPUA NEW GUINEA MEDICAL JOURNAL 26(3-4):174-177, September-December 1983.

Tubal ligation: a misnomer [letter], by J. T. Parente, et al. AMERICAN JOURNAL OF OBSTETRICS AND GYNECOLOGY 151(6):829, March 15, 1985.

Tubal plug and clip method for female sterilization, by C. I. Meeker, et al. OBSTET-RICS AND GYNECOLOGY 65(3):430-435, March 1985.

Tubal pregnancy after a previous tubal ligation and hysterectomy, by D. Beuthe, et al. GEBURTSHILFE UND FRAUENHEILKUNDE 45(3):188, March 1985.

Tubal sterilization. A historical review, by P. E. Børdahl. JOURNAL OF REPRODUC-TIVE MEDICINE 30(1):18-24, January 1985.

Tubal sterilization in women 15-24 years of age: demographic trends in the United States, 1970-1980, by N. C. Lee, et al. AMERICAN JOURNAL OF PUBLIC HEALTH 74(12):1363-1366, December 1984.

Tubal sterilization. A prospective long term investigation of 218 sterilized women, by P. E. Børdahl. ACTA OBSTETRICIA ET GYNECOLOGICA SCANDINAVICA 128: 1-56, 1984.

Tubal sterilization with the Falope ring in an ambulatory-care surgical facility, by S. G. Kaali, et al. NEW YORK STATE JOURNAL OF MEDICINE 85(3):98-100, March 1985.

Tubal sterilization with Filshie Clip. A multicentre study of the ICMR task force on female sterilization. CONTRACEPTION 30(4):339-353, October 1984.

Tunnel vision [A. H. Robins' Dalkon Shield intrauterine device], by S. N. Chakravarty. FORBES 133:214+, May 21, 1984.

20 years for beseda. NORTHWEST PASSAGE 25(6):4, February 1985.

Two trident missiles [overriding Reagan administration decision to cut family planning aid], by R. W. Peterson. AUDUBON 87:4, July 1985.

US antics stifled population debate, by A. Smart. GOODWINS 2(2):11, Fall 1984.

U.S. attacks abortions, by P. Thompson. CHARTIST (101):6, September 1984.

U.S. bishops' efforts to affirm consistent life ethic will help refurbish damaged credibility. NATIONAL CATHOLIC REPORTER 21:14, November 2, 1984.

U.S. churches debate abortion, South Africa, and pornography. CHRISTIANITY TODAY 29:64-65, September 6, 1985.

U. S. control of abortion rights abroad. NEW WOMEN'S TIMES 10(9):4, October 1984.

U.S. denies population crisis, by J. Knox. NOT MAN APART 14(8):12, October 1984.

United States Senate votes to uphold Roe versus Wade, by D. Granberg. LATION RESEARCH AND POLICY REVIEW 4:115-131, June 1985.

U.S. Supreme Court officers angry over weapons ban during March-For-Life. SECURITY SYSTEMS DIGEST 16(3):10, February 4, 1985.

Ultrasonic diagnosis and mini-abortions, by J. Doucha, et al. CESKOSLOVENSKA GYNEKOLOGIE 49(7):481-484, August 1984.

Ultrasound and estradiol plasma levels in threatened abortion, by G. B. Melis, et al. ACTA EUROPAEA FERTILITATIS 15(4):287-294, July-August 1984.

Ultrasound signs in threatened abortion and their prognostic significance, by M. Mantoni. OBSTETRICS AND GYNECOLOGY 65(4):471-475, April 1985.

Uncontrollable life-threatening status asthmaticus—an indicator for termination of pregnancy by cesarean section, by M. Gelber, et al. RESPIRATION 46(3):320-322, 1984.

Underage girl: a surprising judgment, by K. Slack. CHRISTIAN CENTURY 102:1054 - 1056, November 20, 1985.

Under-age sex: Victorian values. ECONOMIST 290:59-60, March 24, 1984.

Understanding Mario Cuomo [Notre Dame speech], by J. Tagg. NATIONAL REVIEW 37:26-26+, February 8, 1985.

Understanding U.S. fertility: findings from the National Survey of Family Growth, Cycle III, by W. F. Pratt, et al. POPULATION BULLETIN 39:1-40, December 1984.

United Nations International Conference on Population, Mexico City. STUDIES IN FAMILY PLANNING 15(6):29, November-December 1984.

University commitment to the improvement of family health education and services, by R. Rodriquez. HYGIE 4(2):18-22, June 1985.

Unscheduled DNA synthesis caused by norethindrone and related contraceptive steroids in short-term male rat hepatocyte cultures, by D. C. Blakey, et al. CARCINOGENESIS 6(8):1201-1205, August 1985.

Untidiness revisited [discussion of November 30, 1984 article, The case for untidiness], by A. Hertzberg. COMMONWEAL 112:69-70, February 8, 1985.

Unusual use of ultrasound in a paranoid patient [letter], by P. E. Cook, et al. CANADIAN MEDICAL ASSOCIATION JOURNAL 131(6):539, September 15, 1984.

Unwanted pregnancy after careful contraception, by R. W. Bakker, et al. NEDERLANDS TIJDSCHRIFT VOOR GENEESKUNDE 129(12):559-560, March 23, 1985.

Up in smoke [clinic bombings], by S. Baer. CHRISTIANITY TODAY 29:19, April 19, 1985.

Update on other means of contraception, by N. Mallovy. HOME MAGAZINE 20:48H, May 1985.

Urological complications secondary to a contraceptive diaphragm, by D. Staskin, et al. JOURNAL OF UROLOGY 134(1):142-143, July 1985.

Use and effectiveness of norethisterone enanthate for family planning in a rural area, by V. Murillo Velasco, et al. GINECOLOGIA Y OBSTETRICIA DE MEXICO 51(314):163-167, June 1983.

Use effectiveness of the Prentif cervical cap in private practice: a prospective study, by H. Lehfeldt, et al. CONTRACEPTION 30(4):331-338, October 1984.

Use of butorphanol tartrate as an analgesic in salpingoclasia with local anesthesia, by J. R. Gaitán, et al. GINECOLOGIA OBSTETRICIA DE MEXICO 51(309):19-23, January 1983.

Use of cervical caps at the University of California, Berkeley: a survey, by G. G. Smith, et al. CONTRACEPTION 30(2):115-123, August 1984.

Use of a clindamycin phosphate-gentamycin combination in endometritis following induced abortion, by P. Rossi, et al. ANNALI DI OSTETRICIA GINECOLOGIA MEDICINA PERINATALE 105(4):267-271, July-August 1984.

Use of contact hysteroscopy in evaluating postpartum bleeding and incomplete abortion, by J. G. Tchabo. JOURNAL OF REPRODUCTIVE MEDICINE 29(10): 749-751, October 1984.

Use of contraception among abortion applicants, by D. Krishnamoni, et al. CANADIAN JOURNAL OF PUBLIC HEALTH 76(2):93-97, March-April 1985.

Use of copper electropnoresis for the prevention of complications and restoration of the reproductive function after induced abortion of the first pregnancy, by V. M. Strugatskii, et al. AKUSHERSTVO I GINEKOLOGIIA (11):62-64, November 1984.

Use of methyl cyanoacrylate (MCA) for female sterilization. Program for Applied Research on Fertility Regulation Northwestern University Medical School Chicago, Illinois. CONTRACEPTION 31(3):243-252, March 1985.

Use of a modified test system to determine early pregnancy factor (EPF) levels in patients with normal first trimester pregnancy and after therapeutic abortion, by H. R. Tinneberg, et al. ANNALS OF THE NEW YORK ACADEMY OF SCIENCES 442:551-557, 1985.

Use of a new vaginal suppository prostaglandin E1 analog Gemeprost for cervix maturation prior to abortion in the 1st trimester, by T. Rabe, et al. GEBURT-SHILFE UND FRAUENHEILKUNDE 45(6):393-401, June 1985.

Use of oral contraceptives in women with cystic fibrosis, by S. B. Fitzpatrick, et al. CHEST 86(6):863-867, December 1984.

Use of osmotic dilators to facilitate induced midtrimester abortion: clinical evaluations, by M. F. Atienza, et al. CONTRACEPTION 30(3):215-223, September 1984.

Use of prostaglandin F2 alpha for dilating the cervical canal in performing an abortion, by S. Matanyi, et al. AKUSHERSTVO I GINEKOLOGIIA (3):39-41, March 1985.

Use of prostaglandins and their analogues for abortion, by M. Bygdeman. CLINICAL OBSTETRICS AND GYNAECOLOGY 11(3):573-584, December 1984.

Use of prostaglandins in the interruption of pregnancy, by F. Havránek. CESKOSLO-VENSKA GYNEKOLOGIE 49(6):439-448, July 1984.

Use of questionnaires in occupational studies of pregnancy outcome, by G. Axelsson, et al. ANNALS OF THE ACADEMY OF MEDICINE SINGAPORE 13(Suppl. 2):327-330, April 1984.

Use of 16,16-dimethyl-trans delta 2 prostaglandin E1 methyl ester (gemeprost) vaginal pessaries for the termin.. :on of pregnancy in the ealry second trimester. A comparison with extra-amniotic prostaglandin E2, by I. T. Cameron, et al. BRITISH JOURNAL OF OBSTETRICS AND GYNAECOLOGY 91(11):1136-1140, November 1984.

Use of the Today contraceptive sponge in the United States, by B. B. North, et al. INTERNATIONAL JOURNAL OF FERTILITY 30(1):81-84, 1985.

Use of vasectomy, by C. Schirren. ZEITSCHRIFT FUR HAUTKRANKHEITEN 60(14): 1097-1099, July 15, 1985.

Uterine guide to gynecologic laparoscopy, by E. H. Jørgensen, et al. UGESKRIFT FOR LAEGER 146(45):3452-3454, November 5, 1984.

Uterine pathology and infertility, by C. Flamigni, et al. ACTA EUROPAEA FERTILI-TATIS 16(1):25-34, January-February 1985.

Uterine perforation following medical termination of pregnancy by vacuum aspiration, by S. Mittal, et al. INTERNATIONAL JOURNAL OF GYNAECOLOGY AND OB-STETRICS 23(1):45-50, February 1985.

Uterine rupture during induced mid-trimester abortion, by Y. Biale, et al. EUROPEAN JOURNAL OF OBSTETRICS, GYNECOLOGY AND REPRODUCTIVE BIOLOGY 19(3):175-182, March 1985.

Vaginal contraceptive activity of hyaluronidase and cyclooxygenase (prostaglandin synthetase) inhibitors in the rabbit, by C. L. Joyce, et al. FERTILITY AND STER-ILITY 44(3):426-428, September 1985.

Vaginal contraceptive sponge: a new non-prescription barrier contraceptive, by E. Lemberg. NURSE PRACTITIONER 9(10):24-25+, October 1984.

Vaginal sponge and toxic shock. AMERICAN JOURNAL OF NURSING 85:693, June 1985.

Value of ovarian and placental steroid determinations in abnormal early pregnancy, by W. Distler, et al. ARCHIVES OF GYNECOLOGY 236(3):153-160, 1985.

Valued outcomes in the selection of a contraceptive method, by E. M. Wall. WESTERN JOURNAL OF MEDICINE 141(3):335-338, September 1984.

Various aspects of prenatal and perinatal reproductive loss, by F. Cisarik, et al. BRATISLAVSKE LEKARSKE LISTY 83(6):670-677, June 1985.

Vasectomy and tubal ligation: medicopsychological aspects of voluntary sterilization, by M. Bourgeois. PSYCHOLOGIE MEDICALE 14(8):1195-1201, June 1982.

Vasectomy counselling, by M. Redelman. HEALTHRIGHT 4:27-29, August 1985.

Vasectomy reversal, by J. Mickelson. MOTHERING 36:30, Summer 1985.

Vasopressin reduces blood loss from second-trimester dilatation and evacuation abortion, by K. F. Schulz, et al. LANCET 2(8451):353-356, August 17, 1985.

Vatican and nuns reach agreement [abortion rights statement; news]. CHRISTIANITY TODAY 29(14):69, October 4, 1985.

Vatican and population growth control: why an American confrontation?, by S. D. Mumford. HUMANIST 43:18-24+, September-October 1983.

Vatican closes the door on dialogue and dissent, by M. Babbitt. NATIONAL NOW TIMES 18(1):2, January 1985.

Vatican threatens outspoken sisters [Vatican threat to expel 24 religious women from their orders unless they retract support for a statement published in the *New York Times* critical of the Church's crusade against legalized abortion, by A. Baker. NEW DIRECTIONS FOR WOMEN 14:1+, March-April 1985.

Vatican to nuns: "shut up", by E. Bader. GUARDIAN 37(15):2, January 16, 1985.

Various aspects of termination of pregnancy by the vacuum-aspiration method, by E. I. Kal'chenko, et al. AKUSHERSTVO I GINEKOLOGIIA (12):43-44, December 1984.

Vecuronium bromide in anaesthesia for laparoscopic sterilization, by J. E. Caldwell, et al. BRITISH JOURNAL OF ANAESTHESIOLOGY 57(8):765-769, August 1985.

Vesicovaginal fistula and its complications due to prolonged use of vaginal diaphragm, by D. M. Kwa, et al. AUSTRALIAN AND NEW ZEALAND JOURNAL OF OBSTETRICS AND GYNAECOLOGY 24(3):225-226, August 1984.

Viability and the moral status of the fetus, by A. V. Campbell. CIBA FOUNDATION SYMPOSIA 115:228-243, 1985.

Victory for abortion rights. INTERCONTINENTAL PRESS 22(23):727, December 10, 1984.

Viewing abortion from the perspective of transplantation: the ethics of the gift of life, by S. S. Mattingly. SOUNDINGS 67:399-410, Winter 1984.

Violence against abortion clinics escalates despite the opposition of prolife leaders, by R. Frame. CHRISTIANITY TODAY 29:44-46, February 1, 1985.

Virginia doctor acquitted of illegal abortion, by L. S. OFF OUR BACKS 15(5):7, May 1985.

Vitamin metabolism and the effects of multivitamin supplementation in oral contraceptive users, by K. Amatayakul, et al. CONTRACEPTION 30(2):179-196, August 1984.

Vocal prochoice activists launch nationwide offensive, by M. Meehan. CHRISTIANITY TODAY 29:42-43, July 12, 1985.

Voluntary and involuntary childlessness in the United States, 1955-1973. SOCIAL BIOLOGY 30:290-306, August 1983.

Voluntary interruptions of pregnancy in metropolitan France in 1981, by M. Kaminski, et al. REVUE D'EPIDEMIOLOGIE ET DE SANTE PUBLIQUE 33(1):70-71, 1985.

Vomiting after anaesthesia for termination of pregnancy in China, by S. C. Chan, et al. SINGAPORE MEDICAL JOURNAL 24(6):360-362, December 1983.

Vor der Weltbevölkerungskonferenz in Mexico [collection of articles]. ENTWICKLUNG UND ZUSAMMENARBEIT 7:7-17, 1984.

Voting on June 9 1985: initiative 'Right to Life'. KRANKENPFLEGE SOINS INFIRMIERE 78(5):32-33, May 1985.

Vulvar effects of the toilet tissue observational routine in the practice of natural family planning [letter], by C. W. Norris. AMERICAN JOURNAL OF OBSTETRICS AND GYNECOLOGY 152(8):1108-1109, August 15, 1985.

WEBA: voice of experience relates the horrors of abortion [Women exploited by abortion], by D. W. Huff. FUNDAMENTALIST JOURNAL 2(1):34-35, January 1983.

WHO collaborative study. Mental health and female sterilization: a follow-up. JOURNAL OF BIOSOCIAL SCIENCE 17:1-18, January 1985.

WHO collaborative study of neoplasia and steroid contraceptives. BRITISH MEDICAL JOURNAL 290(6473):961-965, March 30, 1985.

War on clinics continues. NEW WOMEN'S TIMES 10(11):1, December 1984.

War on people [myths about population growth], by J. L. Simon. CHALLENGE 28: 50-53, March-April 1985.

Was Margaret Sanger a racist?, by C. Valenza. FAMILY PLANNING PERSPECTIVES 17(1):44-46, January-February 1985.

Washington court bars recovery for expenses of rearing normal child. THE FAMILY LAW REPORTER: COURT OPINIONS 10(46):1632-1633, September 25, 1984.

Water intoxication and oxytocin, by F. T. Mwambingu. BRITISH MEDICAL JOURNAL 290(6462):113, January 12, 1985.

We will not yield nor fall silent nor rest until all our children are safe, by M. Garvey. NATIONAL CATHOLIC REPORTER 20:18, October 19, 1984.

Webster says FBI won't classify abortion clinic bombings as acts of terrorism. CRIME CONTROL DIGEST 18(49):3-4, December 10, 1984.

—. SECURITY SYSTEMS DIGEST 15(26):4-5, December 17, 1984.

What are the determinants of delayed childbearing and permanent childlessness in the United States?, by D. E. Bloom, et al. DEMOGRAPHY 21:591-612, November 1984.

What are the limits of birth control?, by L. H. Levie. NEDERLANDS TIJDSCHRIFT VOOR GENEESKUNDE 128(43):2045-2047, October 27, 1984.

What different Christian churches believe about abortion, by C. Dubois. U.S. CATHOLIC 50:33-38, August 1985.

What every girl should know about the Pill, if her GP will tell her, by A. Veitch, et al. GUARDIAN June 3, 1985, p. 10.

What the FBI won't probe. GUARDIAN 37(11):18, December 12, 1984.

What has happened to America's respect for human life [Soap Box], by J. Savely. FUNDAMENTALIST JOURNAL 4(5):30, May 1985.

What is a person? (editorial). JOURNAL OF CHRISTIAN NURSING 1(3):3, Fall 1984.

What is the role of chlamydia culture, wet smear and general bacterial culture from the cervix before surgical abortion?, by M. Nordenvall, et al. LAKARTIDNINGEN 81(39):3471-3472, September 26, 1984.

What makes the Indonesian family planning programme tick. POPULI 2(3):4, 1984.

What matters is what is left inside not what is removed: how about twins? [letter], by G. Jonas. OBSTETRICS AND GYNECOLOGY 65(2):297-298, February 1985.

What a way to treat a hero. GOODWINS 2(4):4, Spring 1985.

What you haven't heard about Bhopal: shocking reports of infertility, miscarriage and deformity, by S. Lerner, et al. MS MAGAZINE 14:85-88, December 1985.

What's new: new duty to warn for birth control pill manufacturer. AMERICAN BAR ASSOCIATION JOURNAL 71:96+, June 1985.

What's new: New York decides healthy baby is no injury, by J. A. Rajchenbach. AMERICAN BAR ASSOCIATION JOURNAL 71:102, June 1985.

What's the #1 contraceptive? (Guess again), by S. Wernick. REDBOOK 165:36+, September 1985.

When the baby doesn't come home. CHILDREN TODAY 13(2):21-24, 1984.

When Irish eyes are smiling . . . they probably aren't women's, by L. Davis. REFRACTORY GIRL 28:36-38, May 1985.

When is a terrorist not necessarily a terrorist?, by S. Taylor. NATIONAL NOW TIMES 18(1):8, January 1985.

When a mentally ill woman refuses abortion, by M. Mahowald, et al. HASTINGS CENTER REPORT 15:22-23, April 1985.

When the unborn die: the impact on parents can be devastating [miscarriage], by M. Nemeth. ALBERTA REPORT 12:27, July 1, 1985.

Where babies go to, by C. Hitchens. SPECTATOR February 9, 1985, p. 10.

Where the bigger the family means the greater the fortune, by P. Quinn-Judge. FAR EASTERN ECONOMIC REVIEW 126:48-49, October 11, 1984.

Where have all the babies gone [social trends; aboption], by K. Menehan. CHRISTIANITY TODAY 29(15):26-29, October 18, 1985.

Who attends family planning clinics?, by P. Chick, et al. AUSTRALIAN AND NEW ZEALAND JOURNAL OF OBSTETRICS AND GYNAECOLOGY 24(3):213-216, August 1984.

Who confers value?, by J. Garvey. COMMONWEAL 112:423-424, August 9, 1985.

Who gains in the battle to control population, by L. Orendiain. BALAI (11):16, 1985.

Who put the wrong in 'wrongful births?', by T. Eastland. THIS WORLD (5):84-93, 1983.

Who really is like Hitler? (abortionists vs. anti-abortion terrorists), by C. Marshner. CATHOLIC DIGEST 11:28, February 1985.

Who uses natural family planning?, by K. J. Daly, et al. CANADIAN JOURNAL OF PUBLIC HEALTH 76(3):207-208l, May-June 1985.

Who's afraid of population?, by Z. Sardar. GEOGRAPHICAL MAGAZINE 56:506, October 1984.

Who's to blame: adolescent sexual activity, by R. Kornfield. JOURNAL OF ADOLESCENT HEALTH CARE 8:17-31, March 1985.

Whose right to life [abortion], by C. B. Fischer. JOURNAL OF WOMEN AND RELIGION 1(1):61-64, Spring 1981.

Why we can't be silent about anti-abortion tactics [innacuracies in The silent scream]. GLAMOUR 83:52, June 1985.

Why women don't get sterilized: a folow-up of women in Honduras, by B. Janowitz, et al. STUDIES IN FAMILY PLANNING 16(2):106-112, March-April 1985.

Windows into the legal past, by N. Blodgett. AMERICAN BAR ASSOCIATION JOURNAL 71:44-48, January 1985.

Wire next time? PROGRESSIVE 49(9):9, September 1985.

Withdraw this license to kill. [Moral relativism as the link between embroyology, abortion and murder], by P. Johnson. TIMES August 22, 1985, p. 10.

Within our reach: a building consensus could at least put an end to abortion on demand [editorial], by K. S. Kantzer, et al. CHRISTIANITY TODAY 29(7):20-23, April 19, 1985.

Womanpoll. CHATELAINE 58:56, September 1985.

Women and mental health: "Charter of Rts" report, by C. McKague. PHOENIX RISING 5(1):38, February 1985.

Women buy most condoms to avoid pregnancy, VD. JET 69:26, October 14, 1985.

Women in struggle, by H. Lessinger. GUARDIAN 37(25):2, March 27, 1985.

Women may need permission for abortion. BRIARPATCH 14(5):8, June 1985.

Women of Japan [abortion is easy to obtain, divorce is difficult; despite rapid social change, women find they often have little future except as housewives, by C. Moorehead. NEW SOCIETY 70:453-455, December 20-27, 1984.

Women who obtain repeat abortions: a study based on record linkage, by P. G. Steinhoff, et al. FAMILY PLANNING PERSPECTIVES 11(1):30-38, 1979.

Women with nongranulomatous colitis should avoid "the pill". NURSES DRUG ALERT 8(9):69, September 1984.

Women's perceptions of first trimester spontaneous abortion, by C. L. Wall-Hass. JOURNAL OF OBSTETRICS, GYNECOLOGY AND NEONATAL NURSING 14(1):50-53, January-February 1985.

Women's responses to abortion: implications for post-abortion support groups, by A. Mcgettigan, et al. JOURNAL OF SOCIAL WORK AND HUMAN SEXUALITY 3: 119-132, 1984-85.

Women's rights in US under big attack, by D. Jenness. INTERCONTINENTAL PRESS 22(21):650, November 12, 1984.

Work to control populations. BEIJING REVIEW 27:14-15, December 10, 1984.

'Worthy of life and unworthy of life'—not an alternative for the physician (editorial), by H. Berger. PADIATRIE UND PADOLOGIE 20(1):1-6, 1985.

Wrongful life?, by C. Frank. AMERICAN BAR ASSOCIATION JOURNAL 71:26, February 1985.

Wrongful life and wrongful birth: new concepts for the pediatrician, by J. Coplan. 75(1):65-72, January 1985.

Wrongful life: a tort resuscitated, by G. Dorst. THE AMERICAN JOURNAL OF TRIAL ADVOCACY 7(1):167-176, Fall 1983.

Wrongful pregnancy: damages recoverable for the birth of a normal, healthy child, by T. L. Mann. THE AMERICAN JOURNAL OF TRIAL ADVOCACY 7(2):385-391, Spring 1984.

Wyeth's birth control gamble [oral]. CHEMICAL WEEK 135:17, November 28, 1984.

Young adult with diabetes: impact of the disease on marriage and having children, by J. E. Ahlfield, et al. DIABETES CARE 8(1):52-56, January-February 1985.

ABORTION: GENERAL

Abortion. CANADIAN MEDICAL ASSOCIATION JOURNAL 133(4):318A-318B, August 15, 1985.

Abortion [letter], by N. E. MacLean. NEW ZEALAND MEDICAL JOURNAL 98(771):22, January 23, 1985.

Abortion. A viable proposition?, by R. Shapiro. NURSING TIMES 81(32):17-18, August 7-13, 1985.

Abortion and infanticide. Is there a difference?, by D. Cannon. POLICY REVIEW 32:12-17, 1985.

Abortion and medical discipline [letter], by F. R. Duncanson. NEW ZEALAND MEDICAL JOURNAL 98(776):251, April 10, 1985.

Abortion and subsequent pregnancy, by C. F. Bradley. CANADIAN JOURNAL OF PSYCHIATRY 29(6):494-498, October 1984.

Abortion clinic closed; clinic closed because of abuse against women. OFF OUR BACKS 15:3, January 1985.

Abortion clinic violence: How far will it go?, by L. Speare. WOMEN'S PRESS 14(5):1, November 1984.

Abortion debate. CHRISTIAN CENTURY 101:1032, November 7, 1984.

Abortion denied—outcome of mothers and babies [letter], by C. Del Campo. CANADIAN MEDICAL ASSOCIATION JOURNAL 131(6):546+, September 15, 1984.

Abortion: the enduring debate. ECONOMIST 292:26+, September 22, 1984.

Abortion following prenatal diagnosis of genetic defects, by W. Weise. ZENTRALBLATT FUR GYNAEKOLOGIE 107(14):855-862, 1985.

Abortion in early pregnancy [letter], by I. R. Walker. MEDICAL JOURNAL OF AUSTRALIA 142(8):489, April 15, 1985.

Abortion in Thailand and Sweden: health services and short-term consequences, by T. N. Singnomklao. CIBA FOUNDATION SYMPOSIUM 115:54-66, 1985.

Abortion is not convenient [letters]. VILLAGE VOICE 29:8-9, October 16, 1984.

Abortion: no going back. GUARDIAN 37(17):18, January 30, 1985.

Abortion or premature delivery?, by R. Perkins. MEDICAL JOURNAL OF AUSTRALIA 142(5):313-314, March 4, 1985.

Abortion re-examined, by E. Monk. HEALTHSHARING 6(1):20, Winter 1984.

Abortion, right and wrong, by R. S. Smith. MICHIGAN MEDICINE 84(6):350+, June 1985.

Abortion services in Slovenia, by L. Andolsek. CIBA FOUNDATION SYMPOSIA 115:21-25, 1985.

Abortion statistics 1983. HEALTH BULLETIN 42(5):272-273, September 1984.

Abortion: trying to hold on to what we have, by P. Krebs, et al. OFF OUR BACKS15:1-2, February 1985.

Administrative, counseling and medical practices in National Abortion Federation facilities, by U. Landy, et al. FAMILY PLANNING PERSPECTIVES 14(5):257-262, September-October 1982.

Adverse effect of an overdistended bladder on first-trimester sonography, by M. E. Baker, et al. AJR 145(3):597-599, September 1985.

AID turns down IPPF, by C. Holden. SCIENCE 227:37, January 4, 1985.

Alleged miscarriages of Catherine of Aragon and Anne Boleyn, by J. Dewhurst. MEDICAL HISTORY 28(1):49-56, January 1984.

Antecedents and prevention of unwanted pregnancy, by M. Gerrard, et al. ISSUES IN MENTAL HEALTH NURSING 5(1/4):85-101, 1983.

Antiabortion violence. FAMILY PLANNING PERSPECTIVES 17(1):4, January-February 1985.

Antiabortion violence on the rise, by L. C. Wohl. MS MAGAZINE 13:135-136+, October 1984.

Appeal of certainty. ECONOMIST 298:18, December 22, 1984.

Case of the Peacenik Provacateur, by P. Maass. NATION 240(24):751, June 22, 1985.

Caught in the abortion backlash, by V. Safran. PROGRESSIVE 49:16, May 1985.

Cervical cerclage following prior delivery [letter], by J. H. Harger. AMERICAN JOURNAL OF OBSTETRICS AND GYNECOLOGY 151(8):1141-1142, April 15, 1985.

Cervix-dilative effect of PGF2 alpha after intracervical and extraovular administration, by A. Pajor, et al. GINEKOLOGIA POLSKA 55(6):421-425, June 1984.

Characteristics and bioefficacy of monoclonal antigonadotropin releasing hormone antibody, by S. K. Gupta, et al. AMERICAN JOURNAL OF REPRODUCTIVE IMMUNOLOGY AND MICROBIOLOGY 7(3):104-108, March 1985.

Chemistry and abortion, by R. Block. MACLEANS 98:58, May 27, 1985.

Civil war, by J. Hoffman, et al. VILLAGE VOICE 30:14, February 12, 1985.

Clustering of abortion scale scores, by R. Lane, Jr. JSSR 24:403-406, December 1985.

Compulsory pregnancy: it's still 1984. FRYING PAN December 1984, p. 16.

Controlled study of 16,16-dimethyl-trans-delta 2 prostaglandin E1 methyl ester vaginal pessaries prior to suction termination of first trimester pregnancies, by P. R. Fisher, et al. BRITISH JOURNAL OF OBSTETRICS AND GYNAECOLOGY 91(11):1141-1144, November 1984.

Coping with abortion, by L. Cohen, et al. JOURNAL OF HUMAN STRESS 10(3): 140-145, Fall 1984.

Crimes—feticide—statutes—vagueness. THE FAMILY LAW REPORTER: COURT OPINIONS December 11, 1984, p. 1074.

Current aspects of abortion assistance, by P. E. Treffers. NEDERLANDS TIJDSCHRIFT VOOR GENEESKUNDE 128(31):1476-1478, August 4, 1984.

Cytogenetic findings in 311 couples with infertility and reproductive disorders, by B. Raczkiewicz, et al. ACTA ANTHROPOGENETICA 7(4):355-366, 1983.

Cytogenetics of aborters and abortuses: a review, by P. J. Noor, et al. SINGAPORE MEDICAL JOURNAL 25(5):306-312, October 1984.

Cytogenetics of pregnancy wastage, by A. Boué, et al. ADVANCES IN HUMAN GENETICS 14:1-57, 1985.

Dependence, reliance and abortion, by M. Strasser. PHILOSOPHICAL QUARTERLY 35:73-82, January 1985.

Early biopsy of chorionic villi. Personal experience and review of the literature, by A.Treisser, et al. REVUE FRANCAISE DE GYNECOLOGIE ET D'OBSTETRIQUE 80(6):397-412, May 1985.

Early embryonic loss: report of the study group, by A. F. Zakharov. PROGRESS IN CLINICAL AND BIOLOGICAL RESEARCH 163C:3-7, 1985.

Early spontaneous abortion, by J. L. Parmentier. SOINS, GYNECOLOGIE, OBSTETRIQUE, PUERICULTURE, PEDIATRIE 24:5-7, May 1983.

Early total operative occlusion of the cervix in anamnestic abortion and premature labor risk, E. Saling. GYNAKOLOGE 17(4):225-229, December 1984.

Effects of common environmental exposures on spontaneous abortion of defined karyotype, by D. Warburton. PROGRESS IN CLINICAL AND BIOLOGICAL RESEARCH 163C:31-36, 1985.

Endocrine abortions, by J. L. Parmentier. SOINS, GYNECOLOGIE, OBSTETRIQUE, PUERICULTURE, PEDIATRIE 24:15-16, May 1983.

Flames of fanaticism: abortion clinic bombings are only the latest actions in America's little-known history of violence in the name of God, by A. J. Menendez. CHURCH AND STATE 38:4-7, February 1985.

Foetal protection against abortion: is it immunosuppression or immuno-stimulation?, by T. G. Wegmann. ANNALES D'IMMUNOLOGIE 135D(3):309-312, November-December 1984.

Follow-up study of children born to women denied abortion, by Z. Matejcek, et al. CIBA FOUNDATION SYMPOSIA 115:136-149, 1985.

Genetic diseases; problems of prenatal testing, by T. Beardsley. NATURE 314:211, March 21, 1985.

Getting rid of old habits, by M. Lauer. MOTHER JONES 10(2):10, February 1985.

Guilty of trying to self-abort, by E. Rader. GUARDIAN 37(13):2, December 26, 1984.

Helping hand for back-alley abortionists, by R. MacKay. GUARDIAN 37(30):15, May 1,1985.

Hentoff, are you listening, by K. Pollitt. MOTHER JONES 10(2):60, February 1985.

HLA compatibility and human reproduction, by P. F. Bolis, et al. CLINICAL AND EXPERIMENTAL OBSTETRICS AND GYNECOLOGY 12(1-2):9-12, 1985.

Holding the center against "right" rhetoric, by J. M. Wall. CHRISTIAN CENTURY102:203-204, February 27, 1985.

Holy war, by P. Donovan. FAMILY PLANNING PERSPECTIVES 17(1):5-9, January-February 1985.

How patients view mandatory waiting periods for abortion, by M. Lupfer, et al. FAMILY PLANNING PERSPECTIVES 13(2):75-79, 1981.

I had an abortion; I kept my baby, by M. A. Kellogg. SEVENTEEN 43:144-145+, October 1984.

Identification of fetal bloodstains by enzyme-linked immunosorbent assay for human a-fetoprotein, by Y. Katsumata. JOURNAL OF FORENSIC SCI-ENCES 30(4):1210-1215, October 1985.

Immunology of abortion, by J. F. Mowbray, et al. CLINICAL AND EXPERIMENTAL IMMUNOLOGY 60(1):1-7, April 1985.

Incidence of chromosome anomalies in 123 married couples with reproductive loss, by M. Lukácová, et al. BRATISLAVSKE LEKARSKE LISTY 83(6):658-669, June 1985.

Interview with Dr. Henry Morgentaler. CANADIAN MEDICAL ASSOCIATION JOURNAL 133(5):490-495, September 1, 1985.

IVF versus nature [letter], by R. Winston, et al. LANCET 1(8423):284, February 2,1985.

Learning the "real" facts of life [interview with J. Irving]. GLAMOUR 83:118+, July 1985.

Looking past abortion rhetoric, by J. A. Brix. CHRISTIAN CENTURY 101:986-988, October 24, 1984.

Maternal age-specific rates of numerical chromosome abnormalities with special reference to trisomy, by T. Hassold, et al. HUMAN GENETICS 70(1):11-17, 1985.

Medical progress and the social implications of abortion: summing-up, by M. Potts. CIBA FOUNDATION SYMPOSIA 115:263-268, 1985.

Metronidazole prophylaxis in elective first trimester abortion, by L. Heisterberg, et al. OBSTETRICS AND GYNECOLOGY 65(3):371-374, March 1985.

Moderate drinking during pregnancy and foetal outcome, by I. G. Barrison, et al. ALCOHOL AND ALCOHOLISM 19(2):167-172, 1984.

Moral norms: an update, by R. A. McCormick. THEOLOGICAL STUDIES 46:50-64, March 1985.

Need for routine sonography prior to late abortion, by F. A. Chervenak, et al. NEW YORK STATE JOURNAL OF MEDICINE 85(1):4-5, January 1985.

Neither incompetent nor indifferent, by D. N. O'Steen. COMMENTARY 111:179-182, March 23, 1984.

Never again/abortion 1954, by S. Matulis. FEMINIST CONNECTION January 1985, p. 1.

New applications for the assay of placental proteins, by A. Klopper, et al. PLACENTA 6(2):173-184, March-April 1985.

New technology confab, by J. Stein. NEW DIRECTIONS FOR WOMEN 14(2):7, March 1985.

Nightmare of Kiko Martinez, by D. Martinez. GUILD NOTES 9(2):4, Spring 1985.

Not quite the baby I expected . . ., by J. Chase. GOOD HOUSEKEEPING 199:68+, October 1984.

Nova Scotia responds to Morgentaler. HEALTHSHARING 6(3):7, Summer 1985.

Offer they can't refuse, by C.Thomas. CONSERVATIVE DIGEST 11:24, August-September 1985.

Organization of multi-level medical services for women with abortions and for pre-mature infants, by M. F. V'iaskova, et al. AKUSHERSTVO I GINEKOLOGIIA (5):60-61, May 1985.

Parental HLA compatibility, fetal wastage and neural tube defects: evidence for a T/t-like locus in humans, by B. Schacter, et al. AMERICAN JOURNAL OF HUMAN GENETICS 36(5):1082-1091, September 1984.

Pathologic early pregnancy. Evaluation of new pregnancy tests, by J. A. Steier, et al. TIDSSKRIFT FOR DEN NORSKE LAEGEFORENING 105(7):496-498, March 10, 1985.

Pensacola, D C bombers found guilty, by M. Anderson. NATIONAL NOW TIMES 18(4):3, June 1985.

Pill that 'might defuse the abortion issue' [morning after pills], by R. Rhein, Jr., et al. BUSINESS WEEK April 1, 1985, p. 85+.

Pituitary microadenoma. Subsequent pregnancies (clinical cases), by C. Wainstein. REVISTA CHILENA DE OBSTETRICIA Y GINECOLOGIA 46(1):20-24, 1981.

Placenta percreta associated with a second-trimester pregnancy termination, by M. D. Hornstein, et al. AMERICAN JOURNAL OF OBSTETRICS AND GYNE-COLOGY 150(8):1002-1003, December 15, 1984.

Post conception failures in reproduction: infectious diseases and immunitary pro-blems, by G. Scarselli, et al. ACTA EUROPAEA FERTILITATIS 15(5):363-367, September-October 1984.

Pregnancy and systemic sclerosis [letter], by M. Giordano, et al. ARTHRITIS AND RHEUMATISM 28(2):237-238, February 1985.

Pregnancy loss in mothers of multiple births and in mothers of singletons only, by G. Wyshak. ANNALS OF HUMAN BIOLOGY 12(1):85-89, January-February 1985.

Prenatal genetic diagnosis [letter], by R. A. Jones. MEDICAL JOURNAL OF AUSTRALIA 143(3):127, August 5, 1985.

Prenatal selection and fetal development disturbances occurring in carriers of G6PD deficiency, by D. Toncheva, et al. HUMAN GENETICS 69(1):88, by D. Toncheva, et al.

Previous child with trisomy 21 and abortion rate, by S. Aymé, et al. PROGRESS IN CLINICAL AND BIOLOGICAL RESEARCH 163C:15-19, 1985.

Privacy: control over stimulus input, stimulus output, and self-regarding conduct, by P. Siegel. BUFFALO LAW REVIEW 33(1):35-84, 1984.

Pro-life in word or deed?, by E. I. Goulding. JOURNAL OF CHRISTIAN NURSING 1(1):32, Spring 1984.

Pro-puppies, pro-parrots, but not pro-people, by C.Thomas. FUNDAMENTALIST JOURNAL 2(10):34, November 1983.

Promoting abortion, by M. Golden. AFER 27:245-249, August 1985.

Relative body weight as a factor in the decision to abort, by T. H. Thelen, et al. PSYCHOLOGICAL REPORTS 52:763-775, June 1983.

Reproductive loss in man: total and chromosomally determined, by A. F. Zakharov. PROGRESS IN CLINICAL AND BIOLOGICAL RESEARCH 163C:9-14, 1985.

Requests for late termination of pregnancy: Tower Hamlets, 1983, by W. Savage. BRITISH MEDICAL JOURNAL 290(6468):621-623, February 23, 1985.

Sample size needed to assess risk of abortion after chorionic villus sampling [letter], by W. Holzgreve, et al. LANCET 1(8422):223, January 26, 1985.

Second trimester abortions discontinued, by T. Puch. BRIARPATCH 14(1):7, February 1985.

Selective survival of only the healthy fetus following prenatal diagnosis of thalassaemia major in binovular twin gestation, by A. Antsaklis, et al. PRENATAL DIAGNOSIS 4(4):289-296, July-August 1984.

Short-course antibiotic prophylaxis in first-trimester abortion, by J. DiOrio. RHODE ISLAND MEDICAL JOURNAL 67(11):499-500, November 1984.

Shrill! Abrasive! Acerbic! Inflammatory!, by A. Gaylor. FEMINIST CONNECTION January 1985, p. 5.

Sterile debate. NEW SCIENTIST 104:2, November 29, 1984.

Study of occupational exposure to antineoplastic drugs and fetal loss in nurses, by S. G. Selevan, et al. NEW ENGLAND JOURNAL OF MEDICINE 313(19): 1173-1178, November 7, 1985.

Syndrome of thrombosis, abortion, and neurological disease, by G. R. Hughes, et al. CONTRIBUTIONS TO NEPHROLOGY 43:9-11, 1984.

Termination of anencephalic pregnancies, by M. Lancet, et al. HAREFUAH 105(8):211-212, October 16, 1983.

Termination of pregnancy or its prevention?, by L. Hirnle. GINEKOLOGIA POLSKA 55(9):701-703, September 1984.

This old lady, by E. Rogers. SOUTHERN EXPOSURE 13(2):2, March 1985.

Tragedy of abortion [letter], by L. Huapaya. CANADIAN MEDICAL ASSOCIATION JOURNAL132(2):93+, January 15, 1985.

Triplet pregnancy with second trimester abortion and delivery of twins at 35 weeks' gestation, by M. T. Banchi. OBSTETRICS AND GYNECOLOGY 64(5):728-730, November 1984.

20 years for beseda. NORTHWEST PASSAGE 25(6):4, February 1985.

Unusual use of ultrasound in a paranoid patient [letter], by P. E. Cook, et al. CANADIAN MEDICAL ASSOCIATION JOURNAL 131(6):539, September 15, 1984.

Use of contraception among abortion applicants, by D. Krishnamoni, et al. CANADIAN JOURNAL OF PUBLIC HEALTH 76(2):93-97, March-April 1985.

Use of questionnaires in occupational studies of pregnancy outcome, by G. Axelsson, et al. ANNALS OF THE ACADEMY OF MEDICINE SINGAPORE 13(Suppl. 2):327-330, April 1984.

Various aspects of prenatal and perinatal reproductive loss, by F. Cisarik, et al. BRATISLAVSKE LEKARSKE LISTY 83(6):670-677, June 1985.

Viability and the moral status of the fetus, by A. V. Campbell. CIBA FOUNDATION SYMPOSIA 115:228-243, 1985.

Viewing abortion from the perspective of transplantation: the ethics of the gift of life, by S. S. Mattingly. SOUNDINGS 67:399-410, Winter 1984.

What a way to treat a hero. GOODWINS 2(4):4, Spring 1985.

When the baby doesn't come home. CHILDREN TODAY 13(2):21-24, 1984.

Where babies go to, by Christopher Hitchens. SPECTATOR February 9, 1985, p. 10.

Who put the wrong in 'wrongful births?', by T. Eastland. THIS WORLD (5):84-93, 1983.

Whose right to life [abortion], by C. B. Fischer. JOURNAL OF WOMEN AND RE-LIGION 1(1):61-64, Spring 1981.

AFRICA
　　Abortion experience among obstetric patients at Korle-Bu Hospital, Accra, Ghana, by P. Lamptey, et al. JOURNAL OF BIOSOCIAL SCIENCE 17(2):195-203, April1985.

　　Attitude towards abortion among teenagers in Bendel State of Nigeria, by O. G. Oshodin. JOURNAL OF THE ROYAL SOCIETY OF HEALTH 105(1): 22-24, February 1985.

　　Illicit abortion, a public health problem in Kinshasa (Zaire), by K. Tshibangu, et al. JOURNAL DE GYNECOLOGIE, OBSTETRIQUE ET BIOLOGIE DE LA REPRODUCTION 13(7):759-763, 1984.

　　Opinions and opinion changes of white South Africans concerning abortion, by J. D. Venter. HUMANITAS 7(2):131-141, 1981.

　　Profile of contraceptive clients in Katsina, northern Nigeria, by H. P. Naghma-E-Rehan, et al. JOURNAL OF BIOSOCIAL SCIENCE 16:427-436, October 1984.

AUSTRALIA
　　Trends in legalized abortion in South Australia 1970-81, by F. Yusuf, et al. JOURNAL OF BIOSOCIAL SCIENCE 17(2):215-221, April 1985.

BELGIUM
　　Belgium/Women's right to choose on trial. INTERNATIONAL VIEWPOINT 83:26, September 30, 1985.

BRITISH COLUMBIA
Discoveries and dissimulations: the impact of abortion deaths on maternal mortality in British Columbia, by A. McLaren, et al. BC STUDIES 64:3-26, 1984-1985.

CANADA
Abortion in Canada: a new phase in the conflict, by T. Sinclair-Faulkner. CHRISTIAN CENTURY 102:923-926, October 16, 1985.

Analysis of Borowski v. The Attorney -General of Canada and The Minister of Finance of Canada, by T. Campbell. SASKATCHEWAN LAW REVIEW 49:359-367,1984-1985.

Appalling implications of Morgentaler's unjust acquittal, by T. Byfield. ALBERTA REPORT 11:60, November 26, 1984.

Backing down on abortion regulation: Saskatchewan's Tories pass a pro-life hot potato to the courts, by L. Cohen. ALBERTA REPORT 12:49, July 8, 1985.

Canada/abortion-rights doctors targeted Socialist voice. INTERCONTI-NENTAL PRESS 23(1):30, January 21, 1985.

Early complications of legal abortions, Canada, 1975-1979, by S. Wadhera, et al. WORLD HEALTH STATISTICS QUARTERLY 37(1):84-97, 1984.

Implementation of abortion policy in Canada as a women's issue, by S. A. McDaniel. ATLANTIS 10:74-91, Spring 1985.

International dilemma, by A. Finlayson. MACLEANS 97:54, November 19, 1984.

Meaning of Morgentaler [acquittal in Toronto abortion clinic trial; special section]. MACLEANS 97:44-50+, November 19, 1984.

Morgentaler and abortion, by F. Orr. ALBERTA REPORT 12:34-38, January 28, 1985.

Morgentaler's march: acquittal brings his Alberta abortions closer, by A. Elash, et al. ALBERTA REPORT 11:34, November 26, 1984.

Outflanking the abortionists: pro-life street tactics come to Alberta to head off Morgentaler, by M. McKinley. ALBERTA REPORT 12:34, December 31, 1984.

Pro-life gains: a U of A study shows less support for abortions, by J. Davidson, et al. ALBERTA REPORT 12:39, March 18, 1985.

Prolife vs. prochoice. CHRISTIAN CENTURY 102:410, April 24, 1985.

Protesting abortion [Morgentaler clinic, Toronto]. MACLEANS 98:17, August 12, 1985.

Religion and gender: a comparison of Canadian and American student attitudes, by Merlin B. Brinkerhoff, et al. JOURNAL OF MARRIAGE AND THE FAMILY 47(2):415-429, May 1985.

CANADA
Renewed abortion fight, by G. Moir. MACLEANS 98:54, April 8, 1985.

Renewed fight over abortion clinics [trial of H. Morgentaler in Toronto], by S. McKay. MACLEANS 97:48, November 5, 1984.

Stalemate on abortion [H. Morgentaler's clinics], by H. Quinn. MACLEANS 97:66, November 26, 1984.

Womanpoll. CHATELAINE 58:56, September 1985.

CHINA
Abortion question [forced abortions for population control. ECONOMIST 294:44, March 2, 1985.

American scholar on abortion in China, by S. W. Mosher. CATHOLIC DIGEST November 1985, p. 111+.

China: the abortion question. THE ECONOMIST 294:44, March 2, 1985.

Vomiting after anaesthesia for termination of pregnancy in China, by S. C. Chan, et al. SINGAPORE MEDICAL JOURNAL 24(6):360-362, December 1983.

DEVELOPING COUNTRIES
Late complications of medical termination of pregnancy: a study in the civil hospital, Surat, by C. Somasundaram, et al. JOURNAL OF FAMILY WELFARE 30:76-84, June 1984.

ENGLAND
Legal abortion in England and Wales, by D. B. Paintin. CIBA FOUNDATION SYMPOSIA 115:4-20, 1985.

FRANCE
Voluntary interruptions of pregnancy in metropolitan France in 1981, by M. Kaminski, et al. REVUE D'EPIDEMIOLOGIE ET DE SANTE PUBLIQUE 33(1):70-71, 1985.

GERMANY
Contraception and abortion of mentally handicapped female adolescents under German law, by A. Eser. MEDICINE AND LAW 4(6):499-513, 1985.

German euthanasia program [letter], by J. E. McArthur. NEW ZEALAND MEDICAL JOURNAL 98(784):656, August 14, 1985.

GREAT BRITAIN
Abortion in Great Britain: one Act, two laws, by K. M. Norrie. THE CRIMINAL LAW REVIEW August 1985, p. 475-488.

Abortion lottery: it's where you live that counts, by A. Neustatter. SUNDAY TIMES November 10, 1985, p. 36.

And at the end of the day who is holding the baby?, by J. South. NEW STATESMAN November 15, 1985, p. 10-12.

GREAT BRITAIN
Back on the bandwagon: the effect of opinion polls on public opinion, by C. Marsh. BRITISH JOURNAL OF POLITICAL SCIENCE 15:51-74, January 1985.

Great Britain fighting for a woman's right/choos. INTERNATIONAL VIEW-POINT 73:26, April 8,1985.

Late is too late. ECONOMIST August 17, 1985, p. 25.

To the backstreet by the backdoor, by J. South. NEW STATESMAN November 22, 1985, p. 14-15.

GREECE
Abortion in Greece, by S. Ginger. CONTEMPORARY REVIEW 243:253-255, November 1983.

IRELAND
Belfast/on the abortion trial. CHARTIST 104:6, May 1985.

Right to life of the unborn—an assessment of the eighth amendment to the Irish constitution. BRIGHAM YOUNG UNIVERSITY LAW REVIEW 1984, p. 371-402.

When Irish eyes are smiling . . . they probably aren't women's, by L. Davis. REFRACTORY GIRL 28:36-38, May 1985.

ITALY
Effect of legal abortion on teenage fertility in Trieste, Italy, by G. Benussi, et al. FAMILY PLANNING PERSPECTIVES 17(1):23-24, January-February 1985.

Genesis of contemporary Italian feminism, by J. Barkan. RADICAL AMERI-CAN 18(5):31, 1984.

Italy: abortion and nationalized health care, by M. Mori. HASTINGS CENTER REPORT 14:22-23, December 1984.

Legal abortion in Italy: 1980-1981, by S. Landucci Tosi, et al. FAMILY PLAN-NING PERSPECTIVES 17:19-23, January-February 1985.

JAPAN
Feminism in Japan, by A. Henry. OFF OUR BACKS 14(10):12, November 1984.

Women of Japan [abortion is easy to obtain, divorce is difficult; despite rapid social change, women find they often have little future except as house-wives, by C. Moorehead. NEW SOCIETY 70:453-455, December 20-27, 1984.

KOREA
Socio-economic change in Korea, by T. Hongsoon Han. ZEITSCHRIFT FUR MISSIONSWISSENSCHAFT UND RELIGIONSWISSENSCHAFT 69:140-149, April 1985.

MEXICO
Conference de Mexico: l'avortement en vedette, by P. Allen. ACTION NATIONALE 74:185, October 1984.

Global politics in Mexico City, by D. Wulf, et al. FAMILY PLANNING PERSPECTIVES 16(5):228-232, September-October 1984.

Ideology and politics at Mexico City: the United States at the 1984 International Conference on population. POPULATION AND DEVELOPMENT REVIEW 11(1):1, March 1985.

SCOTLAND
Edinburgh diary [General Assembly, Church of Scotland, annual meeting], by K. Slack. CHRISTIAN CENTURY 102:636-637, July 3-10, 1985.

SINGAPORE
Epidemiologic analysis of fetal death in utero in Singapore, by K. C. Tan, et al. INTERNATIONAL JOURNAL OF GYNAECOLOGY AND OBSTETRICS 22(3):181-188, June 1984.

Legalized abortion: the Singapore experience. STUDIES IN FAMILY PLANNING 16(3):170, May-June 1985.

SPAIN
Spain and abortion [news]. CHRISTIAN CENTURY 102:490, May 15, 1985.

SRI LANKA
Screening for biological activity of different plant parts of Tabernaemontana dichotoma, known as divi kaduru in Sri Lanka, by P. Perera, et al. JOURNAL OF ETHNOPHARMACOLOGY 11(2):233-241, July 1984.

SWEDEN
Hospitalization for miscarriage and delivery outcome among Swedish nurses working in operating rooms 1973-1978, by H. A. Ericson, et al. ANESTHESIA AND ANALGESIA 64(10):981-988, October 1985.

SWITZERLAND
Pregnancy termination in Switzerland. Development 1979-1981, by P. A. Gloor, et al. SCHWEIZERISCHE RUNDSCHAU FUR MEDIZIN PRAXIS 74(17):434-438, April 23, 1985.

UNITED KINGDOM
Legal abortion in England and Wales, by D. B. Paintin. CIBA FOUNDATION SYMPOSIA 115:4-20, 1985.

UNITED STATES
Abortion and medical discipline [letter]. NEW ZEALAND MEDICAL JOURNAL 98(778): 348, May 8, 1985.

Abortion and medical discipline [letter], by K. B. Fitzsimons, et al. NEW ZEALAND MEDICAL JOURNAL 98(781):507-508, June 26, 1985.

Abortion and sterilization in the United States: demographic dynamics, by P. J. Sweeney. UNION MEDICALE DU CANADA 113(7):587-593, July 1984.

UNITED STATES
>
> Abortion battle in America, by M. Potts. NEW SOCIETY 71:204-206, February 7, 1985.
>
> Abortion clinics: terror, but not terrorism. ECONOMIST 294:18-19, January 5, 1985.
>
> Abortion cuts in California?, by T. Woody. IN THESE TIMES 8(37):4, October 3, 1984.
>
> Abortion: understanding differences, by S. Callahan, et al. FAMILY PLANNING PERSPECTIVES16(5):219-221, September-October 1984.
>
> AID tightens antiabortion measures, by C. Holden. SCIENCE 227:1318-1319, March 15, 1985.
>
> America's abortion dilemma [special section]. NEWSWEEK 105:20-29, January 14,1985.
>
> America's battle over abortion, by M. Potts. NEW SOCIETY 71(1154):204-206, 1985.
>
> Characteristics of abortion patients in the United States, 1979 and 1980, by S. K. Henshaw, et al. FAMILY PLANNING PERSPECTIVES 15(1):5-8+, January-February 1983.
>
> Colorado voters amend the state's constitution to outlaw public funding of abortions. CHRISTIANITY TODAY 29:46-47, January 18, 1985.
>
> Community reaction to the establishment of an abortion clinic in Duluth, Minnesota, by C. M. MacLeod. NORTH DAKOTA QUARTERLY 52(1): 34-47, 1984.
>
> Contemporary American abortion controversy: stages in the argument by C. C. Railsback. QUARTERLY JOURNAL OF SPEECH 70(4):410-424, 1984.
>
> Control definition in case-control studies of ectopic pregnancy, by N. S. Weiss, et al. AMERICAN JOURNAL OF PUBLIC HEALTH 75:67-68, January 1985.
>
> Doctor couple arrested for phony abortions in N.Y. [M. Samuel and J. Cameau-Samuel]. JET 68:38, April 1, 1985.
>
> Florida: more abortion bombings. NEWSWEEK 105:17, January 7, 1985.
>
> Foundation power [critical views of American foundation funding in the areas of population control and abortion, by M. Meehan. HUMAN LIFE REVIEW 10:42-60, Fall 1984.
>
> Foundation power [critical views of American foundation funding in the areas of population control and abortion, by M. Meehan. HUMAN LIFE REVIEW 10:42-60, Fall 1984.
>
> Holy war in Pensacola, by P. Carlson. PEOPLE WEEKLY 23:20-25, January 21, 1985.

UNITED STATES

Illinois abortion statute for incompetent persons struck down. MENTAL AND PHYSICAL DISABILITY LAW REPORTER 8(5):450, September-October 1984.

Intervention analysis of the effects of legalized abortion upon U. S. fertility [impact of the 1973 decision of the United States Supreme Court invalidating statutes that restrict access to abortion], by T. D. Hogan. POPULATION RESEARCH AND POLICY REVIEW 3:201-218, October 1984.

Legal aspects of medical genetics in Wisconsin, by E. W. Clayton. WISCONSIN MEDICAL JOURNAL 84(3):28-32, March 1985.

Life or death split in America, by C. Thomas. TIMES February 13, 1985, p. 11.

Men with ties to church arrested for abortion clinic bombings. CHRISTIANITY TODAY 29:34-35, March 1, 1985.

New twist in the abortion funding controversy: Planned Parenthood v. Arizona. DEPAUL LAW REVIEW 33:835-355, Summer 1984.

New York's controversial Archbishop, by A. L. Goldman. NEW YORK TIMES MAGAZINE October 14, 1984, p. 38+.

1983 abortion decisions: Virginia distinguished. MEDICO-LEGAL BULLETIN 32(4):1-7, July-August 1983.

Polemic on abortion in the U.S.: lessons from an experience, by A. de Miguel. REVISTA ESPANOLA DE INVESTIGACIONES SOCIOLOGICAS 21:151-179, January-March 1983.

Protection of potential human life in Illinois: policy and law at odds, by J. A. Parness. NORTHERN ILLINOIS UNIVERSITY LAW REVIEW 5:1-30, Winter 1984.

Provision of abortion services in the United States, by D. A. Grimes. CIBA FOUNDATION SYMPOSIA 115:26-40, 1985.

Public policy: contract, abortion, and the CIA, by P. H. Brietzke. VALPARAISO UNIVERSITY LAW REVIEW 18:741-940, Summer 1984.

Religion and gender: a comparison of Canadian and American student attitudes, by M. B. Brinkerhoff, et al. JOURNAL OF MARRIAGE AND THE FAMILY 47(2):415-429, May 1985.

Rhode Island abortion statute is struck down by Federal Court. THE FAMILY LAW REPORTER 11(9):1108-1109, January 8, 1985.

Second-trimester abortions in the United States [1972-1981], by D. A. Grimes. FAMILY PLANNING PERSPECTIVES 16:260-266, November-December 1984.

Tactics of the United States right-to-life movement [letter], by J. C. Willke. LANCET 1(8426):453, February 23, 1985.

UNITED STATES
> U. S. control of abortion rights abroad. NEW WOMEN'S TIMES 10(9):4, October 1984.
>
> U.S. attacks abortions, by P. Thompson. CHARTIST (101):6, September 1984.
>
> U.S. churches debate abortion, South Africa, and pornography. CHRISTIANITY TODAY 29:64-65, September 6, 1985.
>
> U.S. denies population crisis, by J. Knox. NOT MAN APART 14(8):12, October 1984.
>
> Women's rights in US under big attack, by D. Jenness. INTERCONTINENTAL PRESS 22(21):650, November 12, 1984.

WALES
> Legal abortion in England and Wales, by D. B. Paintin. CIBA FOUNDATION SYMPOSIA 115:4-20, 1985.

ABORTION: ADVERTISING
Chewing more than he's bitten off, by A. Cockburn. NATION 241:39, July 20-27, 1985.

Dissent and reaction [controversy over abortion advertisement signed by Catholic religious]. AMERICA 152:37, January 19, 1985.

Is Rome anti-Catholic?, by P. Steinfels. COMMONWEAL 112:4-5, January 11, 1985.

ABORTION: AGENTS
Additional studies on pregnancy termination and inhibition of the monkey corpus luteum with 5-oxa-17-phenyl-18,19,20-trinor-PGF1 apha methyl ester and structurally related prostaglandins, by J. W. Wilks, et al. PROSTAGLANDINS 28(3):323-332, September 1984.

Contragestion by antiprogestin: a new approach to human fertility control, by E. E. Baulieu. CIBA FOUNDATION SYMPOSIA 115:192-210, 1985.

Effect of 7 alpha- and 7 beta-methyl-10 beta, 17 beta-diacetoxy-delta 4-estren-3-one on terminating early pregnancy, by Y. H. Chu, et al. YAO HSUEH HSUEH PAO19(3):173-177, March 1984.

Fetal malformations following progesterone therapy during pregnancy: a preliminary report, by J. A. Rock, et al. FERTILITY AND STERILITY 44(1):17-19, July 1985.

Low-dose prostaglandin E2 analogue for cervical dilatation prior to pregnancy termination, by M. Borten, et al. AMERICAN JOURNAL OF OBSTETRICS AND GYNECOLOGY 150(5 Pt 1):561-565, November 1, 1984.

Mid-trimester pregnancy termination with ethacridine lactate, by S. Shukla, et al. JOURNAL OF THE INDIAN MEDICAL ASSOCIATION 82(12):432-434, December 1984.

Midtrimester termination of pregnancy using intravaginal gemeprost (16,16 dimethyl-trans delta 2 PGE1 methyl ester, cervagem), by G. V. Nair, et al. SINGAPORE MEDICAL JOURNAL 1985.

Pregnancy outcome in the Seveso area after ICDD contamination, by G. M. Fara, et al. PROGRESS IN CLINICAL AND BIOLOGICAL RESEARCH 163B:279-285, 1985.

Pregnancy terminating effect and toxicity of an active constituent of Aristolochia mollissima Hance, aristolochic acid A, by W. H. Wang, et al. YAO HSUEH HSUEH PAO 19(6):405-409, June 1984.

Preoperative cervical priming by intracervical application of a new sulprostone gel, by W. Rath, et al. CONTRACEPTION 31(3):207-216, March 1985.

Reproduction and exposure to lead, by M. Saric. ANNALS OF THE ACADEMY OF MEDICINE, SINGAPORE 13(Suppl. 2):383-388, April 1984.

Teratological evaluation of a novel antiabortifacient, dibenzyloxyindanpropionic acid. I. Dysmorphological and histopathological studies, by F. R. del Vecchio, et al. GENERAL PHARMACOLOGY 15(6):461-469, 1984.

— II. Postnatal morphological and behavioral development, by F. R. Del Vecchio, et al. DRUG AND CHEMICAL TOXICOLOGY 7(4):357-381, 1984.

ABORTION: ANESTHESIA
Anaesthesia for suction termination of pregnancy, by S. L. West, et al. ANAESTHESIA 40(7):669-672, July 1985.

ABORTION: ARTIFICIAL
Artificial termination of pregnancy in patients with uterine myoma, by L. N. Vasilevskaia, et al. AKUSHERSTVO I GINEKOLOGIIA (2):47-50, February 1985.

Case of Evans' syndrome: thrombocytopenia improved by artificial abortion, by T. Ohtsuki, et al. RINSHO KETSUEKI 25(11):1814-1818, November 1984.

On brain death, organ transplantation, artificial abortion, euthanasia and embryo transport, by K. Takagi. NIPPON NAIKA GAKKAIZASSHI 73(8):1111-1127, August 1984.

ABORTION: ATTITUDES
Abortion and the ethics manual [letter], by C. D. Gibson, Jr. ANNALS OF ANNALS OF INTERNAL MEDICINE 102(1):133-134, January 1985.

Abortion and infanticide. Is there a difference?, by D. Cannon. POLICY REVIEW 32:12-17, 1985.

Abortion and moral consensus: beyond Solomon's choice, by M. Kolbenschlag. CHRISTIAN CENTURY 102:179-183, February 20, 1985.

An abortion anniversary, by W. Shapiro. NEWSWEEK 105:22, February 4, 1985.

Abortion as a stigma: in the eyes of the beholder, by G. Weidner, et al. JOURNAL OF RESEARCH IN PERSONALITY 18:359-371, September 1984.

Abortion: a civilized exchange, by E. Van Den Haag, et al. NATIONAL REVIEW 37:37-39, September 6, 1985.

Abortion, contraception, infanticide, by P. E. Devine. PHILOSOPHY 58:513-520, October 1983.

Abortion dialogue, by J. A. Brix. CHRISTIAN CENTURY 102:21-24, January 2-9, 1985.

Abortion is not murder, by G. Scialabba. VILLAGE VOICE 29:8, October 16, 1984.

Abortion: an issue to grieve?, by S. S. Joy. JOURNAL OF COUNSELING AND DEVELOPMENT 63:375-376, February 1985.

Abortion—moral and religious aspects. NATIONAL CATHOLIC REPORTER 21(1):53, February 15, 1985.

Abortion: opinion roundup. charts. PUBLIC OPINION 8:25-28, April-May 1985.

Abortion policy and the argument from uncertainty, by R. S. Pfeiffer. SOCIAL THEORY AND PRACTICE 11(3):371-386, 1985.

Abortion, right and wrong, by R. R. Smith. NEWSWEEK 105:16, March 25, 1985.

Abortion: understanding differences, by S. Callahan, et al. FAMILY PLANNING PERSPECTIVES16(5):219-221, September-October 1984.

Against the might of the moral right, by J. Mellor. SPARE RIB 152:11, March 1985.

Back on the bandwagon: the effect of opinion polls on public opinion, by C. Marsh. BRITISH JOURNAL OF POLITICAL SCIENCE 15:51-74, January 1985.

Between pro-life and pro-choice, by V. A. Sackett. PUBLIC OPINION 8:53-55, April-May 1985.

Born again: how an abortion crusader became a right-to-lifer, by J. Klein. NEW YORK18:40-45, January 7, 1985.

Breath of life and unwanted pregnancy, by J. B. Ashbrook. THE CHRISTIAN MINISTRY 16(4):15-17, July 1985.

Candy wrappers, beer bottles and abortions, J. Lankford. CATHOLIC DIGEST 11:13, March 1985.

Catalogue of killing: a pro-choice film fuels the abortion debate, by O. Roberts, et al. ALBERTA REPORT 11:48-49, October 29, 1984.

Caught in the abortion backlash, by V. Safran. PROGRESSIVE 49:16, May 1985.

Choice vs. life. PEOPLE WEEKLY 24:70-72+, August 5, 1985.

College students' attitudes toward shared responsibility in decisions about abortion: implications for counseling, by I. J. Ryan, et al. JOURNAL OF AMERICAN COLLEGE HEALTH 31:231-235, June 1983.

Cry with the mother, by M. S. Shea. THEOLOGY TODAY 41:325-326, October 1984.

Dear friends of pro-choice, by E. Mcauster. NATIONAL CATHOLIC REPORTER 21:14-15, November 16, 1984.

Determinants of opposition to abortion. An analysis of the hard and soft scales, by M. H. Benin. SOCIOLOGICAL PERSPECTIVES 28(2):199-216, 1985.

Drawing lines: the abortion perplex and the presuppositions of applied ethics, by A. Weston. MONIST 67:589-604, October 1984.

Ethical dilemma of late pregnancy termination in cases of gross fetal malformations, by J. R. Leiberman, et al. ISRAEL JOURNAL OF MEDICAL SCIENCES 20(11):1051-1055, November 1984.

From biotechnology to bioethics: the shock of the future, by E. Boné. PRO MUNDI VITA BULLETIN 101:1-42, 1985.

From biotechnology to bioethics: the shock of the future, by E. Boné. PRO MUNDI VITA BULLETIN 101:1-42, 1985.

Genital infections in women undergoing therapeutic abortion, by D. Avonts, et al. EUROPEAN JOURNAL OF OBSTETRICS, GYNECOLOGY AND REPRO-DUCTIVE BIOLOGY 20(1):53-59, July 1985.

Go thou and do likewise [face the facts], by C. Thomas. FUNDAMENTALIST JOURNAL 3(1):26, January 1984.

Hypocrisy of abortion, by A. J. Longo. CANADIAN MEDICAL ASSOCIATION JOURNAL 133(1):13-14, July 1, 1985.

Importance of replicating a failure to replicate: order effects on abortion items, by G. F. Bishop, et al. PUBLIC OPINION QUARTERLY 49(1):105-114, 1985.

Impossible choice [abortion vs. defective child], by M. V. Hunt. MCCALLS 112:44+, July 1985.

Late abortions and the crime of child destruction: a reply [and] a rejoinder, by Victor Tunkel, et al. CRIMINAL LAW REVIEW March 1985, p. 133-142.

Liberty and family rights, by R. Stott. CANADIAN FORUM 64:20-21+, November 1984.

Liittle changes in 14 years in attitudes on abortion. JET 69:5, September 16, 1985.

Meaning of motherhood [review article], by B. Townsend. AMERICAN DEMO-GRAPHICS 7:8+, January 1985.

New heat over an old issue, by R. T. Zintl. TIME 125:17, February 4, 1985.

Nobel laureate speaks in defense of unborn life, by Mother Teresa. CHRISTIANITY TODAY 29:62-63, September 6, 1985.

Notes from the fringe, by M. H. Brown. HARPERS 270:20, June 1985.

Opinions and opinion changes of white South Africans concerning abortion, by J. D. Venter. HUMANITAS 7(2):131-141, 1981.

Order and disorder in anti-abortion rhetoric: a logological view, by R. A. Lake. QUARTERLY JOURNAL OF SPEECH 70:425-443, November 1984.

People like us [pro-lifers]. NATIONAL REVIEW 37:18, February 22, 1985.

Politics of motherhood, by M. O. Steinfels. CHRISTIANITY AND CRISIS 44:342-343, October 1, 1984.

Pregnant women's attitudes toward the abortion of defective fetuses, by R. C. Faden, et al. POPULATION AND ENVIRONMENT 6(4):197-209, 1983.

Pro-choice vs. pro-life is a moral dilemma, says Daniel Callahan: we carry both traditions within us [interview], by G. Breu. PEOPLE WEEKLY 24:89-91+, August 12, 1985.

Propaganda war over abortion, by A. Spake. MS MAGAZINE 14:88-92+, July 1985.

Religion and gender: a comparison of Canadian and American student attitudes, by M. B. Brinkerhoff, et al. JOURNAL OF MARRIAGE AND THE FAMILY 47(2):415-429, May 1985.

Religion, values and attitudes toward abortion, by R. J. Harris, et al. JOURNAL OF THE SCIENTIFIC STUDY OF RELIGION 24:137-154, June 1985.

Right-to-life convention, by A. J. Fugh-Berman. OFF OUR BACKS 15:7, August-September 1985.

Save-a-baby: a viable alternative. FUNDAMENTALIST JOURNAL 2(1):24-25, January 1983.

Selective abortion-thoughts from several countries, by A. Henry. OFF OUR BACKS 14(10):13, November 1984.

Silent no more [pro-choice advocates], by J. V. Lamar, Jr. TIME 125:32, May 27, 1985.

Slaughter of the innocents, by F. A. Schaeffer, et al. FUNDAMENTALIST JOURNAL 2(1):21-22, January 1983.

Some aspects of sexual knowledge and sexual behavior of local women. Results of a survey. 1. General sexual knowledge and attitude to abortion, pregnancy and contraception, by V. Atputharajah. SINGAPORE MEDICAL JOURNAL 25(3):135-140, June 1984.

Split verdict. What Americans think about abortion. POLICY REVIEW 32(18-19), 1985.

Summary report of the results of a sociological investigation of abortion by means of group discussion, by R. Ramos. REVISTA ESPANOLA DE INVESTI-GACIONES SOCIOLÓGICAS 21:243-254, January-March 1983.

Symposium on the philosophy of Alan Donagan. I. Taking a human life. II. Moral absolutism and abortion: Alan Donagan on the hysterectomy and craniotomy cases. III. Comments on Dan Brock and Terrence Donagan, by D. W. Brock, et al. ETHICS 95(4):851-886, 1985.

Time to catch up with public opinion, by G. Rogerson. BODY POLITIC (113):6, April 1985.

Vocal prochoice activists launch nationwide offensive, by M. Meehan. CHRIS-TIANITY TODAY 29:42-43, July 12, 1985.

What has happened to America's respect for human life [Soap Box], by J. Savely. FUNDAMENTALIST JOURNAL 4(5):30, May 1985.

Who confers value?, by J. Garvey. COMMONWEAL 112:423-424, August 9, 1985.

Withdraw this license to kill. [Moral relativism as the link between embroyology, abortion and murder], by P. Johnson. TIMES August 22, 1985, p. 10.

ABORTION: BIBLIOGRAPHY
Debate continues: recent works on abortion, by J. O'Connor. RELIGIOUS STUDIES REVIEW 11:105-114, April 1985.

ABORTION: COMPLICATIONS
Abortion following recent myocardial infarct, by B. Köhler. ZENTRALBLATT FUR GYNAEHOLOGIE 107(8):508-511, 1985.

About TOP risks and about mammography, by E. Trimmer. MIDWIFE, HEALTH VISITOR AND COMMUNITY NURSE 20(9):322, September 1984.

Acute renal insufficiency in pregnancy. A case of the uremic-hemolytic syndrome In the post-partum period, by S. Federico, et al. MINERVA GINECOLOGIA 36 (7-8): 395-398, July-August 1984

Association between unfavorable outcomes in successive pregnancies, by H. C. Miller, et al. AMERICAN JOURNAL OF OBSTETRICS AND GYNECOLOGY 153(1):20-24, September 1, 1985.

Blood loss and nausea during legal abortion, by J. Carcey, et al. ANNALES FRANCAISES D'ANESTHESIA ET DE REANIMATION 4(3):271-273, 1985.

Complications in pregnancy, by R. K. Smith, et al. TOPICS IN EMERGENCY MEDICINE 7(2):9-18, July 1985.

Fatal in utero salicylism, by T. A. Rejent, et al. JOURNAL OF FORENSIC SCI-ENCES 30(3):942-944, July 1985.

Postabortal pelvic infection associated with Chlamydia trachomatis and the influence of humoral immunity, by S. Osser, et al. AMERICAN JOURNAL OF OBSTETRICS AND GYNECOLOGY 150(6):699-703, November 15, 1984.

Relation between postpartum bleeding and abortion, by A. L. Zhou. CHUNG HUA HU LI TSA CHIH 20(1):13-15, February 1985.

Reproductive patterns and the risk of gestational trophoblastic disease, by F. Parazzini, et al. AMERICAN JOURNAL OF OBSTETRICS AND GYNECOLOGY 152(7 Pt 1):866-870, August 1, 1985.

Safety of abortion and tubal sterilization performed separately versus concurrently, by H. H. Akhter, et al. AMERICAN JOURNAL OF OBSTETRICS AND GYNECOLOGY 152(6 Pt 1):619-623, July 15, 1985.

Serum copper concentation significantly less in abnormal pregnancies, by P. K. Buamah, et al. CLINICAL CHEMISTRY 30(10):1676-1677, October 1984.

Value of ovarian and placental steroid determinations in abnormal early pregnancy, by W. Distler, et al. ARCHIVES OF GYNECOLOGY 236(3):153-160, 1985.

Vomiting after anaesthesia for termination of pregnancy in China, by S. C. Chan, et al. SINGAPORE MEDICAL JOURNAL 24(6):360-362, December 1983.

ABORTION: CRIMINAL
A rare case in gynecologic practice, by K. Durveniashki. AKUSHERSTVO I GINEKOLOGIIA 23(4):364-365, 1984.

Septic shock as a complication of criminal abortion, by A. P. Kiriushchenkov. FEL'DSHER I AKUSHERKA 49(9):48-52, September 1984.

ABORTION: EDUCATION
Adolescents' communication styles and learning about birth control, by R. DePietro, et al. ADOLESCENCE 19:827-837, Winter 1984.

Pro-abortionist infiltrates sex education course. (abortion clinic employee gives talk in public school sex ed course), by P. Schlafly. HUMAN EVENTS 45:20, May 18, 1985.

Teaching about abortion as a public issue. WOMEN'S ROLES 10:885-902, June 1984.

ABORTION: ERA
Abortion and the Christian feminist: a dilemma?, by C. Smith. NEW BLACKFRIARS 66:62-67, February 1985.

Abortion and the Christian feminist: profilers of survival, by S. Dowell. NEW BLACKFRIARS 66:67-72, February 1985.

ABORTION: FAILED
Change of mind following failed abortion doesn't relieve the physician of liability. FORTSCHRITTE DER MEDIZIN 103(9):70-71, March 7, 1985.

ABORTION: FEMINISM
Bombing feminism, by R. P. Petchesky. NATION 240:101, February 2, 1985.

Feminism in Japan, by A. Henry. OFF OUR BACKS 14(10):12, November 1984.

Genesis of contemporary Italian feminism, by J. Barkan. RADICAL AMERICAN 18(5):31, 1984.

Women's rights in US under big attack, by D. Jenness. INTERCONTINENTAL PRESS 22(21):650, November 12, 1984.

ABORTION: HABITUAL

Balanced rearrangement of chromosomes 2, 5, and 13 in a family with duplication 5q and fetal loss, by M. I. Evans, et al. AMERICAN JOURNAL OF MEDICAL GENETICS 19(4):783-790, December 1984.

Complex translocation in habitual abortion, by A. Smith, et al. HUMAN GENETICS 70(3):287, 1985.

Corpus luteum insufficiency, the primary cause of habitual abortion: its successful therapy, by G. Siklósi, et al. ORVOSI HETILAP 125(42):2549-2553, October 14,1984.

Determination of certain physical and chemical characteristics of the activating serum factor from preparturient women and women with habitual abortions, by J. Lukanov, et al. EXPERIENTIA 41(1):68-70, January 15, 1985.

Does diethylstilbestrol also affect the ovaries of the fetus?, by T. K. Eskes, et al. NEDERLANDS TIJDSCHRIFT VOOR GENEESKUNDE 128(34):1601-1603, August 25, 1984.

Efficacy of allylestrenol in the prevention of habitual abortion, by R. Grio, et al. MINERVA GINECOLOGIA 37(4):171-172, April 1985.

Functional state of the pituitary-ovaries system in women with a history of habitual abortion, by T. K. Baituraeva, et al. PROBLEMY ENDOKRINOLOGII I GORMONOTERAPII 30(6):25-27, November-December 1984.

Glucose-6-phosphate dehydrogenase in couples with habitual abortion, by J. Guizar Vázquez, et al. GINECOLOGIA Y OBSTETRICIA DE MEXICO 50(308):325-328, December 1982.

Habitual abortion, by E. Maroni. SCHWEIZERISCHE RUNDSCHAU FUR MEDZIN PRAXIS 74(15):371-377, April 9, 1985.

Habitual abortion of chromosomal etiology, by S. S. Bessudnova, et al. AKUSHERS-TVO I GINEKOLOGIIA (12):8-10, December 1984.

IgM gammopathy and the lupus anticoagulant syndrome in habitual aborters, by N. Gleicher, et al. JAMA 253(22):3278-3281, June 14, 1985.

Nonimmunologically induced habitual abortion, by E. Maroni. GYNAEKOLO-GISCHE RUNDSCHAU 24(Suppl. 1):1-8, 1984.

Repeated pregnancy loss due to alpha-thalassemia—report of 3 cases, by C. K. Kuo, et al. TAIWAN I HSUEH HUI TSA CHIH 83(7):724-729, July 1984.

Reproduction and immune factors in women. Pregnancy, habitual abortion and HLA histocompability, by R. C. Martin-du-Pan, et al. JOURNAL OF GYNE-COLOGIE, OBSTETRIQUE ET BIOLOGIE DE LA REPORDUCTION 14(3): 291-293, 1985.

Results obtained in patients with cerclage, by O. Valderrama. REVISTA CHILENA DE OBSTETRICIA Y GINECOLOGIA 49(4):251-255, 1984.

Segregation and fertility analysis in an autosomal reciprocal translocation, t(1;8)(q41; q23.1), by A. E. Vauhkonen, et al. AMERICAN JOURNAL OF HUMAN GENETICS 37(3):533-542, May 1985.

Subclinical autoimmune disease and unexplained abortion, by S. Cowchock, et al. AMERICAN JOURNAL OF OBSTETRICS AND GYNECOLOGY 150(4): 367-371, October 15, 1984.

Surgical management of habitual abortion caused by uterus bicornis (metro-plasty), by Z. Papp, et al. ORVOSI HETILAP 126(7):389-392+, February 17, 1985.

Treatment for habitual aborters . . . LE-anticoagulant can be suppressed with corticotropin, prednisone or azathioprine. NURSES DRUG ALERT 8(4):28-29, April 1984.

Treatment of women habitually aborting, by N. T. Gudakova, et al. AKUSHERSTVO I GINEKOLOGIIA (12):38-39, December 1984.

Uterine pathology and infertility, by C. Flamigni, et al. ACTA EUROPAEA FERTILITATIS 16(1):25-34, January-February 1985.

ABORTION: ILLEGAL

New method for estimation of illegal abortions, by O. Nørgaard. DANISH MEDICAL BULLETIN 32(1):76-78, March 1985.

Virginia doctor acquitted of illegal abortion, by L. S. OFF OUR BACKS 15(5):7, May 1985.

ABORTION: IMCOMPLETE

Characteristics of patients attending Harare Hospital with incomplete abortion, by C. Crowther, et al. CENTRAL AFRICAN JOURNAL OF MEDICINE 31(4):67-70, April1985.

Genetic amniocentesis: impact of placental position upon the risk of pregnancy loss, by J. P. Crane, et al. AMERICAN JOURNAL OF OBSTETRICS AND GYNECOLOGY 150(7):813-816, December 1984.

Incomplete abortion, by A. P. Kiriushchenkov. FEL'DSHER I AKUSHERKA 49(7):46-50, July 1984.

Intrauterine bone contraceptive device: an accident of nature, by Y. F. Dajani, et al. FERTILITY AND STERILITY 43(1):149-150, January 1985.

Observation on plasma fibrinogen level in cases of incomplete abortions, by R. B. Thakur. JOURNAL OF THE INDIAN MEDICAL ASSOCIATION 82(10):353-354, October 1984.

Spermicidal contraceptives and poor reproductive outcomes the epidemiologic evidence against an association, by M. B. Bracken. AMERICAN JOURNAL OF OBSTETRICS AND GYNECOLOGY 151(5):552-556, March 1, 1985.

Use of contact hysteroscopy in evaluating postpartum bleeding and incomplete, by J. G. Tchabo. JOURNAL OF REPRODUCTIVE MEDICINE 29(10): 749-751, October 1984.

ABORTION: INDUCED

Abortion induction in the 2d pregnancy trimester. Endocervical PGE2 gel administration, intramuscular sulprostone administration and combined treatment, by W. Schmidt, et al. GEBURTSHILFE UND FRAUEN-HEILKUNDE 45(4):261-264, April 1985.

Acceptance of effective contraceptive methods after induced abortion, by A. Bulut. STUDIES IN FAMILY PLANNING 15:281-284, November-December 1984.

Action program on anesthesia gases: pregnant employees should have the right to change positions, by J. Björdal. VARDFACKET 8(13-14):8-9, August 16, 1984.

Acupuncture for the induction of cervical dilatation in preparation for first-trimester abortion and its influence on HCG, by Y. K. Ying, et al. JOURNAL OF REPRODUCTIVE MEDICINE 30(7):530-534, July 1985.

Anesthesia for termination of pregnancy: midazolam compared with methohexital, by R. Verma, et al. ANESTHESIA AND ANALGESIA 64(8):792-794, August 1985.

Antiprogesterones are coming: menses induction, abortion, and labour?, by D. L. Healy, et al. BRITISH MEDICAL JOURNAL 290(6468):580-581, February 23, 1985.

Cervix priming in induced abortion in the 1st trimester using intracervical admini-stration of sulprostone gel, by W. Rath, et al. GEBURTSHILFE UND FRAUENHEILKUNDE 45(1):51-56, January 1985.

Dilatation of the cervix by oral PGE2 before first-trimester termination of pregnancy, by C. Somell, et al. ACTA OBSTETRICIA ET GYNECOLOGICA SCANDINAVICA 63(7):625-628, 1984.

Ectopic pregnancy in relation to previous induced abortion, by J. R. Daling. JAMA 253(7):1005-1008, 1985.

Effect of induced abortion on the state of the cervix uteri in nulliparae, by V. O. Vekhnovskii. AKUSHERSTVO I GINEKOLOGIIA 12:42-43, December 1984.

Ethical implications of alternatives to induced abortion and corrective surgery [letter], by P. Cholnoky. ORVOSI HETILAP 126(2):118, January 13, 1985.

Ethics in caring, by T. Keighley. NURSING STANDARDS 365:8, September 20, 1984.

15(S)-15-methyl-prostaglandin F2 alpha used for induction of delivery in the case of intra-uterine fetal death, by M. Osler, et al. ACTA OBSTETRICIA ET GYNECOLOGICA SCANDINAVICA 64(2):131-132, 1985.

Hypothalamic-pituitary function in women after abortion or premature labor, by H. Morishita, et al. NIPPON SANKA FUJINKA GAKKAI ZASSHI 36(10):1807-1812, October 1984.

Illegally induced abortion observation at Ramathibodi Hospital, by S. Pongthai, et al. JOURNAL OF THE MEDICAL ASSOCIATION OF THAILAND 67(Suppl. 2):50-53, October 1984.

Incidence of gestational trophoblastic disease in induced abortion, by S. Tang-trakul, et al. JOURNAL OF THE MEDICAL ASSOCIATION OF THAILAND 67(Suppl. 2:54-55, October 1984.

Induced abortion by the suction method. An analysis of complication rates, by B. I. Nesheim. ACTA OBSTETRICIA ET GYNECOLOGICA SCANDINAVICA 63(7):591-595, 1984.

Induced abortion operations and their early sequelae. Joint study of the Royal College of General Practitioners and the Royal College of Obstetricians and Gynaecologists. JOURNAL OF THE ROYAL COLLEGE OF GENERAL PRACTITIONERS 35(273):175-180, April 1985.

Intrauterine device insertion following induced abortion, by L. Querido, et al. CONTRACEPTION 31(6):603-610, 1985.

Low-dose prostaglandin E2 analogue for cervical dilatation prior to pregnancy termination, by M. Borten, et al. AMERICAN JOURNAL OF OBSTETRICS AND GYNECOLOGY 150(5 Pt 1):561-565, November 1, 1984.

Naproxen sodium for pain relief in first-trimester abortion, by K. Suprapto, et al. AMERICAN JOURNAL OF OBSTETRICS AND GYNECOLOGY 150(8):1000-1001, December 15, 1984.

New prostaglandin E1 analog in late interruption of pregnancy, in utero deaths and very premature ruptures of the membranes. Apropos of 117 cases, by R. Henrion, et al. JOURNAL DE GYNECOLOGIE, OBSTETRIQUE ET BIOLOGIE DE LA REPRODUCTION 13(8):939-946, 1984.

Outcome of pregnancy following induced abortion. Report from the joint study of the Royal College of General Practitioners and the Royal College of Obstetricians and Gynaecologists, by P. I. Frank, et al. BRITISH JOURNAL OF OBSTETRICS AND GYNAECOLOGY 92(4):308-316, April 1985.

Oxytocin-induced water intoxication. A case report, by F. J. Muller, et al. SOUTH AFRICAN MEDICAL JOURNAL 68(5):340-341, August 1985.

Perforation of angular pregnancy during elective pregnancy termination. A case report, by Y. Rahmani, et al. JOURNAL OF REPRODUCTIVE MEDICINE 30(4): 366-367, April 1985.

Peroperative penicillins, bacteremia, and pelvic inflammatory disease in association with induced first-trimester abortion, by L. Heisterberg, et al. DANISH MEDICAL BULLETIN 32(1):73-75, March 1985.

Postconceptional induction of menses with double prostaglandin F2 alpha impact, by M. Borten, et al. 150(8):1006-1007, December 15, 1984.

Preventing febrile complications of suction curettage abortion, by T. K. Park, et al. AMERICAN JOURNAL OF OBSTETRICS AND GYNECOLOGY 152(3):252-255, June 1, 1985.

Prevention of post-abortion complications, by A. A. Radionchenko, et al. SOVETS-KAIA MEDITSINA (11):108-110, 1984.

Previous experience of induced abortion as a risk factor for fetal death and preterm delivery, by T. K. Park, et al. INTERNATIONAL JOURNAL OF GYNAECOLOGY AND OBSTETRICS 22(3):195-202, June 1984.

Prophylactic antibodies unjustified for unselected abortion patients [letter], by J. A. McGregor. AMERICAN JOURNAL OF OBSTETRICS AND GYNECOLOGY 152(6 Pt 1):722-725, July 15, 1985.

Prophylaxis with lymecycline in induced first-trimester abortion: a clinical, controlled trial assessing the role of Chlamydia trachomatis and Mycoplasma hominis, by L. Heisterberg, et al. SEXUALLY TRANSMITTED DISEASES 12(2):72-75, April-June 1985.

Prospective study of Chlamydia trachomatis in first trimester abortion, by H. Shioøtz, et al. ANNALS OF CLINICAL RESEARCH 17(2):60-63, 1985.

Radioimmunological study of the gonadotropic function of the pituitary in women during reestablishment of the menstrual cycle, by V. I. Chemodanov, et al. MEDITSINSKAIA RADIOLOGIIA 30(3):62-64, March 1985.

Ranitidine prophylaxis before anaesthesia in early pregnancy, by B. L. Duffy, et al. ANAESTHESIA AND INTENSIVE CARE 13(1):29-32, February 1985.

Resorption of prostaglandin E2 following various methods of local administration for ripening of the cervix and end the induction of labor, by R. Reichel, et al. WIENER KLINISCHE WOCHENSCHRIFT 97(11):500-503, May 24, 1985.

Risk of serious complications from induced abortion: do personal characteristics make a difference?, by J. W. Buehler, et al. AMERICAN JOURNAL OF OBSTETRICS AND GYNECOLOGY 153(1):14-20, September 1, 1985.

Second-trimester abortions induced by dinoprost, by J. P. Feldman, et al. REVUE FRANCAISE DE GYNECOLOGIE ET D'OBSTETRIQUE 80(2):93-96, February 1985.

Secondary infertility following induced abortion. STUDIES IN FAMILY PLANNING 15:291-295, November-December 1984.

Sequelae of induced abortion, by P. Frank. CIBA FOUNDATION SYMPOSIA 115:67-82, 1985.

Simplified chromosome preparations from chorionic villi obtained by choriocentesis or derived from induced abortions, by D. Pitmon, et al. ANNALES DE GENETIQUE 27(4):254-256, 1984.

16-Phenoxy-prostaglandin-E2 for inducing abortion in intact and complicated pregnancy, by W. Lichtenegger. GEBURTSHILFE UND FRAUENHEILKUNDE 44(11):752-757, November 1984.

Socioeconomic and demographic characteristics of induced abortion cases, by T. K. Chatterjee. INTERNATIONAL JOURNAL OF GYNAECOLOGY AND OBSTETRICS 23(2):149-152, April 1985.

Support from significant others and loneliness following induced abortion, by J. M. Robbins, et al. SOCIAL PSYCHIATRY 20(2):92-99, 1985.

Tubal infertility in relation to prior induced abortion, by J. R. Daling, et al. FERTILITY AND STERILITY 43(3):389-394, March 1985.

Use of a clindamycin phosphate-gentamycin combination in endometritis following induced abortion, by P. Rossi, et al. ANNALI DI OSTETRICIA GINECOLOGIA MEDICINA PERINATALE 105(4):267-271, July-August 1984.

Use of contraception among abortion applicants, by D. Krishnamoni, et al. CANADIAN JOURNAL OF PUBLIC HEALTH 76(2):93-97, March-April 1985.

Use of copper electropnoresis for the prevention of complications and restoration of the reproductive function after induced abortion of the first pregnancy, by V. M. Strugatskii, et al. AKUSHERSTVO I GINEKOLOGIIA (11):62-64, November 1984.

Use of osmotic dilators to facilitate induced midtrimester abortion: clinical evaluations, by M. F. Atienza, et al. CONTRACEPTION 30(3):215-223, September 1984.

Uterine perforation following medical termination of pregnancy by vacuum aspiration, by S. Mittal, et al. INTERNATIONAL JOURNAL OF GYNAECOLOGY AND OBSTETRICS 23(1):45-50, February 1985.

Uterine rupture during induced mid-trimester abortion, by Y. Biale, et al. EUROPEAN JOURNAL OF OBSTETRICS, GYNECOLOGY AND REPRODUCTIVE BIOLOGY 19(3):175-182, March 1985.

What is the role of chlamydia culture, wet smear and general bacterial culture from the cervix before surgical abortion?, by M. Nordenvall, et al. LAKARTIDNINGEN 81(39):3471-3472, September 26, 1984.

ABORTION: LAWS AND LEGISLATION
Abortion amendments mar Civil Rights Bill. OFF OUR BACKS 15(7):13, July 1985.

Abortion and the conscience of the nation, by R. Reagan. FUNDAMENTALIST JOURNAL 3(1):19-25, January 1984.

Abortion Bill "unconstitutional." BRIARPATCH 14(5):9, June 1985.

Abortion clinic sues protesters [news]. CHRISTIANITY TODAY 29(14):69, October 4, 1985.

Abortion controversy slows radical 'civil rights' bill: but foes still face uphill battle. HUMAN EVENTS 45:1+, August 10, 1985.

Abortion controversy: a study in law and politics, by A. M. Pearson, et al. HARVARD JOURNAL OF LAW AND PUBLIC POLICY Spring 1985, p. 427-464.

Abortion dilemma, by A. Finlayson. WORLD PRESS REVIEW 32:56, January 1985.

Abortion fight gets set for a new round, by T. Gest. U S NEWS AND WORLD REPORT 98:69, January 28, 1985.

Abortion in Great Britain: one Act, two laws, by K. M. Norrie. THE CRIMINAL LAW REVIEW August 1985, p. 475-488.

Abortion is not a crime/Spanish women fight, by E. Lamas. INTERNATIONAL VIEWPOINT 76:28, May 20, 1985.

Abortion: new arguments on an old issue [news]. CHRISTIANITY TODAY 29(18):56-57, December 13, 1985.

Abortion pill goes on trial, by N. Docherty. NEW SCIENTIST 106:5, June 20, 1985.

Abortion wins another round, by H. Quinn. MACLEAN'S 97:46, November 19, 1984.

American Life Lobby strives to outlaw taxes for abortion [news], by A. D. Blanchard. FUNDAMENTALIST JOURNAL 4(5):60, May 1985.

Archbishop, governor, and veep, by M. Novak. NATIONAL REVIEW 36:45, September 21, 1984.

Article III, § 2/14th amendment, § 5 congressional responses to Roe [Roe v. Wade, 93 S. Ct. 705] from Lincoln's Dred Scott [Dred Scott, v. Sanford 60 U. S. 393] viewpoint, by G. S. Swan. LINCOLN LAW REVIEW 16:63-89, 1985.

Ask a lawyer: do I need my husband's consent to have an abortion?, by L. S. Dranoff. CHATELAINE 58:20+, April 1985.

Belfast/on the abortion trial. CHARTIST 104:6, May 1985.

Belgium/Women's right to choose on trial. INTERNATIONAL VIEWPOINT 83:26, September 30, 1985.

Bloodletting continues [abortion; perspective], by L. Mooneyham. FUNDAMENTALIST JOURNAL 2(9):12-13, October 1983.

Child in the womb is a human being, by L. Nogrady. PERCEPTION 8:19-22, March-April 1985.

Child sacrifice to the modern Molech, by M. D. Bray. FUNDAMENTALIST JOURNAL 3(1):15-17, January 1984.

Choice. MS 13:97, March 1985.

Claims for malpractice and complications following legal abortions 1975-1979, by
    E. Ryde-Blomqvist. LAKARTIDNINGEN 81(42):3808-3810, October 17,
    1984.

Colorado voters amend the state's constitution to outlaw public funding of
    abortions. CHRISTIANITY TODAY 29:46-47, January 18, 1985.

Consequences of abortion legislation. Special issue: women changing therapy:
    new assessments, values and strategies in feminist therapy, by M. Braude.
    WOMEN AND THERAPY 2(2-3):81-90, Summer-Fall, 1983.

Constitutional law: the minor's right to consent to abortion: how far is Oklahoma
    from Akron. OKLAHOMA LAW REVIEW 37:780-809, Winter 1984.

Constitutionality of a city ordinance regulating the performance of abortion. US
    Supreme Court. Decision Nos. 81746, 811172, June 15, 1983. MEDICINE
    AND LAW 4(1):85-90, 1985.

Contraception and abortion of mentally handicapped female adolescents under
    German law, by A. Eser. MEDICINE AND LAW 4(6):499-513, 1985.

Court to reconsider abortion issue. CONGRESSIONAL QUARTERLY WEEKLY
    REPORT 43:1002, May 25, 1985.

Crimes against the unborn: protecting and respecting the potentiality of human
    life [through criminal law; United States], by J. A. Parness. HARVARD JOUR-
    NAL OF LEGISLATION 22:97-172, Winter 1985.

Critical look at current regulation of interruption of pregnancy as it is called
    according to section 218 et seq. of the Criminal Code (FRG), by E. Backhaus.
    CONCEPTE 4:95-112, 1984.

Demise of the trimester standard? City of Akron v. Akron Center for Reproductive
    Health, Inc. [103 S. Ct. 2481]. JOURNAL OF FAMILY LAW 23:267-286, Feb-
    ruary 1984.

Doctor cleared in abortion trial, by T. Pugh. GUARDIAN 37(8):12, November 12,
    1984.

Echographic diagnosis of gestational age and law 194, by F. Chiavazza, et al.
    ACTA BIOMEDICA DE L'ATENEO PARMENSE 56(2):63-67, 1985.

Factors related to delay for legal abortions performed at a gestational age of 20
    weeks or more. JOURNAL OF BIOSOCIAL SCIENCE 17(3):327-337, July
    1985.

FBI director was right not to usurp ATF in bombings, by R. J. O'Connell. CRIME
    CONTROL DIGEST 19(7):1-2, February 18, 1985.

FBI director was right not to usurp ATF in bombings, by R. J. O'Connell.
    SECURITY SYSTEMS DIGEST 16(4):4-5, February 18, 1985.

Federal law enforcement role at issue in abortion bombings. CRIMINAL JUSTICE
    NEWSLETTER 16(3):7-8, February 1, 1985.

High court hears horrors of illegal abortion, by E. Bader. GUARDIAN 37(46):3, September 25, 1985.

Ideology of the general interest and legislative issues concerning abortion, by B. M. Pereira. REVUE DE L'INSTITUT DE SOCIOLOGIE 1-2:239-256, 1984.

Illinois abortion statute for incompetent persons struck down. MENTAL AND PHYSICAL DISABILITY LAW REPORTER 8(5):450, September-October 1984.

International dilemma, by A. Finlayson. MACLEANS 97:54, November 19, 1984.

Intervention analysis of the effects of legalized abortion upon U. S. fertility [impact of the 1973 decision of the United States Supreme Court invalidating statutes that restrict access to abortion], by T. D. Hogan. POPULATION RE-SEARCH AND POLICY REVIEW 3:201-218, October 1984.

Judgment without justice: abortion on demand 10 years later, by J. Falwell. FUNDAMENTALIST JOURNAL 2(1):8-35, January 1983.

Judicial decision making and biological fact: Roe v. Wade and the unresolved question of fetal viability, by R. H. Blank. WESTERN POLITICAL QUARTERLY 37: 584-602, December 1984.

Justice asks court to reverse Roe v. Wade (which declared abortion on demand to be a constitutional right). HUMAN EVENTS 45:5, July 27, 1985.

Justice asks Supreme Court to overturn Roe/Wade, by M. Anderson. NATIONAL NOW TIMES 18(5):1, August 1985.

Justice Department wants Roe reversal; NOW protests, by L. Sorrel. OFF OUR BACKS 15(8):10, August 1985.

Late abortions and the crime of child destruction: a reply [and] a rejoinder, by V. Tunkel, et al. CRIMINAL LAW REVIEW March 1985, p. 133-142.

Law pregnancy interruption and the consequences for the nurse burdened by conscience, by H. Hulsebosch. TIJDSCHRIFT VOR ZIEKENVERPLEGING 37(24): 754-757, November 27, 1984.

Legal aspects of medical genetics in Wisconsin, by E. W. Clayton. WISCONSIN MEDICAL JOURNAL 84(3):28-32, March 1985.

Legalized abortion: the Singapore experience. STUDIES IN FAMILY PLANNING 16(3):170, May-June 1985.

Legislation on contraception and abortion for adolescents, by R. Roemer. STUDIES IN FAMILY PLANNING 16:241-251, September-October 1985.

Medical Termination of Pregnancy Act1983 (Barbados), by P. K. Menon. INTER-NATIONAL AND COMPARATIVE LAW QUARTERLY 34:630-636, July 1985.

New civil war, by M. Potts. WORLD PRESS REVIEW 32:44, April 1985.

New Jersey constitutional law: Medicaid funding for abortion after Right to Choose v. Byrne. RUTGERS LAW REVIEW 36:665-702, Spring 1984.

New twist in the abortion funding controversy: Planned Parenthood v. Arizona. DEPAUL LAW REVIEW 33:835-355, Summer 1984.

1983 abortion decisions: clarification of the permissible limits of abortion regulation. UNIVERSITY OF RICHMOND LAW REVIEW Fall 1983, p. 137-159.

Out of the courts and into the streets. CANADA AND THE WORLD 50:11-12, April 1985.

Powell plays tricks with his bill, by S. Ardill. SPARE RIB (155):132, June 1985.

Pregnancy termination: not for family planning. The legal difference between sterilization and pregnancy termination is decisive, by H. Krautkrämer. FORT-SCHRITTE DER MEDIZIN 102(36):78, September 27, 1984.

Pro-choice protest of a pro-choice protest [editorial], by L. M. Delloff. CHRISTIAN CENTURY 102:1084-1085, November 27, 1985.

Pro-lifers winning on many key issues. HUMAN EVENTS 45:6, August 31, 1985.

Protection of potential human life in Illinois: policy and law at odds, by J. A. Parness. NORTHERN ILLINOIS UNIVERSITY LAW REVIEW 5:1-30, Winter 1984.

Public opinion and the legalization of abortion; with French summary, by T. F. Hartnagel, et al. CANADIAN REVIEW OF SOCIOLOGY AND ANTHRO-POLOGY 22:411-430, August 1985.

Rational basis? Strict scrutiny? Intermediate scrutiny? Judicial review in the abortion cases. OKLAHOMA CITY UNIVERSITY LAW REVIEW Summer 1984, 317-353.

Reagan's international war against abortion, by L. Gersing. IN THESE TIMES 9(36):5, September 25, 1985.

Recent cases: constitutional law. JOURNAL OF FAMILY LAW 23(3):462-464, 1984-85.

Rejoinder. [Discussion of late abortions and the crime of child destruction: a reply], by V. Tunkel. CRIMINAL LAW REVIEW March 1985, p. 133-140.

Rep. Jack; Kemp; (R.NY) presses anti-abortion measure. HUMAN EVENTS 45:5+, November 30, 1985.

Requirement that doctor notify husband of abortion struck down. THE FAMILY LAW REPORTER: COURT OPINIONS 10(48):1659-1660, October 9, 1984.

Reversing Roe vs Wade, by P. C. Cunningham. CHRISTIANITY TODAY 29:20-22, September 20, 1985.

Rhode Island abortion statute is struck down by Federal Court. THE FAMILY LAW REPORTER 11(9):1108-1109, January 8, 1985.

Right of privacy—mandatory hospitalization for all second trimester abortions invalidated as not being reasonably related to maternal health—City of Akron v. Akron Center for Reproductive Health, Inc., 103 S. Ct. 2481. SANTA CLARA LAW REVIEW 24:789-801, Summer 1984.

Right to life of the unborn—an assessment of the eighth amendment to the Irish constitution. BRIGHAM YOUNG UNIVERSITY LAW REVIEW 1984, p. 371-402.

RNs take to court in abortion cases. AMERICAN JOURNAL OF NURSING 85:830, July 1985.

Roe v. Wade: a retrospective look at a judicial osymoron, by J. J. Coleman, III. ST. LOUIS UNIVERSITY LAW JOURNAL 29:7-44, December 1984.

Root and branch of Roe v. Wade, by J. T. Noonan, Jr. NEBRASKA LAW REVIEW 63:668-679, 1984.

Senate kills proposal to prevent federal funding of abortions for women inmates. CORRECTIONS DIGEST 16:23, November 6, 1985.

75 years of abortion-law landmarks, by M. Janigan. MACLEANS 97:50, November 19, 1984.

Shot fired into Blackman home believed to be accidental. CRIMINAL JUSTICE NEWSLETTER 16(6):8, March 15, 1985.

Some thoughts on autonomy and equality in relation to Roe v. Wade, by R. B. Ginsburg. NORTH CAROLINA LAW REVIEW 63:375-386, January 1985.

State legislatures versus the Supreme Court: abortion legislation in the 1980's, by B. J. George, Jr. PEPPERDINE LAW REVIEW 12:427-513, January 1985.

Statutes and ordinances—abortion. THE CRIMINAL LAW REPORTER: COURT DECISIONS 37(12):2226, June 19, 1985.

Statutes and ordinances—feticide—vagueness. THE CRIMINAL LAW REPORTER:COURT DECISIONS 36(9):2163, November 28, 1984.

Supreme Court and abortion. THE HASTINGS CENTER REPORT 10(6):14-19, December 1980.

Supreme Court will review state abortion laws, by E. Kennelly. NATIONAL NOW TIMES 18(4):3, June 1985.

Taking Roe to the limits: treating viable feticide as murder. INDIANA LAW REVIEW 17:1119-1142, Winter 1984.

Taste of victory [Planned Parenthood organization; Face the Facts], by C. Thomas. FUNDAMENTALIST JOURNAL 4(3):57, March 1985.

Taxation—child support—abortion. THE FAMILY LAW REPORTER: COURT OPINIONS 11(40):1515, August 20, 1985.

Terror hits the clinics, [Army of God's violent attacks on legalized abortion, by A. Brummer. GUARDIAN January 2, 1985, p. 13.

Testimony on constitutional amendments to negate *Roe v. Wade* given before the Subcommittee on the Constitution of the Senate Judiciary Committee, March 7, 1983. WOMEN'S RIGHTS LAW REPORTER 8:179-183, Summer 1985.

Trends in legalized abortion in South Australia 1970-81, by F. Yusuf, et al. JOURNAL OF BIOSOCIAL SCIENCE 17(2):215-221, April 1985.

U.S. Supreme Court officers angry over weapons ban during March-For-Life. SECURITY SYSTEMS DIGEST 16(3):10, February 4, 1985.

United States Senate votes to uphold Roe versus Wade, by D. Granberg. POPULATION RESEARCH AND POLICY REVIEW 4:115-131, June 1985.

Voting on June 9 1985: initiative 'Right to Life'. KRANKENPFLEGE SOINS INFIRMIERE 78(5):32-33, May 1985.

What the FBI won't probe. GUARDIAN 37(11):18, December 12, 1984.

When a mentally ill woman refuses abortion, by M. Mahowald, et al. HASTINGS CENTER REPORT 15:22-23, April 1985.

Within our reach: a building consensus could at least put an end to abortion on demand [editorial], by K. S. Kantzer, et al. CHRISTIANITY TODAY 29(7):20-23, April 19, 1985.

Wrongful life?, by C. Frank. AMERICAN BAR ASSOCIATION JOURNAL 71:26, February 1985.

Wrongful life: a tort resuscitated, by G. Dorst. THE AMERICAN JOURNAL OF TRIAL ADVOCACY 7(1):167-176, Fall 1983.

ABORTION: LEGAL
Annulment of a medical treatment contract in violation of the abortion prohibition of Paragraph 218 StGB, by G. H. Schlund. GEBURTSHILFE UND FRAUENHEILKUNDE 44(8):537-538, August 1984.

Legal abortion: limits and contributions to human life, by R. J. Cook. CIBA FOUNDATION SYMPOSIA 115:211-227, 1985.

Pregnancy termination: not for family planning. The legal difference between sterilization and pregnancy termination is decisive, by H. Krautkrämer. FORTSCHRITTE DER MEDIZIN 102(36):78, September 27, 1984.

ABORTION: LITERATURE
Debate rages over pro-abortion book. FUNDAMENTALIST JOURNAL 3(9):64, October 1984.

ABORTION: MALES
Gender slap, by J. Lukomnik. HEALTH PAC BULLETIN 15(4):11, July 1984.

Baclofen as an analgesic in operations for uterine dilation, aspiration and curettage, by O. Corli, et al. MINERVA ANESTESIOLOGICA 50(7-8):401-405, July-August 1984.

Cervical dilatation for early abortion (new approach), by M. B. Purwar, et al. ASIA-OCEANIA JOURNAL OF OBSTETRICS AND GYNAECOLOGY 10(3):275-279, September 1984.

Chorion biopsy, cytogenetic diagnosis, and selective termination in a twin pregnancy at risk of haemophilia, by M. T. Mulcahy, et al. LANCET 2(8407):866-867, October 13, 1984.

Comparative safety of second-trimester abortion methods, by D. A. Grimes, et al. CIBA FOUNDATION SYMPOSIA 115:83-101, 1985.

Comparison of the methods for terminating pregnancy, by V. M. Sadauskas, et al. AKUSHERSTVO I GINEKOLOGIIA 3:37-39, March 1985.

Comparison of prostaglandin E2 pessaries and laminaria tents for ripening the cervix before termination of pregnancy, by S. R. Killick, et al. BRITISH JOURNAL OF OBSTETRICS AND GYNAECOLOGY 92(5):518-521, 1985.

Contragestion by antiprogestin: a new approach to human fertility control, by E. E. Baulieu. CIBA FOUNDATION SYMPOSIA 115:192-210, 1985.

Cytologic identification of trophoblastic epithelium in products of first-trimester abortion, by E. S. Jacobson, et al. OBSTETRICS AND GYNECOLOGY 66(1):124-126, July 1985.

Decidual morphology and F prostaglandin in amniotic fluid in stretch-induced abortion, by Y. Manabe, et al. OBSTETRICS AND GYNECOLOGY 64(5):661-665, November 1984.

Diagnosis of extrauterine pregnancy in mini-abortions, by M. Dejmek, et al. CESKOSLOVENSKA GYNEKOLOGIE 49(7):484-487, August 1984.

Diagnostic efficacy of 'routine' thoracic radiography preparatory to abortion, by M. Hanisch. RADIOLOGIA DIAGNOSTICA 26(2):233-238, 1985.

Diazepam and ketamine for voluntary interruptions of pregnancy, by G. Bovyn. CAHIERS D'ANESTHESIOLOGIE 30(8):1019-1025, December 1982.

Early and late abortion methods, by D. A. van Lith, et al. CLINICAL OBSTETRICS AND GYNAECOLOGY 11(3):585-601, December 1984.

Echographic and anatomo-pathologic aspects of a blighted ovum. Clinical and prognostic importance, by F. Borruto, et al. MINERVA GINECOLOGIA 36(7-8):413-417, July-August 1984.

Efficacy of using thymalin in different types of peritonitis in obstetrical practice, by B. I. Kuznik, et al. AKUSHERSTVO I GINEKOLOGIIA 9:50-52, September 1984.

Endocrine function of the reproductive system after early abortion by vacuum-aspiration, by T. M. Likhacheva. AKUSHERSTVO I GINEKOLOGIIA 2:37-39, February 1985.

Importance of the ketamine-flunitrazepam combination in elective abortion, by R. Cordebar. CAHIERS D'ANESTHESIOLOGIE 32(Suppl. 8):59-63, December 1984.

In praise of Laminaria . . . seaweed to dilate the cervix. EMERGENCY MEDICINE 17(5):153+, March 15, 1985.

Inhibition of 3 beta-hydroxysteroid dehydrogenase (3 beta-HSD) activity in first- and second-trimester human pregnancy and the luteal phase using Epostane, by N. S. Pattison. FERTILITY AND STERILITY 42(6):875-881, December 1984.

Intracervical administration of prostaglandin E2 prior to vacuum aspiration. A prospective double-blind randomized study, by T. Iversen, et al. INTER-NATIONAL JOURNAL OF GYNAECOLOGY AND OBSTETRICS 23(2):95-99, April 1985.

Intramuscular administration of Prostin for abortion in the second trimester, by F. Curic, et al. JUGOSLAVENSKA GINEKOLOGIJA I OPSTETRICIJA 24(3-4):68-70, May-August 1984.

Maternal reproductive loss and cleft lip with or without cleft palate in human embryos, by K. Shiota. AMERICAN JOURNAL OF MEDICAL GENETICS 19(1):121-129, September 1984.

Medical clinical responsibility in control studies in pregnancy and curettage of the uterus long after fetal death, by G. H. Schlund. GEBURTSHILFE UND FRAUENHEILKUNDE 44(12):827-828, December 1984.

Menstrual induction: surgery versus prostaglandins, by D. T. Baird, et al. CIBA FOUNDATION SYMPOSIA 115:178-191, 1985.

Obstetric-gynecologic day hospital: analgesia for voluntary interruption of pregnancy, by D. Laveneziana, et al. ANNALI DI OSTETRICIA GINE-COLOGIA MEDICINE PERINATALE 106(1):48-51, January-February 1985.

Postconception menses induction using prostaglandin vaginal suppositories, by H. W. Foster, Jr., et al. OBSTETRICS AND GYNECOLOGY 65(5):682-685, May 1985.

Pregnancy prevention by intravaginal delivery of a progesterone antagonist: RU486 tampon for menstrual induction and absorption, by G. D. Hodgen. FERTILITY AND STERILITY 44(2):263-267, August 1985.

Pregnancy terminating effect and toxicity of an active constituent of Aristolochia mollissima Hance, aristolochic acid A, by W. H. Wang, et al. YAO HSUEH HSUEH PAO 19(6):405-409, June 1984.

Pregnancy wastage and prenatal diagnosis, by B. Grünfeld, et al. TIDSSKRIFT FOR DEN NORSKE LAEGEFORENING 105(15):1079-1081, May 30, 1085.

Preoperative cervical priming by intracervical application of a new sulprostone gel, by W. Rath, et al. CONTRACEPTION 31(3):207-216, March 1985.

Prophylactic antibiotics for currettage abortion, by D. A. Grimes, et al. AMERICAN JOURNAL OF OBSTETRICS AND GYNECOLOGY 150(6):689-694, November 15, 1984.

Recurrent thrombotic thrombocytopenic purpura in early pregnancy: effect of uterine evacuation, by E. A. Natelson, et al. OBSTETRICS AND GYNECOLOGY 66(Suppl. 3):54S-56S, September 1985.

Second-trimester abortion: a difficult, unresolved problem, by P. Audra, et al. REVUE FRANCAISE DE GYNECOLOGIE ET D'OBSTETRIQUE 79(4):285-288, April 1984.

Some aspects of late abortion for congenital abnormality, by S. L. Barron. CIBA FOUNDATION SYMPOSIA 115:102-121, 1985.

Stimulation of uterine contraction in fetal death, by B. L. Gurtovoi, et al. AKUSHERSTVO I GINEKOLOGIIA (10):65-67, October 1984.

Successful induction of abortion in intrauterine fetal death and operated pulmonary embolism, by H. Kölbl, et al. ZEITSCHRIFT FUR GEBURTSCHILFE UND PERINATOLOGIE 188(6):285-286, November-December 1984.

Termination of pregnancy by a slow release device containing 16, 16-dimethyl-trans-delta 2 PGE1 methyl ester, by M. Bygdeman, et al. ASIA OCEANIA JOURNAL OF OBSTETRICS AND GYNAECOLOGY 10(3):359-365, September 1984.

Transcervical intra-amniotic induction with PgF2 alpha in missed abortion and labor in the 3d trimester of pregnancy with dead fetus. II, by E. Rizzuto, et al. MINERVA GINECOLOGIA 37(4):137-139, April 1985.

Ultrasonic diagnosis and mini-abortions, by J. Doucha, et al. CESKOSLOVENSKA GYNEKOLOGIE 49(7):481-484, August 1984.

Use of a new vaginal suppository prostaglandin E1 analog Gemeprost for cervix maturation prior to abortion in the 1st trimester, by T. Rabe, et al. GEBURTSHILFE UND FRAUENHEILKUNDE 45(6):393-401, June 1985.

Use of osmotic dilators to facilitate induced midtrimester abortion: clinical evaluations, by M. F. Atienza, et al. CONTRACEPTION 30(3):215-223, September 1984.

Use of prostaglandin F2 alpha for dilating the cervical canal in performing an abortion, by S. Matanyi, et al. AKUSHERSTVO I GINEKOLOGIIA (3):39-41, March 1985.

Use of prostaglandins and their analogues for abortion, by M. Bygdeman. CLINICAL OBSTETRICS AND GYNAECOLOGY 11(3):573-584, December 1984.

Use of 16,16-dimethyl-trans delta 2 prostaglandin E1 methyl ester (gemeprost) vaginal pessaries for the termination of pregnancy in the ealry second trimester. A comparison with extra-amniotic prostaglandin E2, by I. T. Cameron, et al. BRITISH JOURNAL OF OBSTETRICS AND GYNAECOLOGY 91(11): 1136-1140, November 1984.

Various aspects of termination of pregnancy by the vacuum-aspiration method, by E. I. Kal'chenko, et al. AKUSHERSTVO I GINEKOLOGIIA (12):43-44, December 1984.

What matters is what is left inside not what is removed: how about twins? [letter], by G. Jonas. OBSTETRICS AND GYNECOLOGY 65(2):297-298, February 1985.

ABORTION: MISSED
Experimental study of pathological and normal early pregnancy with the E rosette test, by R. R. Strache, et al. ZENTRALBLATT FUR GYNAEKOLOGIE 107(4): 201-207, 1985.

Hydatidiform mole with a coexistent fetus, by H. A. Sande, et al. ACTA OBSTETRICIA ET GYNECOLOGICA SCANDINAVICA 64(4):353-355, 1985.

Transcervical intra-amniotic induction with PgF2 alpha in missed abortion and labor in the 3d trimester of pregnancy with dead fetus. II, by E. Rizzuto, et al. MINERVA GINECOLOGIA 37(4):137-139, April 1985.

ABORTION: MORTALITY AND MORTALITY STATISTICS
Discoveries and dissimulations: the impact of abortion deaths on maternal mortality in British Columbia, by A. McLaren, et al. BC STUDIES 64:3-26, 1984-1985.

Morbidity and mortality from second-trimester abortions, by D. A. Grimes, et al. JOURNAL OF REPRODUCTIVE MEDICINE 30(7):505-514, July 1985.

Mortality due to abortion at Kenyatta National Hospital, 1974-1983, by S. Wanjala, et al. CIBA FOUNDATION SYMPOSIA 115:41-53, 1985.

Safety of termination of pregnancy: NHS versus private [letter], by P. Diggory. LANCET 2(8409):989, October 27, 1984.

Withdraw this license to kill. [Moral relativism as the link between embryology, abortion and murder], by P. Johnson. TIMES August 22, 1985, p. 10.

ABORTION: NURSES AND NURSING
Avoidance of anger, by K. J. Lindgren, et al. MCN 10(5):320-323, September-October 1985.

Nurse confident of acquittal, by T. Pugh. BRIARPATCH 14(2):2, March 1985.

Nurses attitude to therapeutic abortion, by C. Webb. NURSING TIMES 81(1):44-47, January 2-8, 1985.

RNs take to court in abortion cases. AMERICAN JOURNAL OF NURSING 85:830, July 1985.

Royal College of Nursing. Retrograde step. NURSING STANDARD (383):4, February 7, 1985.

This we believe about life and its value: Nurses Christian Fellowship 1980 position statement. JOURNAL OF CHRISTIAN NURSING 1(3):7, Fall 1984.

Aborted sibling factor: a case study, by A. H. Weiner, et al. CLINICAL SOCIAL WORK JOURNAL 12(3):209-215, 1984.

Abortion and subsequent pregnancy, by C. F. Bradley. CANADIAN JOURNAL OF PSYCHIATRY 29(6):494-498, October 1984.

Abortion as a stigma: in the eyes of the beholder, by G. Weidner, et al. JOURNAL OF RESEARCH IN PERSONALITY 18:359-371, September 1984.

Abortion: the devisive issue [editorial], by A. Yankauer. AMERICAN JOURNAL OF PUBLIC HEALTH 75(7):714-715, July 1985.

Abortion outcome as a function of sex-role identification, by R. C. Alter. PSYCHOLOGY OF WOMEN QUARTERLY 8:211-233, Spring 1984.

Abortion, a psychological argument, by J D. Hunt. EMOTIONAL FIRST AID: A JOURNAL OF CRISIS INTERVENTION 1(4):34-42, Winter 1984.

Abortion: understanding differences, by S. Callahan, et al. FAMILY PLANNING PERSPECTIVES16(5):219-221, September-October 1984.

Abortion's other victims. Women discuss post-abortion trauma, by M. Gallagher. POLICY REVIEW 32:20-22, 1985.

Attributions, expectations, and coping with abortion, by B. Major, et al. JOURNAL OF PERSONALITY AND SOCIAL PSYCHOLOGY 48(3):585-599, March 1985.

Avoidance of anger, by K. J. Lindgren, et al. MCN 10(5):320-323, September-October 1985.

Biological paternity, social maternity: on abortion and infanticide as unrecognised Indicators of the cultural character of maternity. THE SOCIOLOGICAL REVIEW MONOGRAPH 28:232-240, June 1979.

Clinical forum. 1. Postabortion counseling, by S. Anthony, et al. NURSING MIRROR156(4):31-37, January 26, 1983.

Comparative study of recidivists and contraceptors along the dimensions of lows of control and impulsivity, by G. D. Gibb. INTERNATIONAL JOURNAL OF PSYCHOLOGY 19(6):581-591, December 1984.

Comparison of the psychosocial situation of 125 abortion patients before and after the abortion, by P. Goebel. ZEITSCHRIFT FUR PSYCHO-SOMATISCHE MEDIZIN UND PSYCHOANALYSE 30(3):270-281, 1984.

Coping with abortion, by L. Cohen, et al. JOURNAL OF HUMAN STRESS 10(3):140-145, Fall 1984.

Death before birth. [Grief after therapeutic abortion], by E. Dunn. SUNDAY TIMES December 8, 1985, p. 38.

Death is also life, by F. Belliard. REVUE DE L'INFIRMIERE 35(2):9-13, January 1985.

Effects of abortion on a marriage, by J. Mattinson. CIBA FOUNDATION SYMPOSIA 115:165-177, 1985.

Female infanticide and amniocentesis, by R. Jeffery, et al. SOCIAL SCIENCE AND MEDICINE 19(11):1207-1212, 1984.

In Turner's syndrome womanhood is important and not chromosomes, by E. M. Sarroe. SYGEPLEJERSKEN 84(31):14-15, August 1, 1984.

Journal from an obscure place: thoughts on abortion from an unborn child, by J. Miles. JOURNAL OF CHRISTIAN NURSING 1(3):8-12, Fall 1984.

Meanings of the notion "desire for a child": some considerations based on an empirical study of 400 patients applying for legal abortion, by A. T. Teichmann. JOURNAL OF PSYCHOSOMATIC OBSTETRICS AND GYNAECOLOGY 3(3-4):215-222, December 1984.

Mini pills, IUDs and abortion, by J. F. Kippley. JOURNAL OF CHRISTIAN NURSING 2(1):32, Winter 1985.

My baby or my life: how could I choose?. . . hyperemesis gravidarum, by V. Kennedy. JOURNAL OF CHRISTIAN NURSING 1(3):4-6, Fall 1984.

Parental response to mid-trimester therapeutic abortion following amniocentesis, by O. W. Jones, et al. PRENATAL DIAGNOSIS 4(4):249-256, July-August 1984.

Peers, parents, and partners. Determining the needs of the support person in an abortion clinic, by P. B. Beeman. JOURNAL OF OBSTETRICS, GYNECOLOGY AND NEONATAL NURSING 14(1):54-58, January-February 1985.

Post-abortion and post-partum psychiatric hospitalization, by H. P. David. CIBA FOUNDATION SYMPOSIA 115:150-164, 1985.

Pregnancy termination for genetic indications: the impact on families, by R. M. Furlong, et al. SOCIAL WORK IN HEALTH CARE 10(1):17-34, Fall 1984.

Psychological aspects of voluntary interruption of pregnancy, by C. Mouniq, et al. PSYCHOLOGIE MEDICALE 14(8):1181-1185, June 1982.

Psychological factors that predict reaction to abortion, by D. T. Moseley, et al. JOURNAL OF CLINICAL PSYCHOLOGY 37(2):276-279, 1981.

Sequelae and support after termination of pregnancy for fetal malformation, by J. Lloyd, et al. BRITISH MEDICAL JOURNAL 290(6472):907-909, March 23, 1985.

Support for prenatal decision following an abnormal amniocentesis: structure, dynamics, and outreach, by P. A. Park. BIRTH DEFECTS 20(6):91-95, 1984.

Support from significant others and loneliness following induced abortion, by J. M. Robbins, et al. SOCIAL PSYCHIATRY 20(2):92-99, 1985.

Therapeutic abortion following midtrimester amniocentesis [letter], by N. J. Leschot, et al. PRENATAL DIAGNOSIS 5(3):243-244, May-June 1985.

Too young to live, by E. Procter. NURSING MIRROR 160(20):31, May 15, 1985.

What is a person? (editorial). JOURNAL OF CHRISTIAN NURSING 1(3):3, Fall 1984.

Women's perceptions of first trimester spontaneous abortion, by C. L. Wall-Hass. JOURNAL OF OBSTETRICS, GYNECOLOGY AND NEONATAL NURSING 14(1):50-53, January-February 1985.

Women's responses to abortion: implications for post-abortion support groups, by A. Mcgettigan, et al. JOURNAL OF SOCIAL WORK AND HUMAN SEXUALITY 3:119-132, 1984-85.

ABORTION: REPEATED

Case of materno-foetal histocompatibility—implications for leucocyte transfusion treatment for recurrent aborters, by D. C. Kilpatrick. SCOTTISH MEDICAL JOURNAL 29(2):110-112, April 1984.

Chromosome aberrations in 334 individuals with various types of abortion (including 144 couples), by J. M. Cantú, et al. REVISTA DE INVESTIGACION CLINICA 37(2):131-134, April-June 1985.

Chromosome analysis in couples with recurrent abortions, by K. Soh, et al. TOHOKU JOURNAL OF EXPERIMENTAL MEDICINE 144(2):151-163, October 1984.

Chromosome studies of 500 couples with two or more abortions, by E. S. Sachs, et al. OBSTETRICS AND GYNECOLOGY 65(3):375-378, March 1985.

Chromosome study in repeated abortions, by K. Larsen, et al. UGESKRIFT FOR LAEGER 147(4):285-287, January 21, 1985.

Clinical, immunologic, and genetic definitions of primary and secondary recurrent spontaneous abortions, by J. A. McIntyre, et al. FERTILITY AND STERILIZATION 42(6):849-855, December 1984.

Congenital afibrinogenemia and recurrent early abortion: a case report, by S. Evron, et al. EUROPEAN JOURNAL OF OBSTETRICS, GYNECOLOGY AND REPRODUCTIVE BIOLOGY 19(5):307, May 1985.

Controlled trial of treatment of recurrent spontaneous abortion by immunisation with paternal cells, by J. F. Mowbray, et al. LANCET 1(8435):941-943, April 27, 1985.

High resolution cytogenetic evaluation of couples with recurring fetal wastage, by T. L. Yang-Feng, et al. HUMAN GENETICS 69(3):246-249, 1985.

HLA typing in couples with repetitive abortion, by P. F. Bolis, et al. BIOLOGICAL RESEARCH IN PREGNANCY AND PERINATOLOGY 5(3):135-137, 1984.

Increased frequency of lymphocytic mitotic non-disjunction in recurrent spontaneous aborters, by R. C. Juberg, et al. JOURNAL OF MEDICAL GENETICS 22(1):32-35, February 1985.

Maternal antipaternal immunity in couples predisposed to repeated pregnancy Losses, by P. R. McConnachie, et al. AMERICAN JOURNAL OF REPRO- DUCTIVE IMMUNOLOGY 5(4):145-150, June 1984.

Paracentric inversion: a study of 2 new cases, by N. Morichon-Delvallez, et al. REVUE FRANCAISE DE GYNECOLOGIE ET D'OBSTETRIQUE 80(5):275- 277, April 1985.

Paternal mosaic 45, X/46, XYq+ and recurrent spontaneous abortions without monosomy X [letter], by V. Izakovic, et al. CLINICAL GENETICS 27(3):285- 286, March 1985.

Paternal Robertsonian translocation t(13q; 14q) and maternal reciprocal translo- cation t(7p; 13q) in a couple with repeated fetal loss, by P. R. Scarbrough, et al. JOURNAL OF MEDICAL GENETICS 21(6):463-464, December 1984.

Plasmapheresis for the treatment of repeated early pregnancy wastage associated with anti-P, by J. A. Rock, et al. OBSTETRICS AND GYNECOLO- GY 66(Suppl. 3):57S-60S, September 1985.

Pregnancy following repeated abortions in uterine abnormalities, by J. Schmid. GYNAEKOLOGISCHE RUNDSCHAU 24(3):140-144, 1984.

Prevention of recurrent spontaneous abortions by leukocyte transfusions, by C. G. Taylor, et al. JOURNAL OF THE ROYAL SOCIETY OF MEDICINE 78(8): 623-627, August 1985.

Recurrent abortions and circulating anticoagulant. Relation to lupic disease: 6 cases, by A. Mathieu, et al. ANNALES DE MEDECINE INTERNE 135(7):502- 506, 1984.

Recurrent abortions, thromboses, and a circulating anticoagulant, by K. Eswaran, et al. AMERICAN JOURNAL OF OBSTETRICS AND GYNECOLOGY 151(6):751-752, March 15, 1985.

Recurrent spontaneous abortion, by M. J. Bennett. HEALTHRIGHT 4:8-13, May 1985.

Recurrent spontaneous abortions associated with lupus anticoagulant in patients with collagen-vascular dieseses, by Y. Ichikawa, et al. RYUMACHI 25(2):87- 94, April 1985.

Repeated first-trimester pregnancy loss: evaluation and management, by P. G. McDonough. AMERICAN JOURNAL OF OBSTETRICS AND GYNECOLOGY 153(1):1-6, September 1, 1985.

Repeated pregnancy loss due to alpha-thalassemia—report of 3 cases, by C. K. Kuo, et al. TAIWAN I HSUEH HUI TSA CHIH 83(7):724-729, July 1984.

Repeated spontaneous abortion, by F. Charvet, et al. REVUE FRANCAISE DE GYNECOLOGIE ET D'OBSTETRIQUE 80(7):555-558, July 1985.

Significance of human leukocyte antigen profiles in human infertility, recurrent abortion, and pregnancy disorders, by A. C. Menge, et al. FERTILITY AND STERILITY 43(5):693-695, May 1985.

Treatment of recurrent spontaneous abortions by immunisation with paternal leucocytes [letter], by M. F. Reznikoff-Etievant, et al. LANCET 1(8442):1398, June 5, 1985.

Women who obtain repeat abortions: a study based on record linkage, by P. G. Steinhoff, et al. FAMILY PLANNING PERSPECTIVES 11(1):30-38, 1979.

ABORTION: RESEARCH
An error in the calculation of the percentage of conceptions with an unbalanced chromosome rearrangement that survive birth, by W. L. Russell. MUTATION RESEARCH 142(4):217, April 1985.

Controversial abortion drug finally approved for use [Preglandin]. BUSINESS JAPAN 29:35, October 1984.

Fetal research and the problem of consent, by C. Perry. WORLD FUTURES 20(1-2):55-67, 1984.

Measuring early pregnancy loss: laboratory and field methods, by A. J. Wilcox, et al. FERTILITY AND STERILITY 44(3):366-374, September 1985.

Pregnancy impairment in mice by antibodies to subcellular placenta fractions, by J. Morenz, et al. INTERNATIONAL JOURNAL OF FERTILITY 29(2):91-97, 1984.

Relative oxytocic properties of fenprostalene compared with cloprostenol, prostaglandin F2 alpha, and oxytocin in the ovarietomized ewe, by R. Garcia-Villar, et al. AMERICAN JOURNAL OF VETERINARY RESEARCH 46(4):841-844, April 1985.

Short term effect of medroxyprogesterone acetate on the rat intestinal digestive and absorptive functions, by R. Singh, et al. INDIAN JOURNAL OF MEDICAL RESEARCH 81:186-192, February 1985.

Studies on implantation traces in rats, by I. Size, observation period and staining, by T. Yamada, et al. JIKKEN DOBUTSU 34(1):17-22, January 1985.

Surgical pathologist examines the placenta, by C. H. Sander. PATHOLOGY ANNUAL 20(Pt 2):235-288, 1985.

ABORTION: SEPTIC
Bacteriology, clinical course, and histoplacental, myometrial and hysterographic findings in the infected ovum between 10 and 26 weeks, by A. Ovalle, et al. REVISTA CHILENA DE OBSTETRICIA Y GINECOLOGIA 48(6):449-462, 1983.

Characteristics of the treatment of pregnant women with septic abortion and pyelonephritis complicated by acute renal failure, by V. L. Cherniakov, et al. AKUSHERSTVO I GINEKOLOGIIA 5:52-53, May 1985.

Considerations in relation to severe toxicoseptic abortion, by M. Buhaciuc, et al. VIATA MEDICALA 32(8):171-172, August 1984.

Microbial flora in septic abortion, by R. M. Nava y Sánchez, et al. GINECOLOGIA Y OBSTETRICIA DE MEXICO 51(317):229-235, September 1983.

Pregnancy in Fanconi's anemia, by H. Zakut, et al. HAREFUAH 107(9):238-239, November 1, 1984.

Preventive use of heparin in women with septic abortion and pyelonephritis in pregnancy, by H. Zrubek, et al. GINEKOLOGIA POLSKA 55(11):855-858, November 1984.

Proteus septicemias. Apropos of 4 cases, by P. Leniaud, et al. MEDECINE TROPICALE 44(2):137-142, April-June 1984.

Septic shock as a complication of criminal abortion, by A. P. Kiriushchenkov. FEL'DSHER I AKUSHERKA 49(9):48-52, September 1984.

T- and B-lymphocyte dynamics in patients following septic abortion, by M. A. Repina, et al. AKUSHERSTVO I GINEKOLOGIIA (3):43-45, March 1985.

ABORTION: SOCIOLOGY
Where have all the babies gone [social trends; aboption], by K. Menehan. CHRISTIANITY TODAY 29(15):26-29, October 18, 1985.

ABORTION: SPONTANEOUS
Accuracy of spontaneous abortion recall, by A. J. Wilcox, et al. AMERICAN JOURNAL OF EPIDEMIOLOGY 120(5):727-733, November 1984.

Acute placentitis and spontaneous abortion caused by chlamydia psittaci of sheeporigin: a histological and ultrastructural study, by S. Y. Wong, et al. JOURNAL OF CLINICAL PATHOLOGY 38(6):707-711, June 1985.

Calculating risk ratios for spontaneous abortions: the problem of induced abortions,by J. Olsen. INTERNATIONAL JOURNAL OF EPIDEMIOLOGY 13(3):347-350, September 1984.

Cell mediated immune response in spontaneous abortion and toxaemia of pregnancy, by J. Naithani, et al. INDIAN JOURNAL OF MEDICAL RESEARCH 81:149-156, February 1985.

Chromosome abnormalities in 118 couples with recurrent spontaneous abortions, by A. Tóth, et al. GYNECOLOGIC AND OBSTETRIC INVESTIGATION 18(2):72-77, 1984.

Chromosome anomalies in spontaneously aborted fetuses and a study of mutagenesis in a human population, by J. Dejmek, et al. BRATISLAVSKE LEKARSKE LISTY 83(6):637-645, June 1985.

Classification and mechanisms of spontaneous abortion, by D. I. Rushton. PERSPECTIVES IN PEDIATRIC PATHOLOGY 8(3):269-287, Fall 1984.

Comparative analysis of methods of the immunotherapy or spontaneous abortions, by V. I. Govallo, et al. AKUSHERSTVO I GINEKOLOGIIA 3:41-43, March 1985.

Controlled trial of treatment of recurrent spontaneous abortion by immunisation with paternal cells, by J. F. Mowbray, et al. LANCET 1(8435):941-943, April 27, 1985.

Course of pregnancy following spontaneous abortion, by B. Rud, et al. ACTA OBSTETRICIA ET GYNECOLOGICA SCANDINAVICA 64(3):277-278, 1985.

Deaths from spontaneous abortion in the United States, by S. M. Berman, et al. JAMA 253(21):3119-3123, June 7, 1985.

Diabetes and spontaneous abortion [letter], by H. Kalter. AMERICAN JOURNAL OF OBSTETRICS AND GYNECOLOGY 152(5):603-604, July 1, 1985.

Down syndrome live births and prior spontaneous abortions of unknown karyotype,by E. B. Hook. PROGRESS IN CLINICAL AND BIOLOGICAL RESEARCH163C:21-24, 1985.

Ectopic pregnancy and spontaneous abortions following in-vitro fertilization and embryo transfer, by S. Lindenberg, et al. ACTA OBSTETRICIA ET GYNECOLOGICA SCANDINAVICA 64(1):31-34, 1985.

Embryos from spontaneous abortions with chromosomal aberrations, by J. Kleinebrecht, et al. ANATOMISCHER ANZEIGER 157(1):3-33, 1984.

Estrogen and progesterone receptors in the decidual tissue of women administered prostaglandins and experiencing spontaneous abortion, by M. K. Asribekova, et al. PROBLEMY ENDOKRINOLOGII I GORMONOTERAPII 31(2):26-29, March-April 1985.

Fever during pregnancy and spontaneous abortion, by J. Kline, et al. AMERICAN JOURNAL OF EPIDEMIOLOGY 121(6):832-842, June 1985.

Fragile sites and chromosome breakpoints in constitutional rearrangements II. Spontaneous abortions, stillbirths and newborns, by F. Hecht, et al. CLINICAL GENETICS 26(3):174-177, September 1984.

Histology of the placenta in spontaneous abortion, by V. Bianco, et al. ANNALI DI OSTETRICIA GINECOLOGIA MEDICINA PERINATALE 105(4):219-224, July-August 1984.

HLA sharing and spontaneous abortion in humans, by M. L. Thomas, et al. AMERICAN JOURNAL OF OBSTETRICS AND GYNECOLOGY 151(8):1053-1058, April 15, 1985.

Hormone levels in amniotic fluid and maternal serum in women who undergo spontaneous abortion after second trimester amniocentesis, by K. Bremme, et al. GYNECOLOGIC AND OBSTETRIC INVESTIGATION 18(2):78-82, 1984.

Immunogenetic studies of spontaneous abortion in mice. Preimmunization of females with allogeneic cells, by N. Kiger, et al. JOURNAL OF IMMUNOLOGY 134(5):2966-2970, May 1985.

In vitro growth and chromosome constitution of placental cells. I. Spontaneous and elective abortions, by P. A. Hunt, et al. CYTOGENETICS AND CELL GENETICS 39(1):1-6, 1985.

Karyotype in couples with spontaneous abortion, by F. Bernardi, et al. MINERVA GINECOLOGIA 36(7-8):391-394, July-August 1984.

Malformations and chromosome anomalies in spontaneously aborted fetuses with single umbilical artery, by J. Byrne, et al. AMERICAN JOURNAL OF OBSTETRICS AND GYNECOLOGY 151(3):340-342, February 1, 1985.

Maternal employment and the chromosomal characteristics of spontaneously aborted conceptions, by J. Silverman, et al. JOURNAL OF OCCUPATIONAL MEDICINE 27(6):427-438, June 1985.

Moral significance of spontaneous abortion, by T. F. Murphy. JOURNAL OF MEDICAL ETHICS 11(2):79-83, June 1985.

Mycoplasma, ureaplasma and spontaneous abortion. AMERICAN FAMILY PHYSICIAN 27:256, April 1983.

Negative effect of the IUCD on the occurrence of heteroploidy—correlated abnormalities in spontaneous abortions: an update, by L. H. Honoré. CONTRACEPTION 31(3):253-260, March 1985.

Reciprocal balanced translocation of the long arm of chromosome 8 to the short arm of chromosome 7 in a woman with two spontaneous abortions, by H. Hatzissevastou-Loukidou, et al. HUMAN GENETICS 70(4):379, 1985.

Recurrent spontaneous abortion, by M. J. Bennett. HEALTHRIGHT 4:8-13, May 1985.

Recurrent spontaneous abortions associated with lupus anticoagulant in patients with collagen-vascular dieseses, by Y. Ichikawa, et al. RYUMACHI 25(2):87-94, April 1985.

Relationship of maternal age and trisomy among trisomic spontaneous abortions, by T. Hassold, et al. AMERICAN JOURNAL OF HUMAN GENETICS 36(6):1349-1356, November 1984.

Repeated spontaneous abortion, by F. Charvet, et al. REVUE FRANCAISE DE GYNECOLOGIE ET D'OBSTETRIQUE 80(7):555-558, July 1985.

Risk of spontaneous abortion after early prenatal diagnosis performed by chorion biopsy, by B. Gustavii. LAKARTIDNINGEN 82(21):1959-1960, May 22, 1985.

Risk of spontaneous abortion in ultrasonically normal pregnancies [letter], by R. D. Wilson, et al. LANCET 2(8408):920-921, October 20, 1984.

Role of Brucella abortus in spontaneous abortion among the black population, by T. J. Fernihough, et al. SOUTH AFRICAN MEDICAL JOURNAL 68(6):379-380, September 14, 1985.

Spontaneous abortion among insulin-dependent diabetic women, by M. Miodovnik, et al. AMERICAN JOURNAL OF OBSTETRICS AND GYNE-COLOGY 150(4):372-376, October 15, 1984.

Spontaneous abortions among female industrial workers, by I. Figá-Talamanca. INTERNATIONAL ARCHIVES OF OCCUPATIONAL AND ENVIRONMENTAL HEALTH 54(2):163-171, 1984.

Spontaneous abortions and malformations in the offspring of nurses exposed to anaesthetic gases, cytostatic drugs, and other potential hazards in hospitals, based on registered information of outcome, by K. Hemminki, et al. JOURNAL OF EPIDEMIOLOGY AND COMMUNITY HEALTH 39(2):141-147, June 1985.

Spontaneous abortions and newborn infants with malformations, by A. Cvejic. MEDICINSKI PREGLED 37(9-10):401-407, 1984.

Spontaneous abortions and stillbirths in relation to prenatal examinations in Denmark. Report from the Cytogenetic Central Register, by U. Friedrich, et al. UGESKRIFT FOR LAEGER 146(25):1848-1849, June 18, 1984.

Spontaneous fetal loss rate in early pregnancy [letter], by D. H. Gilmore, et al. LANCET 1(8420):107, January 12, 1985.

Systematic karyotyping of couples in early spontaneous abortion: a reliable examination in the prevention of chromosome anomalies, by A. Salesses. PROGRESS IN CLINICAL AND BIOLOGICAL RESEARCH 163C:25-29, 1985.

Temporal changes in chromosome abnormality rate in human spontaneous abortions: evidence for an association between sex-chromosome monosomy and trisomy 16, by T. Hassold, et al. CYTOGENETICS AND CELL GENETICS 38(3):200-205, 1984.

Too young to live, by E. Procter. NURSING MIRROR 160(20):31, May 15, 1985.

Transferrin and HLA: spontaneous abortion, neural tube defects, and natural selection, by L. R. Weitkamp, et al. NEW ENGLAND JOURNAL OF MEDICINE 313(15):925-932, October 10, 1985.

Treatment of recurrent spontaneous abortions by immunisation with paternal leucocytes [letter], by M. F. Reznikoff-Etievant, et al. LANCET 1(8442):1398, June 5, 1985.

Women's perceptions of first trimester spontaneous abortion, by C. L. Wall-Hass. JOURNAL OF OBSTETRICS, GYNECOLOGY AND NEONATAL NURSING 14(1):50-53, January-February 1985.

ABORTION: STATISTICS
Comparative study of applications for abortions for the years 1979 and 1980, by E. G. Pérez. TEMAS DE TRABOJO SOCIAL 4(1):67-82, January-June 1982.

Reports and surveys for the Center for Sociological Investigation on Abortion: 1979-1983. REVISTA ESPAÑOLA DE INVESTIGACIONES SOCI-OLOGICAS 21:255-302, January-March 1983.

Second-trimester abortions in the United States [1972-1981], by D. A. Grimes. FAMILY PLANNING PERSPECTIVES 16:260-266, November-December 1984.

Vasopressin reduces blood loss from second-trimester dilatation and evacuation abortion, by K. F. Schulz, et al. LANCET 2(8451):353-356, August 17, 1985.

ABORTION: THERAPEUTIC

Amenorrhoea traumatica following therapeutic abortion: an approach to management, by W. K. Tang. ASIA-OCEANIA JOURNAL OF OBSTETRICS AND GYNAECOLOGY 10(4):479-483, December 1984.

Cervical occlusion due to adhesions following therapeutic abortion: an uncommon sequel to vacuum curettage, by I. S. Fraser. AUSTRALIAN AND NEW ZEALAND JOURNAL OF OBSTETRICS AND GYNAECOLOGY 24(4):292-293, November 1984.

Cervix ripening and labor induction in therapeutic abortion in the middle and late 2d trimester using intracervical and extra-amniotic prostaglandin gel administration, by W. Rath, et al. WIENER KLINISCHE WOCHENSCHRIFT 97(11):486-493, May 24, 1985.

Critical analysis of 75 therapeutic abortions, by N. J. Leschot, et al. EARLY HUMAN DEVELOPMENT 10(3-4):287-293, January 1985.

Death before birth. [Grief after therapeutic abortion], by E. Dunn. SUNDAY TIMES December 8, 1985, p. 38.

Genital infections in women undergoing therapeutic abortion, by D. Avonts, et al. EUROPEAN JOURNAL OF OBSTETRICS, GYNECOLOGY AND REPRO-DUCTIVE BIOLOGY 20(1):53-59, July 1985.

Hormone load tests in the first half of pregnancy—a diagnostic and therapeutic approach, by I. Gerhard, et al. BIOLOGICAL RESEARCH IN PREGNANCY AND PERINATOLOGY 5(4):157-173, 1984.

Mid-trimester therapeutic abortion by vaginal suppository of 16, 16-dimethyl-trans-delta 2-prostaglandin E1, by K. Kato, et al. ASIA OCEANIA JOURNAL OF OBSTETRICS AND GYNAECOLOGY 11(2):163-167, June 1985.

Nurses attitude to therapeutic abortion, by C. Webb. NURSING TIMES 81(1):44-47, January 2-8, 1985.

Parental response to mid-trimester therapeutic abortion following amniocentesis, by O. W. Jones, et al. PRENATAL DIAGNOSIS 4(4):249-256, July-August 1984.

Sequelae of therapeutic abortion [letter], by S. D. Clarke. MEDICAL JOURNAL OF AUSTRALIA 142(7):425, April 1, 1985.

Therapeutic abortion following midtrimester amniocentesis [letter], by N. J. Leschot, et al. PRENATAL DIAGNOSIS 5(3):243-244, May-June 1985.

Therapeutic abortions following rubella infection in pregnancy: the potential impact on the incidence of congenital rubella syndrome, by M. K. Serdula, et al. AMERICAN JOURNAL OF PUBLIC HEALTH 74:1249-1251, November 1984.

Therapeutic use of prostaglandins, by J. Hruda, et al. CASOPIS LEKARU CESKYCH 123(50):1527-1530, December 14, 1984.

Uncontrollable life-threatening status asthmaticus—an indicator for termination of pregnancy by cesarean section, by M. Gelber, et al. RESPIRATION 46(3): 320-322, 1984.

Use of a modified test system to determine early pregnancy factor (EPF) levels in patients with normal first trimester pregnancy and after therapeutic abortion, by H. R. Tinneberg, et al. ANNALS OF THE NEW YORK ACADEMY OF SCIENCES 442:551-557, 1985.

Water intoxication and oxytocin, by F. T. Mwambingu. BRITISH MEDICAL JOURNAL 290(6462):113, January 12, 1985.

ABORTION: THREATENED

Anemia in the etiology of threatened late abortion and premature labor, by T. Mardesic. CESKOSLOVENSKA GYNEKOLOGIE 50(5):356-359, June 1985.

Blood hormone levels in threatened abortion, by M. V. Fedorova, et al. AKUSHERSTVO I GINEKOLOGIIA 12:31-33, December 1984.

Cardiomonitoring in the evaluation of fetal condition in threatened abortion in the second and third trimesters, by I. D. Khokhlova. AKUSHERSTVO I GINEKOLOGIIA 10:35-38, October 1984.

Circulating immune complexes and ribonuclease and 5'-nucleotidase activity in the blood of women with threatened abortion treated with acupuncture-reflexotherapy, by L. I. Ksendzov, et al. AKUSHERSTVO I GINEKOLOGIIA 12:36-37, December 1984.

Does ultrasound examination render biochemical tests obsolete in the prediction ofearly pregnancy failure?, by J. G. Westergaard, et al. BRITISH JOURNAL OF OBSTETRICS AND GYNAECOLOGY 92(1):77-83, January 1985.

Effectiveness of Bricanyl (terbutaline) treatment in the prevention and management of threatened abortion and premature delivery, respectively, within the frames of out-patients' services, by B. Toth, et al. THERAPIA HUNGARICA 30(2):88-92,1982.

Electroimpulse test as a method for the diagnosis of threatened abortion and to evaluate the effectiveness of treatment, by V. I. Orlov. AKUSHERSTVO I GINEKOLOGIIA 12:33-35, December 1984.

Hormone load tests in the first half of pregnancy—a diagnostic and therapeutic approach, by I. Gerhard, et al. BIOLOGICAL RESEARCH IN PREGNANCY AND PERINATOLOGY 5(4):157-173, 1984.

Interactions between beta-mimetics and indices of feto-placental function, by M. Forcucci-Zulli, et al. MINERVA GINECOLOGIA 37(3):89-92, March 1985.

Intrauterine hematoma: a prognostic enigma in threatened abortion, by F. R. Raymond, et al. JOURNAL OF THE AMERICAN OSTEOPATHIC ASSOCIATION 85(1):65-70, January 1985.

Intrauterine synechiae complicated with threatened abortion and preterm labor. Combined therapy with terbutaline and magnesium sulfate, by T. Kawara-bayashi, et al. ASIA-OCEANIA JOURNAL OF OBSTETRICS AND GYNAE-COLOGY 10(4): 449-455, December 1984.

Medroxyprogesterone acetate does not perturb the profile of steroid metabolites in urine during pregnancy, by J. L. Yovich, et al. JOURNAL OF ENDO-CRINOLOGY 104(3):453-459, March 1985.

Outcome of pregnancy after threatened abortion, by J. B. Hertz, et al. ACTA OBSTETRICIA ET GYNECOLOGICA SCANDINAVICA 64(2):151-156, 1985.

Prognostic significance of various hormonal parameters in pregnancies complicated by threatened abortion, by S. Marsico, et al. MINERVA GINE-COLOGIA 36(7-8):381-389, July-August 1984.

Prognostic value of ultrasonic scanning and serum estradiol in threatened abortion, by S. J. Sederberg-Olsen, et al. UGESKRIFT FOR LAEGER 146(25):1853-1855, June 18, 1984.

A rare case in gynecologic practice, by K. Durveniashki. AKUSHERSTVO I GINE-KOLOGIIA 23(4):364-365, 1984.

Serum progesterone levels in early imminent abortion, by A. Balogh, et al. ACTA PHYSIOLOGICA HUNGARICA 65(3):275-279, 1985.

Structuro-functional activity of lymphocyte chromatin in abortion, by M. G. Kubatova, et al. AKUSHERSTVO I GINEKOLOGIIA (5):39-41, May 1985.

Study of local fibrinolysis in abortion, by M. Ikeuchi. NIPPON SANKA FUJINKA GAKKAI ZASSHI 37(7):1215-1223, July 1985.

Treatment of threatened abortion with traditional Chinese medicine—a clinical analysis of 62 cases, by H. Y. Huang. CHUNG HSI I CHIEH HO TSA CHIH 5(4):214-216, April 1985.

Ultrasound and estradiol plasma levels in threatened abortion, by G. B. Melis, et al. ACTA EUROPAEA FERTILITATIS 15(4):287-294, July-August 1984.

Ultrasound signs in threatened abortion and their prognostic significance, by M. Mantoni. OBSTETRICS AND GYNECOLOGY 65(4):471-475, April 1985.

ABORTION:VOLUNTARY
Double-blind placebo-controlled trial of baclofen, alone and in combination, in patients undergoing voluntary abortion, by O. Corli, et al. CLINICAL THERA-PEUTICS 6(6):800-807, 1984.

ABORTION AND COLLEGE STUDENTS
College students' attitudes toward shared responsibility in decisions about abortion: implications for counseling, by I. J. Ryan, et al. JOURNAL OF AMERICAN COLLEGE HEALTH 31:231-235, June 1983.

ABORTION AND DEVELOPING COUNTRIES
Aid and abortion: leave it to Malthus. ECONOMIST 291:27, June 30, 1984.

Abortion bills and smokescreens, by T. L. Langford. TEXAS OBSERVER 77(3):12-14, February 22, 1985.

AID tightens antiabortion measures, by C. Holden. SCIENCE 227:1318-1319, March15, 1985.

American Life Lobby strives to outlaw taxes for abortion [news], by A. D. Blanchard. FUNDAMENTALIST JOURNAL 4(5):60, May 1985.

No aid for abortion. ECONOMIST 294:32, February 16, 1985.

Population update [Reagan administration stand on cutting aid to governments that sanction abortion]. HUMANIST 45:43, May-June 1985.

Taxation—child support—abortion. THE FAMILY LAW REPORTER: COURT OPINIONS 11(40):1515, August 20, 1985.

ABORTION AND ERA
E.R.A. and abortion: really separate issues?, by D. Johnson, et al. AMERICA 150:432-437, June 9, 1984.

Empirical investigation of the determinants of congressional voting on federal financing of abortions and the ERA, by J. M. Netter. JOURNAL OF LEGAL STUDIES 14:245-257, January 1985.

ABORTION AND FEMINISM
Abortion and the Christian feminist: a dilemma?, by C. Smith. NEW BLACK-FRIARS 66:62-67, February 1985.

Abortion and the Christian feminist: profilers of survival, by S. Dowell. NEW BLACKFRIARS 66:67-72, February 1985.

Abortion as "violence against women", by R. Petchesky. RADICAL AMERICAN 18(2):64, 1984.

Abortion: the issue is women's rights, by P. Grogan. MILITANT 48(44):11, November 30, 1984.

Actions refocus nation's abortion debate/women's, by L. Lederer. NATIONAL NOW TIMES 18(1):1, January 1985.

Jerry Falwell meets the sisters of Justice [Columbus, Ohio, radical feminist group protests Falwell's ideas, especially the opposition to abortion rights], by B. Khan. OFF OUR BACKS 16:15, February 1986.

Male ideology of privacy! A feminist perspective on the right of abortion, by C. MacKinnon. RADICAL AMERICAN 17(4):23-35, 1983.

ABORTION AND HORMONES
Evaluation of intra-amniotic administration of 120 gm of urea with 5 mg of prostaglandin F2 alpha for midtrimester termination of pregnancy between 20 and 24 weeks' gestation, by R. V. Haning, Jr., et al. AMERICAN JOURNAL OF OBSTETRICS AND GYNECOLOGY 151(1):92-96, January 1, 1985.

Menstrual induction: surgery versus prostaglandins, by D. T. Baird, et al. CIBA FOUNDATION SYMPOSIA 115:178-191, 1985.

Postconception menses induction using prostaglandin vaginal suppositories, by H. W. Foster, Jr., et al. OBSTETRICS AND GYNECOLOGY 65(5):682-685, May 1985.

Role of prostaglandins in human fertility, by M. P. Embrey. RECENTI PROGRESSI IN MEDICINA 76(1):34-47, January 1985.

Use of prostaglandins and their analogues for abortion, by M. Bygdeman. CLINICAL OBSTETRICS AND GYNAECOLOGY 11(3):573-584, December 1984.

Use of prostaglandins in the interruption of pregnancy, by F. Havránek. CESKOSLOVENSKA GYNEKOLOGIE 49(6):439-448, July 1984.

ABORTION AND HOSPITALS
Abortion issues reach into hospital ORs. AMERICAN JOURNAL OF NURSING 84:1535, December 1984.

Adolescent and voluntary interruption of pregnancy in the hospital milieu, by C. Mazière, et al. SOINS, GYNECOLOGIE, OBSTETRIQUE, PUERICULTURE, PEDIATRIE 45:37-44, February 1985.

Contraception and voluntary pregnancy interruption in public hospital establishments. Circular DGS/2A No. 12-82 of 12 October 1982, by J. Latrille. SOINS, GYNECOLOGIE, OBSTETRIQUE, PUERICULTURE, PEDIATRIE (27-28):61-64, August-September 1983.

Residential care as an alternative to abortion. HOSPITAL PROGRESS 60(1):41-44, 1979.

ABORTION AND INSURANCE
Abortion using health insurance, by O. Gritschneder. GEBURTSHILFE UND FRAUENHEILKUNDE 44(9):604-607, September 1984.

Health insurance study: no increased risk for fetal abnormalities in women working with video display terminals, by A. Ericson, et al. LAKARTIDNINGEN 82(23): 2180-2184, June 5, 1985.

Medicaid and abortion, by R. A. McCormick. THEOLOGICAL STUDIES 45(4):715-721, 1984.

ABORTION AND JOURNALISM
Publishers disagree over controversial ad, by A. Radolf. EDITOR AND PUBLISHER-THE FOURTH ESTATE 118:15, March 30, 1985.

ABORTION AND MALES
Men and abortion. FUTURIST 19:60-62, April 1985.

Requirement that doctor notify husband of abortion struck down. THE FAMILY LAW REPORTER: COURT OPINIONS 10(48):1659-1660, October 9, 1984.

ABORTION AND PARENTAL CONSENT
Minors' right of privacy: access to abortions without parental notification. JOURNAL OF JUVENILE LAW 9:101-105, 1985.

Abortion and medical discipline [letter]. NEW ZEALAND MEDICAL JOURNAL 98(780):451-452, June 12, 1985.

Abortion conflict: what it does to one doctor, by D. Clendinan. NEW YORK TIMES MAGAZINE August 11, 1985, p. 18-22+.

Change of mind following failed abortion doesn't relieve the physician of liability. FORTSCHRITTE DER MEDIZIN 103(9):70-71, March 7, 1985.

Doctor cleared in abortion trial, by T. Pugh. GUARDIAN 37(8):12, November 12, 1984.

From the viewpoint of the hospital physician. 7 years after the reform of paragraph 218, by A. Kayser. KRANKENPFLEGE JOURNAL 22(11):28-32, November 1,1984.

Interruption of pregnancy by private physicians. Opinion of the Baden-Würtemberg Superior Court of 1-30-1985, by H. J. Rieger. DEUTSCHE MEDIZINISCHE WOCHENSCHRIFT 110(13):519-521, March 29, 1985.

Medical criminals: physicians and white-collar offenses, by P. D. Jesilow, et al. JUSTICE QUARTERLY 2(2):149-165, June 1985.

Physician's counseling in conflict about pregnancy. Dilemma and chance, by W. Schuth, et al. DEUTSCHE MEDIZINISCHE WOCHENSCHRIFT 110(30):1175-1178, July 26, 1985.

Virginia doctor acquitted of illegal abortion, by L. S. OFF OUR BACKS 15(5):7, May 1985.

'Worthy of life and unworthy of life'—not an alternative for the physician (editorial), by H. Berger. PADIATRIE UND PADOLOGIE 20(1):1-6, 1985.

Wrongful life and wrongful birth: new concepts for the pediatrician, by J. Coplan. 75(1):65-72, January 1985.

ABORTION AND POLITICS

Abortion and elections/Bishops try to do in dems, by E. Bader. GUARDIAN 37(1):91, October 3, 1984.

Abortion and the right, by J. Hardisty. SHMATE 11:36, Summer 1985.

Abortion and the state. OFF OUR BACKS 15(4):4, April 1985.

Abortion bias: how network coverage has tilted to the prolifers: even anti-abortion forces acknowledge that the nightly news is paying more attention to their side of the explosive issue, by J. Kalter. TV GUIDE 33:6, November 9, 1985.

Abortion clinic bombings and the Reagan administration, by L. Woehrle. OFF OUR BACKS 15:2, January 1985.

Abortion controversy slows radical 'civil rights' bill: but foes still face uphill battle. HUMAN EVENTS 45:1+, August 10, 1985.

Abortion controversy: a study in law and politics, by A. M. Pearson, et al. HARVARD JOURNAL OF LAW AND PUBLIC POLICY Spring 1985, p. 427-464.

Abortion issue is not so simple, by T. C. Fox. NATIONAL CATHOLIC REPORTER 20:12, October 19, 1984.

Abortion policy in Canada as a women's issue, by S. McDaniel. ATLANTIS 10(2):74,Spring 1985.

Abortion rights: some setbacks but more gains. GUARDIAN 37(10):9, December 5,1984.

Abortion, the state and freedom, by N. Hunter. OFF OUR BACKS 14(10):15, November 1984.

Abortion: stories from North and South. HEALTHSHARING 6(1):21, Winter 1984.

Abortion: understanding differences, by S. Callahan, et al. FAMILY PLANNING PERSPECTIVES16(5):219-221, September-October 1984.

Abortions rights actions planned, by D. Wang. INTERCONTINENTAL PRESS 23(17):544, September 9, 1985.

AID tightens antiabortion measures, by C. Holden. SCIENCE 227:1318-1319, March 15, 1985.

Anti-abortion efforts fail in 5 out of 6 states. NATIONAL NOW TIMES 17(6):5, November 1984.

As the abortion issue reaches a political flashpoint, two Catholic experts clash in debate, by D. Grogan. PEOPLE WEEKLY 22:93+, October 22, 1984.

Attacks of anti-abortionists, by C. Walter. WOMANEWS 6(2):1, February 1985.

Baby killers and fetus fetishists, by P. Addelson. WOMEN'S REVIEW OF BOOKS 2(2):14, November 1984.

Backing down on abortion regulation: Saskatchewan's Tories pass a pro-life hot potato to the courts, by L. Cohen. ALBERTA REPORT 12:49, July 8, 1985.

Beyond "choice," by S. Clancy. LESBIAN CONTRADICTION 11:16, Summer 1985.

California referendum on abortion?, by E. Baaer. GUARDIAN 37(43):2, September 4,1985.

Can Congress settle the abortion issue?, by M. C. Segers. HASTINGS CENTER REPORT 12(3), June 20-28.

Canada/abortion-rights doctors targeted Socialist voice. INTERCONTINENTAL PRESS 23(1):30, January 21, 1985.

Capital punishment: helplessness and power, by R. M. Cooper. ENCOUNTER 46:163-175, Spring 1985.

Catholic politicians and abortion, by J. F. Donceel. AMERICA 152:81-83, February 2,1985.

Church and Cuomo [Catholic Church]. COMMONWEAL 111:517-518, October 5, 1984.

Congress facing a bitter battle on population control abroad; tighter abortion controls?, by J. Felton. CONGRESSIONAL QUARTERLY WEEKLY REPORT 42:2142-2146, September 1, 1984.

Conscientious objection, by J. S. O'Neill. NEW ZEALAND LAW JOURNAL 272-274+, August 1984.

Consistency for the sake of life [abortion and nuclear weapons], by P. Narciso. SOJOURNERS 14(8):12, August-September 1985.

Contemporary American abortion controversy: stages in the argument by C. C. Railsback. QUARTERLY JOURNAL OF SPEECH 70(4):410-424, 1984.

Cuomo and the lay voice, by A. McCarthy. COMMONWEAL 111:550-551, October 19, 1984.

Current antiabortion propaganda, by S. L. Polchanova. FEL'DSHER I AKUSHERKA 49(8):43-48, August 1984.

Debating abortion again [H. Morgentaler's clinic in Toronto], by S. MacKay. MACLEANS 97:40, December 24, 1984.

Defending against assaults on abortion rights, by E. Bader. GUARDIAN 37(3):9, October 17. 1984.

Empirical investigation of the determinants of congressional voting on federal financing of abortions and the ERA, by J. M. Netter. JOURNAL OF LEGAL STUDIES 14:245-257, January 1985.

Equal-opportunity banning, by N. Hentoff. VILLAGE VOICE 29:8, October 30, 1984.

Family issues and the right, by S. Sturgis. OFF OUR BACKS 15(8):17, August 1985.

—, by V. Hardisty. SHMATE 11:33, Summer 1985.

Feminist morality; excerpt from *Not an easy choice: a feminist re-examines abortion*, by K. McDonnell. CANADIAN FORUM 64:18-20, November 1984.

Fight for abortion rights, by S. Arnott. GAY COMMUNITY 12(28):1, February 2, 1985.

Genetics and a woman's rights [letter], by A. B. Masters. CANADIAN MEDICAL ASSOCIATION JOURNAL 131(12):1433, December 15, 1984.

Geraldine Ferraro's abortion dilemma: hypothetical dialogue with the candidate, by D. D'Souza. HUMAN EVENTS 44:23, November 3, 1984.

Getting rid of old habits, by M. Lauer. MOTHER JONES 10(2):10, February 1985.

Government steps up attacks on abortion rights, by J. Baker. INTERNATIONAL VIEWPOINT 81:4, July 29, 1985.

Governmental abortion policies and the right to privacy: the rights of the individual and the rights of the unborn. BROOKLYN JOURNAL OF INTERNATIONAL LAW 11:103-126, Winter 1985.

Governor and the bishops [M. Cuomo at Notre Dame]. NEW REPUBLIC 191:7-9, October 8, 1984.

Groups protest: abortion is not an erotic act. COMMUNIQU'ELLES 10(6):6, November 1984.

High court to re-examine state abortion regulations, by E.Witt. CONGRES-SIONAL QUARTERLY WEEKLY REPORT 43:2153-2155, October 26, 1985.

Horizons unclear for herizons, by P. Duchesne. COMMUNIQU'ELLES 11(4):4, July 1985.

House prohibits use of DC funds for abortion, by L. Sorrel. OFF OUR BACKS 15(8):10, August 1985.

Impact of the Hyde amendment on Congress, by S. Tolchin. WOMEN AND POLITICS 5(1):1, Spring 1985.

In defense of women's right to abortion, by P. Grogan. MILITANT 48(45):5, December 7, 1984.

Interview with a pro-choice activist. INTERNATIONAL VIEWPOINT 71:26, March 11, 1985.

Jerry Falwell meets the sisters of Justice [Columbus, Ohio, radical feminist group protests Falwell's ideas, especially the opposition to abortion rights], by B. Khan. OFF OUR BACKS 16:15, February 1986.

Justice asks court to reverse Roe v. Wade (which declared abortion on demand to be a constitutional right). HUMAN EVENTS 45:5, July 27, 1985.

Justice O'Connor, the constitution, and the trimester approach to abortion: a liberty on a collision course with itself, by R. F. Duncan. CATHOLIC LAWYER 29:275-285, Summer 1984.

Life or death split in America, by C. Thomas. TIMES February 13, 1985, p. 11.

Little give-and-take in abortion debate, by J. Walsh. IN THESE TIMES 9(10):3, January 30, 1985.

Long view of elder activists, by A. Braden. SOUTHERN EXPOSURE 13(2):34, March 1985.

Making distinctions [discussion of February 8, 1985 article, Understanding Mario Cuomo], by J. Tagg. NATIONAL REVIEW 37:36+, April 5, 1985.

Mario and Gerry had it coming. (their lambasting from American bishops over abortion), by P. J. Buchanan. HUMAN EVENTS 44:5, August 23, 1984.

Mario slips through [views of M. Cuomo], by D. R. Carlin, Jr. COMMONWEAL 112:392-393, July 12, 1985.

Meaning of the abortion conflict, by Ca. Joffe. CONTEMPORARY SOCIOLOGY 14(1):26-29, January 1985.

Morality struggle: anti-abortionists gain as the furor spreads and uneasiness grows; they exploit progress made in treatment of fetuses; President's support helps, by E. Hume. WALL STREET JOURNAL 205:1+, April 15, 1985.

Mother Church and daughter Geraldine. (Geraldine Ferraro and her difficulties with the Church over her stand on abortion). HUMAN EVENTS 44:4+, August 11, 1984.

NARAL Speakout, by P. De La Fuente. NEW DIRECTIONS FOR WOMEN 14(3): 1, May 1985.

Nation since "Blood Monday."(political aspects of the abortion issue), by P. B. Gemma, Jr. CONSERVATIVE DIGEST 11:16, February 1985.

Necessity defense aids protestors, by M. Byrne. IN THESE TIMES 9(27):16, June 12, 1985.

New Jersey constitutional law: Medicaid funding for abortion after Right to Choose v. Byrne. RUTGERS LAW REVIEW 36:665-702, Spring 1984.

No monolithic view [discussion of September 7, 1984 article, Religion and politics: clearing the air]. COMMONWEAL 111:548+, October 19, 1984.

Now what?, by J. Walsh. IN THESE TIMES 9(21):2, April 24, 1985.

On the barricades for abortion rights, by J. Sutherland. FREE SOCIETY 9(1):32, Fall 1984.

Politics and abortion, by J. I. Rosoff. CIBA FOUNDATION SYMPOSIA 115:244-262, 1985.

Politics of abortion, by N. Hentoff. VILLAGE VOICE 29:8, October 2, 1984.

Politics of motherhood, by M. O. Steinfels. CHRISTIANITY AND CRISIS 44:342-343, October 1, 1984.

Politics, morality, and the Catholic Church, by G. A. Kelly. USA TODAY 113:68-73, March 1985.

Population update [Reagan administration stand on cutting aid to governments that sanction abortion]. HUMANIST 45:43, May-June 1985.

Pro life equals violence, by I. Lloyd. SPARE RIB (152):11, March 1985.

Pro-abortion media shaken by "Silent Scream" (new film shows horrors of abortion), by W. F. Willoughby. HUMAN EVENTS 45:18+, March 23, 1985.

Pro-abortionists to battle "Silent Scream." (angry over anti-abortion film). HUMAN EVENTS 45:4+, March 9, 1985.

Pro-choice and "Silent No More", by M. Bowen. GUARDIAN 37(35):2, June 5, 1985.

Pro-choice and still catholic, by E. Bader. GUARDIAN 37(5):6, October 31, 1984.

Pro-choice movement: new directions, reexaminations, by K. Dubinsky, et al. PERCEPTION 8:16-18, March-April 1985.

Pro-choice pioneer recalls the bad old days, by A. Camen. GUARDIAN 37(46):3, September 25, 1985.

Pro-life delegate protest party's platform: "Shutout of party." HUMAN EVENTS 44(28):4+, July 28, 1984.

Pro-life gains: a U of A study shows less support for abortions, by J. Davidson, et al. ALBERTA REPORT 12:39, March 18, 1985.

Pro-lifers sense impending victory: new court majority eyed. HUMAN EVENTS 45:5+, February 2, 1985.

Pro-lifers winning on many key issues. HUMAN EVENTS 45:6, August 31, 1985.

Prolife activists escalate the war against abortion, by R. Frame. CHRISTIANITY TODAY 28:40-42, November 9, 1984.

Propaganda war over abortion, by A. Spake. MS MAGAZINE 14:88-92+, July 1985.

Protection of potential human life in Illinois: policy and law at odds, by J. A. Parness. NORTHERN ILLINOIS UNIVERSITY LAW REVIEW 5:1-30, Winter 1984.

Prudence, politics and the abortion issue [Catholic position], by D. A. Degnan. AMERICA 152:121-124, February 16, 1985.

Public policy: contract, abortion, and the CIA, by P. H. Brietzke. VALPARAISO UNIVERSITY LAW REVIEW 18:741-940, Summer 1984.

Reagan's international war against abortion, by L. Gersing. IN THESE TIMES 9(36):5, September 25, 1985.

Reagan's world agenda for women, by L. Woods. INTERNATIONAL VIEWPOINT (71):25, March 11, 1985.

Religious belief and public morality, by M. Cuomo. NEW YORK REVIEW OF BOOKS 31:32-37, October 25, 1984.

Rep. Henry J. Hyde challenges Cuomo on church-state issue. HUMAN EVENTS 44:8+, October 6, 1984.

Rep. Jack; Kemp; (R.NY) presses anti-abortion measure. HUMAN EVENTS 45:5+, November 30, 1985.

Reversing Roe vs Wade, by P. C. Cunningham. CHRISTIANITY TODAY 29:20-22, September 20, 1985.

'Right-to-life' bombers strike again, by J. Callum. GUARDIAN 37(4):9, October 24, 1984.

Right-to-life convention, by A. J. Fugh-Berman. OFF OUR BACKS 15:7, August-September 1985.

Sandra Day O'Connor and the justification of abortion, by P. H. Werhane. THEORETICAL MEDICINE 5(3):360-363, October 1984.

Shaming 'Dr. Death': pro-lifers picket abortionists' homes, by A. Elash. ALBERTA REPORT 12:45-46, July 29, 1985.

Silent scream airs at White House, by J. McManus, et al. NATIONAL CATHOLIC REPORTER 21:5, February 22, 1985.

"Silent scream" a study in deception. HERIZONS 3(6):11, September 1985.

Supreme Court and abortion. THE HASTINGS CENTER REPORT 10(6):14-19, December 1980.

Terrorism or not? GUILD NOTES 9(1):6, Winter 1985.

Terrorsim for the glory of God, by B. Quinn. NORTHWEST PASSAGE 25(6):5, February 1985.

Testimony on constitutional amendments to negate *Roe v. Wade* given before the Subcommittee on the Constitution of the Senate Judiciary Committee, March 7, 1983. WOMEN'S RIGHTS LAW REPORTER 8:179-183, Summer 1985.

Tidewater NOW uncover abortion scam, by M. Franke. OFF OUR BACKS 14(9):10, October 1984.

Tooley's immodest proposal, by C. H. Sommers. HASTINGS CENTER REPORT 15:39-42, June 1985.

Truth behind a moving piece of propaganda. [Controversial] US-made anti-abortion video], by A. Kent. GUARDIAN January 9, 1985, p. 8.

U.S. Supreme Court officers angry over weapons ban during March-For-Life. SECURITY SYSTEMS DIGEST 16(3):10, February 4, 1985.

Understanding Mario Cuomo [Notre Dame speech], by J. Tagg. NATIONAL REVIEW 37:26-26+, February 8, 1985.

United States Senate votes to uphold Roe versus Wade, by D. Granberg. POPULATION RESEARCH AND POLICY REVIEW 4:115-131, June 1985.

Victory for abortion rights. INTERCONTINENTAL PRESS 22(23):727, December 10, 1984.

Voting on June 9 1985: initiative 'Right to Life'. KRANKENPFLEGE SOINS INFIRMIERE 78(5):32-33, May 1985.

Webster says FBI won't classify abortion clinic bombings as acts of terrorism. CRIME CONTROL DIGEST 18(49):3-4, December 10, 1984.

—. SECURITY SYSTEMS DIGEST 15(26):4-5, December 17, 1984.

What the FBI won't probe. GUARDIAN 37(11):18, December 12, 1984.

When is a terrorist not necessarily a terrorist?, by S. Taylor. NATIONAL NOW TIMES 18(1):8, January 1985.

Who really is like Hitler? (abortionists vs. anti-abortion terrorists), by C. Marshner. CATHOLIC DIGEST 11:28, February 1985.

Wire next time? PROGRESSIVE 49(9):9, September 1985.

Women may need permission for abortion. BRIARPATCH 14(5):8, June 1985.

ABORTION AND PRISONERS
Senate kills proposal to prevent federal funding of abortions for women inmates. CORRECTIONS DIGEST 16:23, November 6, 1985.

ABORTION AND RELIGION
Abortion and the Catholic Church. HUMANIST 8(1):28, Spring 1985.

Abortion and the Christian feminist: a dilemma?, by C. Smith. NEW BLACK-FRIARS 66:62-67, February 1985.

Abortion and the Christian feminist: profilers of survival, by S. Dowell. NEW BLACKFRIARS 66:67-72, February 1985.

Abortion and elections/Bishops try to do in dems, by E. Bader. GUARDIAN 37(1):91, October 3, 1984.

Abortion and the Holocaust, by R. M. Brown. CHRISTIAN CENTURY 101:1004-1005, October 31, 1984.

Abortion and moral consensus: beyond Solomon's choice, by M. Kolbenschlag. CHRISTIAN CENTURY 102:179-183, February 20, 1985.

Abortion and theology [views of K. Luker], by M. E. Marty. CHRISTIAN CENTURY 101:1018-1020, October 31, 1984.

Abortion: a christian response, by S. J. Grenz. CONRAD GREBEL REVIEW 2(1):21-30, 1984.

Abortion, contraception, infanticide, by P. E. Devine. PHILOSOPHY 58:513-520, October 1983.

Abortion—moral and religious aspects. NATIONAL CATHOLIC REPORTER 21(1): 53, February 15, 1985

Abortion: why don't we all get smart [editorial]. CHRISTIANITY AND CRISIS 45:123-125, April 15, 1985.

Affirmation of life: a nurse wrestles with questions of abortion and justice [photos], by L. Rozzell. SOJOURNERS 14(6):34-37, June 1985.

AID tightens antiabortion measures, by C. Holden. SCIENCE 227:1318-1319, March15, 1985.

American nuns face Vatican ultimatum, by J. M. Wall. CHRISTIAN CENTURY 102:
67-68, January 23, 1985.

Archbishop, governor, and veep, by M. Novak. NATIONAL REVIEW 36:45,
September 21, 1984.

As the abortion issue reaches a political flashpoint, two Catholic experts clash in
debate, by D. Grogan. PEOPLE WEEKLY 22:93+, October 22, 1984.

Baby Doe and Ginny: a reason for treating "the least of these", by D. Brown.
EVANGELICAL JOURNAL 3(1):13-20, 1985.

Baby's first breath not always welcomed [live birth abortions; news]. FUNDA-
MENTALIST JOURNAL 2(1):58-59, January 1983.

Bible, abortion, and common sense, by N. L. Geisler. FUNDAMENTALIST JOUR-
NAL 4(5):24-27, May 1985.

Book withdrawn [Brave new people by D. G. Jones withdrawn by Inter-Varsity
Press]. CHRISTIAN CENTURY 101:920, October 10, 1984.

Cardinal Bernardin and the need for Catholic social teaching. CENTER JOUR-
NAL 1:9-28, Winter 1984.

Case for untidiness, by A. Hertzberg. COMMONWEAL 111:655-656, November
30,1984.

Catholic politicians and abortion, by J. F. Donceel. AMERICA 152:81-83,
February 2,1985.

Catholic theologian at an abortion clinic, by D. C. Maguire. MS MAGAZINE
13:129-132, December 1984.

Catholics and abortion: authority vs. dissent, by R. R. Ruether. CHRISTIAN
CENTURY 102:859-862, October 2, 1985.

Christmas and abortion [sermon; Luke 2:12; Matthew 2:16], by J. Killinger.
THE CHRISTIAN MINISTRY 16(6):26-27, November 1985.

Church and Cuomo [Catholic Church]. COMMONWEAL 111:517-518, October
5, 1984.

Churches' response to abortion [official positions of 16 US churches], by R. J.
Enquist. WORD AND WORLD 5,414:425, Fall 1985.

Crack in the Catholic Monolith, by B. Maschinot. IN THESE TIMES 9(1):7,
November 7, 1984.

Cry with the mother, by M. S. Shea. THEOLOGY TODAY 41:325-326, October
1984.

Cuomo and the lay voice, by A. McCarthy. COMMONWEAL 111:550-551,
October 19, 1984.

Democrats versus Catholic church, by J. Judis. IN THESE TIMES 8(37):7,
October 3, 1984.

Dissent and reaction [controversy over abortion advertisement signed by Catholic religious]. AMERICA 152:37, January 19, 1985.

Diversity claimed [survey of Catholic theologians and scholars]. CHRISTIAN CENTURY 102:240, March 6, 1985.

Drawing lines: the abortion perplex and the presuppositions of applied ethics, by A. Weston. MONIST 67:589-604, October 1984.

Edinburgh diary [General Assembly, Church of Scotland, annual meeting], by K. Slack. CHRISTIAN CENTURY 102:636-637, July 3-10, 1985.

Eerdmans takes over publication of controversial InterVarsity book [Brave new people, by D. G. Jones]. CHRISTIANITY TODAY 28:53, December 14, 1984.

Ethical issues in reproductive medicine: a Mormon perspective [photo], by L. E. Bush. DIALOGUE 18:40-66, Summer 1985.

Extermination of Jews in self-defense? The legends around Theodore N. Kaufman, by W. Benz. VIERTELJAHRSHEFTE FUR ZEITGESCHICHTE 29(4):615-630,1981.

"F factor": the New Testament in some white, feminist, Christian theological construction, by J. C. Lambert. JOURNAL OF FEMINIST STUDIES IN RELIGION 1(2):93-113, Fall 1985.

Feminist morality; excerpt from *Not an easy choice: a feminist re-examines abortion*, by K. McDonnell. CANADIAN FORUM 64:18-20, November 1984.

Focus on life issues [editorial]. NATIONAL CATHOLIC REPORTER 21:16, January 25, 1985.

Foetuses, famous violinists, and the right to continued aid, by M. Davis. PHILOSOPHICAL QUARTERLY 33:259-278, July 1983 and 35:73-82, January 1985.

Genetic medicine in the perspective of Orthodox halakhah, by R.M. Green. JUDAISM 34:261-277, Summer 1985.

Getting rid of old habits, by M. Lauer. MOTHER JONES 10(2):10, February 1985.

Governor and the bishops [M. Cuomo at Notre Dame]. NEW REPUBLIC 191:7-9, October 8, 1984.

Gradualist response to Robert Wennberg, by W. Hasker. CHRISTIAN SCHOLAR'S REVIEW 14(4,362)):369, 1985.

Groping for God's kind face again, by J. G. Swank. CHRISTIANITY TODAY 29:68, June 14, 1985.

Hardest question, by K. L. Woodward. NEWSWEEK 105:29, January 14, 1985.

HHS discriminates religiously, by C. Schiff. WOMANEWS 6(3):5, March 1985.

Holocaust, Nazism and abortion [euphemisms], by Wi. Brennan. FUNDA-
MENTALIST JOURNAL 2(1):30-33, January 1983.

Holy war [violence against abortion-related facilities; United States], by P.
Donovan. FAMILY PLANNING PERSPECTIVES 17(1):5-9,
January-February 1985.

InterVarsity Press bows to pressure, withdraws abortion book, by D. G. Jones.
FUNDAMENTALIST JOURNAL 3(10):64, November 1984.

Is the boycott against the Upjohn Company working. CHRISTIANITY TODAY
29(15):45-46, October 18, 1985.

Is Rome anti-Catholic?, by P. Steinfels. COMMONWEAL 112:4-5, January 11,
1985.

Jerry Falwell meets the sisters of Justice [Columbus, Ohio, radical feminist group
protests Falwell's ideas, especially the opposition to abortion rights], by B.
Khan. OFF OUR BACKS 16:15, February 1986.

Legacy of life, by T. Elkins. CHRISTIANITY TODAY 29(1):18-25, January 18,
1985.

Maguires' ire [discussion of January 11, 1985 article, Is Rome anti-Catholic?], by
P. Steinfels. COMMONWEAL 112:130+, March 8, 1985.

Mainline churches reassess prochoice stand on abortion [Protestant denomina-
tions]. CHRISTIANITY TODAY 28:72, December 14, 1984.

Mario and Gerry had it coming. (their lambasting from American bishops over abortion), by P. J. Buchanan. HUMAN EVENTS 44:5, August 23, 1984.

Marriage in the Greek Orthodox Church, by Demetrios J. Constantelos. JOUR-
NAL OF ECUMENICAL STUDIES 22:21-27, Winter 1985.

Medicaid and abortion, by R. A. McCormick. THEOLOGICAL STUDIES 45(4):
715-721, 1984.

Morality struggle: anti-abortionists gain as the furor spreads and uneasiness
grows; they exploit progress made in treatment of fetuses; President's
support helps, by E. Hume. WALL STREET JOURNAL 205:1+, April 15,
1985.

Mother Church and daughter Geraldine. (Geraldine Ferraro and her difficulties
with the Church over her stand on abortion) HUMAN EVENTS 44:4+, August
11, 1984.

New York's controversial Archbishop, by A. L. Goldman. NEW YORK TIMES
MAGAZINE October 14, 1984, p. 38+.

No monolithic view [discussion of September 7, 1984 article, Religion and
politics: clearing the air]. COMMONWEAL 111:548+, October 19, 1984.

Notes on moral theology, by R. A. McCormick. THEOLOGICAL STUDIES
46(1):50-114, 1985.

NOW challenges hierarchy. NATIONAL NOW TIMES 18(4):1, June 1985.

NY Diocese blocks abortion clinic, by L. S. OFF OUR BACKS 15(3):16, March 1985.

Order and disorder in anti-abortion rhetoric: a logological view, by R. A. Lake. QUARTERLY JOURNAL OF SPEECH 70:425-443, November 1984.

Pathos and promise of Christian ethics: a study of the abortion debate, by W. Werpehowski. HORIZONS 12:284-310, Fall 1985.

Personhood, covenant, and abortion, by M. R. Maguire. AMERICAN JOURNAL OF THEOLOGY AND PHILOSOPHY 6(1):28-46, 1985.

Politics, morality, and the Catholic Church, by G. A. Kelly. USA TODAY 113:68-73, March 1985.

Politics of motherhood, by M. O. Steinfels. CHRISTIANITY AND CRISIS 44:342-343, October 1, 1984.

Prayer for the woman who has miscarried, by G. Nefyodov. JOURNAL OF THE MOSCOW PATRIARCHATE 8:77-78, 1983.

Presbyterian Church (USA) decides to give higher priority to evangelism, by R. L. Frame. CHRISTIANITY TODAY 29(10):36+, July 12, 1985.

Presbyterians in Indianapolis [197th general assembly of Presbyterian Church (USA), June 1985; editorial], by D. J. Brouwer. REFORMED JOURNAL 35(7):3-4, July 1985.

Pro-choice and still catholic, by E. Bader. GUARDIAN 37(5):6, October 31, 1984.

Pro-choice movement: new directions, reexaminations, by K. Dubinsky, et al. PERCEPTION 8:16-18, March-April 1985.

Prohibition analogy as a dry try to make free abortion palatable, by T. Blackburn. NATIONAL CATHOLIC REPORTER 21:14-15, November 2, 1984.

Protestants push pro-life: Evangelicals now fight on their own terms, by T. Fennell. ALBERTA REPORT 12:46, May 13, 1985.

Recant or else [American nuns, diversity of opinion on morality of abortion; news]. CHRISTIAN CENTURY 102:9, January 2-9, 1985.

Recantation or dismissal [nuns asking for dialogue on Catholic antiabortion stand: news]. CHRISTIAN CENTURY 102:793, September 11-18, 1985.

Religion and gender: a comparison of Canadian and American student attitudes, by M. B. Brinkerhoff, et al. JOURNAL OF MARRIAGE AND THE FAMILY 47(2):415-429, May 1985.

Religion and opposition to abortion reconsidered, by A. Lewis Rhodes. REVIEW OF RELIGIOUS RESEARCH 27(2):158-168, December 1985.

Religion, values and attitudes toward abortion, by R. J. Harris, et al. JOURNAL OF THE SCIENTIFIC STUDY OF RELIGION 24:137-154, June 1985.

Religious belief and public morality, by M. Cuomo. NEW YORK REVIEW OF BOOKS 31:32-37, October 25, 1984.

Religious influences and congressional voting on abortion, by R. A. Dentler. JOURNAL FOR THE SCIENTIFIC STUDY OF RELIGION 16(2):145-164, 1984.

Rep. Henry J. Hyde challenges Cuomo on church-state issue. HUMAN EVENTS 44:8+, October 6, 1984.

Rev. Stone and his ghoulish tactics, by R. Sharpe. MS MAGAZINE 14:20, August 1985.

Rules for liberals [Catholics opposed to abortion], by D. R. Carlin, Jr. COMMON-WEAL 111:486-487, September 21, 1984.

"Seamless garment": life in its beginnings, by L. S. Cahill. THEOLOGICAL STUDIES 46:64-80, March 1985.

Shutting the door on dissent [American nuns threatened with expulsion for disagreeing with the Vatican's stand], by J. Castro. TIME 125:83, January 7, 1985.

Sister Margaret Traxler and the Vatican 24—standing up to the Pope on choice and the church, by C. Kleiman. MS MAGAZINE 13:124, April 1985.

Terror hits the clinics, [Army of God's violent attacks on legalized abortion, by A. Brummer. GUARDIAN January 2, 1985, p. 13.

Terrorsim for the glory of God, by B. Quinn. NORTHWEST PASSAGE 25(6):5, February 1985.

This we believe about life and its value: Nurses Christian Fellowship 1980 position statement. JOURNAL OF CHRISTIAN NURSING 1(3):7, Fall 1984.

U.S. bishops' efforts to affirm consistent life ethic will help refurbish damaged credibility. NATIONAL CATHOLIC REPORTER 21:14, November 2, 1984.

U.S. churches debate abortion, South Africa, and pornography. CHRISTIANITY TODAY 29:64-65, September 6, 1985.

Understanding Mario Cuomo [Notre Dame speech], by J. Tagg. NATIONAL REVIEW 37:26-26+, February 8, 1985.

Untidiness revisited [discussion of November 30, 1984 article, The case for untidiness], by A. Hertzberg. COMMONWEAL 112:69-70, February 8, 1985.

Vatican and nuns reach agreement [abortion rights statement; news]. CHRISTIANITY TODAY 29(14):69, October 4, 1985.

Vatican closes the door on dialogue and dissent, by M. Babbitt. NATIONAL NOW TIMES 18(1):2, January 1985.

Vatican threatens outspoken sisters [Vatican threat to expel 24 religious women from their orders unless they retract support for a statement published in the

New York Times critical of the Church's crusade against legalized abortion, by A. Baker. NEW DIRECTIONS FOR WOMEN 14:1+, March-April 1985.

Vatican to nuns: "shut up", by E. Bader. GUARDIAN 37(15):2, January 16, 1985.

We will not yield nor fall silent nor rest until all our children are safe, by M. Garvey. NATIONAL CATHOLIC REPORTER 20:18, October 19, 1984.

What different Christian churches believe about abortion, by C. Dubois. U.S. CATHOLIC 50:33-38, August 1985.

Within our reach: a building consensus could at least put an end to abortion on demand [editorial], by K. S. Kantzer, et al. CHRISTIANITY TODAY 29(7):20-23, April 19, 1985.

ABORTION AND SOCIOLOGY
Abortion: medical progress and social implications. CIBA FOUNDATION SYMPOSIA 115:1-285, 1985.

Destiny and liberty. Notes on the interruption of pregnancy in Western Societies, by A. Ines. REVISTA ESPANOLA DE INVESTGAGIONES SOCIOLOGICAS 21:135-150, January-March 1983.

ABORTION AND SUICIDE
Attempted suicide in response to refusal of elective abortion, by L. Gabinet. OHIO STATE MEDICAL JOURNAL 80(11):801-803, November 1984.

ABORTION AND THE MENTALLY RETARDED
Contraception and abortion of mentally handicapped female adolescents under German law, by A. Eser. MEDICINE AND LAW 4(6):499-513, 1985.

When a mentally ill woman refuses abortion, by M. Mahowald, et al. HASTINGS CENTER REPORT 15:22-23, April 1985.

ABORTION AND THE MILITARY
Psychopathological effects of voluntary termination of pregnancy on the father called up for military service, by J.-C. DuBouis-Bonnefond, et al. PSYCHO-LOGIE MEDICALE 14(8):1187-1189, June 1982.

Tell it to the Marines [letter], by P. Gerber. MEDICAL JOURNAL OF AUSTRALIA 142(9):530-531, April 29, 1985.

ABORTION AND THE PERFORMING ARTS
Bitter silent scream, by M. McDonald. MACLEANS 98:58, February 25, 1985.

Right-to-life porn, by J. Morley. NEW REPUBLIC 192:8-10, March 25, 1985.

Silent scream [antiabortion film], by C. Wallis. TIME 125:62, March 25, 1985.

Silent scream airs at White House, by J. McManus, et al. NATIONAL CATHOLIC REPORTER 21:5, February 22, 1985.

Silent scream, population, parochiaid, by E. Doerr. HUMANIST 45:41-42, July-August 1985.

Silent scream: seeking an audience. NEWSWEEK 105:37, February 25, 1985.

Some prochoice advocates acknowledge prolife impact of film depicting an abortion [The silent scream], by S. Anderson. CHRISTIANITY TODAY 29:46-47, April 5, 1985.

Truth about The silent scream, by A. Spake. MS MAGAZINE 14:92, July 1985.

Why we can't be silent about anti-abortion tactics [innacuracies in The silent scream]. GLAMOUR 83:52, June 1985.

ABORTION AND WOMEN

Gender slap, by J. Lukomnik. HEALTH PAC BULLETIN 15(4):11, July 1984.

Pregnant women's attitudes toward the abortion of defective fetuses, by R. C. Faden, et al. POPULATION AND ENVIRONMENT 6(4):197-209, 1983.

Some aspects of sexual knowledge and sexual behavior of local women. Results of a survey. 1. General sexual knowledge and attitude to abortion, pregnancy and contraception, by V. Atputharajah. SINGAPORE MEDICAL JOURNAL 25(3):135-140, June 1984.

WEBA: voice of experience relates the horrors of abortion [Women exploited by abortion], by D. W. Huff. FUNDAMENTALIST JOURNAL 2(1):34-35, January 1983.

Womanpoll. CHATELAINE 58:56, September 1985.

Women of Japan [abortion is easy to obtain, divorce is difficult; despite rapid social change, women find they often have little future except as house-wives, by C. Moorehead. NEW SOCIETY 70:453-455, December 20-27, 1984.

ABORTION AND YOUTH

Abortion experience among obstetric patients at Korle-Bu Hospital, Accra, Ghana, by P. Lamptey, et al. JOURNAL OF BIOSOCIAL SCIENCE 17(2): 195-203, April1985.

Adolescent and voluntary interruption of pregnancy in the hospital milieu, by C. Mazière, et al. SOINS, GYNECOLOGIE, OBSTETRIQUE, PUERICULTURE, PEDIATRIE 45:37-44, February 1985.

Adolescent mothers and fetal loss, what is learned from experience, by P. B. Smith,et al. PSYCHOLOGICAL REPORTS 55:775-778, December 1984.

Adolescents' values, sexuality, and contraception in a rural New York county, by N. McCormick, et al. ADOLESCENCE 20:385-395, Summer 1985.

Attack on teen abortion, by E. Bader. GUARDIAN 37(23):1, March 13, 1985.

Attitude towards abortion among teenagers in Bendel State of Nigeria, by O. G. Oshodin. JOURNAL OF THE ROYAL SOCIETY OF HEALTH 105(1):22-24, February 1985.

Confronting the teenage pregnancy issue: social marketing as an interdisciplinary approach, by W. Marsiglio. HUMAN RELATIONS 38(10):983-1000, 1985.

A-bombs and abortions, by C. R. Wood. FUNDAMENTALIST JOURNAL 3(7):66, July-August 1984.

Abortion clinic bombings and the Reagan administration, by L. Woehrle. OFF OUR BACKS 15:2, January 1985.

Abortion clinic bombings present new American crime and security problems. POLICE AND SECURITY BULLETIN 16(9):1, January 1985.

Abortion clinic: what goes on, by S. K. Reed. PEOPLE WEEKLY 24:103-106, August 26, 1985.

Abortion clinics intensify security to avert bombings. SECURITY SYSTEMS DIGEST16(2):7, January 21, 1985.

Abortion clinics lose coverage after attacks, by S. Taravella. BUSINESS INSURANCE19:3+, January 21, 1985.

Abortion clinics: terror, but not terrorism. ECONOMIST 294:18-19, January 5, 1985.

Abortion clinics under fire. GUILD NOTES 9(1):1, Winter 1985.

Abortion conflict: what it does to one doctor, by D. Clendinan. NEW YORK TIMES MAGAZINE August 11, 1985, p. 18-22+.

Abortion service of Ste-Therese in danger, by P. Duchesne. COMMUNIQU 'ELLES11(3):6, May 1985.

Abortion terrorism: the toll rises. MS MAGAZINE 13:19, March 1985.

Activists urge fightback against bombers, by A. Finger. GUARDIAN 37(16):3, January 23, 1985.

Bombing feminism, by R. P. Petchesky. NATION 240:101, February 2, 1985.

Bombings: abortion clinic attacks not called terrorism, but may bring FBI action. SECURITY LETTER 15(1):2, January 2, 1985.

Book maps out reproductive battle, by A. Dermansky. NEW DIRECTIONS FOR WOMEN November1984, p. 5.

Catholic theologian at an abortion clinic, by D. C. Maguire. MS MAGAZINE 13:129-132, December 1984.

Clinic bombings: government policy incarnate, by S. Poggi. GAY COMMUNITY 12(27):3, January 26, 1985.

Community reaction to the establishment of an abortion clinic in Duluth, Minnesota, by C. M. MacLeod. NORTH DAKOTA QUARTERLY 52(1):34-47, 1984.

Computerized histories facilitate patient care in a termination of pregnancy clinic: the use of a small computer to obtain and reproduce patient information, by R. J. Lilford, et al. BRITISH JOURNAL OF OBSTETRICS AND GYNAECOLOGY 92(4):333-340, April 1985.

D. A. pickets abortion clinic, by Barbara Fischkin. [Denis Dillon pickets clinic in Nassau County, New York, run by Bill Baird]. MS 14:19, December 1985.

Doctor couple arrested for phony abortions in N.Y. [M. Samuel and J. Cameau-Samuel]. JET 68:38, April 1, 1985.

Doctor's dilemma [H. Morgentaler's clinics], by R. Block. MACLEANS 97:52, December 17, 1984.

Dorval's erotic zone, by P. Duchesne. COMMUNIQU'ELLES 11(3):7, May 1985.

Double standard [bombings, Planned Parenthood offices, abortion clinics; editorial], by B. C. Harris. WITNESS 68(2):16, February 1985.

Explosions over abortion [terrorist bombings of clinics], by E. Magnuson. TIME 125:16-17, January 14, 1985.

Fight for abortion rights, by S. Arnott. GAY COMMUNITY 12(28):1, February 2, 1985.

Florida: more abortion bombings. NEWSWEEK 105:17, January 7, 1985.

Freestanding abortion clinics: services, structure, fees, by S. K. Henshaw. FAMILY PLANNING PERSPECTIVES 14(5):248-250+, September-October 1982.

Holy war in Pensacola, by P. Carlson. PEOPLE WEEKLY 23:20-25, January 21, 1985.

In the bombsight: abortion clinics. U S NEWS AND WORLD REPORT 98:8, January 14, 1985.

Jury discards abortion law; AG ponder appeal, by L. Waldorf. BODY POLITIC (109):9, December 1984.

Meaning of Morgentaler [acquittal in Toronto abortion clinic trial; special section]. MACLEANS 97:44-50+, November 19, 1984.

Men with ties to church arrested for abortion clinic bombings. CHRISTIANITY TODAY 29:34-35, March 1, 1985.

Morgentaler's escalating crusade, by S. McKay. MACLEANS 98:12, August 19, 1985.

New attacks on abortion clinics, by M. Koppel. INTERCONTINENTAL PRESS 23(3): 87, February 18, 1985.

NOW holds over 30 weekend vigils in abortion clinic, by M. Anderson. NATIONAL NOW TIMES 18(1):3, January 1985.

NY Diocese blocks abortion clinic, by L. S. OFF OUR BACKS 15(3):16, March 1985.

On the barricades for abortion rights, by J. Sutherland. FREE SOCIETY 9(1):32, Fall 1984.

Peers, parents, and partners. Determining the needs of the support person in an abortion clinic, by P. B. Beeman. JOURNAL OF OBSTETRICS, GYNECOLO-GY AND NEONATAL NURSING 14(1):54-58, January-February 1985.

Police raid abortion clinic, by J. Walkington. INTERCONTINENTAL PRESS 23(13):393, July 1985.

Pro-abortionist infiltrates sex education course. (abortion clinic employee gives talk in public school sex ed course), by P. Schlafly. HUMAN EVENTS 45:20, May 18, 1985.

Protesting abortion [Morgentaler clinic, Toronto]. MACLEANS 98:17, August 12, 1985.

Raegan fiddles at the clinic burns, E. Bader. RIGHTS AND BILL OF RIGHTS JOURNAL 31(2):5, July 1985.

Referrals vetoed [shelter operated by J. Vaughan, Los Angeles; news]. CHRISTIAN CENTURY 102:177, February 20, 1985.

Renewed abortion fight, by G. Moir. MACLEANS 98:54, April 8, 1985.

Renewed fight over abortion clinics [trial of H. Morgentaler in Toronto], by S. McKay. MACLEANS 97:48, November 5, 1984.

'Right-to-life' bombers strike again, by J. Callum. GUARDIAN 37(4):9, October 24, 1984.

Right to life or right to lie?, by B. Abas. PROGRESSIVE 49:24-25, June 1985.

Stalemate on abortion [H. Morgentaler's clinics], by H. Quinn. MACLEANS 97:66, November 26, 1984.

Strange definition of terrorism, by P. Simpson. WORKING WOMAN 10:44, April 1985.

Terror hits the clinics, [Army of God's violent attacks on legalized abortion, by A. Brummer. GUARDIAN January 2, 1985, p. 13.

Terrorist attacks intensify. NATIONAL NOW TIMES 17(6):5, November 1984.

Terrorist attacks on abortion clinics, by I. Canright. SOUTHERN EXPOSURE 12(6):111, November 1984.

Trials target abortion clinics, by I. Dequeecker. INTERCONTINENTAL PRESS 23(17):543, July 8, 1985.

Up in smoke [clinic bombings], by S. Baer. CHRISTIANITY TODAY 29:19, April 19, 1985.

Violence against abortion clinics escalates despite the opposition of prolife leaders, by R. Frame. CHRISTIANITY TODAY 29:44-46, February 1, 1985.

War on clinics continues. NEW WOMEN'S TIMES 10(11):1, December 1984.

Webster says FBI won't classify abortion clinic bombings as acts of terrorism. CRIME CONTROL DIGEST 18(49):3-4, December 10, 1984.

—. SECURITY SYSTEMS DIGEST 15(26):4-5, December 17, 1984.

ABORTION FUNDING

Abortion cuts in California?, by T. Woody. IN THESE TIMES 8(37):4, October 3, 1984.

Colorado voters amend the state's constitution to outlaw public funding of abortions. CHRISTIANITY TODAY 29:46-47, January 18, 1985.

Empirical investigation of the determinants of congressional voting on federal financing of abortions and the ERA, by J. M. Netter. JOURNAL OF LEGAL STUDIES 14:245-257, January 1985.

House prohibits use of DC funds for abortion, by L. Sorrel. OFF OUR BACKS 15(8):10, August 1985.

New twist in the abortion funding controversy: Planned Parenthood v. Arizona. DEPAUL LAW REVIEW 33:835-355, Summer 1984.

No aid for abortion. ECONOMIST 294:32, February 16, 1985.

Oops! There goes your right to choose, by H. Levine. GUARDIAN 37(41):7, August 7, 1985.

Public findings of contraceptive, sterilization and abortion services, 1983 [United States], by R. B. Gold, et al. FAMILY PLANNING PERSPECTIVES 17:25-30, January-February 1985.

Senate kills proposal to prevent federal funding of abortions for women inmates. CORRECTIONS DIGEST 16:23, November 6, 1985.

BIRTH CONTROL: GENERAL

After contraception: dispelling rumors about later childbearing. POPULATION REPORTS 12(5):697-731, September-October 1984.

Antecedents and prevention of unwanted pregnancy, by M. Gerrard, et al. ISSUES IN MENTAL HEALTH NURSING 5(1/4):85-101, 1983.

Birth control after 35. PREVENTION 37:57-61, August 1985.

Birth control: the appeal of certainty. ECONOMIST 293:18, December 22, 1984.

Birth control gap, by D. Kinnon. HEALTHSHARING 6(2):15, Spring 1985.

Birth control update, by A. B. Eagan. MCCALLS 112:18+, February 1985.

—, by K. McCoy. SEVENTEEN 44:75-76+, September 1985.

Birth control: surprising news!, by M. H. J. Farrell. GOOD HOUSEKEEPING 200:315, May 1985.

Corporate bottom line. HEALTHSHARING 5(4):4, Fall 1984.

Daughters of the sexual revolution. Judy Sadgrove. GUARDIAN November 12, 1985, p. 10.

High-and low-tech control, by L. R. Brown. NATURAL HISTORY 94:77, April 1985.

Pill's eclipse [survey on forms of birth control]. TIME 124:79, December 17, 1984.

Popular contraception. AMERICAN FAMILY PHYSICIAN 31:290, April 1985.

Precautionary tales . . . , by C. Doyle. OBSERVER January 20, 1985, p. 24-29.

Recent cases: children, by M. A. Jones. THE JOURNAL OF SOCIAL WELFARE LAW May 1985, p. 157-162.

Risky business: why you gamble with birth control [excerpt from Swept away], by C. Cassell. MADEMOISELLE 90:194-195+, October 1984.

Stopping population growth, by L. R. Brown. STATE OF THE WORLD 1985, p. 200-221.

Structure of pregnancy intervals by planning status, by N. B. Ryder. POPULATION STUDIES 39:193-211, July 1985.

Theory of marital fertility transition, by R. D. Retherford. POPULATION STUDIES 39:249-268, July 1985.

To have and have not [children], by A. Hinde. TIMES HIGHER EDUCATIONAL SUPPLEMENT 666:13, August 9, 1985.

To have or have not. (Is sterilization the contraceptivefor you?), by E. Michaud. PHILADELPHIA MAGAZINE 76:121+, March 1985.

What are the limits of birth control?, by L. H. Levie. NEDERLANDS TIJDSCHRIFT VOOR GENEESKUNDE 128(43):2045-2047, October 27, 1984.

Who gains in the battle to control population, by L. Orendiain. BALAI (11):16, 1985.

Who's afraid of population?, by Z. Sardar. GEOGRAPHICAL MAGAZINE 56:506, October 1984.

Wrongful pregnancy: damages recoverable for the birth of a normal, healthy child, by T. L. Mann. THE AMERICAN JOURNAL OF TRIAL ADVOCACY 7(2):385-391, Spring 1984.

Wyeth's birth control gamble [oral]. CHEMICAL WEEK 135:17, November 28, 1984.

AFRICA
Economic and demographic interrelationships in sub-Saharan Africa, by E. Boserup. POPULATION AND DEVELOPMENT REVIEW 11:383-397, September 1985.

AFRICA
Persistence of high fertility in Kenya, by I. Sindiga. SOCIAL SCIENCE AND MEDICINE 20(1):71-84, 1985.

Regulation of births in Africa, by J. C. Cazenave, et al. SOINS, PATHOLOGIE TROPICALE (46):3-6, March-April 1984.

Religious identity and attitudes toward contraceptives among university students in Nigeria, by I. Owie. SOCIAL BIOLOGY 30:101-105, Spring 1983.

2d papal visit to Kenya and the 43rd International Eucharist Congress [news]. AFER 27:196+, August 1985.

Work to control populations. BEIJING REVIEW 27:14-15, December 10, 1984.

ASIA
Population in the Asian scene questions, by R. Toledo. BALAI (11):2, 1985.

BRITISH COLUMBIA
First campaigns for birth control clinics in British Columbia, by A. McLaren. JOURNAL OF CANADIAN STUDIES 19(3):50-64, 1984.

CANADA
Canadian birth control movement on trial, 1936-1937, by D. Dodd. SOCIAL HISTORY16(32):411-428, 1983.

CHINA
China pushes efforts to reduce population growth. CHEMICAL AND ENGI-NEERING NEWS 63:50-51, January 14, 1985.

China's fertility transition: the one-child campaign, by E. Platte. PACIFIC AFFAIRS 57:646-671, Winter 1984-1985.

China's population policy, by G. Iver. OFF OUR BACKS 15(3):15, March 1985.

China's population policy: 'fewer but better' children. UN MONTHLY CHRONICLE 21:xiv, June 1984.

Chinese express views on Mosher to Stanford, by M. Sun. SCIENCE 226: 28-29, October 5, 1984.

Education related to birth control. BEIJING REVIEW 28:27-28, August 19, 1985.

Mosher affair, by P. V. Ness. WILSON QUARTERLY 8(1):160-172, 1984.

One-child population policy, modernization, and the extended Chinese family, by C. Xiangming. JOURNAL OF MARRIAGE AND THE FAMILY 47:193-202, February 1985.

Population control vs. freedom in China, by V. Bullough, et al. FREE INQUIRY 4:12-15, Winter 1983-84.

CHINA
> Population policy and trends in China, 1978-83, by J. Banister. CHINA QUARTERLY December 1984, p. 717-741.

> Survey reveals childbirth attitudes. BEIJING REVIEW 28:30, June 17, 1985.

DEVELOPING COUNTRIES
> Population policy: country experience [Mexico, Indonesia, and India], by M. Ainsworth. FINANCE AND DEVELOPMENT 21:18-20, September 1984.

> Rural poverty breeds fertility, by A. Vajpayee. NATURE 316:773, August 29, 1985.

EGYPT
> Mass media and population problem in Egypt [3 articles]. POPULATION STUDIES 11:41-60, April-June 1984.

GREAT BRITAIN
> Birth control movement in England and the United States: the first 100 years, by T. Perse. JOURNAL OF THE AMERICAN MEDICAL WOMEN'S ASSOCIATION 40(4):119-122, July-August 1985.

> Gains and losses for women, by M. Simms. NEW HUMANIST 100:18-21, Spring 1985.

> Open all hours . . . birth control clinic, by J. Seymour. NURSNG MIRROR AND MID-WIVES JOURNAL 161(16):22-24, October 16, 1985.

> Under-age sex: Victorian values. ECONOMIST 290:59-60, March 24, 1984.

GUATEMALA
> Public opinion on and potential demand for vasectomy in semi-rural Guatemala, by R. Santiso, et al. JOURNAL OF PUBLIC HEALTH 75:73-75, January 1985.

INDIA
> Compulsory birth control and fertility measures in India: a simulation approach, by S. S. Halli. SIMULATION AND GAMES 14(4):429-444, December 1983.

> Rajiv steps in where Sanjay failed, by R. Ford. TIMES August 29, 1985, p. 10.

INDONESIA
> Angels who wear not a halo but a coil, by J. Tweedie. GUARDIAN 19:11, July 1985.

IRELAND
> Irish bastards, by S. G. Davies. SPECTATOR 254:11, February 2, 1985.

> Learning the facts of life [legal contraception], by T. Clifton. NEWSWEEK 105:48, March 11, 1985.

KOREA
Socio-economic change in Korea, by T. H. Han. ZEITSCHRIFT FUR MIS-
SIONSWISSENSCHAFT UND RELIGIONSWISSENSCHAFT 69:140-
149, April 1985.

LATIN AMERICA
Go forth and multiply—like rabbits?[Latin America], by A. Hiller. HUMANIST
44:15-19, November-December 1984.

MEXICO
Vor der Weltbevölkerungskonferenz in Mexico [collection of articles].
ENTWICKLUNG UND ZUSAMMENARBEIT 7:7-17, 1984.

NEW GUINEA
Role of maternal and child health clinics in education and prevention: a case
study from Papua New Guinea, by J. Reid. SOCIAL SCIENCE AND
MEDICINE 19(3): 291-303, 1984.

SCOTLAND
Becoming voluntarily childless: an exploratory study in a Scottish city, by E.
Campbell. SOCIAL BIOLOGY 30(3):307-317, Fall 1983.

SINGAPORE
Social discipline in Singapore: an alternative for the resolution of social
problems, by S. R. Quah. JOURNAL OF SOUTHEAST ASIAN STUDIES
14:266-289, September 1983.

UNITED STATES
American physicians and birth control, 1936-1947, by J. M. Ray, et al. JOUR-
NAL OF SOCIAL HISTORY 18:399-411, Spring 1985.

Birth control clinics in high schools brew controversy nationwide [Chicago's
DuSable High School]. JET 69:10-11, October 14, 1985.

Birth control movement in England and the United States: the first 100 years,
by T. Perse. JOURNAL OF THE AMERICAN MEDICAL WOMEN'S
ASSOCIATION 40(4):119-122, July-August 1985.

Economic and other determinants of annual change in U. S. fertility: 1917-
1976. SOCIAL SCIENCE RESEARCH 13(3):250-267, September
1984.

Recovery for rearing healthy child ruled out in District of Columbia. THE
FAMILY LAW REPORTER: COURT OPINIONS 10(39):1532-1533,
August 7, 1984.

Reproductive rights in North Carolina, by S. Poggi. GAY COMMUNITY
13(5):2, August 10, 1985.

U.S. denies population crisis, by J. Knox. NOT MAN APART 14(8):12,
October 1984.

Understanding U.S. fertility: findings from the National Survey of Family
Growth, Cycle III, by W. F. Pratt, et al. POPULATION BULLETIN 39:1-40,
December 1984.

UNITED STATES
US antics stifled population debate, by A. Smart. GOODWINS 2(2):11, Fall 1984.

Voluntary and involuntary childlessness in the United States, 1955-1973. SOCIAL BIOLOGY 30:290-306, August 1983.

What's new: New York decides healthy baby is no injury, by J. A. Rajchenbach. AMERICAN BAR ASSOCIATION JOURNAL 71:102, June 1985.

VIET NAM
Where the bigger the family means the greater the fortune, by P. Quinn-Judge. FAR EASTERN ECONOMIC REVIEW 126:48-49, October 11, 1984.

BIRTH CONTROL: ADVERTISING
End this TV taboo: Sets' run birth control ads during "Dallas" and "Dynasty," by J. Kalter. TV GUIDE 33:30, November 23, 1985.

Role of advertising in birth control use and sexual decision making, by J. McKillip, et al. JOURNAL OF SEX EDUCATION AND THERAPY 10:44-48, Fall-Winter 1984.

BIRTH CONTROL: ATTITUDES
Contraceptive knowledge and use of birth control as a function of sex guilt, by C. Berger, et al. INTERNATIONAL JOURNAL OF WOMEN'S STUDIES 8:72-79, January-February 1985.

Development of a scale to measure attitude toward the condom as a method of birth control, by I. S. Brown. JOURNAL OF SEX RESEARCH 20:255-263 August1984.

Go forth and multiply—like rabbits?[Latin America], by A. Hiller. HUMANIST 44:15-19, November-December 1984.

Religious identity and attitudes toward contraceptives among university students in Nigeria, by I. Owie. SOCIAL BIOLOGY 30:101-105, Spring 1983.

Russell rominates: his stand on birth control shocks some pro-lifers, by A. Singer. ALBERTA REPORT 12:28, July 1, 1985.

Short-term effects of teenage parenting programs on knowledge and attitudes, by M. W. Roosa. ADOLESCENCE 19(75):659-666, Fall 1984.

Survey reveals childbirth attitudes. BEIJING REVIEW 28:30, June 17, 1985.

War on people [myths about population growth], by J. L. Simon. CHALLENGE 28:50-53, March-April 1985.

BIRTH CONTROL: BARRIER
Remove that shield, by A. Henry. OFF OUR BACKS 14(11):12, December 1984.

Shielding dalkon. OFF OUR BACKS 14(9):7, October 1984.

American physicians and birth control, 1936-1947, by J. M. Ray, et al. JOURNAL OF SOCIAL HISTORY 18:399-411, Spring 1985.

Birth control movement in England and the United States: the first 100 years, by T. Perse. JOURNAL OF THE AMERICAN MEDICAL WOMEN'S ASSOCIATION 40(4):119-122, July-August 1985.

Case for birth control before 1850: Nantucket reexamined, by B. J. Logue. JOURNAL OF INTERDISCIPLINARY HISTORY 15:371-391, Winter 1985.

Effects of birth rank, maternal age, birth interval, and sibship size on infant and child mortality: evidence from 18th and 19th century reproductive histories, by J. Knodel, et al. AMERICAN JOURNAL OF PUBLIC HEALTH 74:1098-1106, October 1984.

Public policy on human reproduction and the historian, by J. Reed. JOURNAL OF SOCIAL HISTORY 18:383-398, Spring 1985.

Windows into the legal past, by N. Blodgett. AMERICAN BAR ASSOCIATION JOURNAL 71:44-48, January 1985.

BIRTH CONTROL: IUD
Primary tubal infertility in relation to the use of an intrauterine device [also tubal i infertility and the intrauterine device by Daniel W. Cramer, pp. 941-947, and current status of intrauterine devices by Daniel R. Mishell (editorial), pp. 984-985], by J. R. Daling, et al. NEW ENGLAND JOURNAL OF MEDICINE 312: 937-941, April 11, 1985.

BIRTH CONTROL: LAWS AND LEGISLATION
Failed tubal ligation: bringing a wrongful birth case to trial, by G. I. Strausberg. TRIAL 21(5):30-33, May 1985.

Picture costs ten thousand words, by D. O. Stewart. AMERICAN BAR ASSO-CIATION JOURNAL 71:62-66, January 1985.

Reproduction law and medical consent, by B. M. Dickens. UNIVERSITY OF TORONTO LAW JOURNAL 35:255-286, Summer 1985.

Reproductive rights in North Carolina, by S. Poggi. GAY COMMUNITY 13(5):2, August 10, 1985.

'Squeal rule' and a minor's right to privacy, by P. A. Olah. SPECIALTY LAW DIGEST HEALTH CARE 7(4):5-37, June 1985.

Torts—medical malpractice—wrongful birth. THE FAMILY LAW REPORTER: COURT OPINIONS 11(32):1397, June 18, 1985.

Washington court bars recovery for expenses of rearing normal child. THE FAMILY LAW REPORTER: COURT OPINIONS 10(46):1632-1633, September 25, 1984.

What's new: new duty to warn for birth control pill manufacturer. AMERICAN BAR ASSOCIATION JOURNAL 71:96+, June 1985.

Does a man give a damn—about birth control?, by P. Nelson. MADEMOISELLE 91:100, June 1985.

Pill for men, by G. Levoy. NEW AGE February 1985, p. 19.

BIRTH CONTROL: METHODS
Mucus and moonlight: low-tech birth control. UTNE READER 10:17, June 1985.

On pills, IUDs and condoms, by S. Evangelista. BALAI 11:21, 1985.

Pregnancy protection index: a framework for the Systematic Study of Pregnancy Protection. JOURNAL OF SEX RESEARCH 20(3):14, August 1984.

BIRTH CONTROL: POSTCOITAL
Post-coital birth control family planning. OFF OUR BACKS 15(2):7, February 1985.

BIRTH CONTROL: PSYCHOLOGY AND PSYCHIATRY
Physiological basis of birth control, by W. X. Li, et al. SHENG LI KO HSUEH CHIN CHAN 15(1):87-92, January 1984.

BIRTH CONTROL: RESEARCH
Billings method of family planning: an assessment. STUDIES IN FAMILY PLANNING15:253-266, November-December 1984.

Contraception—the morning after. FAMILY PLANNING PERSPECTIVES 16:266-270, November-December 1984.

Effects of paced coital stimulation on estrus duration in intact cycling rats and ovariectomized and ovariectomized-adrenal-octomized hormone-primed rats, by M. S. Erskine. BEHAVIORAL NEUROSCIENCE 99(1):151-161, February 1985.

Seeking better contraceptives. POPULI 2(2):24, 1984.

BIRTH CONTROL: RURAL
Islamic populations: limited demographic transition, by J. I. Clarke. GEOGRAPHY 70:118-128, April 1985.

BIRTH CONTROL AND AGING
Birth control after 35. PREVENTION 37:57-61, August 1985.

BIRTH CONTROL AND CHEMOTHERAPY
Birth control considerations during chemotherapy, by C. C. Tarpy. ONCOLOGY NURSING FORUM 12(2):75-78, March-April 1985.

BIRTH CONTROL AND ECONOMICS
Economic and other determinants of annual change in U. S. fertility: 1917-1976. SOCIAL SCIENCE RESEARCH 13(3):250-267, September 1984.

Rural poverty breeds fertility, by A. Vajpayee. NATURE 316:773, August 29, 1985.

BIRTH CONTROL AND EDUCATION
Education related to birth control. BEIJING REVIEW 28:27-28, August 19, 1985.

Price of unemployment, by M. Olesen. BRIARPATCH 14(5):14, June 1985.

BIRTH CONTROL AND THE FDA
Gyn game: FDA and contraceptive sponge, by D. St. Clair. HEALTH PAC BULLETIN 15(5):13, September 1984.

BIRTH CONTROL AND FEMINISM
Socialist-feminism and reproductive rights. SOCIALIST REVIEW (78):110, November 1984.

BIRTH CONTROL AND PARENTAL CONSENT
Parental consent—does doctor know best after all? The Gillick case, by D. Brahams. NEW LAW JOURNAL 135:8-10, January 4, 1985.

'Squeal rule' and a minor's right to privacy, by P. A. Olah. SPECIALTY LAW DIGEST HEALTH CARE 7(4):5-37, June 1985.

BIRTH CONTROL AND PHYSICIANS
American physicians and birth control, 1936-1947, by J. M. Ray, et al. JOURNAL OF SOCIAL HISTORY 18:399-411, Spring 1985.

Obstacles to successful fertility control in Nigeria, by E. O. Udjo. SOCIAL SCIENCE AND MEDICINE 19(11):1167-1171, 1984.

Reproduction law and medical consent, by B. M. Dickens. UNIVERSITY OF TORONTO LAW JOURNAL 35:255-286, Summer 1985.

BIRTH CONTROL AND POLITICS
Canadian birth control movement on trial, 1936-1937, by D. Dodd. SOCIAL HISTORY16(32):411-428, 1983.

Communist Party and woman question 1922-1929, by J. Sangster. LABOUR/LE TRAVAIL 15:25, Spring 1985.

Foreign aid birth control campaigns: the disability connection—in whose interest?, by A. Gajerski-Cauley. RESOURCES FOR FEMINIST RESEARCH 14:14-18, March 1985.

House panel rejects birth control notification. CONGRESSIONAL QUARTERLY WEEKLY REPORT 43:943, May 18, 1985.

Muslims battle over birth control, by D. MacKenzie. NEW SCIENTIST 107:21, July 18, 1985.

Not Reagan's way. ECONOMIST 292:30+, August 11, 1984.

Politics of population control, by L. Sundberg. HERIZONS 2(7):9, November1984.

"Right-to-life" scores new victory at AID, by C. Holden. SCIENCE 229:1065-1067, September 13, 1985.

Russell rominates: his stand on birth control shocks some pro-lifers, by A. Singer. ALBERTA REPORT 12:28, July 1, 1985.

Washington court bars recovery for expenses of rearing normal child. THE FAMILY LAW REPORTER: COURT OPINIONS 10(46):1632-1633, September 25, 1984.

BIRTH CONTROL AND RELIGION

American Catholic family: signs of cohesion and polarization, by W. V. D'Antonio. JOURNAL OF MARRIAGE AND THE FAMILY 47(2):395-405, May 1985.

Bitter pill [pro life opposition to birth control], by A. E. Schwartz. NEW REPUBLIC 192:10-12, February 18, 1985.

Bold stand on birth control [views of John Paul II], by R. N. Ostling. TIME 124:66, December 3, 1984.

Catholic father of the pill, by D. Nyhan. NATIONAL CATHOLIC REPORTER 21:7, December 28, 1984.

Catholic physician, the contraception issue and the three questions of ethics, by J. A. O'Donohoe. JOURNAL OF PASTORAL COUNSELING 18:34-46, Spring-Summer 1983.

Ethical issues in reproductive medicine: a Mormon perspective [photo], by L. E. Bush. DIALOGUE 18:40-66, Summer 1985.

First aid in pastoral care: pastoral care in marriage, by J. Thompson. EXPOSITORY TIMES 96:324-329, August 1985.

Go forth and multiply—like rabbits?[Latin America], by A. Hiller. HUMANIST 44:15-19, November-December 1984.

Marriage in Roman Catholicism, by D. L. Carmody. JOURNAL OF ECUMENICAL STUDIES 22:28-40, Winter 1985.

Muslims battle over birth control, by D. MacKenzie. NEW SCIENTIST 107:21, July 18, 1985.

Reciprocal influences of family and religion in a changing world, by A. Thornton. JOURNAL OF MARRIAGE AND THE FAMILY 47(2):381-394, May 1985.

Religious affiliation and the fertility of married couples, by W. D. Mosher, et al. JOURNAL OF MARRIAGE AND THE FAMILY 46:671-677, August 1984.

Religious identity and attitudes toward contraceptives among university students in Nigeria, by I. Owie. SOCIAL BIOLOGY 30:101-105, Spring 1983.

2d papal visit to Kenya and the 43rd International Eucharist Congress [news]. AFER 27:196+, August 1985.

Vatican and population growth control: why an American confrontation?, by S. D. Mumford. HUMANIST 43:18-24+, September-October 1983.

BIRTH CONTROL AND WOMEN

Communist Party and woman question 1922-1929, by J. Sangster. LABOUR/LE TRAVAIL 15:25, Spring 1985.

Population control: no-women decide, by A. Henry. OFF OUR BACKS 14(9):2, October 1984.

Women in struggle, by H. Lessinger. GUARDIAN 37(25):2, March 27, 1985.

BIRTH CONTROL AND YOUTH

Adolescents' communication styles and learning about birth control, by R. DePietro, et al. ADOLESCENCE 19:827-837, Winter 1984.

Birth control clinic controversy [teen-age pregnancy; Chicago's DuSable High School; editorial], by J. M. Wall. CHRISTIAN CENTURY 102:907-908, October 16, 1985.

Birth control clinics in high schools brew controversy nationwide [Chicago's DuSable High School]. JET 69:10-11, October 14, 1985.

Birth control: facts you should know [teenagers], by S. S. Soria. TEEN 29:6+, February 1985.

Birth control in school [DuSable High School, Chicago]. CHRISTIANITY TODAY 29(16):58, November 8, 1985.

Birth control use by teenagers: 1 and 2 years postabortion, by M. Abrams. JOURNAL OF ADOLESCENT HEALTH CARE 6(3):196-200, 1985.

China's population policy: 'fewer but better' children. UN MONTHLY CHRONICLE 21:xiv, June 1984.

Correlation of moral development with use of birth control and pregnancy among teenage girls, by J. Jurs. PSYCHOLOGICAL REPORTS 55:1009-1010, December 1984.

Health belief model approach to adolescents' fertility control: some pilot program findings, by M. Eisen, et al. HEALTH EDUCATION QUARTERLY 12(2):185-210, Summer 1985.

Parental consent—does doctor know best after all? The Gillick case, by D. Brahams. NEW LAW JOURNAL 135:8-10, January 4, 1985.

Predictors of repeat pregnancies among low-income adolescents, by M. Gispert, et al. HOSPITAL AND COMMUNITY PSYCHIATRY 35:719-723, July 1984.

Prevention of pregnancy and abortion in adolescence, by L. Ruusuvaara. DUODECIM 101(2):156-158, 1985.

Risk of premarital first pregnancy among metropolitan-area teenagers: 1976 and 1979, by M. A. Koenig, et al. FAMILY PLANNING PERSPECTIVES 14(5):239-241+, September-October 1982.

Sex and the under-age girl, by M. McFadyean. NEW SOCIETY 72:386-388, June 14, 1985.

Short-term effects of teenage parenting programs on knowledge and attitudes, by M. W. Roosa. ADOLESCENCE 19(75):659-666, Fall 1984.

'Squeal rule' and a minor's right to privacy, by P. A. Olah. SPECIALTY LAW DIGEST HEALTH CARE 7(4):5-37, June 1985.

Under-age sex: Victorian values. ECONOMIST 290:59-60, March 24, 1984.

What every girl should know about the Pill, if her GP will tell her, by A. Veitch, et al. GUARDIAN June 3, 1985, p. 10.

BIRTH CONTROL CLINICS
Birth control clinic controversy [teen-age pregnancy; Chicago's DuSable High School; editorial], by J. M. Wall. CHRISTIAN CENTURY 102:907-908, October 16, 1985.

Birth control clinics in high schools brew controversy nationwide [Chicago's DuSable High School]. JET 69:10-11, October 14, 1985.

First campaigns for birth control clinics in British Columbia, by A. McLaren. JOURNAL OF CANADIAN STUDIES 19(3):50-64, 1984.

Increasing appointment keeping by reducing the call-appointment interval, by J. Benjamin-Bauman, et al. JOURNAL OF APPLIED BEHAVIOR ANALYSIS 17:295-301, Fall 1984.

Influence of client-provider relationships on teenage women's subsequent use of contraception, by C. A. Nathanson, et al. AMERICAN JOURNAL OF PUBLIC HEALTH 75(1):33-38, January 1985.

Open all hours . . . birth control clinic, by J. Seymour. NURSNG MIRROR AND MID-WIVES JOURNAL 161(16):22-24, October 16, 1985.

Reducing noncompliance to follow-up appointment keeping at a family practice center, by J. M. Rice, et al. JOURNAL OF APPLIED BEHAVIOR ANALYSIS 17:303-311, Fall 1984.

Role of maternal and child health clinics in education and prevention: a case study from Papua New Guinea, by J. Reid. SOCIAL SCIENCE AND MEDICINE 19(3): 291-303, 1984.

CONTRACEPTION
Contraception—the morning after. FAMILY PLANNING PERSPECTIVES 16:266-270, November-December 1984.

CONTRACEPTION: FEMALE: ORAL: COMPLICATIONS
Pill and thrombosis, by I. Thranov, et al. UGESKRIFT FOR LAEGER 146(36):2709-2711, September 3, 1984.

CONTRACEPTION: METHODS
Maternal lactation as a contraception method? 3. Comparison of maternal Lactation with current methods of contraception, by A. Fourati, et al. TUNISIE MEDICALE 62(2):137-141, March-April 1984.

Maternal lactation as a method of contraception? 1. The epidemiology of maternal lactation in a suburban region of Tunis, by S. Khadraoui, et al. TUNIS MEDI-CALE 61(6):431-437, November-December 1983.

Maternal lactation as a method of contraception? 2. The epidemiology of postpartum amenorrhea, by H. Chaabouni, et al. TUNISIE MEDICALE 62(1):83-90, January-February 1984.

Risk of current methods in contraception, by M. M. Zufferey. REVUE MEDICALE DE LA SUISSE ROMANDE 105(2):147-150, February 1985.

Risks of new contraception methods, by M. M. Zufferey. GYNAEKOLOGISCHE RUNDSCHAU 24(Suppl. 1):40-42, 1984.

Tomorrow's contraception, by C. C. Standley, et al. REVUE DE'L'INFIRMIERE 35(4):16-19, February 1985.

CONTRACEPTION: POSTCOITAL
Experience with levonorgestrel in postcoital contraception, by E. Canzler, et al. ZENTRALBLATT FUR GYNAEKOLOGIE 106(17):1182-1191, 1984.

Post-coital contraception using a combination of d-norgestrel and ethinylo-estradiol, by C. N. Duy, et al. JOURNAL DE GYNECLOGIE, OBSTETRIQUE ET BIOLOGIE DE LA REPRODUCTION 14(4):523-526, 1985.

Post-coital contraception with estrogens. Mechanism of action, results and sequelae in a caseload of 123 cases, by F. Monasterolo. MINERVA GINECOLOGIA 36(7-8):451-454, July-August 1984.

Post-coital contraception, by A. A. Kubba. JOURNAL OF THE ROYAL SOCIETY OF HEALTH 104(6):212-213, December 1984.

—, by A. A. Yuzpe. CLINICAL OBSTETRICS AND GYNAECOLOGY 11(3):787-797, December 1984.

— [letter], by G. Kovacs, et al. MEDICAL JOURNAL OF AUSTRALIA 142(7):424-425, April 1, 1985.

—, by P. Draca, et al. MEDICINSKI PREGLED 38(3-4):205-206, 1985.

— (without prostaglandins), by R. Wyss. GYNAKOLOGE 17(3): 200-203, September 1984.

Postcoital contraception with steroid hormones, by G. Köhler, et al. ZENTRAL-BLATT FUR GYNAEKOLOGIE 106(17):1173-1181, 1984.

Potential use of postcoital contraception to prevent unwanted pregnancy, by T. A. Johnston, et al. BRITISH MEDICAL JOURNAL 290(6474):1040-1041, April 6, 1985.

CONTRACEPTION AND CONTRACEPTIVES: GENERAL
After contraception: dispelling rumors about later childbearing. POPULATION REPORTS 12(5):697-731, September-October 1984.

Antecedents and prevention of unwanted pregnancy, by M. Gerrard, et al. ISSUES IN MENTAL HEALTH NURSING 5(1/4):85-101, 1983.

Bankruptcy of contraception?, by F. P. Wibaut. NEDERLANDS TIJDSCHRIFT VOOR GENEESKUNDE 128(50):2349-2353, December 15, 1984.

Breastfeeding and contraception: why the inverse association?, by S. Millman. STUDIES IN FAMILY PLANNING 16(2):61-75, March-April 1985.

Breastfeeding—the leading contraceptive in the world, by S. Bergström. LAKARTIDNINGEN 82(6):398-403, February 6, 1985.

Communicating contraception. POPULI 2(2):31, 1984.

Comparison of a 2-phase preparation (Oviol 22) with a low-dose 1-phase preparation, by M. Dik, et al. GEBURTSHILFE UND FRAUENHEILKUNDE 44(12):808-812, December 1984.

Continuation and effectiveness of contraceptive practice: a cross-sectional approach, by J. E. Laing. STUDIES IN FAMILY PLANNING 16(3):138-153, May-June 1985.

Contraception and the use of care systems, by M. H. Bouvier-Colle, et al. JOURNAL DE GYNECOLOGIE, OBSTETRIQUE ET BIOLOGIE DE LA REPRODUCTION 14(2):155-162, 1985.

Contraception: dilemmas for the relatively infertile, by S. Craig, et al. HEALTH-RIGHT 4:13-16, February 1985.

Contraception update. CLINICAL OBSTETRICS AND GYNAECOLOGY 11(3):549-819, December 1984.

Contraceptives for the relatively infertile, by G. T. Kovacs. HEALTHRIGHT 4:17-19, February 1985.

Cosmo's update on contraception, by A. Ferrar. COSMOPOLITAN 197:240-243, October 1984.

Effect of marital dissolution on contraceptive protection, by L. Bumpass, et al. FAMILY PLANNING PERSPECTIVES 16:271-284, November-December 1984.

Fertility of couples following cessation of contraception, by N. Spira, et al. JOURNAL OF BIOSOCIAL SCIENCE 17(3):281-290, July 1985.

Impacts of behavioral intentions, social support, and accessibility on contraception: a cross-cultural study, by S. Kar, et al. POPULATION AND ENVIRON-MENT 7(1):17-31, Spring 1984.

Lactation promoting contraception, by K. Biering-Sørensen, et al. UGESKRIFT FOR LAEGER 147(14):1213, April 1, 1985.

Missed pill conception: fact or fiction? [letter], by S. R. Killick, et al. BRITISH MEDICAL JOURNAL 291(6493):487, August 17, 1985.

Pregnancy protection index: a framework for the Systematic Study of Pregnancy Protection. JOURNAL OF SEX RESEARCH 20(3):14, August 1984.

Psychosocial and psychosexual aspects of contraception, by M. Guay. INFIRMIERE CANADIENNE 27(1):23-26, January 1985.

"Right-to-life" scores new victory at AID, by C. Holden. SCIENCE 229:1065-1067, September 13, 1985.

Statistical comparison of pearl rates, by J. E. Higgins, et al. AMERICAN JOURNAL OF OBSTETRICS AND GYNECOLOGY 151(5):656-659, March 1, 1985.

Structural approach to the evaluation of the quality of contraception services, by J. Ananijevic-Pandey, et al. JUGOSLAVENSKA GINEKOLOGIJA I OPSTETRICIJA 24(5-6):91-95, September-December 1984.

Taking precautions, by R. Shapiro. NURSING TIMES 81(9):20-21, February - March 1985.

Treatment of mitral cardiomyopathies 3. Gynecologic-obstetric prevention and treatment, by J. Droniou. SOINS CARDIOLOGIE (24):17-18, February 1985.

Unwanted pregnancy after careful contraception, by R. W. Bakker, et al. NEDERLANDS TIJDSCHRIFT VOOR GENEESKUNDE 129(12):559-560, March 23, 1985.

Update on other means of contraception, by N. Mallovy. HOME MAGAZINE 20:48H, May 1985.

Use of contraception among abortion applicants, by D. Krishnamoni, et al. CANADIAN JOURNAL OF PUBLIC HEALTH 76(2):93-97, March-April 1985.

PAKISTAN
Changing pattern of contraception in Lahore, Pakistan: 1963-1980, by F. Yusuf, et al. JOURNAL OF BIOSOCIAL SCIENCE 17(3):317-325, July 1985.

UNITED STATES
Voluntary and involuntary childlessness in the United States, 1955-1973. SOCIAL BIOLOGY 30:290-306, August 1983.

CONTRACEPTION AND CONTRACEPTIVES: HISTORY
Cervical cap as a contraceptive alternative, by M. A. Johnson. NURSE PRACTITIONER 10(1):37+, January 1985.

CONTRACEPTION AND CONTRACEPTIVES: RESEARCH
Chemical fertility control and wildlife management, by J. F. Kirkpatrick, et al. BIOSCIENCE 35:485-491, September 1985.

Comparative evaluation of contraceptive efficacy of norethisterone oenanthate (200 mg) injectable contraceptive given every two or three monthly. Indian Council of Medical Research Task Force on hormonal contraception, by S. K. Banerjee, et al. CONTRACEPTION 30(6):561-574, December 1984.

Comparison of high-dose estrogens versus low-dose ethinylestradiol and norgestrel combination in postcoital interception: a study in 493 women, by M. R. Van Santen, et al. FERTILITY AND STERILIZATION 43(2):206-213, February 1985.

Seeking better contraceptives. POPULI 2(2):24, 1984.

Some aspects of sexual knowledge and sexual behavior of local women. Results of a survey. 1. General sexual knowledge and attitude to abortion, pregnancy and contraception, by V. Atputharajah. SINGAPORE MEDICAL JOURNAL 25(3):135-140, June 1984.

CONTRACEPTION AND YOUTH

Adolescent pregnancy and sex roles, by C. J. Ireson. SEX ROLES 11:189-201, August 1984.

Adolescent pregnancy: contributing factors, consequences, treatment and plausible solutions, by C. Black, et al. ADOLESCENCE 20:281-290, Summer1985.

Contraception for teenagers. SOCIETY 23:35-52, November-December 1985.

CONTRACEPTIVES: GENERAL

After contraception: dispelling rumors about later childbearing. POPULATION REPORTS 12(5):697-731, September-October 1984.

Choice of contraception for the diabetic woman, by N. Athea, et al. JOURNEES ANNUELLES DE DIABETOLOGIE DE L'HOTEL-DIEU 253:61, 1983.

Contraception: introduction, by J. C. Guillat. SOINS, GYNECOLOGIE, OBSTET-RIQUE, PUERICULTURE, PEDIATRIE, July-August 1982.

Contraception with progesterone pellets during lactation, by O. Peralta, et al. REVISTA CHILENA DE OBSTETRICIA Y GINECOLOGIA 49(5):337-345, 1984.

Contraceptive advice for the postpartum period, by I. Couvreur, et al. SOINS, GYNECOLOGIE, OBSTETRIQUE, PUERICULTURE, PEDIATRIE 35:39-41, April 1984.

Contraceptive futurology or 1984 in 1984, by E. Diczfalusy. CONTRACEPTION 31(1):1-10, January 1985.

Contraceptive role of breastfeeding, by J. P. Habicht, et al. POPULATION STUDIES 39:213-232, July 1985.

Contraceptive use and efficacy in a genetically counseled population, by D. C. Wertz, et al. SOCIAL BIOLOGY 30:328-334, August 1983.

Contraceptive use before tubal sterilization, by G. S. Grubb, et al. JOURNAL OF REPRODUCTIVE MEDICINE 30(4):345-350, April 1985.

Cross-country study of commercial contraceptive sales programs: factors that lead to success, by M. S. Boone, et al. STUDIES IN FAMILY PLANNING 16(1):30-39, January-February 1985.

Favorable response to Metrulen in Von Willebrand's disease (type III), by J. Moreb, et al. HAREFUAH 107(10):283-285, November 15, 1984.

Hyperprolactinemia and contraception: a prospective study, by A. A. Luciano, et al. OBSTETRICS AND GYNECOLOGY 65(4):506-510, April 1985.

Initiating contraceptive use: how do young women decide, by J. E. White. PEDI-ATRIC NURSING 10(5):347-352, September-October 1984.

Long-term experience with Norplant contraceptive implants in Finland, by P. Holma. CONTRACEPTION 31(3):231-241, March 1985.

Natural family planning [discussion of May 1985 article, comparing contraceptives], by J. Willis. FDA CONSUMER 19:2, September 1985.

Paying high price for the pill [damages awarded in P. Buchan's suit against Ortho Pharmaceutical Canada], by R. Block. MACLEANS 97:52, April 30, 1984.

Real and false risks of contraceptive information, by M. D. Béran. GYNAEKOLO-GISCHE RUNDSCHAU 24(Suppl. 1):49-53, 1984.

Retinal manifestations of thrombotic thrombocytopenic purpura (TTP) following use of contraceptive treatment, by M. Snir, et al. ANNALS OF OPHTHAL-MOLOGY 17(2):109-112, February 1985.

AFRICA
Contraceptive continuation rates in Papua, New Guinea, by P. K. Townsend. PAPUA NEW GUINEA MEDICAL JOURNAL 26(2):114-121, June 1983.

Profile of contraceptive clients in Katsina, northern Nigeria, by H. P. Naghma-E-Rehan, et al. JOURNAL OF BIOSOCIAL SCIENCE 16:427-436, October 1984.

Regulation of births in Africa, by J. C. Cazenave, et al. SOINS, PATHOLOGIE TROPICALE (46):3-6, March-April 1984.

ASIA
Determinants of contraceptive use in Nepal, by J. M. Tuladhar. JOURNAL OF BIOSOCIAL SCIENCE 17(2):185-193, April 1985.

Early symptoms and discontinuation among users of oral contraceptives in Sri Lanka. STUDIES IN FAMILY PLANNING 15(6):285, November-December 1984.

BANGLADESH
General yeast infection in Bangladeshi women using contraceptives, by K. M. Rahman, et al. BANGLADESH MEDICAL RESEARCH COUNCIL BULLE-TIN 10(2):65-70, December 1984.

Noncompliance among oral contraceptive acceptors in rural Bangladesh, by B. Seaton. STUDIES IN FAMILY PLANNING 16(1):52-59, January-February 1985.

Oral contraception in Bangladesh, by S. Bhatia, et al. STUDIES IN FAMILY PLANNING 15:233-241, September-October 1984.

CANADA
Affecting fatherhood: a research team at the University of Western Ontario may have found a low-risk reversible male contraceptive, by S. Bars. SCIENCE DIMENSION 17(2):14-19, 1985.

CANADA
Sex supplies: Calgary's free condom shop starts charging, by T. Fennell. ALBERTA REPORT 11:41, November 5, 1984.

DENMARK
Cardiovascular disease mortality in Denmark before and after the introduction of oral contraceptives, by E. H. Larsen, et al. UGESKRIFT FOR LAEGER 146(36):2677-2680, September 3, 1984.

Mortality caused by cardiovascular diseases in Denmark before and after the Introduction of the pill (letter), by O. Lidegaard. UGESKRIFT FOR LAEGER 147(1):39-40, December 31, 1984.

DEVELOPING COUNTRIES
Breastfeeding, contraception, and birth intervals in developing countries, by D. P. Smith. STUDIES IN FAMILY PLANNING 16(3):154-163, May-June 1985.

EGYPT
How the number of living sons influences contraceptive use in Menoufia Governor-ate, Egypt, by S. Gadalla, et al. STUDIES IN FAMILY PLAN-NING 16(3):164-169, May-June 1985.

Islam and birth planning: an interview with the Grand Mufti of Egypt. POPULI 2(2):40, 1984.

GERMANY
Contraception and abortion of mentally handicapped female adolescents under German law, by A. Eser. MEDICINE AND LAW 4(6):499-513, 1985.

New woman, the new family and the rationalization of sexuality; the sex reform movement in Germany 1928 to 1933, by A. Grossmann. DAI:THE HUMANITIES AND SOCIAL SCIENCES 45(7), January 1985.

Oral contraceptives containing chlormadinone acetate and cancer incidence at selected sites in the German Democratic Republic—a correlation analysis, by P. Nischan, et al. INTERNATIONAL JOURNAL OF CANCER 34(5):671-674, November 15, 1984.

GREAT BRITAIN
Contraceptive controversy [in British media; Law Lords decision; news]. CHRISTIAN CENTURY 102:994, November 6, 1985.

Doctor and the underage girl [contraception; from our British correspondent, by K. Slack. CHRISTIAN CENTURY 102:174-176, February 20, 1985.

Fertility of couples following cessation of contraception, by N. Spira, et al. JOURNAL OF BIOSOCIAL SCIENCE 17(3):281-290, July 1985.

Underage girl: a surprising judgment, by K. Slack. CHRISTIAN CENTURY 102:1054-1056, November 20, 1985.

GUATEMALA
Contraceptive use and fertility in Guatemala. Tables, by R. S. Monteith, et al. 16:279-288, September-October 1985.

INDIA
Demographic transition in a Punjab village. POPULATION AND DEVELOP-
MENT REVIEW 10(4):661, December 1984.

Determinants of contraceptive use in Nepal, by J. M. Tuladhar. JOURNAL OF
BIOSOCIAL SCIENCE 17(2):185-193, April 1985.

IRELAND
Ireland sex and violence in the Dail. ECONOMIST 294:40+, February 23,
1985.

Learning the facts of life [legal contraception], by T. Clifton. NEWSWEEK
105:48, March 11, 1985.

ISRAEL
Contraception and religiousness in a general practice population in Israel, by
A. Sandiuk, et al. FAMILY PRACTICE 1(1):37-41, March 1984.

KENYA
Impacts of behavioral intentions, social support, and accessibility on contra-
ception: a cross-cultural study, by S. Kar, et al. POPULATION AND
ENVIRONMENT 7(1):17-31, Spring 1984.

MEXICO
Effectiveness of injectable contraceptives in Mexican women, by J. Garza-
Flores, et al. BOLETIN DE LA OFICINA SANITARIA PAN AMERICANA
98(2):181-186, February 1985.

NETHERLANDS
Contraception and fertility in the Netherlands, by E. Ketting. FAMILY PLAN-
NING PERSPECTIVES 15(1):19-25, January-February 1983.

PHILIPPINES
Impacts of behavioral intentions, social support, and accessibility on contra-
ception: a cross-cultural study, by S. Kar, et al. POPULATION AND
ENVIRONMENT 7(1):17-31, Spring 1984.

SRI LANKA
Ethnic differences in contraceptive use in Sri Lanka, by K. R. Murty, et al.
STUDIES IN FAMILY PLANNING 15:222-232, September-October 1984.

SWEDEN
Oral contraceptive use and breast cancer in young women in Sweden [letter],
by H. Olsson, et al. LANCET 1(8431):748-749, March 30, 1985.

THAILAND
Multilevel model of family planning availability and contraceptive use in rural
Thailand, by B. Entwisle, et al. DEMOGRAPHY 21:559-574, November
1984.

UNITED STATES
Contraceptive practice among American women, 1973-1982, by C. A.
Bachrach. FAMILY PLANNING PERSPECTIVES 16:253-259,
November-December 1984.

UNITED STATES
Contraceptive practice among American women, 1973-1982, by C. A. Bachrach. FAMILY PLANNING PERSPECTIVES 16:253-259, November-December 1984.

Contraceptive practices of women attending the Sexually Transmitted Disease Clinic in Nashville, Tennessee, by R. W. Quinn, et al. SEXUALLY TRANSMITTED DISEASES 12(3):99-102, July-September 1985.

Contraceptive use in Georgia: estimation by telephone survey, by A. M. Spitz, et al. SOUTHERN MEDICAL JOURNAL 78(3):323-328, March 1985.

Contraceptive use, pregnancy and fertility patterns among single American women in their 20s, by K. Tanfer, et al. FAMILY PLANNING PERSPEC-TIVES 17(1):10-19, January-February 1985.

Gallup poll shows Americans are mistaken about contraceptives. AMERICAN FAMILY PHYSICIAN 31:18, April 1985.

Prevalence and trends in oral contraceptive use in premenopausal females ages 12-54 years, United States, 1971-1980, by R. Russell-Briefel, et al. AMERICAN JOURNAL OF PUBLIC HEALTH 75(10):1173-1176, October 1985.

Public findings of contraceptive, sterilization and abortion services, 1983 [United States], by R.I B. Gold, et al. FAMILY PLANNING PERSPEC-TIVES 17:25-30, January-February 1985.

Use of the Today contraceptive sponge in the United States, by B. B. North, et al. INTERNATIONAL JOURNAL OF FERTILITY 30(1):81-84, 1985.

VENEZUELA
Impacts of behavioral intentions, social support, and accessibility on contraception: a cross-cultural study, by S. Kar, et al. POPULATION AND ENVIRONMENT 7(1):17-31, Spring 1984.

CONTRACEPTIVES: ADVERTISING
Condom spots stun Spanish, by M. Specht. ADVERTISING AGE 55:3+, October 4, 1984.

Nets pressed to run contraceptive ads, by M. Christopher. ADVERTISING AGE 55:66+, October 8, 1984.

New contraceptive tries again, by D. A. Fuller. AD FORUM 6:11+, January 1985.

TV, sex and prevention, by K. Foltz. NEWSWEEK 106:72, September 9, 1985.

CONTRACEPTIVES: AGENTS
Antifertility activity and general pharmacological properties of ORF 13811: a synthetic analog of zoapatanol, by D. W. Hahn, et al. 30(1):39-53, July1984.

Are there adverse effects of periconceptual spermicide use?, by J. L. Mills, et al. FERTILITY AND STERILITY 43(3):442-446, 1985.

Barring the way to gonococci . . . synergistic effect between spermicides and barrier contraceptives. EMERGENCY MEDICINE 16(20):92, November 30, 1984.

Concentration-dependent mechanisms of ovulation inhibition by the progestin ST-1435, by P. L. Lähteenmäki, et al. FERTILITY AND STERILIZATION 44(1):20-24, July 1985.

Contraception update. CLINICAL OBSTETRICS AND GYNAECOLOGY 11(3):549-819, December 1984.

Depot medroxyprogesterone acetate: clinical and metabolic effects (lipids, glucose,hemostasis), by Y. Hyjazi, et al. JOURNAL DE GYNECOLOGIE, OBSTETRIQUE ET BIOLOGIE DE LA REPRODUCTION 14(1):93-103, 1985.

Effect of anionic polymeric hydrogels on spermatozoa motility, by H. Singh, et al. BIOMATERIALS 5(5):307-309, September 1984.

Effect of chemical intravaginal contraceptives and Betadine on Ureaplasma urealyticum, by A. J. Amortegui, et al. CONTRACEPTION 30(2):135-141, August1984.

Effect of a topical contraceptive on endocervical culture for Neisseria gonor-rhoeae, by C. H. Livengood, et al. AMERICAN JOURNAL OF OBSTETRICS AND GYNECOLOGY 150(3):319-320, October 1, 1984.

In vitro amplification of toxic shock syndrome toxin-1 by intravaginal devices, by P. M. Tierno, Jr., et al. CONTRACEPTION 31(2):185-194, February 1985.

In vitro and in vivo evaluation of latex condoms using a two-phase nonoxynol 9 system, by N. Rodgers-Neame, et al. FERTILITY AND STERILITY 43(6):931-936, June 1985.

Long-term follow-up of children breast-fed by mothers receiving depot-medroxy-progesterone acetate, by J. Jimenez, et al. CONTRACEPTION 30(6):523-5 33, December 1984.

Luteinizing hormone releasing hormone analogues for contraception, by S. J. Nillius. CLINICAL OBSTETRICS AND GYNECOLOGY 11(3):551-572, December 1984.

New aid in fighting AIDS? [spermicide nonoxynol-9]. NEWSWEEK 105:85, February 18, 1985.

Pediatric drug information, by R. G. Fischer. PEDIATRIC NURSING 11(5):384, September-October 1985.

PID associated with fertility regulating agents. Task Force on intrauterine devices, special programme of research, development and research training in human reproduction, World Health Organization. CONTRACEPTION 30(1):1-21, July 1984.

Pregnancy terminating effect and toxicity of an active constituent of Aristolochia mollissima Hance, aristolochic acid A, by W. H. Wang, et al. YAO HSUEH HSUEH PAO 19(6):405-409, June 1984.

Real and false risks of local contraception: spermicides and the diaphragm, by M. M. Zufferey. JOURNAL DE GYNECOLOGIE, OBSTETRIQUE ET BIOLOGIE DE LA REPRODUCTION 14(3):359-363, 1985.

Spermicides and congenital malformations: no relation. AMERICAN JOURNAL OF NURSING 85:699, June 1985.

—. NURSES DRUG ALERT 9(6): 47, June 1985.

Spermicides and pregnancy. AMERICAN FAMILY PHYSICIAN 31:248, June 1985.

Spermicides and teratgenesis. Family Planning Association of NSW. Medical advisory board. HEALTHRIGHT 4:31, May 1985.

Spermicides given green light [study by James L. Mills and Joe L. Simpson], by J. Silberner. SCIENCE NEWS 127:326, May 25, 1985.

Steroid chemistry: history and recent developments, by P. Crabbé. IMPACT OF SCIENCE ON SOCIETY 136:389-396, 1984.

Studies in antifertility agents—Part XLI: Secosteroids—X syntheses of various stereoisomers of (+/-) 2,6 beta—diethyl-7 alpha -ethynyl-3-(p-hydroxy-phenyl)-trans-bicyclo[4.30]nonan beta-ol, by A. G. Thingran, et al. STEROIDS 42(6):627-634, December 1983.

Studies in spiro heterocycles. Part 4(1): investigation of the reactions of fluori-nated 3-aroylmethylene-indol-2-ones with hydrazine and phenylhydrazine and synthesis of spiro [indole-3,3'-pyrazol]-2-ones, by K. C. Joshi, et al. PHARMAZIE 40(1):21-22, January 1985.

CONTRACEPTIVES: AGENTS: COMPLICATIONS
Spermicides and birth defects: no clear link, by M. Engel. GLAMOUR 83:160, August 1985.

CONTRACEPTIVES: AGENTS: MALE
Studies on fertility control-the formation and antifertility effect of polyvinyl-pyrolidone-gossypol complex, by Z. W. Gu, et al. BIOMATERIALS, MEDICAL DEVICES AND ARTIFICIAL ORGANS 12(1-2):1-14, 1984.

CONTRACEPTIVES: ATTITUDES
Comparison of three social-psychological models of attitude and behavioral plan: prediction of contraceptive behavior, by M. D. Pagel, et al. JOURNAL OF PERSONALITY AND SOCIAL PSYCHOLOGY 47:517-533, September 1984.

Contraceptive attitudes and practice in women choosing sterilization, by K. D. Bledin, et al. JOURNAL OF THE ROYAL COLLEGE OF GENERAL PRACTITIONERS 34(268):595-599, November 1984.

Contraceptive compatibility, S. Bryant-Johnson. ESSENCE 16:20+, September 1985.

Effect of contraceptive knowledge source upon knowledge accuracy and contra-ceptive behavior, by A. J. Pope, et al. HEALTH EDUCATION 16:41-44, June-July 1985.

Group discussion on contraceptive issues, by B. A. Rienzo. HEALTH EDUCA-
TION 16:52-53, August-September 1985.

Just the facts [networks reject a TV spot]. TIME 126:57, August 19, 1985.

Predicting contraceptive behavior among university men: the role of emotions
and behavioral intentions, by W. A. Fisher. JOURNAL OF APPLIED SOCIAL
PSYCHOLOGY 14:104-123, March-April 1984.

Public misinformed about safety of the pill. GALLUP REPORT March 1985, p.
27-29.

Survey of attitudes concerning contraception and the resolution of teenage
pregnancy, by C. Rinck, et al. ADOLESCENCE 18(72):923-929, Winter
1983.

What's the #1 contraceptive? (Guess again), by S. Wernick. REDBOOK 165:36+,
September 1985.

CONTRACEPTIVES: BARRIER
AIDS. Condoms and gay abandon [letter], by C. J. Mitchell. MEDICAL JOURNAL
OF AUSTRALIA 142(11):617, May 27, 1985.

Are there adverse effects of periconceptual spermicide use?, by J. L. Mills, et al.
FERTILITY AND STERILITY 43(3):442-446, 1985.

Barrier contraception, by A. Mills. CLINICAL OBSTETRICS AND GYNECOLOGY
11(3):641-660, December 1984.

Barrier methods of contraception, by R. L. Skrine. PRACTITIONER
229(1403):441-446, May 1985.

Cabbages and condoms: packaging and channels of distribution, by M. Potts.
CLINICAL OBSTETRICS AND GYNAECOLOGY 11(3):799-809, December
1984.

Collagen sponge as vaginal contraceptive barrier: critical summary of seven years
of research, by M. Chvapil, et al. AMERICAN JOURNAL OF OBSTETRICS
AND GYNECOLOGY 151(3):325-329, February 1, 1985.

Comparative clinical trial of the contraceptive sponge and Neo Sampoon tablets,
by E.Borko, et al. OBSTETRICS AND GYNECOLOGY 65(4):511-515, April
1985.

Comparative trial of the Today contraceptive sponge and diaphragm, by D. A.
Edelman, et al. AMERICAN JOURNAL OF OBSTETRICS AND GYNE-
COLOGY150(7):869-876, December 1, 1984.

Contraceptive sponge patient insert warns of TSS. FDA DRUG BULLETIN
14(2):18-19, August 1984.

Dalkon Shield is finally recalled. CONSUMER REPORTS 50:447, August 1985.

Diaphragm: an accomplice in recurrent UTI [letter], by G. E. Leach. UROLOGY
24(5):524, November 1984.

Electroconvulsive therapy [letter], by S. Barza. CANADIAN JOURNAL OF PSYCHIATRY 30(4):310, June 1985.

CONTRACEPTIVES: DEVELOPING COUNTRIES
Contraceptive use during lactation in developing countries, by A. R. Pebley, et al. STUDIES IN FAMILY PLANNING 16(1):40-51, January-February 1985.

CONTRACEPTIVES: EDUCATION
Magazine versus physicians: the influence of information source on intentions to use oral contraceptives, by D. F. Halpern, et al. WOMEN AND HEALTH 1 0(1):9-23, Spring 1985.

CONTRACEPTIVES: FEMALE
Contraceptive habits in women born in 1936. Results of a health survey at the ages of 40 and 45, by K. Garde, et al. UGESKRIFT FOR LAEGER 147(4):314-318, January 21, 1985.

Contraceptive practice among American women, 1973-1982, by C. A. Bachrach. FAMILY PLANNING PERSPECTIVES 16:253-259, November-December 1984.

'Missed pill' conception: fact of fiction?, by B. G. Molloy, et al. BRITISH MEDICAL JOURNAL 290(6480):1474-1475, May 18, 1985.

Relationship of the menstrual cycle and thyroid hormones to whole-body protein turnover in women, by D. R. Garrel, et al. HUMAN NUTRITION 39C:29-37, January 1985.

CONTRACEPTIVES: FEMALE: BARRIER
Adverse effects of contraceptive sponges. NURSES DRUG ALERT 9(2):9, February 1985.

Bankruptcy 'shield' against Dalkon claims. NEW SCIENTIST 107:21, August 29, 1985.

Barring the way to gonococci . . . synergistic effect between spermicides and barrier contraceptives. EMERGENCY MEDICINE 16(20):92, November 30, 1984.

Beyond the pill?. . . vaginal contraceptive sponge, by P. Holmes. NURSING TIMES 81(7):19, 13-19, February 1985.

Cervical cap as a contraceptive alternative, by M. A. Johnson. NURSE PRACTI-TIONER 10(1):37+, January 1985.

Etymology of condom, by Z. P. Thundy. AMERICAN SPEECH 60:177-179, Summer 1985.

How Robins will go on paying for the Dalkon Shield, by C. S. Eklund, et al. BUSI-NESS WEEK April 15, 1985, p. 50.

Ireland sex and violence in the Dail. ECONOMIST 294:40+, February 23, 1985.

Promoting the sponge: learning from experience. PUBLIC RELATIONS JOURNAL 41:20-21, March 1985.

Real and false risks of local contraception: spermicides and the diaphragm, by M. M. Zufferey. JOURNAL DE GYNECOLOGIE, OBSTETRIQUE ET BIOLOGIE DE LA REPRODUCTION 14(3):359-363, 1985.

—. GYNAEKOLOGISCHE RUNDSCHAU 24(Suppl. 1):26-28, 1984.

Sex supplies: Calgary's free condom shop starts charging, by T. Fennell. ALBERTA REPORT 11:41, November 5, 1984.

$615 million reserve set for Dalkon Shield claims, by M. Fletcher. BUSINESS INSURANCE 19:3+, April 8, 1985.

Spermicides given green light [study by James L. Mills and Joe L. Simpson], by J. Silberner. SCIENCE NEWS 127:326, May 25, 1985.

Sponge is selling again, by T. Carson. BUSINESS WEEK June 17, 1985, p. 65+.

Urological complications secondary to a contraceptive diaphragm, by D. Staskin, et al. JOURNAL OF UROLOGY 134(1):142-143, July 1985.

Use effectiveness of the Prentif cervical cap in private practice: a prospective study, by H. Lehfeldt, et al. CONTRACEPTION 30(4):331-338, October 1984.

Use of cervical caps at the University of California, Berkeley: a survey, by G. G. Smith, et al. CONTRACEPTION 30(2):115-123, August 1984.

Use of the Today contraceptive sponge in the United States, by B. B. North, et al. INTERNATIONAL JOURNAL OF FERTILITY 30(1):81-84, 1985.

Vaginal contraceptive sponge: a new non-prescription barrier contraceptive, by E. Lemberg. NURSE PRACTITIONER 9(10):24-25+, October 1984.

Vesicovaginal fistula and its complications due to prolonged use of vaginal diaphragm, by D. M. Kwa, et al. AUSTRALIAN AND NEW ZEALAND JOURNAL OF OBSTETRICS AND GYNAECOLOGY 24(3):225-226, August 1984.

Women buy most condoms to avoid pregnancy, VD. JET 69:26, October 14, 1985.

CONTRACEPTIVES: FEMALE: BARRIER: COMPLICATIONS
Aetna's defense costs capped under Dalkon Shield agreement, by S. Tarnoff. BUSINESS INSURANCE 18:1+, November 26, 1984.

After a lawyer turns whistle-blower, the company that made the Dalkon Shield warns women of its dangers, by J. S. Podesta. PEOPLE WEEKLY 23:61+, January 14,1985.

Association between diaphragm use and urinary tract infection, by S. D. Fihn, et al. JAMA 254:240-245, July 12, 1985.

Big payout [A. H. Robins' liability for Dalkon Shield]. TIME 125:86, April 15, 1985.

Case study. A. H. Robins and the Dalkon Shield, by C. Policano. PUBLIC RELATIONS JOURNAL 41:16-19+, March 1985.

Days of our Dalkon [A. H. Robins Co., manufacturer of the Dalkon Shield, reported a deficit because of a special fund set up to deal with lawsuits by Injured women], by A. Fugh-Berman. OFF OUR BACKS 15:6, May 1985.

Hepatitis and diaphragm fitting, by L. A. Lettau, et al. JAMA 254(6):752, August 9,1985.

How Robins will go on paying for the Dalkon Shield, by C. S. Eklund, et al. BUSINESS WEEK April 15, 1985, p. 50.

Is Depo Provera still being incautiously used?, by P. Cohen. NEW STATESMAN 108:6, October 19, 1984.

Make sure your diaphragm is still protecting you. GLAMOUR 83:80, April 1985.

Possible hepatitis from diaphragm fitting [letter], by L. C. Wislicki. JAMA 252(23): 3251, December 21, 1984.

Risks from Dalkon Shield, by J. Willis. FDA CONSUMER 19:35, May 1985.

Robins nuns for shelter [files for bankruptcy to cope with Dalkon Shield disaster], by C. P. Alexander. TIME 126:32-33, September 2, 1985.

Robins sees continuing Dalkon problem. CHEMICAL MARKETING REPORT 227:9+, June 3, 1985.

Robins sets fund for Dalkon Shield claims. CHEMICAL AND ENGINEERING NEWS 63:8, April 8, 1985.

Take out Dalkon Shield. FDA CONSUMER 19:37, February 1985.

Toxic shock syndrome associated with the use of the vaginal contraceptive sponge [letter], by R. C. Dart, et al. JAMA 253(13):1877, April 5, 1985.

Tunnel vision [A. H. Robins' Dalkon Shield intrauterine device], by S. N. Chakravarty. FORBES 133:214+, May 21, 1984.

Vaginal sponge and toxic shock. AMERICAN JOURNAL OF NURSING 85:693, June 1985.

CONTRACEPTIVES: FEMALE: COMPLICATIONS
Depression and self-blame [women who use contraception and become pregnant anyway], by C. Turkington. PSYCHOLOGY TODAY 18:18, December 1984.

Ovulation inhibitors and tumors, by G. Freund, et al. DEUTSCHE MEDIZINISCHE WOCHENSCHRIFT 110(35):1346-1350, August 30, 1985.

CONTRACEPTIVES: FEMALE: IMPLANTED
Contraceptive implant [Norplant], by M. Clark. NEWSWEEK 105:70, March 11, 1985.

New birth control implant safer than taking pill [Norplant]. JET 68:29, March 25, 1985.

Six small capsule implants may change the way the world conceives of birth control [Norplant system gradually releases levonorgestrel]. PEOPLE WEEKLY 23:137, March 18, 1985.

CONTRACEPTIVES: FEMALE: INJECTED
Menstrual regulation by (15S)-15 methyl prostaglandin F2 alpha by intramuscular route, by P. R. Bhattacharaya, et al. ASIA-OCEANIA JOURNAL OF OBSTET-RICS AND GYNAECOLOGY 10(4):435-437, December 1984.

CONTRACEPTIVES: FEMALE: IUD
Clinical chemistry in women treated with six levonorgestrel covered rods or with a copper IUD, by S. Díaz, et al. CONTRACEPTION 31(4):321-330, April 1985.

Current status of intrauterine devices, by D. R. Mishell, Jr. NEW ENGLAND JOURNAL OF MEDICINE 312:984-985, April 11, 1985.

Evolution of the minor complications due to the use of copper intrauterine device, by A. Albert, et al. CLINICA E INVESTIGACION EN GINECOLOGIA Y OBSTETRICIA 10(1):16-22, 1983.

Hormonal contraception and IUDs in adolescents, by M. Mall-Haefeli. FORT-SCHRITTE DER MEDIZIN 102(33):823-824, September 6, 1984.

Intra-uterine contraceptive devices, by J. Elias. PRACTITIONER 229(1403):431-436, May 1985.

Intrauterine devices and long-term risks, by E. Michaels. CHATELAINE 58:18, February 1985.

IUD alert [Dalkon Shield], by C. SerVaas. SATURDAY EVENING POST 257:108-109, January-February 1985.

IUD-infertility link, by J. Silberner. SCIENCE NEWS 127:229, April 13, 1985.

Mini pills, IUDs and abortion, by J. F. Kippley. JOURNAL OF CHRISTIAN NURSING 2(1):32, Winter 1985.

Post-cesarean section insertion of intrauterine devices, by I. C. Chi, et al. AMERICAN JOURNAL OF PUBLIC HEALTH 74:1281-1282, November 1984.

Primary tubal infertility in relation to the use of an intrauterine device [also tubal i infertility and the intrauterine device by Daniel W. Cramer, pp. 941-947, and current status of intrauterine devices by Daniel R. Mishell (editorial), pp. 984-985], by Janet R. Daling, et al. NEW ENGLAND JOURNAL OF MEDICINE 312:937-941, April 11, 1985.

Tubal infertility and the intrauterine device, by D. W. Cramer, et al. NEW ENGLAND JOURNAL OF MEDICINE 312:941-947, April 11, 1985.

CONTRACEPTIVES: FEMALE: IUD: COMPLICATIONS
Contraceptive dilemma [Dalkon Shield IUD recall and counterfeit Ovulen-21 pills], by P. Ohlendorf. MACLEANS 97:74+, November 26, 1984.

How IUDs cause infertility, by I. Anderson. NEW SCIENTIST 106:6, April 18, 1985.

Intrauterine device insertion following induced abortion, by L. Querido, et al. CONTRACEPTION 31(6):603-610, 1985.

IUD-infertility link, by J. Silberner. SCIENCE NEWS 127:229, April 13, 1985.

IUDs and infertility. AMERICAN FAMILY PHYSICIAN 31:244+, June 1985.

—. MCCALLS 112:57, August 1985.

Robins' costly reserve fund [for lawsuits brought by users of its Dalkon Shield intrauterine birth-control device]. DUNS BUSINESS MONTHLY 125:22, May 1985.

Searle closes its eyes to a health hazard? [Copper 7 IUD], by W. B. Glaberson. BUSINESS WEEK October 14, 1985, p. 120-122.

CONTRACEPTIVES: FEMALE: ORAL

Absence of correlation between oral contraceptive usage and cardiovascular mortality, by R. A. Wiseman. INTERNATIONAL JOURNAL OF FERTILITY 29(4):198-208, 1984.

Acne and oral contraceptives, by H. L. van der Meeren, et al. NEDERLANDS TIJDSCHRIFT VOOR GENEESKUNDE 128(28):1333-1337, July 14, 1984.

Alternative approach to initiating oral contraceptives. AMERICAN FAMILY PHYSICIAN 31:137, March 1985.

Are there any absolute medical contraindications to the progestogen only oral contraceptive?, by J. Guillebaud. BRITISH MEDICAL JOURNAL 289(6451): 1079, October 20, 1984.

At last, good news about the pill, by J. Langone. DISCOVER 6:8, February 1985.

Benefits of oral contraceptives, by A. A. Kubba. JOURNAL OF THE ROYAL SOCIETY OF HEALTH 105(2):73-74, April 1985.

Birth control use means more clinic visits. JET 67:37, January 28, 1985.

Breaking up with the pill: is it hard to do?, by E. Goldbaum. MADEMOISELLE 91:52+, February 1985.

Case-control study of galactorrhea and its relationship to the use of oral contraceptives, by S. J. Taler, et al. OBSTETRICS AND GYNECOLOGY 65(5):665-668, May 1985.

Clinical evaluation of Rigevidon used for contraception, by L. Marianowski, et al. GINEKOLOGIA POLSKA 55(8):631-635, August 1984.

Combined hormonal oral contraceptive. Comparative study of 4 schemes, by Ron L. Reynoso, et al. GINECOLOGIA Y OBSTETRICIA DE MEXICO 52(329):221-223, September 1984.

Comparative métabolic effects of oral contraceptive preparations containing different progestagens. Effects of desogestrel + ethinylestradiol on the haemostatic balance, by I. Rákoczi, et al. ARZNEIMITTEL-FORSCHUNG 35(3):630-633,1985.

Comparison of plasma cholesterol, triglycerides and high density lipoprotein cholesterol levels in women using contraceptive pills and a control group, by D. Yeshurun, et al. GYNECOLOGIC AND OBSTETRIC INVESTIGATION 18(4):169-173, 1984.

Conception-waits in fertile women after stopping oral contraceptives, by S. Harlap, et al. INTERNATIONAL JOURNAL OF FERTILITY 29(2):73-80, 1984.

Contraceptive dilemma [Dalkon Shield IUD recall and counterfeit Ovulen-21 pills], by P. Ohlendorf. MACLEANS 97:74+, November 26, 1984.

Day of the yam, by A. Rosser. NURSING TIMES 81(18):47, May 1-7, 1985.

Deep vein thrombosis and the oestrogen content in oral contraceptives. An epidemiological analysis, by A. Kierkegaard. CONTRACEPTION 31(1):29-41, January 1985.

Effect of a once-a-month oral contraceptive on serum prolactin levels, by M. C. Jia, et al. CHUNG HUA FU CHAN KO TSA CHIH 20(2):113-116, March 1985.

Effect of oral contraceptive drug on cardiovascular system, liver and kidneys, by C. Chaudhuri, et al. INDIAN HEART JOURNAL 37(2):96-100, March-April 1985.

Effect of oral contraceptive formulation and field-workers: a cautionary tale, by P. C. Miller, et al. INTERNATIONAL JOURNAL OF GYNAECOLOGY AND OBSTETRICS 23(1):13-20, February 1985.

Effect of oral contraceptives and some psychological factors on the menstrual experience, by C. M. Harding, et al. JOURNAL OF BIOSOCIAL SCIENCE 17(3):291-304, July 1985.

Effects of oral contraceptives on vitamins B6, B12, C, and folacin, by K. S. Veninga. JOURNAL OF NURSE-MIDWIFERY 29(6):386-390, November-December 1984.

Electroconvulsive therapy [letter], by S. Barza. CANADIAN JOURNAL OF PSYCHIATRY 30(4):310, June 1985.

Fibrinopeptide A plasma levels during low-estrogen oral contraceptive treatment, by G. B. Melis, et al. CONTRACEPTION 30(6):575-583, December 1984.

Formulation and noncontraceptive uses of the new, low-dose oral contraceptive, by F. R. Batzer. JOURNAL OF REPRODUCTIVE MEDICINE 29(7 Suppl):503-512, July 1984.

Gonadal steroids in athletic women contraception, complications and performance, by J. C. Prior, et al. SPORTS MEDICINE 2(4):287-295, July-August 1985.

Good news about the pill, by N. Mallovy. HOME MAGAZINE 20:48E-48H, May 1985.

How to go off the pill. MCCALLS 112:79-80, November 1984.

Impairment of caffeine clearance by chronic use of low-dose oestrogen-containing oral contraceptives, by D. R. Abernethy, et al. EUROPEAN JOURNAL OF CLINICAL PHARMACOLOGY 28(4):425-428, 1985.

Instructions for starting the use of oral contraceptives [letter], by N. B. Loudon, et al. NEW ENGLAND JOURNAL OF MEDICINE 311(25):1634-1635, December 20,1984.

Judging risks versus benefits of oral contraceptives [editorial], by J. K. Jones, et al. CLINICAL PHARMACY 3(5):521-522, September-October 1984.

Latest views on pill prescribing, by C. R. Kay. JOURNAL OF THE ROYAL COLLEGE OF GENERAL PRACTITIONERS 34(268):611-614, November 1984.

Magazine versus physicians: the influence of information source on intentions to use oral contraceptives, by D. F. Halpern, et al. WOMEN AND HEALTH 1 0(1):9-23, Spring 1985.

Making of the pill, by C. Djerassi. SCIENCE 5:127-129, November 1984.

Managing patients on oral contraceptives, by M. Block, et al. AMERICAN FAMILY PHYSICIAN 32(2):154-168, August 1985.

Menstrual cycle from a bio-behavioral approach: a comparison or oral contraceptive and non-contraceptive users, by K. F. Garrett, et al. INTERNATIONAL JOURNAL OF PSYCHOPHYSIOLOGY 1(2):209-214, February 1984.

Metabolism of 14-C-arachidonic acid in platelets and antiaggregatory potency of prostacyclin in women taking oral contraceptives, by K. Jaschonek, et al. PROSTAGLANDINS LEUKOTRIENES AND MEDICINE 15(2):275-276, August 1984.

Mini pills, IUDs and abortion, by J. F. Kippley. JOURNAL OF CHRISTIAN NURSING 2(1):32, Winter 1985.

'Missed pill' conception: fact or fiction? [letter]. BRITISH MEDICAL JOURNAL 291(6488):136-137, July 13, 1985.

—, by P. Bye. BRITISH MEDICAL JOURNAL 290(6485):1905, June 22, 1985.

New HWC guidelines for oral contraceptive users, manufacturers and health professionals, by P. LaCroix. CANADIAN NURSE 81:13, October 1985.

New pill: should you take it?, by A. B. Eagan. MS MAGAZINE 14:35-36+, October 1985.

No more griseofulvin for pill users: another clinically important inteaction?, by L. Offerhaus. NEDERLANDS TIJDSCHRIFT VOOR GENEESKUNDE 128(33):1579-1580, August 18, 1984.

Noncompliance among oral contraceptive acceptors in rural Bangladesh, by B. Seaton. STUDIES IN FAMILY PLANNING 16(1):52-59, January-February 1985.

Oral contraception and coagulation, by M. Notelovitz. CLINICAL OBSTETRICS AND GYNAECOLOGY 28(1):73-83, March 1985.

Oral contraception and metabolism, by A. Harlay. INFIRMIERE FRANCAISE (257):19-21, July 1984.

Oral contraception for the adolescent, by L. B. Tyrer. JOURNAL OF REPRO-DUCTIVE MEDICINE 29(Suppl. 7):551-559, July 1984.

Oral contraception in Bangladesh, by S. Bhatia, et al. STUDIES IN FAMILY PLAN-NING 15:233-241, September-October 1984.

Oral contraception, coital frequency, and the time required to conceive, by C. F. Westoff, et al. SOCIAL BIOLOGY 29:157-167, Spring-Summer, 1982.

Oral contraception—starting, stopping or changing. DRUG THERAPY BULLETIN 23(10):37-39, May 20, 1985.

Oral contraceptive PPI: its effect on patient knowledge, feelings, and behavior, by C. D. Sands, et al. DRUG INTELLIGENCE AND CLINICAL PHARMACY 18(9):730-735, September 1984.

Oral contraceptive use: prospective follow-up of women with suspected glucose intolerance, by T. J. Duffy, et al. CONTRACEPTION 30(3):197-208, September 1984.

Oral contraceptives, by R. P. Shearman. AUSTRALIAN FAMILY PHYSICIAN 13(9): 685-691, September 1984.

Oral contraceptives and pituitary response to GnRH: comparative study of progestin-related effects, by A. Römmler, et al. CONTRACEPTION 31(3): 295-303, March 1985.

Oral contraceptives, Chlamydia trachomatis infection, and pelvic inflammatory disease. A word of caution about protection, by A. E. Washington, et al. JAMA 253(15):2246-2250, April 19, 1985.

Oral contraceptives containing chlormadinone acetate and cancer incidence at selected sites in the German Democratic Republic—a correlation analysis, by P. Nischan, et al. INTERNATIONAL JOURNAL OF CANCER 34(5):671-674, November 15, 1984.

Oral contraceptives in the 1980s, by S. R. Miliken. PHYSICIAN ASSISTANT 9(5):29-30+, May 1985.

Oral contraceptives market benefits from new products. CHEMICAL MARKETING REPORT 227:20-21, March 25, 1985.

Oral contraceptives, 1985: a synopsis, by D. Woods. CANADIAN MEDICAL ASSOCIATION JOURNAL 133(5):463-465, September 1, 1985.

Paying high price for the pill [damages awarded in P. Buchan's suit against Ortho Pharmaceutical Canada], by R. Block. MACLEANS 97:52, April 30, 1984.

Photosensitized decomposition of contraceptive steroids: a possible explanation for the observed (photo) allergy of the oral contraceptive pill, by A. Sedee, et al. ARCHIV DER PHARMAZIE 318(2):111-119, February 1985.

Pill that 'might defuse the abortion issue' [morning after pills], by R. Rhein, Jr., et al. BUSINESS WEEK April 1, 1985, p. 85+.

Pill that might defuse the abortion issue [morning-after pills], by R. Rhein, Jr., et al. BUSINESS WEEK April 1, 1985, p. 85+.

Pill/25 years of uncertainty, by P. Duchesne. COMMUNIQU'ELLES 11(4):6, July 1985.

Pill's eclipse [survey on forms of birth control]. TIME 124:79, December 17, 1984.

Possible antidepressant effect of oral contraceptives: case report, by P. Roy-Byrne, et al. 45(8):350-352, August 1984.

Prescribing contraceptives for under-age-girls—the doctor's legal position, by D. Brahams. PRACTITIONER 229(1403):461-463, May 1985.

Prescribing oral contraceptives in 1985, by L. H. Labson. PATIENT CARE 19(6):16-18+, March 30, 1985.

Prevalence and trends in oral contraceptive use in premenopausal females ages 12-54 years, United States, 1971-1980, by R. Russell-Briefel, et al. AMERICAN JOURNAL OF PUBLIC HEALTH 75(10):1173-1176, October 1985.

Progress in oral contraception. Advantages of a levonorgestrel-containing 3-stage preparation over low-dose levonorgestrel and desogestrel containing monophasic combination preparations, by U. Lachnit-Fixson. FORTSCHRITTE DER MEDIZIN 102(33):825-830, September 6, 1984.

Public and the pill: is the pill making a comeback?, by J. D. Forrest. AMERICAN JOURNAL OF PUBLIC HEALTH 75(10):1131-1132, October 1985.

Reflections on a new generation of oral contraceptives, by U. Gaspard. JOURNAL DE GYNECOLOGIE, OBSTETRIQUE ET BIOLOGIE DE LA REPRODUCTION 14(1):85-92, 1985.

Response of patients and doctors to the 1983 'pill scare', by L. D. Ritchie, et al. JOURNAL OF THE ROYAL COLLEGE OF GENERAL PRACTITIONERS 34(268):600-602, November 1984.

Safety of the contraceptive pill—a 24 year trial [letter], by Y. R. Dugas. SOUTH AFRICAN MEDICAL JOURNAL 68(1):9-10, July 6, 1985.

Serum lipid and lipoprotein changes induced by new oral contraceptives containing ethinylestradiol plus levonorgestrel or desogestrel, by U. J. Gaspard, et al. CONTRACEPTION 31(4):395-408, April 1985.

Tri-Norinyl and Ortho-Novum 7/7/7—two triphasic oral contraceptives. MEDICAL LETTER ON DRUGS AND THERAPEUTICS 26(672):93-94, October 12, 1984.

207

Triphasil—a new triphasic oral contraceptive. MEDICAL LETTER ON DRUGS AND THERAPEUTICS 27(688):48, May 24, 1985.

Vitamin metabolism and the effects of multivitamin supplementation in oral contraceptive users, by K. Amatayakul, et al. CONTRACEPTION 30(2):179-196, August 1984.

CONTRACEPTIVES: FEMALE: ORAL: COMPLICATIONS
Analysis of outcome predictors of migraine towards chronicity, by A. Baldrati, et al. CEPHALALGIA 5(Suppl. 2):195-199, May 1985.

An association with birth control pills. Moyamoya, by W. Sequeira, et al. IMJ 166(6): 434-436, December 1984.

Benign breast disease, oral contraceptive use, and the risk of breast cancer [letter], by C. La Vecchia. JOURNAL OF CHRONIC DISEASES 37(11):869-870, 1984.

Breast cancer and oral contraceptives: critique of the proposition that high potency progestogen products confer excess risk, by F. M. Sturtevant. BIOMEDICAL PHARMACOTHERAPY 38(8):371-379, 1984.

Cardiovascular disease mortality in Denmark before and after the introduction of oral contraceptives, by E. H. Larsen, et al. UGESKRIFT FOR LAEGER 146(36):2677-2680, September 3, 1984.

Cervical dysplasia: association with sexual behavior, smoking, and oral contraceptive use?, by E. A. Clarke, et al. AMERICAN JOURNAL OF OBSTETRICS AND GYNECOLOGY 151(5):612-616, March 1985.

Chromosomal abnormalities in the Kaiser-Permanente Birth Defects Study, with special reference to contraceptive use around the time of conception, by S. Harlap, et al. TERATOLOGY 31(3):381-387, June 1985.

Clinical and pathological comparison of young adult women with hepatocellular carcinoma with and without exposure to oral contraceptives, by R. A. Hromas, et al. AMERICAN JOURNAL OF GASTROENTEROLOGY 80(6):479-485, June1985.

Contact lens wear problems: implications of penicillin allergy, diabetic relatives, and use of birth control pills, by D. P. Harrison. AMERICAN JOURNAL OF OPTOMETRY AND PHYSIOLOGICAL OPTICS 61(11):674-678, November 1984.

Early symptoms and discontinuation among users of oral contraceptives in Sri Lanka. STUDIES IN FAMILY PLANNING 15(6):285, November-December 1984.

Effect of oral contraceptive formulation and field-workers: a cautionary tale, by P. C. Miller, et al. INTERNATIONAL JOURNAL OF GYNAECOLOGY AND OBSTETRICS 23(1):13-20, February 1985.

Effect of oral contraceptives in malaria infections in rhesus monkey, by W. E. Collins, et al. WHO BULLETIN 62(4):627-637, 1984.

Effects of elevated female sex steroids on ethanol and acetaldehyde metabolism in humans, by C M. Jeavons, et al. ALCOHOLISM: CLINICAL AND EXPERIMENTAL RESEARCH 8(4):352-358, July-August 1984.

Effects of oral contraceptives and obesity on protein C antigen, by T. W. Meade, et al. THROMBOSIS AND HAEMOSTASIS 53(2):198-199, April 22, 1985.

Estroprogestational minipills: breast diseases and functional cysts of the ovary. Apropos of 87 cases, by M. Vincens, et al. THERAPIE 40(3):177-180, May-June 1985.

Evidence of immunosuppressor factor in the serum of women taking oral contraceptives, by J. Bousquet, et al. GYNECOLOGIC AND OBSTETRIC INVESTIGATION 18(4):178-182, 1984.

Foreign travel alert for women on the pill. GLAMOUR 83:51, June 1985.

Gallbladder disease related to use of oral contraceptives and nausea in pregnancy, by A.Järnfelt-Samsioe, et al. SOUTHERN MEDICAL JOURNAL 78(9):1040-1043, September 1985.

Hepatic adenoma and oral contraception: apropos of a hemorrhagic complication, by J. Maurice, et al. REVUE MEDICALE DE LA SUISSE ROMANDE 105(3): 211-217, March 1985.

Hepatobiliary complications of female hormonal contraception, by F. Darnis. SOINS (437):3-7, September 1984.

Hormonal factors and melanoma in women, by A. Green, et al. MEDICAL JOURNAL OF AUSTRALIA 142(8):446-448, April 15, 1985.

Hormones in the etiology and prevention of breast and endometrial cancer, by R. D. Gambrell, Jr. SOUTHERN MEDICAL JOURNAL 77(12):1509-1515, December 1984.

How risky is the pill? ECONOMIST 295:16, April 6, 1985.

Immunogenicity and the vascular risk of oral contraceptives, by C. Plowright, et al. BRITISH HEART JOURNAL 53(5):556-561, May 1985.

Increased UDP-glucuronyltransferase in putative preneoplastic foci of human liver after long-term use of oral contraceptives, by G. Fischer, et al. NATURWISSENSCHAFTEN 72(5):277-278, May 1985.

Influence of client-provider relationships on teenage women's subsequent use of contraception, by C. A. Nathanson, et al. AMERICAN JOURNAL OF PUBLIC HEALTH 75(1):33-38, January 1985.

Invasive cervical cancer and combined oral contraceptives [letter], by J. A. Fortney, et al. BRITISH MEDICAL JOURNAL 290(6481):1587, May 25, 1985.

Iron stores in users of oral contraceptive agent, by E. P. Frassinelli-Gunderson, et al. AMERICAN JOURNAL OF CLINICAL NUTRITION 41:703-712, April 1985.

Mesenteric vein thrombosis associated with oral contraceptive administration during pregnancy, by M. Friedman, et al. ANNALES CHIRURGIAE ET GYNACOLOGIAE 73(5):296-298, 1984.

Mesenteric venous thrombosis and oral contraceptive use, by V. Naraynsingh, et al. TROPICAL AND GEOGRAPHICAL MEDICINE 37(2):192-193, June 1985.

Mortality caused by cardiovascular diseases in Denmark before and after the Introduction of the pill (letter), by O. Lidegaard. UGESKRIFT FOR LAEGER 147(1):39-40, December 31, 1984.

No link is found between 'pill' and breast cancer. JET 68:39, June 24, 1985.

Nutrition and the pill, by L. B. Tyrer. JOURNAL OF REPRODUCTIVE MEDICINE 29(Suppl. 7):547-550, July 1984.

On the origin and histological structure of adenocarcinoma of the endocervix in women under 50 years of age, by G. Dallenbach-Hellweg. PATHOLOGY, RESEARCH, AND PRACTICE 179(1):38-50, September 1984.

Oral contraception and cancer of the female reproductive system, by K. L. Woods. JOURNAL OF CLINICAL AND HOSPITAL PHARMACY 10(2):123-135, June 1985.

Oral contraception and serious psychiatric illness: absence of an association, by M. P. Vessey, et al. BRITISH JOURNAL OF PSYCHIATRY 146:45-49, January 1985.

Oral contraceptive failure. AMERICAN JOURNAL OF NURSING 85:694, June 1985.

Oral contraceptive failure . . . drugs taken concurrently can reduce its effectiveness. NURSES DRUG ALERT 9(6):42-43, June 1985.

Oral contraceptive pill and benign intracranial hypertension [letter], by N. D. Soysa. 98(784):656, August 14, 1985.

Oral contraceptives. The current risk-benefit ratio, by E. B. Connell. JOURNAL OF REPRODUCTIVE MEDICINE 29(Suppl. 7):513-523, July 1984.

Oral contraceptives and breast cancer: the current controversy, by M. C. Pike, et al. JOURNAL OF THE ROYAL SOCIETY OF HEALTH 105(1):5-10, February 1985.

Oral contraceptives and cardiovascular disease: a critique of the epidemiologic studies, by J. P. Realini, et al. AMERICAN JOURNAL OF OBSTETRICS AND GYNECOLOGY 152(6 Pt 2):729-798, July 15, 1985.

Oral contraceptives and cervical cancer, by J. M. Piper. GYNECOLOGIC ONCOLOGY 22(1):1-14, September 1985.

Oral contraceptives and the cobalamin (vitamin B12) metabolism, by K. Hjelt, et al. ACTA OBSTETRICIA ET GYNECOLOGICA SCANDINAVICA 64(1):59-63, 1985.

Oral contraceptives and neoplasia, by P. G. Stubblefield. JOURNAL OF REPRO-DUCTIVE MEDICINE 29(Suppl. 7):524-529, July 1984.

Oral contraceptives and nonfatal vascular disease, by J. B. Porter, et al. OBSTET-RICS AND GYNECOLOGY 66(1):1-4, July 1985.

Oral contraceptives and reproductive mortality [letter], by W. M. Gerhold. NEW ENGLAND JOURNAL OF MEDICINE 311(24):1583, December 13, 1984.

Oral contraceptives and surgery: reduced antithrombin and antifactor Xa levels without postoperative venous thrombosis in low-risk patients, by A. S. Gallus, et al. THROMBOSIS RESEARCH 35(5):513-526, September 1, 1984.

Oral contraceptives and venous thrombosis [letter], by C. Hougie. WESTERN JOURNAL OF MEDICINE 141(5):688-689, November 1984.

Oral contraceptives come of age . . . decreases the susceptibility to many diseases. CANADIAN OPERATING ROOM NURSES JOURNAL 3(3):44, May-June 1985.

Oral contraceptives, Chlamydia trachomatis infection, and pelvic inflammatory disease. A word of caution about protection, by A. E. Washington, et al. JAMA 253(15):2246-2250, April 19, 1985.

Patient understanding of oral contraceptive side effects, by N. Goldfield, et al. WESTERN JOURNAL OF MEDICINE 142(3):417-418, March 1985.

Pelvic inflammatory disease: pill risk, by D. D. Bennett. SCIENCE NEWS 127:263, April 27, 1985.

Pill and the liver, by L. Schiff. ACTA GASTROENTEROLOGICA LATINOAMERI-CANA 13(2):188-191, 1983.

Pill formulations and their effect on lipid and carbohydrate metabolism, by P. G. Brooks. JOURNAL OF REPRODUCTIVE MEDICINE 29(Suppl. 7):539-546, July 1984.

Pill's armed competitor. DISCOVER 6:7, May 1985.

Pitfalls of linking cancer to the pill, by S. Connor. NEW SCIENTIST 105:3, April 4, 1985.

Plasma pyridoxal phosphate in women taking oral contraceptives since at least five years, by A. Hamfelt, et al. UPSALA JOURNAL OF MEDICAL SCIENCES 89(3): 285-286, 1984.

Possible potentiation of suicide risk in patients with EEG dysrhythmias taking oral contraceptives: a speculative empirical note, by F. A. Struve. CLINICAL ELECTROENCEPHALOGRAPHY 16(2):88-90, April 1985.

Real and false risks of hormonal contraceptives, by J. Belaïsch. GYNAEKOLO-GISCHE RUNDSCHAU 24(Suppl. 1):12-19, 1984.

Reexamining the oral contraceptive issues, by R. Orne, et al. JOURNAL OF OBSTETRICS, GYNECOLOGY AND NEONATAL NURSING 14(1):30-36, January-February 1985.

Regenerative nodular hyperplasia, hepatocellular carcinoma and oral contraceptives (letter), by J. F. Bretagne, et al. GASTROENTEROLOGIE CLINIQUE ET BIOLOGIQUE 8(10):768-679, October 1984.

Relationship of estrogen and progesterone to breast disease, by P. G. Brooks. JOURNAL OF REPRODUCTIVE MEDICINE 29(Suppl. 7):530-538, July 1984.

Renin-angiotensin mechanisms in oral contraceptive hypertension in conscious rats, by W. L. Fowler, Jr., et al. AMERICAN JOURNAL F PHYSIOLOGY 248(5 Pt 2):H695-699, May 1985.

Role of tobacco and oral contraception in myocardial infarction in the female. Description of a case, by A. Leone, et al. PATHOLOGICA 76(1044):493-498, July-August 1984.

Surgery and the pill [editorial], by J. Guillebaud. BRITISH MEDICAL JOURNAL 291(6494):498-499, August 24, 1985.

Use of oral contraceptives in women with cystic fibrosis, by S. B. Fitzpatrick, et al. CHEST 86(6):863-867, December 1984.

WHO collaborative study of neoplasia and steroid contraceptives. BRITISH MEDICAL JOURNAL 290(6473):961-965, March 30, 1985.

Women with nongranulomatous colitis should avoid "the pill". NURSES DRUG ALERT 8(9):69, September 1984.

CONTRACEPTIVES: FEMALE: POST-COITAL
Pill that 'might defuse the abortion issue' [morning after pills], by R. Rhein, Jr., et al. BUSINESS WEEK April 1, 1985, p. 85+.

Raising a child of rape[woman sues Dr. J. Novoa because morning-after pill Estrace proves ineffective], by P. Carlson. PEOPLE WEEKLY 23:30-35, March 25, 1985.

CONTRACEPTIVES: FUNDING
Public findings of contraceptive, sterilization and abortion services, 1983 [United States], by R. B. Gold, et al. FAMILY PLANNING PERSPECTIVES 17:25-30, January-February 1985.

CONTRACEPTIVES: HISTORY
Contraceptive behavior in 1877 dispensary users. Which to use? What were the motives for their suspension?, by R. Maggi, et al. ANNALI DI OSTETRICIA GINECOLOGIA MEDICINA PERINATALE 105(1):5-13, January-February 1984.

Oral contraceptives in 1984, by E. K. Chapler. IOWA MEDICINE 74(10):439-440, October 1984.

Was Margaret Sanger a racist?, by C. Valenza. FAMILY PLANNING PERSPECTIVES 17(1):44-46, January-February 1985.

Contraception with long-acting subdermal implants. A five-year clinical trial with Silastic covered rod implants containing levonorgestrel. The International Committee for Contraception Research (ICCR) of the Population Council, by D. N. Robertson, et al. CONTRACEPTION 31(4):351-359, April 1985.

Subdermal contraceptive implants [letter], by H. J. Orford. SOUTH AFRICAN MEDICAL JOURNAL 67(3):80, January 19, 1985.

CONTRACEPTIVES: INJECTED
Case against Depo-Provera. MULTINATIONAL MONITOR 6:3-22, February-March 1985.

Comparative evaluation of contraceptive efficacy of norethisterone oenanthate (200 mg) injectable contraceptive given every two or three monthly. Indian Council of Medical Research Task Force on hormonal contraception, by S. K. Banerjee, et al. CONTRACEPTION 30(6):561-574, December 1984.

Depo-Provera: blessing or curse?, by U. Vaid. THE NATIONAL PRISON PROJECT JOURNAL 4:1+, Summer 1985.

Development of a low-dose monthly injectable contraceptive system: I. Choice of compounds, dose and administration route, by J. Garza-Flores, et al. CONTRACEPTION 30(4):371-379, October 1984.

Effectiveness of injectable contraceptives in Mexican women, by J. Garza-Flores, et al. BOLETIN DE LA OFICINA SANITARIA PAN AMERICANA 98(2):181-186, February 1985.

Injectable contraception using depot progestagens, by V. V. Murillo, et al. GINECOLOGIA Y OBSTETRICIA DE MEXICO 51(315):191-197, July 1983.

Injectable contraception, by M. G. Elder. CLINICAL OBSTETRICS AND GYNAE-COLOGY 11(3):723-741, December 1984.

Intraperitoneal bleeding from ectopic decidua following hormonal contraception. Case report, by L. C. Tang, et al. BRITISH JOURNAL OF OBSTETRICS AND GYNAECOLOGY 92(1):102-103, January 1985.

Long-term effects of Depo-Provera on carbohydrate and lipid metabolism, by D. F. Liew, et al. CONTRACEPTION 31(1):51-64, January 1985.

Panel says Depo-Provera not proved safe, by M. Sun. SCIENCE 226:950-951, November 23, 1984.

Pharmacokinetic and pharmacodynamic investigations with monthly injectable contraceptive preparations, by A. R. Aedo, et al. CONTRACEPTION 31(5):453-469, May 1985.

Public board of inquiry advises that Depo-Provera not be approved for use as contraceptive in U. S. FAMILY PLANNING PERSPECTIVES 17(1):38-39, January-February 1985.

Real and false risks of injectable hormonal contraception, by C. Revaz. GYNAKOLOGISCHE RUNDSCHAU 24(Suppl. 1):20-25, 1984.

Reduced risk of pelvic inflammatory disease with injectable contraceptives [letter], by R. H. Gray. LANCET 1(8436):1046, May 4, 1985.

Retreat on Depo-provera, by P. Prakash. ECONOMIC AND POLITICAL WEEKLY 19:2072-2073, December 8, 1984.

CONTRACEPTIVES: IUD

How IUDs cause infertility, by I. Anderson. NEW SCIENTIST 106:6, April 18, 1985.

IUD, by P. Duchesne. COMMUNIQU'ELLES 11(4):5, July 1985.

CONTRACEPTIVES: IUD: COMPLICATIONS

Dalkon Shield IUD health risk hushed, by G. Evans. SPARE RIB 156:10, July 1985.

Dalkon Shield/a very serious business, by P. Duchesne. COMMUNIO 11(4):6, July 1985.

PID associated with fertility regulating agents. Task Force on intrauterine devices, special programme of research, development and research training in human reproduction, World Health Organization. CONTRACEPTION 30(1):1-21, July 1984.

CONTRACEPTIVES: LAWS AND LEGISLATION

Abortion pill goes on trial, by N. Docherty. NEW SCIENTIST 106:5, June 20, 1985.

After a lawyer turns whistle-blower, the company that made the Dalkon Shield warns women of its dangers, by J. S. Podesta. PEOPLE WEEKLY 23:61+, January 14,1985.

Contraception and abortion of mentally handicapped female adolescents under German law, by A. Eser. MEDICINE AND LAW 4(6):499-513, 1985.

Contraceptive controversy [in British media; Law Lords decision; news]. CHRISTIAN CENTURY 102:994, November 6, 1985.

Days of our Dalkon [A. H. Robins Co., manufacturer of the Dalkon Shield, reported a deficit because of a special fund set up to deal with lawsuits by Injured women], by A. Fugh-Berman. OFF OUR BACKS 15:6, May 1985.

Demise of the trimester standard? City of Akron v. Akron Center for Reproductive Health, Inc. [103 S. Ct. 2481]. JOURNAL OF FAMILY LAW 23:267-286, February 1984.

Doctors ordered to consult parents before prescribing. College regrets appeal banon contraception for girls under 16. NURSING STANDARD 379:2, January 10,1985.

Judge biased against Robins, court says, by S. Tarnott. BUSINESS INSURANCE 18:2+, November 12, 1984.

Laws and policies affecting fertility: a decade of change. POPULATION REPORTS 12(6):105, November 1984.

Legislation on contraception and abortion for adolescents, by R.Roemer. STUDIES IN FAMILY PLANNING 16:241-251, September-October 1985.

Prescribing contraceptives for under-age-girls—the doctor's legal position, by D. Brahams. PRACTITIONER 229(1403):461-463, May 1985.

Reproduction law and medical consent, by B. M. Dickens. UNIVERSITY OF TORONTO LAW JOURNAL 35:255-286, Summer 1985.

CONTRACEPTIVES: MALE

Affecting fatherhood: a research team at the University of Western Ontario may have found a low-risk reversible male contraceptive, by S. Bars. SCIENCE DIMENSION 17(2):14-19, 1985.

AIDS. Condoms and gay abandon [letter], by C. J. Mitchell. MEDICAL JOURNAL OF AUSTRALIA 142(11):617, May 27, 1985.

Clastogenicity of a male contraceptive, gossypol, in mammalian cell cultures with and without the metabolic activation by S9 mix, by J. C. Liang, et al. ENVIRONMENTAL RESEARCH 36:138-143, February 1985.

Clinical trial of gossypol as a male contraceptive: a randomized controlled study, by G. Z. Liu. CHUNG HUA I HSUEH TSA CHIH 65(2):107-109, February 1985.

Condom a day keeps the doctor away, by J. McBeth. FAR EASTERN ECONOMIC REVIEW 126:49-50, October 11, 1984.

Contraceptive behavior in college-age males related to Fishbein model, B. M. Ewald, et al. ANS 7(3):63-69, April 1985.

Effect of oral medroxyprogesterone acetate and methyltestosterone on sexual functioning in a male contraceptive trial, by K. Doody, et al. CONTRA-CEPTION 31(1):65-70, January 1985.

Etymology of condom, by Z. P. Thundy. AMERICAN SPEECH 60:177-179, Summer 1985.

Low risk reversible [male] contraceptive tested. CANADIAN NURSE 81:15, September 1985.

Male contraception. Gonadal and adrenal functions in men treated with medroxy-progesterone, by M. Roger, et al. PATHOLOGIE BIOLOGIE 32(8):895-898, October 1984.

Male contraception—a review, by D. Donaldson. JOURNAL OF THE ROYAL SOCIETY OF HEALTH 105(3):91-98, June 1985.

(-)-Gossypol: an active male antifertility agent, by S. A. Matlin, et al. CONTRACEP-TION 31(2):141-149, February 1985.

Pharmacological basis of therapeutics: gossypol, an oral male contraceptive?, by S. M. Penningroth. JOURNAL OF THE MEDICAL SOCIETY OF NEW JERSEY 81(8):663-665, August 1984.

Predicting contraceptive behavior among university men: the role of emotions and behavioral intentions, by W. A. Fisher. JOURNAL OF APPLIED SOCIAL PSYCHOLOGY 14:104-123, March-April 1984.

Real and false risks of male contraception, by J. Belaïsch. GYNAEKOLOGISCHE RUNDSCHAU 24(Suppl. 1):43-48, 1984.

Regulation of male fertility: an immunological approach, by A. Tjokronegoro. ASIAN PACIFIC JOURNAL OF ALLERGY AND IMMUNOLOGY 1(2):161-167, December 1983.

Religious correlates of male sexual behavior and contraceptive use, by M. Young. HEALTH EDUCATION 16:20-25, August-September 1985.

Revival of the male pill, by E. Fogg. NEW SCIENTIST 104:25, December 20-27, 1984.

Sex supplies: Calgary's free condom shop starts charging, by T. Fennell. ALBERTA REPORT 11:41, November 5, 1984.

Transient reduction in serum HDL-cholesterol following medroxyprogesterone acetate and testosterone cypionate administration to healthy men, by K. E. Friedl, et al. CONTRACEPTION 31(4):409-420, April 1985.

Trojan horse goes to court: Bolger v. Youngs Drug Products Corp., by M. Mason. AMERICAN JOURNAL OF LAW AND MEDICINE 10(2):203-227, Summer 1984.

Women buy most condoms to avoid pregnancy, VD. JET 69:26, October 14, 1985.

CONTRACEPTIVES: MALE: BARRIER
Condom spots stun Spanish, by M. Specht. ADVERTISING AGE 55:3+, October 4, 1984.

In vitro and in vivo evaluation of latex condoms using a two-phase nonoxynol 9 system, by N. Rodgers-Neame, et al. FERTILITY AND STERILITY 43(6):931-936, June 1985.

CONTRACEPTIVES: METHODS
Acceptance of effective contraceptive methods after induced abortion, by A. Bulut. STUDIES IN FAMILY PLANNING 15:281-284, November-December 1984.

Antifertility effect of citrus hystrix DC, by P. Piyachaturawat, et al. JOURNAL OF ETHNOPHARMACOLOGY 13(1):105-110, March 1985.

Basic considerations in the choice of contraceptive methods for male and female, by J. Hammerstein. GYNAKOLOGE 17(3):156-174, September 1984.

Classic methods of contraception, by G. A. Hauser. GYNAKOLOGE 17(3):194-199, September 1984.

Comparative clinical trial of the contraceptive sponge and Neo Sampoon tablets, by E.Borko, et al. OBSTETRICS AND GYNECOLOGY 65(4):511-515, April 1985.

Comparing contraceptives, by J. Willis. FDA CONSUMER 19:28-35, May 1985.

Contraception consultation. Choice of contraception method, by J. C. Guillat. SOINS, GYNECOLOGIE, OBSTETRIQUE, PUERICULTURE, PEDIATRIE (14-15):29-31, July-August 1982.

Contraception with subdermal ST-1435 capsules: side-effects, endocrine profiles and liver function related to different lengths of capsules, by H. Kurunmäki, et al. CONTRACEPTION 31(3):305-318, March 1985.

Effect of marital dissolution on contraceptive protection, by L. Bumpass, et al. FAMILY PLANNING PERSPECTIVES 16:271-284, November-December 1984.

Effect of a new contraceptive ring releasing 20 micrograms levonorgestrel daily on blood lipid levels and glucose tolerance, by M. G. Elder, et al. CONTRA-CEPTION 30(1):55-60, July 1984.

Hormonal contraceptive methods, by J. McEwan. PRACTITIONER 229(1403): 415-423, May 1985.

Influence of sexual level of knowledge in contraceptive devices and venereal diseases on pelvic infections, by M. Shiloach. AHOT BE YISRAEL 39(124):9-12, June 1984.

Inhibiting effect of artificial cryptorchidism on spermatogenesis, by R. Mieusset, et al. FERTILITY AND STERILITY 43(4):589-594, April 1985.

Investigations on Dierrenbachia amoena Gentil. I: Endocrine effects and contraceptive activity, by R. Costa de Pasquale, et al. JOURNAL OF ETHNOPHARMACOLOGY 12(3):293-303, December 1984.

—. II: Use of compounds of the muramyl dipeptide (MDP) family as adjuvants, by H. A. Nash, et al. JOURNAL OF REPRODUCTIVE IMMUNOLOGY 7(2):151-162, February 1985.

—. III. Evaluation of various vehicles and adjuvants, by C. C. Chang, et al. JOUR-NAL OF REPRODUCTIVE IMMUNOLOGY 7(2):163-169, February 1985.

Microbiological and histological findings in the fallopian tubes of women using various contraceptive methods, by J. A. Collins, et al. CONTRACEPTION 30(5):457-466, November 1984.

On pills, IUDs and condoms, by S. Evangelista. BALAI 11:21, 1985.

Regulation of fertility by means of vaginal rings medicated with estradiol and levonorgestrel, by S. Diaz, et al. REVISTA CHILENA DE OBSTETRICIA Y GINECOLOGIA 47(4):266-273, 1982.

Relationship between contraceptive method and vaginal flora, by B. A. Peddie, et al. AUSTRALIAN AND NEW ZEALAND JOURNAL OF OBSTETRICS AND GYNAECOLOGY 24(3):217-218, August 1984.

Spermicides and birth defects: no clear link, by M. Engel. GLAMOUR 83:160, August 1985.

Subcutaneous implantation of gestagens. A new alternative for safe contraception, by V. Odlind, et al. LAKARTIDNINGEN 81(39):3494-3496, September 26, 1984.

Valued outcomes in the selection of a contraceptive method, by E. M. Wall. WESTERN JOURNAL OF MEDICINE 141(3):335-338, September 1984.

CONTRACEPTIVES: NURSES AND NURSING
Royal College of Nursing. Retrograde step. NURSING STANDARD (383):4, February 7, 1985.

CONTRACEPTIVES: ORAL
Idolized pill: a pill to be gilded . . . or resistance to oral contraception, by M. Debout. PSYCHOLOGIE MEDICALE 14(8):1173-1179, June 1982.

Oral contraceptives in 1984, by E. K. Chapler. IOWA MEDICINE 74(10):439-440, October 1984.

Placing of antifertility drugs in food supplies: one answer to our global population crisis?, by S. Lesse. AMERICAN JOURNAL OF PSYCHOTHERAPY 39(2):155-158, April 1985.

Relation between Trichomonas vaginalis and contraceptive measures, by H. A. el-Boulaqi, et al. JOURNAL OF THE EGYPTIAN SOCIETY OF PARASITOLOGY 14(2):495-499, December 1984.

CONTRACEPTIVES: ORAL: COMPLICATIONS
Effects of a combination of cigarette smoking and oral contraception on coagulation and fibrinolysis in human females, by J. Harenberg, et al. KLINISCHE WOCHENSCHRIFT 63(5):221-224, March 1, 1985.

Oral contraceptives, lipids and cardiovascular disease, by K. Fotherby. CONTRACEPTION 31(4):367-394, April 1985.

CONTRACEPTIVES: POSTCOITAL
Comparison of high-dose estrogens versus low-dose ethinylestradiol and norgestrel combination in postcoital interception: a study in 493 women, by M. R. Van Santen, et al. FERTILITY AND STERILIZATION 43(2):206-213, February 1985.

Contraception—the morning after. FAMILY PLANNING PERSPECTIVES 16:266-270, November-December 1984.

Contraception the 'morning after.' A too little used opportunity, by C. Schumann. FORTSCHRITTE DER MEDIZIN 102(33):807-810, September 6, 1984.

Effect of postcoital oestradiol treatment upon transport, growth, differentiation and viability of preimplantation mouse embryos, by L. S. Roblero, et al. ARCHIVOS DE BIOLOGIA Y MEDICINA EXPERIMENTALES 16(1):55-59, August 1983.

Effect of a single midcycle administration of 0.5 or 2.0 mg dienogest (17 alpha-cyanomethyl-17beta-hydroxy-estra-4,9-dien-3-one) on pituitary and ovarian function—investigation for the use as a postcoital contraceptive, by G. Köhler, et al. EXPERIMENTAL AND CLINICAL ENDOCRINOLOGY 84(3):299-304, December 1984.

Interception II: postcoital low-dose estrogens and norgestrel combination in 633 women, by M. R. Van Santen, et al. CONTRACEPTION 31(3):275-293, March 1985.

Pill that might defuse the abortion issue [morning-after pills], by R. Rhein, Jr., et al. BUSINESS WEEK April 1, 1985, p. 85+.Pill/25 years of uncertainty, by P. Duchesne. COMMUNIQU'ELLES 11(4):6, July 1985.

Post-coital birth control family planning. OFF OUR BACKS 15(2):7, February 1985.

Post-coital contraception, by P. D. Bromwich. PRACTITIONER 229(1403):427-429, May 1985.

Postcoital pill, by E. Weisberg. HEALTHRIGHT 4:17-19, August 1985.

Study of the intravaginal insert (IVI): acceptability, side effects, and post-coital spermicidal activity, by M. Ahmad, et al. ACTA EUROPAEA FERTILITATIS 15(5):369-376, September-October 1984.

CONTRACEPTIVES: PSYCHOLOGY AND PSYCHIATRY
Antecedents and prevention of unwanted pregnancy, by M. Gerrard, et al. ISSUES IN MENTAL HEALTH NURSING 5(1/4):85-101, 1983.

Aspects of the choice of contraceptives after legal abortion in relation to psychological masculinity: femininity and psychosocial functions, by L. Jacobsson, et al. JOURNAL OF PSYCHOSOMATIC OBSTETRICS AND GYNAECOLOGY 3(1):53-58, May 1984.

Bankruptcy of contraception?, by F. P. Wibaut. NEDERLANDS TIJDSCHRIFT VOOR GENEESKUNDE 128(50):2349-2353, December 15, 1984.

Breastfeeding and contraception: why the inverse association?, by S. Millman. STUDIES IN FAMILY PLANNING 16(2):61-75, March-April 1985.

Comparison of three social-psychological models of attitude and behavioral plan: prediction of contraceptive behavior, by M. D. Pagel, et al. JOURNAL OF PERSONALITY AND SOCIAL PSYCHOLOGY 47:517-533, September 1984.

Contraceptive practices and reproductive patterns in sickle cell disease, by J. H. Samuels-Reid, et al. JOURNAL OF THE NATIONAL MEDICAL ASSOCIATION 76(9):879-883, September 1984.

Depression and self-blame [women who use contraception and become pregnant anyway], by C. Turkington. PSYCHOLOGY TODAY 18:18, December 1984.

Impacts of behavioral intentions, social support, and accessibility on contraception: a cross-cultural study, by S. Kar, et al. POPULATION AND ENVIRONMENT 7(1):17-31, Spring 1984.

Influence of client-provider relationships on teenage women's subsequent use of contraception, by C. A. Nathanson, et al. AMERICAN JOURNAL OF PUBLIC HEALTH 75(1):33-38, January 1985.

Oral contraception and serious psychiatric illness: absence of an association, by M. P. Vessey, et al. BRITISH JOURNAL OF PSYCHIATRY 146:45-49, January 1985.

Premarital contraceptive use: a discriminant analysis approach, by A. R. Sack, et al. ARCHIVES OF SEXUAL BEHAVIOR 14(2):165-182, April 1985.

Psychosexual problems, by P. Tunnadine. PRACTITIONER 229(1403):453-455+, May 1985.

Psychosocial and psychosexual aspects of contraception, by M. Guay. INFIRMIERE CANADIENNE 27(1):23-26, January 1985.

Psychosomatic complications of contraception, by P. Cepicky, et al. CESKO-SLOVENSKA GYNEKOLOGIE 49(10):758-759, December 1984.

CONTRACEPTIVES: RESEARCH

Absence of histopathology in somatic tissues of rats made infertile with gossypol, by S. J. Engler, et al. ARCHIVES OF ANDROLOGY 13(1):93-100.

Affecting fatherhood: a research team at the University of Western Ontario may have found a low-risk reversible male contraceptive, by S. Bars. SCIENCE DIMENSION 17(2):14-19, 1985.

Alteration of convulsive threshold and conditioned avoidance response in mice fed diets containing contraceptive steroids, by H. C. Yen-Koo, et al. DRUG AND CHEMICAL TOXICOLOGY 7(6):541-549, 1984.

Chromosome analysis of female baboons following treatment with STS 557 and levonorgestrel, by J. Strecke, et al. ZENTRALBLATT FUR GYNAEKOLOGIE 107(5):304-307, 1985.

Combined contraceptives in experimental liver damage, by A. Kulcsár, et al. ACTA PHARMACEUTICA HUNGARICA 54(6):272-279, November 1984.

Contraception research lagging [news], by C. Holden. SCIENCE 229(4718): 1066, September 13, 1985.

Contraceptive update, by H. Pengelley. PROTECT YOURSELF August 1985, p. 50-57.

Current trends in antifertility vaccine research, by D. C. Covey, et al. WESTERN JOURNAL OF MEDICINE 142(2):197-202, February 1985.

Effect of aspirin containing silastic implants placed adjacent to epididymis on fertility of rats, by W. D. Ratnasooriya, et al. INDIAN JOURNAL OF EXPERIMENTAL BIOLOGY 22(2):75-77, February 1984.

Effect of continuous local microdose norethisterone enanthate on the epididymis of adult rat, by U. K. Srivastava. ANDROLOGIA 15(4):333-338, July-August 1983.

Effect of gossypol on macromolecular synthesis in rat testis. An in vitro study, by P. Kainz, et al. CONTRACEPTION 31(2):151-158, February 1985.

Effect of oral contraceptives in malaria infections in rhesus monkey, by W. E. Collins, et al. WHO BULLETIN 62(4):627-637, 1984.

Effects of the ovarian and contraceptive cycles on absolute thresholds, auditory fatigue and recovery from temporary threshold shifts at 4 and 6 kHz, by J.-C. Petiot, et al. AUDIOLOGY 23(6):581-598, November-December 1984.

Fertility control in the bitch by active immunization with porcine zonae pellucidae: use of different adjuvants and patterns of estradiol and progesterone levels in estrous cycles, by C. A. Mahi-Brown, et al. BIOLOGY OF REPRODUCTION 32(4):761-772, May 1985.

Formulation of a potential antipregnancy vaccine based on the beta-subunit of human chorionic gonadotropin (beta-hCG). I. Alternative macromolecular carriers, by Y. Y. Tsong, et al. JOURNAL OF REPRODUCTIVE IMMUNOLOGY 7(2):139-149, February 1985.

Germ cell survival, differentiation, and epididymal transit kinetics in mouse testis subjected to high in vivo levels of testosterone enanthate, by R. B. Goldberg. CELL AND TISSUE RESEARCH 237(2):337-342, 1984.

Gossypol in female fertility control: ovum implantation and early pregnancy Inhibited in rats, by Y. C. Lin, et al. LIFE SCIENCES 37(1):39-47, July 8, 1985.

Influence of cigarette smoke and treatment with contraceptive hormones on the fibrinolytic activity in the rat, by A. Kjaeldgaard, et al. THROMBOSIS RESEARCH 36(6):571-578, December 15, 1984.

Inhibition by gossypol of testosterone production by mouse Leydig cells in vitro, by A. Donaldson, et al. CONTRACEPTION 31(2):165-171, February 1985.

Inhibition of luteal phase progesterone levels in the rhesus monkey by epostane, by B. W. Snyder, et al. CONTRACEPTION 31(5):479-486, May 1985.

Intestinal absorption of ST-1435 in rats, by P. L. Lähteenmäki. CONTRACEP-TION 30(2):143-151, August 1984.

Marvelon—an OC with a new progestagen. DRUG AND THERAPEUTICS BULLETIN 22(18):69-70, September 1984.

Migraine drug could be a new contraceptive, by L. Veltman. NEW SCIENTIST 105: 22, March 7, 1985.

New class of non-hormonal contragestational agents: pharmacodynamic-pharmacokinetic relationships, by A. Assandri, et al. QUARTERLY REVIEWS ON DRUG METABOLISM AND DRUG INTERACTIONS 4(2-3):237-261, 1982.

Non-hormonal methods of contraception in diabetic women. Reliability, risks, pre-cautions, surveillance, by D. Buchsenschutz. JOURNEES ANNUELLES DE DIABETOLOGIE DE L'HOTEL-DIEU 1983, p. 239-252.

On the immunogenicity of the beta subunit of ovine luteinizing hormone (oLH beta) and equine chorionic gonadotropin (eCG) in the chimpanzee (Pan troglodytes): effect of antiserum on monkey cycle and early pregnancy, by N.

R. Moudgal, et al. AMERICAN JOURNAL OF REPRODUCTIVE IMMUNOLO-GY AND MICROBIOLOGY 8(4):120-124, August 1985.

Pharmacokenetic observations on ST-1435 administered subcutaneously and Intravaginally, by P. L. Lähteenmäki, et al. CONTRACEPTION 30(4):381-389, October 1984.

PID associated with fertility regulating agents. Task Force on intrauterine devices, special programme of research, development and research training in human reproduction, World Health Organization. CONTRACEPTION 30(1):1-21, July 1984.

Renin-angiotensin mechanisms in oral contraceptive hypertension in conscious rats, by W. L. Fowler, Jr., et al. AMERICAN JOURNAL F PHYSIOLOGY 248(5 Pt 2):H695-699, May 1985.

Sexual reformation and counterreformation in law and medicine, by J. Money. MEDICINE AND LAW 4(5):479-488, 1985.

Tomorrow's contraception, by C. C. Standley, et al. REVUE DE'L'INFIRMIERE 35(4):16-19, February 1985.

Unscheduled DNA synthesis caused by norethindrone and related contraceptive steroids in short-term male rat hepatocyte cultures, by D. C. Blakey, et al. CARCINOGENESIS 6(8):1201-1205, August 1985.

Vaginal contraceptive activity of hyaluronidase and cyclooxygenase (prosta-glandin synthetase) inhibitors in the rabbit, by C. L. Joyce, et al. FERTILITY AND STERILITY 44(3):426-428, September 1985.

CONTRACEPTIVES: SOCIOLOGY
Socio-economic correlates of fertility and contraceptive practices amongst target couples of a rural community, by M. Bhattacharya, et al. INDIAN JOURNAL OF PUBLIC HEALTH 28(3):139-146, July--September 1984.

CONTRACEPTIVES: STATISTICS
Continuation and effectiveness of contraceptive practice: a cross-sectional approach, by J. E. Laing. STUDIES IN FAMILY PLANNING 16(3):138-153, May-June 1985.

Contraceptive trends [editorial], by K. Wellings, et al. BRITISH MEDICAL JOURNAL 289(6450):939-940, October 13, 1984.

Contraceptive usage during lactation: analysis of 1973 and 1976 national survey of family growth: age and race, by M. Labbok, et al. AMERICAN JOURNAL OF PUBLIC HEALTH 75:75-77, January 1985.

Contraceptive use, pregnancy and fertility patterns among single American women in their 20s, by K. Tanfer, et al. FAMILY PLANNING PERSPECTIVES 17(1):10-19, January-February 1985.

Gallup poll shows Americans are mistaken about contraceptives. AMERICAN FAMILY PHYSICIAN 31:18, April 1985.

Royal College of General Practitioners' oral contraception study: some recent observations, by C. R. Kay. CLINICAL OBSTETRICS AND GYNAECOLOGY 11(3):759-786, December 1984.

Understanding U.S. fertility: findings from the National Survey of Family Growth, Cycle III, by W. F. Pratt, et al. POPULATION BULLETIN 39:1-40, December 1984.

CONTRACEPTIVES AND BREASTFEEDING

Contraceptive usage during lactation: analysis of 1973 and 1976 national survey of family growth: age and race, by M. Labbok, et al. AMERICAN JOURNAL OF PUBLIC HEALTH 75:75-77, January 1985.

Contraceptive use during lactation in developing countries, by A. R. Pebley, et al. STUDIES IN FAMILY PLANNING 16(1):40-51, January-February 1985.

CONTRACEPTIVES AND COLLEGE STUDENTS

Beliefs, attitudes, intentions and contraceptive behavior of college students, by D. McLittle. DAI: HUMANITIES AND SOCIAL SCIENCES 45(7), January 1985.

Contraceptive behavior in college-age males related to Fishbein model, by B. M. Ewald, et al. ANS 7(3):63-69, April 1985.

Health belief model and the contraceptive behavior of college women: implications for health education, by N. R. Hester, et al. JOURNAL OF AMERICAN COLLEGE HEALTH 33:245-252, June 1985.

Predicting contraceptive behavior among university men: the role of emotions and behavioral intentions, by W. A. Fisher. JOURNAL OF APPLIED SOCIAL PSYCHOLOGY 14:104-123, March-April 1984.

CONTRACEPTIVES AND ECONOMICS

Cross-country study of commercial contraceptive sales programs: factors that lead to success, by M. S. Boone, et al. STUDIES IN FAMILY PLANNING 16(1):30-39, January-February 1985.

CONTRACEPTIVES AND HORMONES

Comparison of high-dose estrogens versus low-dose ethinylestradiol and norgestrel combination in postcoital interception: a study in 493 women, by M. R. Van Santen, et al. FERTILITY AND STERILIZATION 43(2):206-213, February 1985.

Contraceptive efficacy and hormonal profile of ferujoi: a new coumarin from Ferula jaeschkeana, by M. M. Singh, et al. PLANTA MEDICA 3:268-270, June 1985.

Estrogen-progestogen agents and megaloblastic anemia, by D. Mottier, et al. JOURNAL DE GYNECOLOGIE, OBSTETRIQUE ET BIOLOGIE DE LA REPRODUCTION 13(6):707-710, 1984.

Estrogen treatment for victims of rape [letter]. NEW ENGLAND JOURNAL OF MEDICINE 312(15):988-989, April 11, 1985.

Exogenous hormone use and fibrocystic breast disease by histopathologic component, by G. S. Berkowitz, et al. INTERNATIONAL JOURNAL OF CANCER 34(4): 443-449, October 15, 1984.

Germ cell survival, differentiation, and epididymal transit kinetics in mouse testis subjected to high in vivo levels of testosterone enanthate, by R. B. Goldberg. CELL AND TISSUE RESEARCH 237(2):337-342, 1984.

Hormonal contraception and IUDs in adolescents, by M. Mall-Haefeli. FORT-SCHRITTE DER MEDIZIN 102(33):823-824, September 6, 1984.

Hormonal contraceptive methods, by J. McEwan. PRACTITIONER 229(1403): 415-423, May 1985.

Immediate postabortal contraception with Norplant: levonorgestrel, gonado-tropin, estradiol, and progesterone levels over two postabortal months and return of fertility after removal of Norplant capsules, by H. Kurunmäki, et al. CONTRACEPTION 30(5):431-442, November 1984.

Immunogenicity of synthetic sex hormones and thrombogenesis, by V. Beaumont, et al. PATHOLOGIE BIOLOGIE 33(4):245-249, April 1985.

Intraperitoneal bleeding from ectopic decidua following hormonal contraception. Case report, by L. C. Tang, et al. BRITISH JOURNAL OF OBSTETRICS AND GYNAECOLOGY 92(1):102-103, January 1985.

Luteinizing hormone releasing hormone analogues for contraception, by S. J. Nillius. CLINICAL OBSTETRICS AND GYNECOLOGY 11(3):551-572, December 1984.

Metabolic and vascular consequences of hormonal contraception in non-diabetics, by A. Basdevant, et al. JOURNEES ANNUELLES DE DIABETOLOGIE DE L'HOTEL DIEU 1983, p. 223-237.

New look at progestogens, by K. Fotherby. CLINICAL OBSTETRICS AND GYNAECOLOGY 11(3):701-722, December 1984.

Post-coital contraception with estrogens. Mechanism of action, results and sequelae in a caseload of 123 cases, by F. Monasterolo. MINERVA GINECOLOGIA 36(7-8):451-454, July-August 1984.

Real and false risks of injectable hormonal contraception, by C. Revaz. GYNAKOLOGISCHE RUNDSCHAU 24(Suppl. 1):20-25, 1984.

Regulation of fertility by means of vaginal rings medicated with estradiol and levonorgestrel, by S. Diaz, et al. REVISTA CHILENA DE OBSTETRICIA Y GINECOLOGIA 47(4):266-273, 1982.

Relationship of estrogen and progesterone to breast disease, by P. G. Brooks. JOURNAL OF REPRODUCTIVE MEDICINE 29(Suppl. 7):530-538, July 1984.

Synthetic gestagens and endocervical adenocarcinoma [letter], by G. Dallenbach-Hellweg. INTERNATIONAL JOURNAL OF GYNECOLOGY AND PATHOLOGY 3(2):241, 1984.

Contraception and voluntary pregnancy interruption in public hospital establish-ments. Circular DGS/2A No. 12-82 of 12 October 1982, by J. Latrille. SOINS, GYNECOLOGIE, OBSTETRIQUE, PUERICULTURE, PEDIATRIE (27-28):61-64, August-September 1983.

CONTRACEPTIVES AND MALES
Adolescent contraceptive use and pregnancy: the role of the male partner, by P. E. Abrons. DAI: SCIENCES AND ENGINEERING 45(12), June 1985.

CONTRACEPTIVES AND THE MENTALLY RETARDED
Contraception and abortion of mentally handicapped female adolescents under German law, by A. Eser. MEDICINE AND LAW 4(6):499-513, 1985.

CONTRACEPTIVES AND PARENTAL CONSENT
Mandatory parental involvement in contraceptive services for minors, by K. H. Gould. SOCIAL WORK IN EDUCATION 7(1):7-12, 1984.

Right of privacy and minors' confidential access to contraceptives, by S. Ebers. NEW YORK LAW SCHOOL HUMAN RIGHTS ANNUAL 2:131-149, Fall 1984.

Teenage confidence and consent. BRITISH MEDICAL JOURNAL 290(6462): 144-145, January 12, 1985.

CONTRACEPTIVES AND PHYSICIANS
Doctor and the underage girl [contraception; from our British correspondent, by K. Slack. CHRISTIAN CENTURY 102:174-176, February 20, 1985.

Grappling with the population programme, by A. Maranan. BALAI 11:22, 1985.

Magazine versus physicians: the influence of information source on intentions to use oral contraceptives, by D. F. Halpern, et al. WOMEN AND HEALTH 1 0(1):9-23, Spring 1985.

Response of patients and doctors to the 1983 'pill scare', by L. D. Ritchie, et al. JOURNAL OF THE ROYAL COLLEGE OF GENERAL PRACTITIONERS 34(268):600-602, November 1984.

CONTRACEPTIVES AND POLITICS
Black fertility patterns—Cape Town and Ciskei, by M. Roberts, et al. SOUTH AFRICAN MEDICAL JOURNAL 66(13):481-484, September 29, 1984.

CONTRACEPTIVES AND RELIGION
Contraception and religiousness in a general practice population in Israel, by A. Sandiuk, et al. FAMILY PRACTICE 1(1):37-41, March 1984.

Contraceptive use among Mormons, 1965-1975, by B. Heaton, et al. DIALOGUE 16(3):106-109, 1983.

Factors in adolescent contraceptive use . . . knowledge, self-esteem and religiosity, by K. G. Kellinger. NURSE PRACTITIONER 10(9):55+, September 1985.

Religious correlates of male sexual behavior and contraceptive use, by M. Young. HEALTH EDUCATION 16:20-25, August-September 1985.

Social class, religion and contraceptive failure in a sample of pregnant women in Brisbane, by J. M. Najman, et al. COMMUNITY HEALTH STUDIES 8(3):323-331, 1984.

CONTRACEPTIVES AND SPORTS

Gonadal steroids in athletic women contraception, complications and performance, by J. C. Prior, et al. SPORTS MEDICINE 2(4):287-295, July-August 1985.

CONTRACEPTIVES AND VITAMINS

Effects of oral contraceptives on vitamins B6, B12, C, and folacin, by K. S. Veninga. JOURNAL OF NURSE-MIDWIFERY 29(6):386-390, November-December 1984.

CONTRACEPTIVES AND WEIGHT CONTROL

Effects of oral contraceptives and obesity on protein C antigen, by T. W. Meade, et al. THROMBOSIS AND HAEMOSTASIS 53(2):198-199, April 22, 1985.

CONTRACEPTIVES AND WOMEN

Foreign travel alert for women on the pill. GLAMOUR 83:51, June 1985.

Guide to contraceptive choices for women with disabilities. RESOURCES FOR FEMINIST RESEARCH 14:106-108, March 1985.

Gynaecology of middle-aged women—menstrual and reproductive histories, by A. Hagstad, et al. MATURITAS 7(2):99-113, July 1985.

Laparoscopic findings and contraceptive use in women with signs and symptoms suggestive of acute salpingitis, by P. Wølner-Hanssen, et al. OBSTETRICS AND GYNECOLOGY 66(2):233-238, August 1985.

Microbiological and histological findings in the fallopian tubes of women using various contraceptive methods, by J. A. Collins, et al. CONTRACEPTION 30(5):457-466, November 1984.

CONTRACEPTIVES AND YOUTH

Adolescent contraception: factors to consider before you prescribe, by L. B. Tyrer, et al. CONSULTANT 25(10):75-79+, July 1985.

Adolescent contraceptive use and pregnancy: the role of the male partner, by P. E. Abrons. DAI: SCIENCES AND ENGINEERING 45(12), June 1985.

Adolescents' values, sexuality, and contraception in a rural New York county, by N. McCormick, et al. ADOLESCENCE 20:385-395, Summer 1985.

Age variation in use of a contraceptive service by adolescents, by S. G. Philliber, et al. PUBLIC HEALTH REPORTS 100:34-40, January-February 1985.

Communication and contraceptive practices in adolescent couples, by P. O'Hara. ADOLESCENCE 20:33-43, September 1985.

Contraception and abortion of mentally handicapped female adolescents under German law, by A. Eser. MEDICINE AND LAW 4(6):499-513, 1985.

Contraception for the adolescent, by R. B. Shearin, et al. POSTGRADUATE MEDICINE 78(3):209-211+, September 1, 1985.

Contraception in adolescents, by G. Freund. FORTSCHRITTE DER MEDIZIN 103(22):610-612, June 13, 1985.

Contraceptive decision-making in urban, black female adolescents: its relationship to cognitive development, by B. Sachs. INTERNATIONAL JOURNAL OF NURSING STUDIES 22(2):117-126, 1985.

Contraceptive knowledge of 14 to 17-year-old students of a suburban district, by I. Mehlan, et al. ZEITSCHRIFT FUR AERZTLICHE FORTBILDUNG 79(5):205-207,1985.

Contraceptive method switching among American female adolescents, 1979, by M. B. Hirsch, et al. JOURNAL OF ADOLESCENT HEALTH CARE 6(1):1-7, January 1985.

Contraceptive risktaking among never-married youth, by S. Krishnamoorthy, et al. AUSTRALIAN JOURNAL OF SEX, MARRIAGE AND FAMILY 4(3):151-157, August 1983.

Contraceptive risk-taking behavior among young women: an investigation of psycho-social variables, by M. A. Gutman. DAI: SCIENCES AND ENGINEER-ING 46(6), December 1986.

Contraceptive use, pregnancy and fertility patterns among single American women in their 20s, by K. Tanfer, et al. FAMILY PLANNING PERSPECTIVES 17(1):10-19, January-February 1985.

Doctors ordered to consult parents before prescribing. College regrets appeal banon contraception for girls under 16. NURSING STANDARD 379:2, January 10,1985.

Double standard [bombings, Planned Parenthood offices, abortion clinics; editorial], by B. C. Harris. WITNESS 68(2):16, February 1985.

Factors in adolescent contraceptive use . . . knowledge, self-esteem and religiosity, by K. G. Kellinger. NURSE PRACTITIONER 10(9):55+, September 1985.

Fertility of couples following cessation of contraception, by N. Spira, et al. JOURNAL OF BIOSOCIAL SCIENCE 17(3):281-290, July 1985.

Hormonal contraception and IUDs in adolescents, by M. Mall-Haefeli. FORT-SCHRITTE DER MEDIZIN 102(33):823-824, September 6, 1984.

Influence of client-provider relationships on teenage women's subsequent use of contraception, by C. A. Nathanson, et al. AMERICAN JOURNAL OF PUBLIC HEALTH 75(1):33-38, January 1985.

Know thyself—adolescents self-asessment of compliance behavior, by I. F. Litt. PEDIATRICS 75(4):693-696, April 1985.

Mandatory parental involvement in contraceptive services for minors, by K. H. Gould. SOCIAL WORK IN EDUCATION 7(1):7-12, 1984.

Oral contraception for the adolescent, by L. B. Tyrer. JOURNAL OF REPRO-DUCTIVE MEDICINE 29(Suppl. 7):551-559, July 1984.

Prescribing contraceptives for under-age-girls—the doctor's legal position, by D. Brahams. PRACTITIONER 229(1403):461-463, May 1985.

Survey of attitudes concerning contraception and the resolution of teenage pregnancy, by C. Rinck, et al. ADOLESCENCE 18(72):923-929, Winter 1983.

Teenage confidence and consent. BRITISH MEDICAL JOURNAL 290(6462): 144-145, January 12, 1985.

Teens just want to have fun?, by K. Mitchell. PEDIATRIC NURSING 11(4):256+, July-August 1985.

Time for new thinking about teenage pregnancy . . . young women may want and need more direct personal guidance about contraception, by J. G. Dryfoos. AMERICAN JOURNAL OF PUBLIC HEALTH 75(1):13-14, January 1985.

Underage girl: a surprising judgment, by K. Slack. CHRISTIAN CENTURY 102: 1054-1056, November 20, 1985.

Who's to blame: adolescent sexual activity, by R. Kornfield. JOURNAL OF ADOLESCENT HEALTH CARE 8:17-31, March 1985.

FAMILY PLANNING: GENERAL
Achieving expected parities: a reanalysis of Freedman, et al's data, 1962-1977, by D. M. Sloane, et al. DEMOGRAPHY 21(3):413-422, August 1984.

Breast-feeding, birth spacing and pregnancy care: prevalence and outcome, by R. P. Bernard, et al. JOURNAL OF TROPICAL PEDIATRICS 30(5):279-286, October 1984.

CNA position on family planning. CANADIAN NURSE 80:8, December 1984.

Contraceptive use and efficacy in a genetically counseled population, by D. C. Wertz, et al. SOCIAL BIOLOGY 30:328-334, August 1983.

Crucial new direction for international family planning, by F. P. Hosken. HUMANIST 44:5-8+, January-February 1984.

Educating for marriage and responsible parenthood in the field of health care, by J. Dunovsky. CASOPIS LEKARU CESKYCH 124(10):289-292, March 1985.

Effect of marital dissolution on contraceptive protection, by L. Bumpass, et al. FAMILY PLANNING PERSPECTIVES 16:271-284, November-December 1984.

Elevating ambulatory record systems: a case study, by L. Brooks. TOPICS IN HEALTH RECORD MANAGEMENT 5(3):47-50, March 1985.

Ethnicity, locus of control for family planning, and pregnancy counselor credibility, by D. R. Atkinson, et al. JOURNAL OF COUNSELING PSYCHOLOGY 32:417-421, July 1985.

Family planning and culture, by B. Qureshi. JOURNAL OF THE ROYAL SOCIETY OF HEALTH 105(1):11-14, February 1985.

Family planning experience. POPULI 2(1):36, 1984.

Family planning: general practice and clinic services, by S. Rowlands. JOURNAL OF THE ROYAL COLLEGE OF GENERAL PRACTITIONERS 35(273):199-200, April 1985.

Family planning: the global challenge, by J. A. Loraine. PRACTITIONER 229(1403):407-412, May 1985.

Family planning in the service of human development, by H. Mahler. WHO CHRONICLE 38(6):239-242, 1984.

Family planning performance at a major hospital in Sri Lanka, by S. Tennakoon. CEYLON MEDICAL JOURNAL 28(4):233-238, December 1983.

Further reflections on changes in fertility expectations and preferences, by A. D. Thornton, et al. DEMOGRAPHY 21(3):423-429, August 1984.

Gender slap, by J. Lukomnik. HEALTH PAC BULLETIN 15(4):11, July 1984.

Generation of one-child families? FUTURIST 19:49-50, June 1985.

Global prospects, by Brown, et al. NOT MAN APART 15(3):12, March 1985.

Grappling with the population programme, by A. Maranan. BALAI 11:22, 1985.

Health education and beyond: a Soviet women's group experience, by M. Coughlin, et al. JOURNAL OF JEWISH COMMUNAL SERVICE 60(1):65-69, 1983.

Impact of family planning service in rural Yangoru, by P. Roscoe. PAPUA NEW GUINEA MEDICAL JOURNAL 27(1):16-19, March 1984.

Impact of PKU on the reproductive patterns in collaborative study families, by J. K. Burns, et al. AMERICAN JOURNAL OF MEDICAL GENETICS 19(3):515-524, November 1984.

Late infertile days in early postpartum cycles, by L. I. Hatherley. CLINICAL REPRODUCTION AND FERTILITY 3(1):73-80, March 1985.

Mrs Gillick and the Wisbech Area Health Authority, by J. Griffiths. BRISTOL MEDICO-CHIRURGICAL JOURNAL 100(374):37, April 1985.

Myth of the month. HEALTH 17:82, February 1985.

No one is realistic about family planning, by Y. A. Eraj. INTERNATIONAL NURSING REVIEW 31(6):179, November-December 1984.

Oxford-Family Planning Association contraceptive study, by M. P. Vessey, et al. CLINICAL OBSTETRICS AND GYNAECOLOGY 11(3):743-757, December 1984.

Population control: no-women decide, by A. Henry. OFF OUR BACKS 14(9):2, October 1984.

229

Family planning experience. POPULI 2(1):36, 1984.

Family planning: general practice and clinic services, by S. Rowlands. JOURNAL OF THE ROYAL COLLEGE OF GENERAL PRACTITIONERS 35(273):199-200, April 1985.

Family planning: the global challenge, by J. A. Loraine. PRACTITIONER 229(1403):407-412, May 1985.

Family planning in the service of human development, by H. Mahler. WHO CHRONICLE 38(6):239-242, 1984.

Family planning performance at a major hospital in Sri Lanka, by S. Tennakoon. CEYLON MEDICAL JOURNAL 28(4):233-238, December 1983.

Further reflections on changes in fertility expectations and preferences, by A. D. Thornton, et al. DEMOGRAPHY 21(3):423-429, August 1984.

Gender slap, by J. Lukomnik. HEALTH PAC BULLETIN 15(4):11, July 1984.

Generation of one-child families? FUTURIST 19:49-50, June 1985.

Global prospects, by Brown, et al. NOT MAN APART 15(3):12, March 1985.

Grappling with the population programme, by A. Maranan. BALAI 11:22, 1985.

Health education and beyond: a Soviet women's group experience, by M. Coughlin, et al. JOURNAL OF JEWISH COMMUNAL SERVICE 60(1):65-69, 1983.

Impact of family planning service in rural Yangoru, by P. Roscoe. PAPUA NEW GUINEA MEDICAL JOURNAL 27(1):16-19, March 1984.

Impact of PKU on the reproductive patterns in collaborative study families, by J. K. Burns, et al. AMERICAN JOURNAL OF MEDICAL GENETICS 19(3):515-524, November 1984.

Late infertile days in early postpartum cycles, by L. I. Hatherley. CLINICAL REPRODUCTION AND FERTILITY 3(1):73-80, March 1985.

Mrs Gillick and the Wisbech Area Health Authority, by J. Griffiths. BRISTOL MEDICO-CHIRURGICAL JOURNAL 100(374):37, April 1985.

Myth of the month. HEALTH 17:82, February 1985.

No one is realistic about family planning, by Y. A. Eraj. INTERNATIONAL NURSING REVIEW 31(6):179, November-December 1984.

Oxford-Family Planning Association contraceptive study, by M. P. Vessey, et al. CLINICAL OBSTETRICS AND GYNAECOLOGY 11(3):743-757, December 1984.

Population control: no-women decide, by A. Henry. OFF OUR BACKS 14(9):2, October 1984.

Potential impact of changes in fertility on infant, child and maternal mortality, by J. Trussell, et al. STUDIES IN FAMILY PLANNING 15:267-280, November-December 1984.

Proximate determinants of fertility: sub-national variations. POPULATION STUDIES 39(1):113, March 1985.

Putting off children. AMERICAN DEMOGRAPHICS 6(9):30, September 1984.

Reproduction law—part one, by B. M. Dickens. HEALTH MANAGEMENT FORUM 6(2):22-34, Summer 1985.

To have or not to have a pregnancy, by L. Klein. OBSTETRICS AND GYNE-COLOGY 65(1):1-4, January 1985.

Two trident missiles [overriding Reagan administration decision to cut family planning aid], by R. W. Peterson. AUDUBON 87:4, July 1985.

Young adult with diabetes: impact of the disease on marriage and having children, by J. E. Ahlfield, et al. DIABETES CARE 8(1):52-56, January-February 1985.

AFRICA
Black fertility patterns—Cape Town and Ciskei, by M. Roberts, et al. SOUTH AFRICAN MEDICAL JOURNAL 66(13):481-484, September 29, 1984.

Characteristics of family planning acceptors at a primary health care project in Lagos, Nigeria, by A. A. Olukoya. PUBLIC HEALTH 99(1):37-44, January 1985.

Film program in health and family planning in rural Zaire, by M. Carael, et al. HUMAN ORGANIZATION 43:341-348, Winter 1984.

Household fertility decisions in West Africa: a comparison of male and female survey results, by F. L. Mott, et al. STUDIES IN FAMILY PLANNING 16(2): 88-99, March-April 1985.

Knowledge, attitude and practice of family planning in Hausa women, by N. Rehan. SOCIAL SCIENCE AND MEDICINE 18(10):839-844, 1984.

Male attitudes towards family planning in Khartoum, Sudan, by M. A. Mustafa, et al. JOURNAL OF BIOSOCIAL SCIENCE16(4):437-449, October 1984.

Multivariate analysis of family planning knowledge differentials in rural Ghana. JOURNAL OF FAMILY WELFARE 30:47-60, June 1984.

Nairobi conference [includes outside the Nairobi conference, inside Nairobi, trip to Kibwezi, family planning, International Council of African Women report, find markets (workshop)], by A. Henry. OFF OUR BACKS 15:1-9, November 1985.

No one is realistic about family planning, by Y. A. Eraj. INTERNATIONAL NURSING REVIEW 31(6):179, November-December 1984.

Obstacles to successful fertility control in Nigeria, by E. O. Udjo. SOCIAL SCIENCE AND MEDICINE 19(11):1167-1171, 1984.

231

AFRICA
   Persistence of high fertility in Kenya, by I. Sindiga. SOCIAL SCIENCE AND
      MEDICINE 20(1):71-84, 1985.

   Public opinion on and potential demand for vasectomy in semi-rural
      Guatemala, by R. Santiso, et al. JOURNAL OF PUBLIC HEALTH 75:73-
      75, January 1985.

AUSTRALIA
   AFFPA medical task force guidelines. Medical Task Force of the Australian
      Federation of Family Planning Associations. MEDICAL JOURNAL OF
      AUSTRALIA 143(4):162-163, August 19, 1985.

BANGLADESH
   Nuptiality, fertility and family planning practices in rural Bangladesh: a case
      study, by S. B. Bhuyan, et al. JOURNAL OF FAMILY WELFARE 31:62-
      75, September 1984.

   Strengthening government health and family planning programs: findings
      from an Action Research Project in rural Bangladesh, by R. Simmons, et
      al. STUDIES IN FAMILY PLANNING 15:212-221, September-October
      1984.

CARIBBEAN
   Family planning services in the commonwealth Caribbean [editorial], by L.
      Matadial. WEST INDIAN MEDICAL JOURNAL 34(1):1-2, March 1985.

CHINA
   Birth planning and fertility transition [People's Republic of China: conference
      paper]. ANNALS OF THE AMERICAN ACADEMY OF POLITICAL AND
      SOCIAL SCIENCE 476:128-141, November 1984.

   Population dynamics and policy in the People's Republic of China [compared
      with Japan, Korea, and Taiwan; conference paper], by L.-J. Cho.
      ANNALS OF THE AMERICAN ACADEMY OF POLITICAL AND SOCIAL
      SCIENCE 476:111-127, November 1984.

   Population policy and trends in China, 1978-83, by J. Banister. CHINA
      QUARTERLY December 1984, p. 717-741.

DEVELOPING COUNTRIES
   Demography comes of age [World Bank's World Development Report].
      ECONOMIST 292:76-77, July 14, 1984.

   Effects of social setting and family planning programs on recent fertility
      declines indeveloping countries: a reassessment, by S. E. Tolnay, et al.
      SOCIOLOGY AND SOCIAL RESEARCH 69(1):72-89, October 1984.

   Family planning in rural and semirural areas, by M. R. Santamaría Valladolid.
      REVISTA DE ENFERMAGEN 7(74):63-66, October 1984.

   Population policy analysis and development planning, by O. G. Simmons.
      JOURNAL OF DEVELOPING AREAS 18:433-448, July 1984.

DEVELOPING COUNTRIES
Population policy: country experience [Mexico, Indonesia, and India], by M. Ainsworth. FINANCE AND DEVELOPMENT 21:18-20, September 1984.

Threshold hypothesis. Evidence from less developed Latin American countries, 1950 to 1980. DEMOGRAPHY 21(4):459, November 1984.

Use and effectiveness of norethisterone enanthate for family planning in a rural area, by V. M. Velasco, et al. GINECOLOGIA Y OBSTETRICIA DE MEXICO 51(314):163-167, June 1983.

DOMINICAN REPUBLIC
Multiple interventions: a lesson on utility and weakness—Dominican Republic, by J. A. Ballweg. PUBLIC HEALTH REVIEWS 12(3-4):240-245, 1984.

EGYPT
Islam and birth planning: an interview with the Grand Mufti of Egypt. POPULI 2(2):40, 1984.

Population policy in Egypt: a case in public policy analysis [family planning policies adopted since 1962], by A. S. Hassan. POPULATION STUDIES 11:19-25, April-June 1984.

GREAT BRITAIN
Facing the facts. TIMES EDUCATIONAL SUPPLEMENT 3596:35, May 31, 1985.

HUNGARY
Comments on two Hungarian television educational series, by A. Pázsy. PROGRESS IN CLINICAL AND BIOLOGICAL RESEARCH 163C:351-354, 1985.

INDIA
Barriers to effective family planning in Nepal, by S. R. Schuler, et al. STUDIES IN FAMILY PLANNING 16:260-270, September-October 1985.

Coevcion in a soft state: the family planning program of India, by M. Vicziany. PACIFIC AFFAIRS 55:373-402, Fall 1982.

Demographic transition in a Punjab village. POPULATION AND DEVELOP-MENT REVIEW 10(4):661, December 1984.

Educational transition in rural South India. POPULATION AND DEVELOP-MENT REVIEW 11(1):29, March 1985.

Family planning programme in India: the non governmental sector, by A. B. Wadia. JOURNAL OF FAMILY WELFARE 30:11-46, June 1984.

National Family Welfare Programme in India, by C. S. Dawn. JOURNAL OF THE INDIAN MEDICAL ASSOCIATION 82(5):177-180, May 1984.

Natural family planning in Mauritas, Indian Ocean: utilization patterns and continuance predictors, by G. L. Conner, et al. JOURNAL OF SOCIAL SERVICE RESEARCH 8(1):29-48, 1984.

INDIA
Socioeconomic status and fertility in rural Bangladesh, by K. Shaikh, et al. JOURNAL OF BIOSOCIAL SCIENCE 17:81-90, January 1985.

INDONESIA
"Beyond family planning" in Indonesia. POPULI 2(3):20, 1984.

Determinants of birth-interval length in the Philippines, Malaysia and Indonesia: a hazard model. DEMOGRAPHY 22(2):145, May 1985.

What makes the Indonesian family planning programme tick. POPULI 2(3):4, 1984.

JAPAN
Family planning in Japanese society, by N. Engel. BULLETIN OF CONCERNED ASIAN SCHOLARS 17(2):71, April 1985.

Population dynamics and policy in the People's Republic of China [compared with Japan, Korea, and Taiwan; conference paper], by L.-J. Cho. ANNALS OF THE AMERICAN ACADEMY OF POLITICAL AND SOCIAL SCIENCE 476:111-127, November 1984.

KOREA
Measuring the effect of sex preference on fertility: the case of Korea. DEMOGRAPHY 22(2):280, May 1985.

LATIN AMERICA
Threshold hypothesis. Evidence from less developed Latin American countries, 1950 to 1980. DEMOGRAPHY 21(4):459, November 1984.

MALAYSIA
Determinants of birth-interval length in the Philippines, Malaysia and ndonesia: a hazard model. DEMOGRAPHY 22(2):145, May 1985.

MEXICO
Global politics in Mexico City, by D. Wulf, et al. FAMILY PLANNING PERSPECTIVES 16(5):228-232, September-October 1984.

Ideology and politics at Mexico City: the United States at the 1984 International Conference on population. POPULATION AND DEVELOPMENT REVIEW 11(1):1, March 1985.

United Nations International Conference on Population, Mexico City. STUDIES IN FAMILY PLANNING 15(6):29, November-December 1984.

NEW GUINEA
Role of maternal and child health clinics in education and prevention: a case study from Papua New Guinea, by J. Reid. SOCIAL SCIENCE AND MEDICINE 19(3): 291-303, 1984.

NIGERIA
Integrated family planning services: a Nigerian experience, by O. Ayangade. EAST AFRICAN MEDICAL JOURNAL 61(5):412-419, May 1984.

234

PAKISTAN
Effect of birth spacing on childhood mortality in Pakistan, by J. G. Cleland, et al. POPULATION STUDIES 38:401-418, November 1984.

PHILIPPINES
Determinants of birth-interval length in the Philippines, Malaysia and I Indonesia: a hazard model. DEMOGRAPHY 22(2):145, May 1985.

PUERTO RICO
Model of fertility control in a Puerto Rican Community, by S. L. Schensul, et al. URBAN ANTHROPOLOGY 11(1):81-99, Spring 1982.

SCOTLAND
Motivation for parenthood: a factor analytic study of attitudes towards having children, by J. S. Bell, et al. JOURNAL OF COMPARATIVE FAMILY STUDIES 16(1):111-119, Spring 1985.

SINGAPORE
Family planning in Singapore, by C. Ng. ASIA-OCEANIA JOURNAL OF OBSTETRICS AND GYNAECOLOGY 10(4):559-563, December 1984.

SOUTHEAST ASIA
Malaysian integrated population program performance: its relation to organizational and integration factors [family planning with health], by C. O. Fong. MANAGEMENT SCIENCE 31:50-65, January 1985.

SRI LANKA
Early symptoms and discontinuation among users of oral contraceptives in Sri Lanka. STUDIES IN FAMILY PLANNING 15(6):285, November-December 1984.

Ethnic differences in contraceptive use in Sri Lanka, by K. R. Murty, et al. STUDIES IN FAMILY PLANNING 15:222-232, September-October 1984.

SWEDEN
Swedish solutions, by J. Trost. SOCIETY 23:44-48, November-December 1985.

THAILAND
Measuring accessibility to family planning services in rural Thailand, by N. Chayovan, et al. STUDIES IN FAMILY PLANNING 15:201-211, September-October 1984.

Multilevel model of family planning availability and contraceptive use in rural Thailand, by B. Entwisle, et al. DEMOGRAPHY 21:559-574, November 1984.

Social communication, organization and community development: family planning in Thailand, by L. J. Duhl. ASSIGNMENT CHILDREN 65(68): 117-136, 1984.

TURKEY
Psychological and social disorders of Turkish women during an unaccepted pregnancy in a foreign country, by H. Berzewski. INTERNATIONAL JOURNAL OF SOCIAL PSYCHIATRY 30(4):275-282, Winter 1984.

UNITED STATES
Contraceptive practice among American women, 1973-1982, by C. A. Bachrach. FAMILY PLANNING PERSPECTIVES 16:253-259, November-December 1984.

Costs and benefits of Title XX and Title XIX family planning services in Texas, by D. Malitz. EVALUATION REVIEW 8:519-536, August 1984.

Family planning and female sterilization in the United States, by T. M. Shapiro, et al. SOCIAL SCIENCE AND MEDICINE 17(23):1847-1855, 1983.

Family planning clinic services in the United States, 1983, by A. Torres, et al. FAMILY PLANNING PERSPECTIVES 17(1):30-35, January -February 1985.

Family planning: U. S. policy changing?, by J. Raloff. SCIENCE NEWS 128: 55, July 27, 1985.

Foundation power [critical views of American foundation funding in the areas of population control and abortion, by M. Meehan. HUMAN LIFE REVIEW 10:42-60, Fall 1984.

Overpopulation problem as it affects the United States: a step toward a societal response [Catholic Church position], by S. D. Mumford. HUMANIST 45:14-17+, July-August 1985.

Patterns of contraceptive method of use by California family planning clinic clients, 1976-84, by B. M. Aved. AMERICAN JOURNAL OF PUBLIC HEALTH 75(10):1210-1212, October 1985.

US antics stifled population debate, by A. Smart. GOODWINS 2(2):11, Fall 1984.

What are the determinants of delayed childbearing and permanent childless-ness in the United States?, by David E. Bloom, et al. DEMOGRAPHY 21:591-612, November 1984.

USSR
Family planning in USSR found wanting. CURRENT DIGEST OF THE SOVIET PRESS 37:10-12+, October 23, 1985.

FAMILY PLANNING: ATTITUDES
Attitudes toward marriage and childbearing of individuals at risk for Huntington's disease, by M. Schoenfeld, et al. SOCIAL WORK IN HEALTH CARE 9(4):73-81, Summer 1984.

Population policies and proposals: when big brother becomes big daddy [family planning and other population policies as functions of the state and as indi-vidual human rights], by L. E. Farrell. BROOKLYN JOURNAL OF INTERNA-TIONAL LAW 10:83-114, Winter 1984.

FAMILY PLANNING: EDUCATION
Education. Gaining and giving insight, by K. Hills. NURSING MIRROR AND MID-WIVE'S JOURNAL 160(6):28-29, February 6, 1985.

University commitment to the improvement of family health education and services, by R. Rodriquez. HYGIE 4(2):18-22, June 1985.

FAMILY PLANNING: LAWS AND LEGISLATION
Age of consent and the sexual dilemma, by A. Langslow. AUSTRALASIAN NURSES JOURNAL 14(8):50-51, March 1985.

Court of Appeals rules DHSS notice on family planning contrary to law, by D. Brahams. LANCET 1(8419):59-61, January 5, 1985.

Family planning: U. S. policy changing?, by J. Raloff. SCIENCE NEWS 128:55, July 27, 1985.

Laws and policies affecting fertility: a decade of change. POPULATION REPORTS 12(6):105, November 1984.

Pregnancy termination: not for family planning. The legal difference between sterilization and pregnancy termination is decisive, by H. Krautkrämer. FORT-SCHRITTE DER MEDIZIN 102(36):78, September 27, 1984.

Rights threatened [on amendments proposed by Jesse Helms, Orrin Hatch and Jack Kemp to legislation funding Title X placing severe limitations on the use of private and federal fund for family planning], by P. Sheldrick. NEW DIREC-TIONS FOR WOMEN 15:1+, January-February 1986.

FAMILY PLANNING: METHODS
Billings method of family planning: an assessment. STUDIES IN FAMILY PLANNING15:253-266, November-December 1984.

Symptothermal method of natural family planning, by K. Hamilton. PHYSICIAN ASSISTANT 8(11):143-144+, November 1984.

FAMILY PLANNING: MORTALITY AND MORTALITY STATISTICS
Potential impact of changes in fertility on infant, child and maternal mortality, by J. Trussell, et al. STUDIES IN FAMILY PLANNING 15:267-280, November-December 1984.

FAMILY PLANNING: NATURAL
Aged gametes, adverse pregnancy outcomes and natural family planning. An epide-miologic review, by R. H. Gray. CONTRACEPTION 30(4):297-309, October 1984.

More about natural family planning [letter], by L. A. Bennett. AUSTRALIAN FAMILY PHYSICIAN 13(6):396-397, June 1984.

Natural family planning (NFP) (letter), by G. Luh-Hardegg. GEBURTSHILFE UND FRAUENHEILKUNDE 44(12):829-830, December 1984.

Natural family planning [discussion of May 1985 article, comparing contraceptives], by J. Willis. FDA CONSUMER 19:2, September 1985.

Natural family planning in Mauritas, Indian Ocean: utilization patterns and continuance predictors, by G. L. Conner, et al. JOURNAL OF SOCIAL SERVICE RESEARCH 8(1):29-48, 1984.

Natural methods of family planning, by A. M. Flynn. CLINICAL OBSTETRICS AND GYNECOLOGY 11(3):661-678, December 1984.

Sex ratio associated with natural family planning [letter], by A. Perez, et al. FERTILITY AND STERILITY 43(1):152-153, January 1985.

Symptothermal method of natural family planning, by K. Hamilton. PHYSICIAN ASSISTANT 8(11):143-144+, November 1984.

Vulvar effects of the toilet tissue observational routine in the practice of natural family planning [letter], by C. W. Norris. AMERICAN JOURNAL OF OBSTETRICS AND GYNECOLOGY 152(8):1108-1109, August 15, 1985.

Who uses natural family planning?, by K. J. Daly, et al. CANADIAN JOURNAL OF PUBLIC HEALTH 76(3):207-208l, May-June 1985.

FAMILY PLANNING: NURSES AND NURSING
Paving the way for parenthood . . . family planning nurse, by G. Rands. NURSING TIMES 81(4):46-47, January 23-29, 1985.

FAMILY PLANNING: PLANNED PARENTHOOD
Double standard [bombings, Planned Parenthood offices, abortion clinics; editorial], by B. C. Harris. WITNESS 68(2):16, February 1985.

Margaret Sanger and the International Planned Parenthood Federation, by M. Golden. AFER 27:109-114, April 1985.

FAMILY PLANNING: RESEARCH
Family planning for deer, by T. Levenson. DISCOVER 5:34-35+, December 1984.

Guidelines for overcoming design problems in family planning operations research, by A. A. Fisher, et al. STUDIES IN FAMILY PLANNING 16(2):100-105, March-April 1985.

Strengthening government health and family planning programs: findings from an Action Research Project in rural Bangladesh, by R. Simmons, et al. STUDIES IN FAMILY PLANNING 15:212-221, September-October 1984.

FAMILY PLANNING: RURAL
Film program in health and family planning in rural Zaire, by M. Carael, et al. HUMAN ORGANIZATION 43:341-348, Winter 1984.

Measuring accessibility to family planning services in rural Thailand, by N. Chayovan, et al. STUDIES IN FAMILY PLANNING 15:201-211, September-October 1984.

FAMILY PLANNING: SOCIOLOGY
Generational differences in fertility among Mexican Americans: implications for assessing the effects of immigration, by F. D. Bean, et al. SOCIAL SCIENCE QUARTERLY 65:573-582, June 1984.

Socio-economic and demographic factors and their influence on family planning behavior among non-adopters, by M. M. Reddy. JOURNAL OF FAMILY WELFARE 30:92, June 1984.

Bioethics seminar 10. The roots and overview of family planning, by T. Kimura. KANGOGAKU ZASSHI 48(11):1301-1304, November 1984.

Childlessness: a panel study of expressed intentions and reported fertility, by L. G. Pol. SOCIAL BIOLOGY 30:318-327, August 1983.

Commons debates the Warnock Report, by N. Fowler. NURSING STANDARD 376:8, December 6, 1984.

Economic and other determinants of annual change in U. S. fertility: 1917-1976. SOCIAL SCIENCE RESEARCH 13(3):250-267, September 1984.

Fertility survey of different birth cohort women in Beijing city, S. X. Wang. CHUNG HUA FU CHAN KO TSA CHIH 20(1):30-33, January 1985.

Professional satisfaction and client outcomes: a comparative organizational analysis, by C. S. Weisman, et al. MEDICAL CARE 23(10):1179-1192, October 1985.

Understanding U.S. fertility: findings from the National Survey of Family Growth, Cycle III, by W. F. Pratt, et al. POPULATION BULLETIN 39:1-40, December 1984.

FAMILY PLANNING AND MALES
Male attitudes towards family planning in Khartoum, Sudan, by M. A. Mustafa, et al. JOURNAL OF BIOSOCIAL SCIENCE16(4):437-449, October 1984.

FAMILY PLANNING AND PLANNED PARENTHOOD
Education and the timing of motherhood: disentangling causation, by R. R. Rindfuss. JOURNAL OF MARRIAGE AND THE FAMILY 46:981-984, November1984.

FAMILY PLANNING AND POLITICS
Adolescent Family Life Act and the promotion of religious doctrine, by P. Donovan. FAMILY PLANNING PERSPECTIVES16(5):222-228, September-October 1984.

Array of anti-abortion amendments planned, by N. Cohodas. CONGRESSIONAL QUARTERLY WEEKLY REPORT 43:2201-2202, November 2, 1985.

Family planning: U. S. policy changing?, by J. Raloff. SCIENCE NEWS 128:55, July 27, 1985.

Ideology and politics at Mexico City: the United States at the 1984 International Conference on population. POPULATION AND DEVELOPMENT REVIEW 11(1):1, March 1985.

Population and politics. HEALTHSHARING (1):16, Winter 1984.

Shared dreams/disability/reproductive rights. RADICAL AMERICAN 18(4):51, 1984.

Strengthening government health and family planning programs: findings from an Action Research Project in rural Bangladesh, by R. Simmons, et al. STUDIES IN FAMILY PLANNING 15:212-221, September-October 1984.

Two trident missiles [overriding Reagan administration decision to cut family planning aid], by R. W. Peterson. AUDUBON 87:4, July 1985.

US antics stifled population debate, by A. Smart. GOODWINS 2(2):11, Fall 1984.

FAMILY PLANNING AND RELIGION
Adolescent Family Life Act and the promotion of religious doctrine, by P. Donovan. FAMILY PLANNING PERSPECTIVES16(5):222-228, September-October 1984.

Overpopulation problem as it affects the United States: a step toward a societal response [Catholic Church position], by S. D. Mumford. HUMANIST 45:14-17+, July-August 1985.

FAMILY PLANNING AND WOMEN
Contraceptive use, pregnancy and fertility patterns among single American women in their 20s, by K. Tanfer, et al. FAMILY PLANNING PERSPECTIVES 17(1):10-19, January-February 1985.

Family planning and female sterilization in the United States, by T. M. Shapiro, et al. SOCIAL SCIENCE AND MEDICINE 17(23):1847-1855, 1983.

Population control: no-women decide, by A. Henry. OFF OUR BACKS 14(9):2, October 1984.

FAMILY PLANNING AND YOUTH
Age of consent and the sexual dilemma, by A. Langslow. AUSTRALASIAN NURSES JOURNAL 14(8):50-51, March 1985.

Are we failing our teenagers? Value of a family planning service for teenagers within the sexually transmitted disease clinic, by J. M. Tobin, et al. BRITISH MEDICAL JOURNAL 290(6465):376-378, February 2, 1985.

Effectiveness of family planning clinics in serving adolescents, by E. E. Kisker. FAMILY PLANNING PERSPECTIVES 16:212-218, September-October 1984.

Factors associated with adolescent use of family planning clinics, by J. A. Shea, et al. AMERICAN JOURNAL OF PUBLIC HEALTH 74(11):1227-1230, November 1984.

Global politics in Mexico City, by D. Wulf, et al. FAMILY PLANNING PERSPEC-TIVES 16(5):228-232, September-October 1984.

Planning programs for pregnant teenagers, by M. R. Burt, et al. PUBLIC WELFARE 43(2):28-36, Spring 1985.

Potential impact of changes in fertility on infant, child and maternal mortality, by J. Trussell, et al. STUDIES IN FAMILY PLANNING 15:267-280, November-December 1984.

School-based health clinics: a new approach to preventing adolescent preg-nancy?, by J. Dryfoos. FAMILY PLANNING PERSPECTIVES 17:70-75, March-April 1985.

Abortion clinic: what goes on, by S. K. Reed. PEOPLE WEEKLY 24:103-106, August 26, 1985.

Birth control use means more clinic visits. JET 67:37, January 28, 1985.

Experience from a local authority clinic for advice on contraception. A consec-utive study of 1000 women attending a clinic for advice on contraception in the Municipality of Fredriksberg, by E. Schroeder, et al. AGESKRIFT FOR LAEGER 146(26):1953-1957, June 25,1984.

Factors associated with adolescent use of family planning clinics, by J. A. Shea, et al. AMERICAN JOURNAL OF PUBLIC HEALTH 74(11):1227-1230, November 1984.

Family planning clinic services in the United States, 1983, by A. Torres, et al. FAMILY PLANNING PERSPECTIVES 17(1):30-35, January -February 1985.

Flipchart nutrition reference for family planning, by J. Van Gurp. JOURNAL OF NUTRITION EDUCATION 17:18B, March 1985.

Institutional factors affecting teenagers' choice and reasons for delay in attending a family planning clinic, by L. S. Jabin, et al. FAMILY PLANNING PERSPECTIVES 15(1):25-29, January-February 1983.

Patterns of contraceptive method of use by California family planning clinic clients, 1976-84, by B. M. Aved. AMERICAN JOURNAL OF PUBLIC HEALTH 75(10):1210-1212, October 1985.

Rubella susceptibility among prenatal and family planning clinic populations, by S. F. Dorfman, et al. MT. SANAI JOURNAL OF MEDICINE 52(4):248-252, April 1985.

Who attends family planning clinics?, by P. Chick, et al. AUSTRALIAN AND NEW ZEALAND JOURNAL OF OBSTETRICS AND GYNAECOLOGY 24(3):213-216, August 1984.

FAMILY PLANNING COUNSELING
Family-planning and sexual counseling . . . the nurse's role, by J. Glover. NURS-ING MIRROR AND MIDWIVE'S JOURNAL 160(3):28-29, January 16, 1985.

FAMILY PLANNING FUNDING
Rights threatened [on amendments proposed by Jesse Helms, Orrin Hatch and Jack Kemp to legislation funding Title X placing severe limitations on the use of private and federal fund for family planning], by P. Sheldrick. NEW DIREC-TIONS FOR WOMEN 15:1+, January-February 1986.

FAMILY PLANNING PROGRAMS
Contraceptive prevalence: the influence of organized family planning programs, by R. J. Lapham, et al. STUDIES IN FAMILY PLANNING 16(3):117-137, May-June 1985.

Effects of social setting and family planning programs on recent fertility declines in developing countries: a reassessment, by S. E. Tolnay, et al. SOCIOLOGY AND SOCIAL RESEARCH 69(1):72-89, October 1984.

Effects of US decision to withdraw aid for worldwide family planning programmes. LANCET 1(8420):97, January 12, 1985.

Impact of family planning programs on fertility, by J. D. Sherris, et al. POPULATION REPORTS (29):1733-1771, January-February 1985.

Planned parenthood seeks support via newspaper ads. EDITOR AND PUBLISHER-THE FOURTH ESTATE 117:30, October 13, 1984.

FEMALE STERILIZATION
Ectopic pregnancies following female sterilization. A matched case-control analysis, by I. C. Chi, et al. ACTA OBSTETRICIA ET GYNECOLOGICA SCANDINAVICA 63(6):517-521, 1984.

FERTILITY AND FERTILITY CONTROL
Becoming voluntarily childless: an exploratory study in a Scottish city, by E. Campbell. SOCIAL BIOLOGY 30(3):307-317, Fall 1983.

Chemical fertility control and wildlife management, by J. F. Kirkpatrick, et al. BIO-SCIENCE 35:485-491, September 1985.

Fertility effects of isolated spouse separations in relation to their timing, by R. G. Potter, et al. SOCIAL BIOLOGY 30:279-289, August 1983.

Fertility of couples following cessation of contraception, by N. Spira, et al. JOURNAL OF BIOSOCIAL SCIENCE 17(3):281-290, July 1985.

Menses induction in rhesus monkeys using a controlled-release vaginal delivery system containing (15S) 15-methyl prostaglandin F2 alpha methyl ester, by C. H. Spilman, et al. FERTILITY AND STERILITY 42(4):638-643, October 1984.

Model of fertility control in a Puerto Rican Community, by S. L. Schensul, et al. URBAN ANTHROPOLOGY 11(1):81-99, Spring 1982.

Population and U. S. policy [U.N. conference on population]. NATIONAL REVIEW 36:13-14, September 7, 1984.

Public opinion on and potential demand for vasectomy in semi-rural Guatemala, by R. Santiso, et al. JOURNAL OF PUBLIC HEALTH 75:73-75, January 1985.

FERTILITY AND FERTILITY STATISTICS
Census-derived estimates of fertility by duration since first marriage in the Republic of Korea. DEMOGRAPHY 21:537-558, November 1984.

Childlessness: a panel study of expressed intentions and reported fertility, by L. G. Pol. SOCIAL BIOLOGY 30:318-327, August 1983.

Economic and other determinants of annual change in U. S. fertility: 1917-1976. SOCIAL SCIENCE RESEARCH 13(3):250-267, September 1984.

FERTILITY: GENERAL
Labor force participation and fertility: a social analysis of their antecedents and simultaneity, by M. Van Loo. HUMAN RELATIONS 37:941-968, November 1984.

Trends in Moslem fertility and the application of the demographic transition model, by M. H. Nagi. SOCIAL BIOLOGY 30:245-262, August 1983.

INDIA
Changes in the age at marriage and its effects on fertility: a study of slum dwellers in Greater Bombay, by P. K. Bhargava. JOURNAL OF FAMILY WELFARE 31:32-36, September 1984.

Impact of development and population policies on fertility in India, by A. K. Jain. STUDIES IN FAMILY PLANNING 16:181-198, July-August 1985.

HYSTERECTOMY
Indications for prevalence and implications of hysterectomy: a discussion, by K. Wijma, et al. JOURNAL OF PSYCHOSOMATIC OBSTETRICS AND GYNE-COLOGY 3(2):69-77, August 1984.

Premath of hysterectomy, by R. Kasrawi, et al. JOURNAL OF PSYCHOSOMATIC OBSTETRICS AND GYNECOLOGY 3(3-4):233-236, December 1984.

Psychological functioning after non-cancer hysterectomy: a review of methods and results, by K. Wijma. JOURNAL OF PSYCHOSOMATIC OBSTETRICS AND GYNAECOLOGY 3(3-4):133-154, December 1984.

Symposium on the philosophy of Alan Donagan. I. Taking a human life. II. Moral absolutism and abortion: Alan Donagan on the hysterectomy and craniotomy cases. III. Comments on Dan Brock and Terrence Donagan, by D. W. Brock, et al. ETHICS 95(4):851-886, 1985.

Tubal pregnancy after a previous tubal ligation and hysterectomy, by D. Beuthe, et al. GEBURTSHILFE UND FRAUENHEILKUNDE 45(3):188, March 1985.

HYSTERECTOMY: PSYCHOLOGY AND PSYCHIATRY
Psychological contributions to understanding gynaecological problems, by M. Tsoi. BULLETIN OF THE HONG KONG PSYCHOLOGICAL SOCIETY 14:9-16, January 1985.

Psychological effects of hysterectomy in premenopausal women, by S. Kav Venaki, et al. JOURNAL OF PSYCHOSOMATIC OBSTETRICS AND GYNECOLOGY 2(2):76-80, June 1983.

Psychological problems following hysterectomy, by L. Millet, et al. PSYCHOLO-GIE MEDICALE 14(8):1239-1244, June 1982.

MARRIAGE AND THE FAMILY
Aborted sibling factor: a case study, by A. H. Weiner, et al. CLINICAL SOCIAL WORK JOURNAL 12(3):209-215, 1984.

American Catholic family: signs of cohesion and polarization, by W. V. D'Antonio. JOURNAL OF MARRIAGE AND THE FAMILY 47(2):395-405, May 1985.

Childlessness and marital stability in remarriages, by J. D. Griffith, et al. JOURNAL OF MARRIAGE AND THE FAMILY 46:577-585, August 1984.

Effect of marital dissolution on contraceptive protection, by L. Bumpass, et al. FAMILY PLANNING PERSPECTIVES 16:271-284, November-December 1984.

First aid in pastoral care: pastoral care in marriage, by J. Thompson. EXPOSITORY TIMES 96:324-329, August 1985.

Marriage in the Greek Orthodox Church, by D. J. Constantelos. JOURNAL OF ECUMENICAL STUDIES 22:21-27, Winter 1985.

Marriage in Roman Catholicism, by D. L. Carmody. JOURNAL OF ECUMENICAL STUDIES 22:28-40, Winter 1985.

Reciprocal influences of family and religion in a changing world, by A. Thornton. JOURNAL OF MARRIAGE AND THE FAMILY 47(2):381-394, May 1985.

MISCARRIAGE

Adolescent mothers and fetal loss, what is learned from experience, by P. B. Smith,et al. PSYCHOLOGICAL REPORTS 55:775-778, December 1984.

Effects of miscarriage on a man, by D. D. Cumings. EMOTIONAL FIRST AID: A JOURNAL OF CRISIS INTERVENTION 1(4):47-50, Winter 1984.

Hospitalization for miscarriage and delivery outcome among Swedish nurses working in operating rooms 1973-1978, by H. A. Ericson, et al. ANESTHESIA AND ANALGESIA 64(10):981-988, October 1985.

Immunisation can prevent miscarriage. NEW SCIENTIST 106:20, May 9, 1985.

Japanese miscarriages blamed on computer terminals. NEW SCIENTIST 106:7, May 23, 1985.

Miscarriage: a loss that must be acknowledged. EMOTIONAL FIRST AID: A JOURNAL OF CRISIS INTERVENTION 1(4):43-46, Winter 1984.

Prayer for the woman who has miscarried, by G. Nefyodov. JOURNAL OF THE MOSCOW PATRIARCHATE 8:77-78, 1983.

What you haven't heard about Bhopal: shocking reports of infertility, miscarriage and deformity, by S. Lerner, et al. MS MAGAZINE 14:85-88, December 1985.

When the baby doesn't come home. CHILDREN TODAY 13(2):21-24, 1984.

When the unborn die: the impact on parents can be devastating [miscarriage], by M. Nemeth. ALBERTA REPORT 12:27, July 1, 1985.

PLANNED PARENTHOOD

Planned Parenthood [Planned Parenthood Ass'n v. Dep't of Human Resources, 687 p.2d 785 (Or.)] aborts state funding limits. WILLIAMETTE LAW REVIEW 21:405-410, Spring 1985.

SEX AND SEXUALITY

Abortion outcome as a function of sex-role identification, by R. C. Alter. PSYCHOLOGY OF WOMEN QUARTERLY 8:211-233, Spring 1984.

Adolescent pregnancy and sex roles, by C. J. Ireson. SEX ROLES 11:189-201, August 1984.

Cervical dysplasia: association with sexual behavior, smoking, and oral contraceptive use?, by E. A. Clarke, et al. AMERICAN JOURNAL OF OBSTETRICS AND GYNECOLOGY 151(5):612-616, March 1985.

Contraceptive knowledge and use of birth control as a function of sex guilt, by C. Berger, et al. INTERNATIONAL JOURNAL OF WOMEN'S STUDIES 8:72-79, January-February 1985.

Daughters of the sexual revolution. J. Sadgrove. GUARDIAN November 12, 1985, p. 10.

Influence of parents, church, and peers on the sexual attitudes and behaviors of college students, by L. R. Daugherty, et al. ARCHIVES OF SEXUAL BEHAVIOR 13(4):351-359, August 1984.

Measuring the effect of sex preference on fertility: the case of Korea. DEMOGRAPHY 22(2):280, May 1985.

New woman, the new family and the rationalization of sexuality; the sex reform movement in Germany 1928 to 1933, by A. Grossmann. DAI:THE HUMANITIES AND SOCIAL SCIENCES 45(7), January 1985.

Psychosexual problems, by P. Tunnadine. PRACTITIONER 229(1403):453-455+, May 1985.

"Right-to-life" scores new victory at AID, by C. Holden. SCIENCE 229:1065-1067, September 13, 1985.

Sex and the under-age girl, by M. McFadyean. NEW SOCIETY 72:386-388, June 14, 1985.

Some aspects of sexual knowledge and sexual behavior of local women. Results of a survey. 1. General sexual knowledge and attitude to abortion, pregnancy and contraception, by V. Atputharajah. SINGAPORE MEDICAL JOURNAL 25(3):135-140, June 1984.

—. V. Sexual intercourse, by V. Atputharajah. SINGAPORE MEDICAL JOURNAL 26(2):155-160, April 1985.

TV, sex and prevention, by K. Foltz. NEWSWEEK 106:72, September 9, 1985.

Who's to blame: adolescent sexual activity, by R. Kornfield. JOURNAL OF ADOLESCENT HEALTH CARE 8:17-31, March 1985.

STERILIZATION: GENERAL
Decision to undergo tubal ligation, by J. G. Fontaine. UNION MEDICALE DU CANADA 113(7):604-606, July 1984.

Indrani and Nirmaladevi speak out. OFF OUR BACKS 14(10):4, November 1984.

Parents right to decide [letter], by H. C. Moss. INDIANA MEDICINE 77(1):28, January 1984.

Safe sterilization, by F. Diamond. HEALTHSHARING 6(1):6, Winter 1984.

Sterilisation. PRACTITIONER 229(1403):449-451, May 1985.

Sterilization, by J. R. Newton. CLINICAL OBSTETRICS AND GYNAECOLOGY 11(3):603-640, December 1984.

Sterilization: an informed decision?, by C. Toomey. TIMES August 9, 1985, p. 9.

To have or have not. (Is sterilization the contraceptivefor you?), by E. Michaud. PHILADELPHIA MAGAZINE 76:121+, March 1985.

AFRICA

Outpatient interval female sterilization at the University College Hospital, Ibadan, Nigeria, by E. O. Otolorin, et al. AFRICAN JOURNAL OF MEDICINE AND MEDICAL SCIENCES 14(1-2):3-9, March-June 1985.

ASIA

Making news: Asian women in the west, by U. Butalia. ISIS 1984, p. 114.

BANGLADESH

Bangladesh: involuntary sterilization. NATION 239(22):705, December 29, 1984.

BRAZIL

Sterilization in the northeast of Brazil, by B. Janowitz, et al. SOCIAL SCIENCE AND MEDICINE 20(3):215-221, 1985.

CHINA

Sterilization methods in China [letter], by V. L. Bullough, et al. AMERICAN JOURNAL OF PUBLIC HEALTH 75(6):689, June 1985.

HONDURAS

Why women don't get sterilized: a folow-up of women in Honduras, by B. Janowitz, et al. STUDIES IN FAMILY PLANNING 16(2):106-112, March-April 1985.

INDIA

Compulsory birth control and fertility measures in India: a simulation approach, by S. S. Halli. SIMULATION AND GAMES 14(4):429-444, December 1983.

Inflationary note from India: the going rate for sterilization, by C. Levine. HASTINGS CENTER REPORT 15:3, April 1985.

One son is no sons [India], by S. A. Freed, et al. NATURAL HISTORY 94:10+, January 1985.

NEW GUINEA

Tubal ligation in Milne Bay Province, Papua New Guinea, by P. Barss, et al. PAPUA NEW GUINEA MEDICAL JOURNAL 26(3-4):174-177, September-December 1983.

NIGERIA

Pattern and attitude of Nigerian women in Benin City towards female steriliza-tion, by A. F. Omu, et al. ASIA OCEANIA JOURNAL OF OBSTETRICS AND GYNAECOLOGY 11(1):17-21, March 1985.

PUERTO RICO
Model of fertility control in a Puerto Rican Community, by S. L. Schensul, et al. URBAN ANTHROPOLOGY 11(1):81-99, Spring 1982.

UNITED STATES
Abortion and sterilization in the United States: demographic dynamics, by P. J. Sweeney. UNION MEDICALE DU CANADA 113(7):587-593, July 1984.

Contraceptive practice among American women, 1973-1982, by C. A. Bachrach. FAMILY PLANNING PERSPECTIVES 16:253-259, November-December 1984.

Family planning and female sterilization in the United States, by T. M. Shapiro, et al. SOCIAL SCIENCE AND MEDICINE 17(23):1847-1855, 1983.

Reproductive rights in North Carolina, by S. Poggi. GAY COMMUNITY 13(5):2, August 10, 1985.

Sterilization among American Indian and Chicano Mothers, by K. I. Hunter, et al. INTERNATIONAL QUARTERLY OF COMMUNITY HEALTH AND EDUCATION 4(4):343-352, 1983-84.

Tubal sterilization in women 15-24 years of age: demographic trends in the United States, 1970-1980, by N. C. Lee, et al. AMERICAN JOURNAL OF PUBLIC HEALTH 74(12):1363-1366, December 1984.

STERILIZATION: ATTITUDES
Attitudes of sterilized women to contraceptive sterilization, by P. E. Børdahl. SCANDINAVIAN JOURNAL OF SOCIAL MEDICINE 12(4):191-194, 1984.

Husband or wife? A multivariate analysis of decision making for voluntary sterilization, by M. D. Clark, et al. JOURNAL OF FAMILY ISSUES 3(3):341-360, 1982.

Sterilization: making the choice, by P. A. Hillard. PARENTS MAGAZINE 60:124+, March 1985.

What's the #1 contraceptive? (Guess again), by S. Wernick. REDBOOK 165:36+, September 1985.

STERILIZATION: COMPLICATIONS
Sterilization failures and their causes, by R. M. Soderstrom. AMERICAN JOURNAL OF OBSTETRICS AND GYNECOLOGY 152(4):395-403, June 15, 1985.

Sterilization failures with bipolar tubal cautery, by J. W. Ayers, et al. FERTILITY AND STERILITY 42(4):526-530, October 1984.

STERILIZATION: ECONOMICS
Comparative risks and costs of male and female sterilization, by G. L. Smith, et al. AMERICAN JOURNAL OF PUBLIC HEALTH 75:370-374, April 1985.

Contraceptive attitudes and practice in women choosing sterilization, by K. D. Bledin, et al. JOURNAL OF THE ROYAL COLLEGE OF GENERAL PRACTITIONERS 34(268):595-599, November 1984.

Effects of sterilization on menstruation, by J. Foulkes, et al. SOUTHERN MEDICAL JOURNAL 78(5):544-547, May 1985.

Family planning and female sterilization in the United States, by T. M. Shapiro, et al. SOCIAL SCIENCE AND MEDICINE 17(23):1847-1855, 1983.

Female sterilization: free choice and oppression, by C. Barroso. REVISTA DE SAUDE PUBLICA 18(2):170-180, April 1984.

Female sterilization—safe and irreversible?, by O. Lalos, et al. LAKARTIDNINGEN 81(38):3358-3360, September 19, 1984.

Filshie clip for female sterilization [letter], by D. Casey. CONTRACEPTION 31(4):441-442, April 1985.

Four-year follow-up of insertion of quinacrine hydrochloride pellets as a means of nonsurgical female sterilization, by R. Bhatt, et al. FERTILITY AND STERILI-ZATION 44(3):303-306, September 1985.

How reliable is female sterilization? 211 pregnancies after 35,599 operations, by V. Odlind, et al. LAKARTIDNINGEN 81(38):3357-3358, September 19, 1984.

Making the decision for female sterilization, by A. A. Durán, et al. GINECOLOGIA Y OBSTETRICIA DE MEXICO 51(313):131-136, May 1983.

Menstrual patterns after female sterilization: variables predicting change, by L. P. Cole, et al. STUDIES IN FAMILY PLANNING 15:242, September-October 1984.

Mental health and female sterilization: a follow-up. Report of a WHO Collaborative prospective study. JOURNAL OF BIOSOCIAL SCIENCE 17(1):1-18, January 1985.

Outpatient interval female sterilization at the University College Hospital, Ibadan, Nigeria, by E. O. Otolorin, et al. AFRICAN JOURNAL OF MEDICINE AND MEDICAL SCIENCES 14(1-2):3-9, March-June 1985.

Pattern and attitude of Nigerian women in Benin City towards female sterilization, by A. F. Omu, et al. ASIA OCEANIA JOURNAL OF OBSTETRICS AND GYNAECOLOGY 11(1):17-21, March 1985.

Quinacrine nonsurgical female sterilization: a reassessment of safety and efficacy, by E. Kessel, et al. FERTILITY AND STERILITY 44(3):293-298, September 1985.

Reversibility of female sterilization, by A. M. Siegler, et al. FERTILITY AND STERILIZATION 43(4):499-510, April 1985.

Social and gynaecological background of 218 sterilized women, by P. E. Børdahl. SCANDINAVIAN JOURNAL OF SOCIAL MEDICINE 12(4):183-190, 1984.

Sterilization of women, by H. A. Hirsch. GYNAKOLOGE 17(3):210-215, September 1984.

Use of methyl cyanoacrylate (MCA) for female sterilization. Program for Applied Research on Fertility Regulation Northwestern University Medical School Chicago, Illinois. CONTRACEPTION 31(3):243-252, March 1985.

WHO collaborative study. Mental health and female sterilization: a follow-up. JOURNAL OF BIOSOCIAL SCIENCE 17:1-18, January 1985.

STERILIZATION: INVOLUNTARY
Sterilization: all the dif between forced and free, by E. Bader. GUARDIAN 37(20):5, February 20, 1985.

STERILIZATION: LAWS AND LEGISLATION
Carrie Buck's daughter [forced eugenic sterilization], by S. J. Gould. NATURAL HISTORY 93:14-18, July 1984.

Legal aspects of medical genetics in Wisconsin, by E. W. Clayton. WISCONSIN MEDICAL JOURNAL 84(3):28-32, March 1985.

Legal issues in sterilization using tubal coagulation, by G. H. Schlund. GEBURT-SHILFE UND FRAUENHEILKUNDE 44(10):692-693, October 1984.

Pregnancy termination: not for family planning. The legal difference between sterilization and pregnancy termination is decisive, by H. Krautkrämer. FORT-SCHRITTE DER MEDIZIN 102(36):78, September 27, 1984.

STERILIZATION: MALE
Comparative risks and costs of male and female sterilization, by G. L. Smith, et al. AMERICAN JOURNAL OF PUBLIC HEALTH 75:370-374, April 1985.

More pick sterilization, but not many black men do. JET 68:39, August 5, 1985.

STERILIZATION: METHODS
Can anesthesia be employed for male or female sterilization with impunity?, by O. Zaffiri. MINERVA ANESTESIOLOGICA 51(1-2):57-59, January-February 1985.

Pulling the plug on sterilization [fallopian tube plug allows reversible sterilization; work of C. Irving Meeker and Wilfred Roth], by J. Silberner. SCIENCE NEWS 127:166, March 16, 1985.

Sterilization methods in China [letter], by V. L. Bullough, et al. AMERICAN JOURNAL OF PUBLIC HEALTH 75(6):689, June 1985.

STERILIZATION: MORTALITY AND MORTALITY STATISTICS
On risks, costs of sterilization [letter], by D. A. Grimes, et al. AMERICAN JOURNAL OF PUBLIC HEALTH 75(10):1230, October 1985.

STERILIZATION: PSYCHOLOGY AND PSYCHIATRY
Contraceptive attitudes and practice in women choosing sterilization, by K. D. Bledin, et al. JOURNAL OF THE ROYAL COLLEGE OF GENERAL PRACTITIONERS 34(268):595-599, November 1984.

Effects of female sterilization: one year follow-up in a prospective controlled study of psychological and psychiatric outcome, by J. E. Cooper, et al. JOURNAL OF PSYCHOSOMATIC RESEARCH 29(1):13-22, 1985.

Effects of information on patient stereotyping, by B. M. DeVellis, et al. RESEARCH IN NURSING AND HEALTH 7(3):237-244, September 1984.

Exotic reaction to tubal ligation, by S. Lockwood. AUSTRALIAN FAMILY PHYSICIAN 13(6): 446-447, June 1984.

Mental health and female sterilization: a follow-up. Report of a WHO Collaborative prospective study. JOURNAL OF BIOSOCIAL SCIENCE 17(1):1-18, January 1985.

Psychological considerations in the wish for refertilization, by H. Herrmann, et al. GEBURTSHILFE UND FRAUENHEILKUNDE 45(3):170-175, March 1985.

Psychological factors related to adjustment after tubal ligation, by M. M. Tsoi, et al. JOURNAL OF REPRODUCTIVE AND INFANT PSYCHOLOGY 2(1):1-6, April 1984.

Regret after decision to have a tubal sterilization, by G. S. Grubb, et al. 44(2):248-253, August 1985.

Social and psychological perspectives on voluntary sterilization: a review, by S. G. Philliber, et al. STUDIES IN FAMILY PLANNING 16(1):1-29, January-February 1985.

Vasectomy and tubal ligation: medicopsychological aspects of voluntary sterilization, by M. Bourgeois. PSYCHOLOGIE MEDICALE 14(8):1195-1201, June 1982.

STERILIZATION: RESEARCH
Cruelty to animals [letter], by C. E. Horner. AUSTRALIAN VETERINARY JOURNAL 61(12):414-415, December 1984.

Laparoscopic sterilization of the bitch and queen by uterine horn occlusion, by D. E. Wildt, et al. AMERICAN JOURNAL OF VETERINARY RESEARCH 46(4):864-869, April 1985.

Long-term regret among 216 sterilized women. A six-year follow-up investigation, by P. E. Børdahl. SCANDINAVIAN JOURNAL OF SOCIAL WORK 13(1):41-47, 1985.

New technology leaves spayed heifers with ovary tissue [ovarian autograft technique]. SUCCESSFUL FARMING 83:B1, August 1985.

Ovarian function in monkeys after bilateral salpingectomy, by J. R. Zhao, et al. INTERNATIONAL JOURNAL OF FERTILITY 29(2):118-121, 1984.

Seeking better contraceptives. POPULI 2(2):24, 1984.

Sex and the single cat, by S. L. Gerstenfeld. PARENTS MAGAZINE 60:166, June 1985.

American Association of Gynecologic Laparoscopists' 1982 membership survey, by J. M Phillips, et al. JOURNAL OF REPRODUCTIVE MEDICINE 29(8):592-594, August 1984.

Sterilizing statistics [survey by National Center for Health Statistics]. CONSUMERS RESEARCH MAGAZINE 68:38, March 1985.

Tubal sterilization in women 15-24 years of age: demographic trends in the United States, 1970-1980, by N. C. Lee, et al. AMERICAN JOURNAL OF PUBLIC HEALTH 74(12):1363-1366, December 1984.

STERILIZATION: TECHNIQUES

Bipolar coagulation in surgical laparoscopy, by I. Les, et al. CESKOSLOVENSKA GYNEKOLOGIE 50(4):289-290, May 1985.

Claims for malpractice and complications following female sterilization 1975-1979, by E. Ryde-Blomqvist. LAKARTIDNINGEN 81(42):3810-3812, October 17, 1984.

Elective sterilization: no guarantees, by J. K. Avery. JOURNAL OF THE TENNESSEE MEDICAL ASSOCIATION 77(9):540-541, September 1984.

Evolution and reversibility of damage to rabbit fallopian tubes after five sterilization methods, by N. Garcea, et al. MICROSURGERY 6(1):20-25, 1985.

Experience with laparoscopic interval sterilization with fallopian tube rings, by A. F. Haenel, et al. FORTSCHRITTE DER MEDIZIN 103(5):87-90, February 7, 1985.

Female sterilization monitored by laparoscopy. Evaluation of 2 electrosurgical occlusive technics, by L. C. Uribe Ramirez, et al. GINECOLOGIA Y OBSTETRICIA DE MEXICO 52(322):33-40, February 1984.

Human sterilization emerging technologies and reemerging social issues. SCIENCE, TECHNOLOGY AND HUMAN VALUES 9(3):8, Summer 1984.

Laparoscopic salpingoclasia. Comparative study of 3 methods, by J. Vázquez Méndez, et al. GINECOLOGIA Y OBSTETRICIA DE MEXICO 53(335):75-78, March 1985.

Laparoscopic sterilization in a free-standing clinic: a report of 1,092 cases, by S. Y. Lee, et al. CONTRACEPTION 30(6):545-553, December 1984.

Menstrual pattern changes following minilap/Pomeroy, minilap/ring and laparoscopy/ring sterilization: a review of 5982 cases, by P. P. Bhiwandiwala, et al. INTERNATIONAL JOURNAL OF GYNAECOLOGY AND OBSTETRICS 22(3):251-256, June 1984.

Minilaparotomy and laparoscopy: safe, effective, and widely used, by L. Liskin, et al. POPULATION REPORTS (9):C125-167, May 1985.

Ovabloc. Five years of experience, by T. P. Reed. JOURNAL OF REPRODUCTIVE MEDICINE 29(8):601-602, August 1984.

Ovarian function following ligation of the fallopian tubes, by X. D. Sun. CHUNG HUA FU CHAN KO TSA CHIH 19(3):166-167, July 1984.

Prostaglandins mediate postoperative pain in Falope ring sterilization, by B. L. Brodie, et al. AMERICAN JOURNAL OF OBSTETRICS AND GYNECOLOGY 151(2):175-177, January 15, 1985.

Search for a tubal ligation, by L. Haught. FEMINIST CONNECTION 5(3):30, December 1984.

Sterilization by composite rubber clip [letter], by P. W. Ashton. AUSTRALIAN AND NEW ZEALAND JOURNAL OF OBSTETRICS AND GYNAECOLOGY 25(1):78, February 1985.

Sterilization via minilaparotomy using a Chinese retractor, by K. Leikanger. TIDS-SKRIFT FOR DEN NORSKE LAEGEFORENING 104(27):1916-1917, September 30, 1984.

Use of butorphanol tartrate as an analgesic in salpingoclasia with local anesthesia, by J. R. Gaitán, et al. GINECOLOGIA OBSTETRICIA DE MEXICO 51(309):19-23, January 1983.

Use of methyl cyanoacrylate (MCA) for female sterilization. Program for Applied Research on Fertility Regulation Northwestern University Medical School Chicago, Illinois. CONTRACEPTION 31(3):243-252, March 1985.

Vecuronium bromide in anaesthesia for laparoscopic sterilization, by J. E. Caldwell, et al. BRITISH JOURNAL OF ANAESTHESIOLOGY 57(8):765-769, August 1985.

STERILIZATION: TUBAL

Bipolar tubal cautery failures [letter]. FERTILITY AND STERILITY 43(6):943-947, June 1985.

Comparative study of topical anesthesia for laparoscopic sterilization with the use of the tubal ring, by S. Koetsawang, et al. AMERICAN JOURNAL OF OBSTETRICS AND GYNECOLOGY 150(8):931-933, December 15, 1984.

Comparison of interval and postabortal/puerperal laparoscopic sterilization with the tubal ring procedure, by L. Heisterberg, et al. ACTA OBSTETRICIA ET GYNECOLOGICA SCANDINAVICA 64(3):223-225, 1985.

Complications and short-term consequences of tubal sterilization. A personal three- and twelve-month follow-up investigation, by P. E. Børdahl, et al. ACTA OBSTETRICIA ET GYNECOLOGICA SCANDINAVICA 63(6):481-486, 1984.

Controlled comparison of the Pomeroy resection technique and laparoscopic electro-coagulation of the tubes, by P. E. Børdahl, et al. ANNALES CHIRURGIAE ET GYNAECOLOGIAE 73(5):288-292, 1984.

Development of a simplified laparoscopic sterilization technique, by S. D. Khandwala. JOURNAL OF REPRODUCTIVE MEDICINE 29(8):586-588, August 1984.

Ectopic pregnancy in a distal tubal remnant, by B. G. Molloy, et al. INTER-NATIONAL JOURNAL OF GYNAECOLOGY AND OBSTETRICS 23(2):135-136, April 1985.

Effects of three techniques of tubal occlusion on ovarian hormones and menstruation, by P. Virutamasen, et al. JOURNAL OF THE MEDICAL ASSOCIATION OF THAILAND 67(4):201-210, April 1984.

Effects on menstruation of elective tubal sterilization: a prospective controlled study, by K. D. Bledin, et al. JOURNAL OF BIOSOCIAL SCIENCE 17:19-30, January 1985.

Experience with laparoscopic interval sterilization with fallopian tube rings, by A. F. Haenel, et al. FORTSCHRITTE DER MEDIZIN 103(5):87-90, February 7, 1985.

Factors associated with married women's selection of tubal sterilization and vasectomy, by R. N. Shain, et al. FERTILITY AND STERILITY 43(2):234-244, February 1985.

Factors influencing the success of microsurgical tuboplasty for sterilization reversal, by P. J. Paterson. CLINICAL REPRODUCTION AND FERTILITY 3(1):57-64, March 1985.

Grand multiparity: benefits of a referral program for hospital delivery and post-partum tubal ligation, by P. Barss, et al. PAPUA NEW GUINEA MEDICAL JOURNAL 28(1):35-39, March 1985.

High failure rate of a plactic tubal (Bleier) clip, by R. Adelman. OBSTETRICS AND GYNECOLOGY 64(5):721-724, November 1984.

Hypergonadotropic amenorrhea following laparoscopic tubal sterilization, by A. W. Kowatsch, et al. WIENER KLINISCHE WOCHENSCHRIFT 97(11):504-505, May 24, 1985.

Incidence, significance and remission of tubal spasm during attempted hysteroscopic tubal sterilization, by J. M. Cooper, et al. JOURNAL OF REPRODUCTIVE MEDICINE 30(1):39-42, January 1985.

Institutional abuse tubal sterilization in a population at risk of ill-treating their children, by Y. Englert, et al. CHILD ABUSE AND NEGLECT 9(1):31-35, 1985.

Interval tubal sterilization in obese women—an assessment of risks, by I. C. Chi, et al. AMERICAN JOURNAL OF OBSTETRICS AND GYNECOLOGY 152(3): 292-297, June 1, 1985.

Intrauterine and ectopic pregnancies after a tubal ligation with documented tubal occlusion, by A. G. Shapiro. SOUTHERN MEDICAL JOURNAL 78(8):1014-1015, August 1985.

Lack of tubal occlusion by intrauterine quinacrine and tetracycline in the primate, by L. J. Zaneveld, et al. CONTRACEPTION 30(2):161-167, August 1984.

Laparoscopic tubal sterilization. Endothermy coagulation and cross-clipping, by O. Storeide, et al. TIDSSKRIFT FOR DEN NORSKE LAEGEFORENING 104(23):1544-1545, August 20, 1984.

Laparoscopy in the puerperium, by A. Molina Sosa, et al. GINECOLOGIA Y OBSTETRICIA DE MEXICO 51(319):301-306, November 1983.

Legal issues in sterilization using tubal coagulation, by G. H. Schlund. GEBURT-SHILFE UND FRAUENHEILKUNDE 44(10):692-693, October 1984.

Long-term risk of menstrual disturbances after tubal sterilization, by F. DeStefano, et al. AMERICAN JOURNAL OF OBSTETRICS AND GYNECOLOGY 152(7 Pt 1): 835-841, August 1, 1985.

Long-term toxicity of a hydrogelic occlusive device in the isthmus of the human oviduct. A light microscopic study, by J. Brundin, et al. ACTA PATHO-LOGICA ET MICROBIOLOGICA SCANDINAVICA 93(3):121-126, May 1985.

Menstrual pattern changes following minilap/Pomeroy, minilap/ring and laparo-scopy/ring sterilization: a review of 5982 cases, by P. P. Bhiwandiwala, et al. INTERNATIONAL JOURNAL OF GYNAECOLOGY AND OBSTETRICS 22(3):251-256, June 1984.

Morbidity in tubal occlusion by laparoscopy, by F. Castro Carvajal, et al. GINECOL-OGIA Y OBSTETRICIA DE MEXICO 52(321):19-22, January 1984.

Personal experience with tubal sterilizations performed by the posterior uterine vault approach, by J. Adamec, et al. CESKOSLOVENSKA GYNEKOLOGIE 50(1):44-47, February 1985.

Plastic (Bleier) clip high failure rate [letter], by L. Hammond. OBSTETRICS AND GYNECOLOGY 66(2):297-298, August 1985.

Post-tubal-ligation syndrome, by J. A. Vázquez. GINECOLOGIA Y OBSTETRICIA DE MEXICO 51(317):237-240, September 1983.

Post-tubal sterilization syndrome—a misnomer, by M. C. Rulin, et al. AMERICAN JOURNAL OF OBSTETRICS AND GYNECOLOGY 151(1):13-19, January 1 1985.

Regret after decision to have a tubal sterilization, by G. S. Grubb, et al. 44(2):248-253, August 1985.

Safety of abortion and tubal sterilization performed separately versus concur-rently, by H. H. Akhter, et al. AMERICAN JOURNAL OF OBSTETRICS AND GYNECOLOGY 152(6 Pt 1):619-623, July 15, 1985.

Salpingitis after laparoscopic sterilization, by J. Blaakaer, et al. UGESKRIFT FOR LAEGER 146(44):3373, October 29, 1984.

Separate stitches tubal sterilization, a modified Pomeroy's technic an analysis of the procedure, complications and failure rate, by P. Rimdusit. JOURNAL OF THE MEDICAL ASSOCIATION OF THAILAND 67(11):602-607, November 1984.

Sequelae of tubal ligation, by C. F. Alvarez. GINECOLOGIA Y OBSTETRICIA DE MEXICO 53(334):35-37, February 1985.

Sequelae of tubal ligation: an anlysis of 75 consecutive hysterectomies, by R. J. Stock. SOUTHERN MEDICAL JOURNAL 77(10):1255-1260, October 1984.

Social and gynecological long-term consequences of tubal sterilization. A personal six-year follow-up investigation, by P. E. Børdahl. ACTA OBSTETRICIA ET GYNECOLOGICA SCANDINAVICA 63(6):487-495, 1984.

Sterilization: making the choice, by P. A. Hillard. PARENTS MAGAZINE 60:124+, March 1985.

Study on ovarian function following tubal ligation, by X. D. Sun, et al. ACTA ACADEMIAE MEDICINAE WUHAN 5(2):119-120, 1985.

Teaching laparoscopic sterilization, by C. L. Cook, et al. JOURNAL OF REPRO-DUCTIVE MEDICINE 29(9):693-696, September 1984.

Torision of the fallopian tube sterilization by electrocoagulation via a laparoscope, by B. Ottesen, et al. EUROPEAN JOURNAL OF OBSTETRICS, GYNE-COLOGY AND REPRODUCTIVE BIOLOGY 19(5):297-300, May 1985.

Tubal ligation by minilaparotomy, by C. Grudsky, et al. REVISTA CHILENA DE OBSTETRICIA Y GINECOLOGIA 46(4):198-205, 1981.

Tubal ligation by a vaginal approach, by S. A. Guzman, et al. GINECOLOGIA Y OBSTETRICIA DE MEXICO 52(327):171-174, July 1984.

Tubal ligation in Milne Bay Province, Papua New Guinea, by P. Barss, et al. PAPUA NEW GUINEA MEDICAL JOURNAL 26(3-4):174-177, September-December 1983.

Tubal ligation: a misnomer [letter], by J. T. Parente, et al. AMERICAN JOURNAL OF OBSTETRICS AND GYNECOLOGY 151(6):829, March 15, 1985.

Tubal plug and clip method for female sterilization, by C. I. Meeker, et al. OBSTETRICS AND GYNECOLOGY 65(3):430-435, March 1985.

Tubal pregnancy after a previous tubal ligation and hysterectomy, by D. Beuthe, et al. GEBURTSHILFE UND FRAUENHEILKUNDE 45(3):188, March 1985.

Tubal sterilization. A historical review, by P. E. Børdahl. JOURNAL OF REPRO-DUCTIVE MEDICINE 30(1):18-24, January 1985.

Tubal sterilization. A prospective long term investigation of 218 sterilized women, by P. E. Børdahl. ACTA OBSTETRICIA ET GYNECOLOGICA SCANDI-NAVICA 128:1-56, 1984.

Tubal sterilization in women 15-24 years of age: demographic trends in the United States, 1970-1980, by N. C. Lee, et al. AMERICAN JOURNAL OF PUBLIC HEALTH 74(12):1363-1366, December 1984.

Tubal sterilization with the Falope ring in an ambulatory-care surgical facility, by S. G. Kaali, et al. NEW YORK STATE JOURNAL OF MEDICINE 85(3):98-100, March 1985.

Tubal sterilization with Filshie Clip. A multicentre study of the ICMR task force on female sterilization. CONTRACEPTION 30(4):339-353, October 1984.

Uterine guide to gynecologic laparoscopy, by E. H. Jørgensen, et al. UGESKRIFT FOR LAEGER 146(45):3452-3454, November 5, 1984.

Effect of tubal ligation on the incidence of epithelial cancer of the ovary, by M. Koch, et al. CANCER DETECTION AND PREVENTION 7(4):241-245, 1984.

STERILIZATION: VOLUNTARY
Social and psychological perspectives on voluntary sterilization: a review, by S. G. Philliber, et al. STUDIES IN FAMILY PLANNING 16(1):1-29, January-February 1985.

STERILIZATION AND CRIMINALS
Depo-Provera: blessing or curse?, by U. Vaid. THE NATIONAL PRISON PROJECT JOURNAL 4:1+, Summer 1985.

Infant K's case. MACLEANS 98:21, May 13, 1985.

Sentencing—castration of rapists—cruel and unusual punishment. THE CRIMINAL LAW REPORTER: COURT DECISIONS 36(24):2463, March 20, 1985.

STERILIZATION AND FEMINISM
International feminists target sterilization programs. OVERTHROW 6(4):7, December 1984.

STERILIZATION AND HORMONES
Corpus luteum function assessed by serial serum progesterone measurements after laparoscopic endotherm sterilization, by R. Kirschner, et al. ACTA EUROPAEA FERTILITATIS 16(3):169-173, May-June 1985.

Interaction between sex hormone binding globulin and levonorgestrel released for vaginal rings in women, by S. Z. Cekan, et al. CONTRACEPTION 31(4):431-439, April 1985.

Oestrogen deficiency after tubal ligation, by J. Cattanach. LANCET 1(8433):847-849, April 13, 1985.

STERILIZATION AND HOSPITALS
Sterilizations in a community hospital, by O. Storeide, et al. TIDSSKRIFT FOR DEN NORSKE LAEGEFORENING 104(23):1534-1535, August 20, 1984.

STERILIZATION AND THE MENTALLY RETARDED
Sterilization of the mentally retarded, by A. Rousso. MEDICINE AND LAW 3(4):353-362, 1984.

Women and mental health: "Charter of Rts" report, by C. McKague. PHOENIX RISING 5(1):38, February 1985.

STERILIZATION AND PHYSICIANS
Postpartum sterilization and the private practitioner, by V. P. DeVilliers. SOUTH AFRICAN MEDICAL JOURNAL 67(4):132-133, January 26, 1985.

STERILIZATION AND POLITICS
Politics of procreation. SCIENCE FOR PEOPLE (57):15, 1985.

STERILIZATION AND SOCIOLOGY
Social class distribution of surgical patients: an assessment of Oxford Record Linkage Study data, by K. Hunt, et al. COMMUNITY MEDICINE 6(4):291-298, November 1984.

Long-term regret among 216 sterilized women. A six-year follow-up investigation, by P. E. Børdahl. SCANDINAVIAN JOURNAL OF SOCIAL WORK 13(1):41-47, 1985.

Making news: Asian women in the west, by U. Butalia. ISIS 1984, p. 114.

Sterilization among American Indian and Chicano Mothers, by K. I. Hunter, et al. INTERNATIONAL QUARTERLY OF COMMUNITY HEALTH AND EDUCATION 4(4):343-352, 1983-84.

Tubal sterilization in women 15-24 years of age: demographic trends in the United States, 1970-1980, by N. C. Lee, et al. AMERICAN JOURNAL OF PUBLIC HEALTH 74(12):1363-1366, December 1984.

STERILIZATION CLINICS
Laparoscopic sterilization in a free-standing clinic: a report of 1,092 cases, by S. Y. Lee, et al. CONTRACEPTION 30(6):545-553, December 1984.

STERILIZATION FUNDING
Public findings of contraceptive, sterilization and abortion services, 1983 [United States], by R. B. Gold, et al. FAMILY PLANNING PERSPECTIVES 17:25-30, January-February 1985.

VASECTOMY
Good news about vasectomies, by E. Michaels. CHATELAINE 58:18, February 1985.

Public opinion on and potential demand for vasectomy in semi-rural Guatemala, by R. Santiso, et al. JOURNAL OF PUBLIC HEALTH 75:73-75, January 1985.

Use of vasectomy, by C. Schirren. ZEITSCHRIFT FUR HAUTKRANKHEITEN 60(14):1097-1099, July 15, 1985.

Vasectomy counselling, by M. Redelman. HEALTHRIGHT 4:27-29, August 1965.

Vasectomy reversal, by J. Mickelson. MOTHERING 36:30, Summer 1985.

AUTHOR INDEX

258

259

Grogan, P. 8, 50
Grossmann, A. 64
Grubb, G. S. 29, 82
Grudsky, C. 98
Grünfeld, B. 75
Gu, Z. W. 93
Guay, M. 79
Gudakova, N. T. 97
Guillat, J. C. 26
Guillebaud, J. 13, 94
Guizar Vázquez, J. 95
Gupta, S. K. 20
Gurtovoi, B. L. 93
Gustavii, B. 85
Gutman, M. A. 28
Guzman, S. A. 98
Habicht, J. P. 28
Haenel, A. F. 39
Hagstad, A. 46
Hahn, D. W. 13
Halli, S. S. 25
Halpern, D. F. 57
Hamilton, K. 94
Hammerstein, J. 15
Hammond, L. 72
Haning, R. V., Jr. 39
Harding, C. M. 36
Hardisty, J. 6
Hardisty, V. 40
Harenberg, J. 37
Harewood, J. 1
Harger, J. H. 20
Harlap, S. 21, 25
Harlay, A. 66
Harper, M. J. K. 1
Harris, B. C. 34
Harris, R. J. 82
Harrison, D. P. 26
Hartnagel, T. F. 79
Hasker, W. 45
Hassan, A. S. 73
Hassold, T. 58, 82, 95
Hatherley, L. I. 56
Hatziessevastou-Loukidou, H. 81
Haught, L. 87
Hauser, G. A. 22
Havránek, F. 101
Healy, D. L. 13
Heaton, B. 28
Hecht, F. 43
Heisterberg, L. 24, 60, 70, 78
Hemfelt, A. 72
Hemminki, K. 91
Henrion, R. 64

Henry, A. 42, 63, 72, 83, 87
Henshaw, S. K. 20, 43
Hentoff, N. 38, 72
Hernandez, D. J. 1
Herrmann, H. 78
Hertz, J. B. 68
Hertzberg, A. 19, 100
Herz, B. K. 2
Hester, N. R. 46
Higgins, J. E. 92
Hillard, P. A. 92
Hiller, A. 45
Hills, K. 35
Himle, L. 95
Hinde, A. 96
Hirsch, H. A. 92
Hirsch, M. B. 28
Hitchens, C. 104
Hjelt, K. 67
Hodgen, G. D. 75
Hoffman, J. 22
Hogan, T. D. 53
Holden, C. 5, 27, 85
Holma, P. 57
Holmes, P. 16
Holzgreve, W. 86
Hongsoon Han, T. 90
Honoré, L. H. 63
Hook, E. B. 34
Horner, C. E. 30
Hornstein, M. D. 71
Hosken, F. P. 30
Hougie, C. 68
Hromas, R. A. 22
Hruda, J. 96
Huang, H. Y. 97
Huapaya, L. 97
Huff, D. W. 103
Hughes, G. R. 94
Hulsebosch, H. 56
Hume, E. 61
Hunt, J. D. 9
Hunt, K. 90
Hunt, M. V. 50
Hunt, P. A. 51
Hunter, K. I. 92
Hunter, N. 9
Hyjazi, Y. 32
Iberger, C. 28
Ichikawa, Y. 81
Ikeuchi, M. 93
Ines, A. 32
Ireson, C. J. 11
Iver, G. 21

266

268

Steinfeis, P. 54
Steinfels, M. O. 72
Steinfels, P. 57
Steinhoff, P. G. 106
Stettner, A. G. 3
Stewart, D. O. 71
Stock, R. J. 88
Storeide, O. 55, 92
Stott, R. 56
Strache, R. R. 40
Strasser, M. 32
Strausberg, G. I. 40
Strecke, J. 22
Strugatskii, V. M. 100
Struve, F. A. 73
Stubblefield, P. G. 67
Sturgis, S. 40
Sturtevant, F. M. 18
Sun, M. 21, 69
Sun, X. D. 69, 93
Sundberg, L. 72
Suprapto, K. 63
Sutherland, J. 66
Swan, G. S. 14
Swank, J. G. 45
Sweeney, P. J. 6
Tagg, J. 57, 99
Takagi, K. 66
Taler, S. J. 19
Tan, K. D. 38
Tanfer, K. 29
Tang, L. C. 53
Tang, W. K. 12
Tangrtrakul, S. 51
Taravella, S. 7
Tarnoff, S. 11, 54
Tarpy, C. C. 16
Taylor, C. G. 76
Taylor, S. 104
Tchabo, J. G. 100
Teichmann, A. T. 59
Tennakoon, S. 41
Teresa, Mother 65
Thakur, R. B. 65
Theile, U. 2
Thelen, T. H. 82
Thingran, A. G. 93
Thomas, C. 45, 56, 66, 78, 95
Thomas, M. L. 46
Thompson, J. 42
Thompson, P. 99
Thornton, A. 81
Thornton, A. D. 44
Thranov, I. 71

Thundy, Z. OP. 39
Tierno, P. M., Jr. 50
Tinneberg, H. R. 101
Tjokronegoro, A. 82
Tobin, J. M. 14
Tolchin, S. 50
Toledo, R. 73
Tolnay, S. e. 37
Toncheva, d. 75
Toomey, C. 92
Torres, A. 41
Tosi, S. L. 56
Toth, B. 36
Townsend, B. 59
Townsend, P. K. 27
Tóth, A. 21
Treffers, P. E. 30
Triesser, A. 34
Trimmer, E. 10
Trost, J. 94
Trussell, J. 74
Tshibangu, K. 49
Tsoi, M. 79
Tsong, Y. Y. 43
Tuladhar, J. M. 32
Tunkel, V. 56, 82
Tunnadine, P. 79
Turkington, C. 32
Tweedie, J. 13
Tyrer, L. B. 11. 65, 67
Udjo, E. O. 66
Uribe Ramirez, L. C. 42
V'iaskova, M. F. 68
Vaid, U. 32
Vajpayee, A. 86
Valderrama, O. 84
Valenza, D. 103
Van Den Haag, E. 6
Van Gurop, J. 43
Van Loo, M. 55
Van Santen, M. R. 24, 52
van der Meeren, H. L. 10
van Lith, D. A. 34
Vasilevskaia, L. N. 14
Vauhkonen, A. E. 87
Vázquez, J. A. 74
Vázquez Méndez, J. 55
Veitch, A. 104
Vekhnovskil, V. O. 35
Veltman, L. 61
Veninga, K. S. 37
Venter, J. D. 66
Verma, R. 13
Vessey, M. P. 67, 69

271